20^{00}

Blacks and Whites
in São Paulo, Brazil

BLACKS & WHITES
in
SÃO PAULO, BRAZIL
1888–1988

George Reid Andrews

The University of Wisconsin Press

The University of Wisconsin Press
114 North Murray Street
Madison, Wisconsin 53715

3 Henrietta Street
London WC2E 8LU, England

Library of Congress Cataloging-in-Publication Data
Andrews, George Reid, 1951–
Blacks and whites in São Paulo, Brazil, 1888–1988
George Reid Andrews.
384 pp.   cm.
Includes bibliographical references and index.
ISBN 0-299-13100-9   ISBN 0-299-13104-1
1. Blacks—Brazil—São Paulo (State)—History—20th century.
2. Blacks—Brazil—History—20th century.
3. São Paulo (Brazil State)—Race relations.
4. Brazil—Race relations.   I. Title.
F2631.A58   1991
981'.6100496—dc20   91-50320
CIP

To My Parents
Barbara Mahler Andrews
and
George Reid Andrews (1915–1977)

Contents

Contents

List of Tables

Acknowledgments

As always, my first and deepest thanks must go to my family, who left friends, home, school, and work in America's most livable city to spend a year in São Paulo. I saw as much that year through their eyes as I did through my own. Several years later, my wife, Roye A. Werner, read the first draft of the manuscript, made valuable editorial suggestions, and contributed her considerable insight into modern Brazilian life.

Several friends and colleagues in the United States helped me get started on this project and carry it through to completion. Emília Viotti da Costa, Seymour Drescher, John French, Ramón Gutiérrez, Thomas Holloway, Harold Sims, and Thomas Skidmore provided support and encouragement in the early stages. As I became more immersed in the project, Enrique Amayo, John French, Dale Graden, Catherine Lugar, and Joel Wolfe offered citations and data from their own research, and Thomas Skidmore made useful criticisms and comments on the penultimate draft of the manuscript. I owe a particular debt to Thomas Holloway, who furnished me with abundant primary material that he had turned up during the course of his own work in São Paulo, and who subjected the manuscript to rigorous and probing criticism from which it benefited greatly. Throughout this project he was a model of generous collegiality.

During my first research trip to Brazil, in 1983, Hamilton Cardoso, Boris Fausto, Florestan Fernandes, Michael Hall, Clóvis Moura, João Baptista Borges Pereira, Paulo Sérgio Pinheiro, Dea Fenelon Ribeiro, and Robert Slenes offered useful advice and suggestions. I was warmly received by the members of the Centro de Estudos de Cultura Contemporânea, at that time under the direction of Regis Castro de Andrade, who invited me to return as a visiting researcher in 1984–1985. During that year of research Yara Maria Aun Khoury and Paulo Sérgio Pinheiro provided indispensable assistance in helping me gain access to the company archives used in chapter 4. And I am deeply indebted to Miriam Nicolau Ferrara, who graciously invited me into her home over a several-month period to work with her collection of Afro-Brazilian newspapers, since donated to the Instituto de Estudos Brasileiros at the University of São Paulo.

My archival work was greatly facilitated by the staffs of the Eletricidade de São Paulo (Eletropaulo) archive, directed by Luiz Carlos de Mello, and the Arquivo Edgar Leuenroth at the University of Campinas, directed by Marco Aurélio Garcia. At the former Jafet textile factory, Maximino Fernandes and Antônio Telassi were cheerful and obliging hosts. I also worked at the Biblioteca Municipal, the Arquivo do Estado de São Paulo, the archive of *O Estado de São Paulo*, the Centro Pastoral Vergueiro, and the libraries of the Instituto Brasileiro de Geografia e Estatística (IBGE) and the Sistema Estadual de Análise de Dados (SEADE). Finally, Ari Cándido Fernandes, of the Secretaria da Cultura; Lúcia Elena Garcia de Oliveira, of IBGE; Ivair Augusto Alves dos Santos, of the Conselho de Participação e Desenvolvimento da Comunidade Negra; and Maria Aparecida Silva Bento Teixeira, of the Secretaria do Trabalho, were very helpful in making available to me publications and working documents prepared by their respective agencies.

Upon my return to the University of Pittsburgh, Philip Sidel, director of the Social Science Computer Research Institute, and Mike Eliot, wrote the programs to convert the company data into usable form. Shirley Kane, also of SSCRI, did the data entry. Rosemary Feldman and Monica Perz were able research assistants.

I was fortunate to have Robin Whitaker as my copy editor. She brought a sharp and sympathetic eye to the manuscript, which was significantly improved as a result of her efforts.

Financial support for this research was provided by grants from the National Endowment for the Humanities, the Fulbright-Hays program, the Social Science Research Council, and, at the University of Pittsburgh, the Center for Latin American Studies, the University Center for International Studies, and the Central Research Fund. I finished the book while on sabbatical leave from the university's Department of History, a uniquely congenial workplace and set of colleagues.

Blacks and Whites
in São Paulo, Brazil

1. Introduction

In 1975 and 1976 my wife and I lived for eighteen months in Argentina while I did research for a book on nineteenth-century black history in that country. On our way home, we spent a month traveling in Brazil. Though I did not realize it at the time, during that trip I reached the decision that some day I would come back. Not only was the country compelling and fascinating in its own right; for anyone interested in black history, particularly black history in Latin America, it was clearly the place to be. Recipient during the colonial period and the nineteenth century of more Africans than any other New World nation, and today the home of the second-largest black[1] population in the world, in sheer numerical terms Brazil is the most important chapter in Afro-American (using the term in its pan-hemispheric sense) history.[2]

Portrayals of that history have undergone a striking evolution over the course of the 1900s. Despite the fact that it enslaved more Africans than any other American nation, and was the last country in Christendom to abolish slavery (in 1888), between 1900 and 1950 Brazil successfully cultivated an image of itself as the world's first "racial democracy," a land in which blacks and whites lived together in harmony under conditions of almost complete equality. That image was not seriously questioned until the 1950s, when UNESCO-sponsored researchers, seeking the explanation for Brazil's racial idyll, instead documented pervasive racial inequality and the widespread diffusion of antiblack attitudes and stereotypes. And after a hiatus of research on racial issues imposed by the military governments of the 1960s, new work done in the 1970s and 1980s has been even more critical of Brazilian racial realities, some of it going so far as to characterize Brazil as a South Africa without apartheid.[3]

A South Africa without apartheid, however, would not be South Africa, or at least not the South Africa which that comparison invokes. Brazilians who compare their country to South Africa are citing the most extreme case of late-twentieth-century racial inequality. But what makes that case extreme is precisely what Brazil lacks: a comprehensive system of racial discrimination imposed on the society by the national state and enforced by the agencies of that state. To say that Brazil is a South Africa without apartheid is to say that it is not South Africa at all—which indeed it is not.

As we shall see over the course of this book, Brazil is a country of marked racial inequality. But it is a country in which, unlike South Africa or the segregationist American South, racial inequality, at least in the twentieth century, has not been imposed by the force of law. This is not a trivial distinction. When racial discrimination is mandated by law, it operates in a much more rigid and inflexible way than in societies in which it is informal and at the discretion of the individual. The very crudeness and visibility of such legally mandated discrimination have proven to be its Achilles' heel. The overt injustices of segregation and apartheid eventually mobilized millions of people to fight against them; and that fight had a compelling focal point in the struggle to overturn racially discriminatory legislation and replace it with laws guaranteeing racial equality.

In societies like the American North or Brazil, by contrast, the absence of state-mandated discrimination has made racial injustice significantly more difficult to struggle against. Discrimination left to the whim of the individual operates in an inconsistent and unpredictable way, and is not always identifiable as such. This can lead to considerable uncertainty over whether discrimination even exists, particularly when other factors offer convincing explanations for the existence of racial inequality in a given society. It is clear, for example, that black people are badly underrepresented in white-collar occupations in Brazil. But much of that underrepresentation can be ascribed to the lower educational levels of black job applicants as compared with whites, or the concentration of the black population in rural areas or in less economically dynamic regions of the country which offer fewer opportunities for white-collar employment.

Nevertheless, recent research by sociologists and economists has made quite clear that structural factors cannot explain all the disparities between the black and white racial groups in Brazil, and that discrimination does in fact play a significant role in reducing black access to jobs, income, education, housing, and the other public and private goods offered by modern industrial society.[4] This research in turn raises a series of questions, the answers to which will form the subject matter of this book.

First, why do prejudice and discrimination exist at all in a country which has historically prided itself on its freedom from both? Second, how has the character of Brazilian race relations, and of Brazilian racial inequality, changed over time? It would be surprising if Brazilian racial hierarchy functioned in the 1980s in the same way that it did in the 1930s, or the 1880s; and indeed it does not. How, concretely, have patterns of Brazilian racial inequality evolved and changed during the hundred-year period since the abolition of slavery?

Having identified *how* race relations in Brazil have evolved during the last hundred years, we then face the most demanding task of all: explaining *why* they have altered. This will require us to situate the recent (post-1888) history of Brazilian race relations within the broader political, economic, and social context within which that history has unfolded. This in turn requires at least the rudiments of a theoretical framework.

Brazilian Perspectives

One logical place to look for the elements of such a framework is in the work of previous historians of Brazilian race relations. When one surveys that literature, one finds that it tends to focus on the experience of slavery both as the most obvious and visible expression of racial hierarchy in Brazil's national experience, and as the most important determinant of Brazil's present-day racial situation.[5] Such a focus is not unreasonable, given that, as those authors have conclusively demonstrated, slavery was so widespread throughout colonial and nineteenth-century Brazil, and was so much at the core of pre-1888 society and economy, that it had an even greater impact in shaping modern Brazil and the problems which that country faces than was the case in the United States. Slavery had been functioning in Brazil for one hundred years before it became an important component of North American society and economy, and was not abolished until twenty-five years after emancipation in the United States; over the course of slavery's existence, nine to twelve times as many Africans were imported into Brazil as into the United States; and at the moment of their respective independences, the proportion of slaves in Brazil's population was more than double the proportion of slaves in the U.S. population.[6] Given slavery's obvious importance in Brazilian history, it is absolutely essential to devote careful attention to the institution and its long-term impacts on that country.

Looking at slavery, however, is only the first step in coming to grips with Brazil's recent racial history, and it is a step that carries with it certain risks. The first is that of focusing on slavery because it is so easy to "see," and in the process neglecting other important dimensions of Brazil's historical past. Slavery was a highly visible legal, social, and economic institution which left extensive written evidence of its existence and of its development over time. The resulting documentary bias toward slaves and masters has helped make slavery a popular topic among the social and economic historians of Brazil's colonial period and nineteenth century.[7] But even historians of slavery have expressed concern over "the hypnotic attraction exerted over scholars by slavery as an institution," and have suggested that future researchers turn their attention to other aspects of colonial society, for example, the free nonelite population. Without a firmer grasp of the broader society which housed and surrounded the slave population, we will be hard pressed to explain the evolution of Brazilian race relations both before and after emancipation.[8]

Mention of the postemancipation period (1888 to the present) raises the second risk of focusing on slavery as the primary determinant of present-day race relations: the temptation simply to extrapolate its story forward in time to explain twentieth-century developments, without taking into account the ways in which new historical conditions altered and ultimately transformed the heritage of slavery. The dangers of such a temptation are particularly visible in the work of the scholar generally credited with the creation of the "racial democracy" concept, sociologist Gilberto Freyre (1900–1987).[9]

In numerous books and articles published from the 1930s through the 1970s, Freyre persuasively developed the argument of a "New World in the tropics," of Brazil as a land almost (not quite, but almost) free of racial prejudice, and one which could serve to the rest of the world as an example of how to resolve its racial problems. He found the roots of that "New World" in Brazil's colonial experience, and especially its allegedly benign experience with slavery. Stressing the relatively low levels of race prejudice among Brazil's Portuguese colonists, and the dearth of European women in the colony, Freyre argued that Brazil provided the setting for widespread race mixture between European masters and African slaves. Extensive miscegenation "dissolved" whatever vestigial race prejudice the Portuguese may have brought with them from Europe, simultaneously producing a large population of mixed race. The result was "one of the most harmonious unions of culture with nature and of one culture with another that the lands of this hemisphere have ever known." And as Brazil moved into the nineteenth and twentieth centuries, this "harmonious union" of blacks with whites formed the basis for the "broad democratization" of Brazilian society, and its inexorable "march toward social democracy."[10]

During the last decades of his life Freyre moved visibly to the right, supporting the post-1964 military dictatorship and joining it in denouncing anyone who questioned the concept of racial democracy as Communist and anti-Brazilian.[11] Foremost among such questioners was sociologist Florestan Fernandes (1920–), a vigorous critic of almost all aspects of Brazilian society, and particularly its system of race relations. One of the coordinators of the UNESCO-sponsored research of the 1940s and 1950s, Fernandes and his collaborators have produced numerous books and articles attacking the "myth" of racial democracy and laying bare the reality of racial inequality and discrimination in their country.[12] The military governments of the 1960s having defined such criticism as an act of subversion, Fernandes was deprived of his professorship at the University of São Paulo in the academic purge of 1969, following which he taught in the United States and Canada. As the country began its gradual transition back to democracy in the late 1970s he was able to resume teaching in São Paulo, and in 1986 was elected to Congress on the Workers' Party ticket, in which capacity he served in the Constituent Assembly which wrote the Constitution of 1988.

Given the fundamental disagreements between Freyre's and Fernandes's perspectives, it is striking to note at least two convergences between them. The first is the emphasis which both authors place on the experience of slavery in determining Brazil's present-day racial situation. They differ completely, of course, on the nature of slavery's impact. Despite his awareness of the brutality and cruelty associated with the institution, Freyre saw slavery as having exerted a basically positive influence on Brazil's social and cultural development. Fernandes, by contrast, saw slavery as deeply destructive, both for its immediate victims and for the future of Brazilian society as a whole. Far from having any potentially democratizing effects, slavery was an inherently authoritarian system which implanted prejudice and a strong sense of racial superiority in the hearts of Brazilian whites. And by denying its victims the most basic human rights and freedoms, and maintaining them as illiterate, unskilled workers who learned, for their own survival, to avoid disciplined work wherever and whenever it presented itself, slavery crippled Afro-Brazilians as a people and completely stripped them of the ability to compete against white people in the twentieth-century contest for jobs, education, and livelihood. As a result, far from entitling them to the fruits of membership in a functioning racial democracy, after emancipation the legacy of slavery would continue to marginalize and exclude Afro-Brazilians through the dual factors of their own incapacity and of white hostility and prejudice.[13]

Freyre and Fernandes differ dramatically in their assessment of how slavery shaped the current state of race relations in Brazil—but that it did so, and did so in fundamental ways, they readily agree. Their agreement on this point reflects and articulates—and, in dialectical fashion, helped to shape—the same belief among Brazilians more generally.[14] Or, to be more precise, among educated white Brazilians. It has been my experience that, in discussing race relations in their country, Afro-Brazilians are more likely to see racial inequality as caused by present-day discrimination. Euro-Brazilians, by contrast, are more likely to explain such inequities in terms of the heritage of slavery, which they often do by combining the Freyre and Fernandes arguments. Although Freyre's position has been subjected to severe criticism in academic circles, it still enjoys substantial currency among the white middle and upper classes, the members of which continue to think of their country as a land of relative racial equality, particularly in comparison, for example, to the United States. The evidence of racial hierarchy in Brazil is so clear, however, and so visible on a day-to-day basis, that most thoughtful Brazilians feel compelled to try to resolve the contradiction between the image of racial democracy and the reality of racial inequality. They do so by stressing the Fernandes thesis of slavery as the root cause of black inability to compete against whites. Blacks failed to enter the mainstream of Brazilian society, not because of discrimination, but because of the illiteracy, malnutrition, criminality, and so on, that were their inheritance from slavery. As that experience recedes into the past, many of these Brazilians go on to argue, and as education and the other benefits of Brazil's material progress are extended to the black population, Afro-Brazilians will be able to take part in that progress on conditions of full equality—because, after all, Brazil *is* a racial democracy which places no obstacles in the way of its black citizens.[15]

Those readers who have had contact with Brazil and its people will recognize such optimism as one of the country's most appealing national traits.[16] Thus it is not entirely surprising, to return to Freyre and Fernandes, that this should be the second point of convergence between them: in spite of their radically different perspectives on the historical experience of slavery and its long-term implications, both conclude with fundamentally optimistic visions of the future of Brazilian race relations. For Freyre, such optimism was the logical consequence of his belief that Brazil had been traveling a basically progressive and positive path over the course of its four hundred–year history, and would simply continue to do so in the future. At the beginning of his career, in the 1930s, he had argued (indeed, it is the final sentence of his book on nineteenth-century Brazil, *The Mansions and the Shanties*) that "Brazil is becoming more and more a racial democracy, characterized by an almost unique combination of diversity and unity." Forty years later he was able to announce that Brazil had achieved its historical mission of obliterating racial barriers altogether by creating, through race mixture, the world's first "meta-race," or "beyond-race" *(alem-raça)*, as a result of which "each Brazilian overcomes his or her consciousness of racial origin or status, of color as an indicator of origin or status. Instead, the Brazilian simply feels—Brazilian."[17]

Optimism seems less justified in the case of Fernandes, until one takes into account the Marxist orientation of much of his work, and his resulting faith in the progressive character of long-term historical change. Slavery had been a perverse and destructive experience for Brazil, Fernandes argued, one which had left deep wounds and scars in the Brazilian psyche. But capitalist development and the "bourgeois revolution" (the title of his masterwork) of the twentieth century would inexorably transform Brazilian society, gradually erasing "the legacy of the white race" (as he subtitled another of his books, *The Integration of the Black into Class Society*) and replacing it with a modern, capitalist society based on class identification rather than racial ascription. Thus, while Freyre saw the heritage of slavery extending in an unbroken line into the late twentieth century and beyond, Fernandes saw that heritage as susceptible to alteration and transformation by subsequent historical developments. Fernandes never underestimated the time, struggle, and effort that that process would take. But he clearly believed that history—and, more specifically, capitalist development—was on the side of racial equality. As a result, despite his criticisms of the Freyre thesis and of the Brazilian model of race relations more generally, he could agree with Freyre that, if the "bourgeois revolution" were allowed to continue its course, "Brazil could become the first major racial democracy in the world created by the expansion of modern Western civilization."[18]

Comparative Perspectives

Such faith in the healing powers of capitalism seems more appropriate to a liberal modernization theorist than to a Marxist. But as political scientist Stanley Greenberg has noted, both theoretical camps in fact share the belief that, over the long run, capitalist development will tend to break down social identities based on race and ethnicity and replace them with the more "modern" categories of class and citizenship. Unfortunately for such theorists, the history of the twentieth century offers little support for such a proposition. Racial and ethnic identities continue to enrich, and bedevil, societies as developed as the United States, Great Britain, Israel, France, the Soviet Union—and Brazil. Indeed, Greenberg argues, "'archaic' social relations, like race and ethnicity, are potentially compatible with and perhaps functional to capitalist development."[19] Superior racial status can be used by one group of workers to compete more effectively against another, or indeed to avoid competition entirely. Employers may exploit racial or ethnic divisions within the work force to lower their wage bill, or to foil efforts by their workers to organize and bargain collectively. Thus, far from doing away with the social categories of race and ethnicity, capitalist growth and development can actually reinforce and strengthen them, in ways suggested by comparative analysis of the evolution of racial orders in different countries.

Some twenty years ago Pierre van den Berghe noted the severe stresses which twentieth-century urbanization and industrialization introduced into systems of racial hierarchy that had come into existence under slavery.[20] He characterized those earlier systems—which in the Americas had their genesis in the plantation-based societies where New World slavery found its home—as traditional, "paternalist" models of race relations governed by deeply rooted, if largely informal and seldom voiced, rules of racial superiority and domination.

By the nineteenth and twentieth centuries, the rural plantation societies in which such systems had originated were experiencing the throes of modernization—or, to use somewhat different language, of structural transformation. The abolition of slavery itself was one such transformation, a political event which had the direct economic consequence of forcing planters to bargain and negotiate with their workers in a "free" wage-labor market. Former slaves were now at liberty to move from plantation to plantation in search of better wages and working conditions, or to leave the countryside entirely and move to nearby or distant cities, where expanding service and industrial economies offered a broader range of opportunities for work, education, and leisure.

As blacks and whites streamed into such rapidly growing turn-of-the-century cities as Atlanta, Chicago, Rio de Janeiro, and São Paulo, they found a more fluid, less rigidly structured social setting than they had known in the countryside. In the absence of the plantation-based social order, which had enforced and been governed by the "paternalist" model of race relations, black people were now free (or freer) to compete openly against whites for jobs, wages, education, housing—and perhaps last, but certainly not least, political participation and power.

Since there was never enough of these goods to go around, the competition for them became correspondingly intense. And as the competition intensified, incentives grew for members of the traditionally dominant racial group to use that dominance, and their racial status, as additional weapons in the struggle. The result, concluded van den Berghe, was the rise of either informal racial exclusion, as in the northern United States or southern Brazil, or comprehensive systems of state-imposed and -enforced racial segregation, as in South Africa or the American South.

Van den Berghe supported and illustrated this theoretical argument with brief comparative examinations of the evolution of race relations in four national settings: Brazil, Mexico, South Africa, and the United States. Recent work on the rise of segregation in the last two of these countries has further enriched his analysis, and goes considerably beyond him in illuminating the specific tensions and stresses which accompany the transition from "paternalist" to "competitive" race relations.[21] Particularly useful in this regard is Stanley Greenberg's work on the role of different class actors in the construction of "racial orders": segregation in the American South, and apartheid in South Africa.

Greenberg argues that the initial driving force behind the creation of such systems was commercial agriculture: the owners of large farms and plantations producing cash crops for national and international markets. These landowners required large, stable supplies of farm labor; and during the "period of intensification" of institutionalized racial domination (1890–1960 in South Africa, 1875–1930 in the American South), they enjoyed preferential access to the state, which they used to influence the formulation of state labor policies. Thus in both cases commercial farmers and planters took the lead in creating institutional mechanisms designed to coerce members of the racially subordinate group (Africans and Afro-Americans, respec-

tively) into entering the wage-labor market and accepting employment on terms dictated by their employers and the state.

Industries created during the late nineteenth and early twentieth
centuries also benefited from such arrangements, especially labor-
intensive, heavy industries like mining, and iron and steel. As those
industries grew, and as mineowners and industrialists acquired increasing political power, they joined with the planters and farmers in
supporting and extending systems of racial control.[22] But not all
capitalists derived such direct benefits from segregation. Owners of
later-developing industries, and retail and service enterprises, often
found that racial controls made it difficult for them to pry workers
away from agriculture and the more established industries. They
therefore tended to prefer a freer, more fluid labor market unencum-
bered by such controls. But given their political weakness in relation
to the planters and major industrialists, these entrepreneurs had little
choice but to accept the racial order as a given, and learn to live
within its strictures.

Like businessmen, white workers also varied in their attitude
toward institutionalized discrimination, depending on their position
in the economy. Skilled workers organized in craft unions found
racial exclusion "enormously congenial," because it facilitated efforts
to restrict entry into, and therefore their control over, the skilled
trades. Industrial unions, on the other hand, could go in one of two
diametrically opposed directions. One, followed by the garment
workers in South Africa and the United States, the United Mine-
workers in the American South, and, after its formation in 1936, the
Congress of Industrial Organizations, was the strategy of racial inclusion, based on organizing pan-racial unions rigorously opposed to
discrimination. But prior to the creation of the CIO in the United
States, and until the present in South Africa, this response was relatively rare in both societies. The more typical tendency was for
industrial unions to work within the framework of segregation, organizing white and black workers into separate locals, or excluding
black workers entirely, and then pressing for either informal or state-
imposed privileges for white workers. How far unions could go with
this approach depended on their degree of organization and political
power. In the American South, where their political clout was nil,

racial discrimination in the labor market tended to remain informal, and was enforced at the firm or industry level rather than mandated by law. In South Africa, where, because of the small size of the white population in relation to the black, workers' power within the white racial group was proportionally greater, unions succeeded in establishing rigid color bars guaranteed by the state.[23]

Greenberg's class-based approach can be very useful in helping us understand how, in the decades after emancipation, societies historically rooted in slavery transformed their systems of racial domination into something new and different from what had gone before. And for the purposes of the present discussion, its utility is further increased by the fact that, in focusing on South Africa and the American South, Greenberg is describing societies similar in a number of respects to Brazil.[24] All three were multiracial, export-oriented societies based in the nineteenth century on commercial agriculture, which during the twentieth century underwent a process of late (in comparison to western Europe and the northern United States) but gradually accelerating and intensifying industrialization. This process of capitalist growth and development produced visible alterations in the class structure of these societies which, Greenberg argues, had significant impacts on patterns of race relations in the United States and South Africa. What do we find when we apply a similar perspective to Brazil?

Inevitably we will find different outcomes from those in the United States and South Africa—two cases which, as the comparative literature makes clear, themselves differed in significant ways from each other. Brazilian workers and elites, and blacks and whites, confronted conditions and challenges different from those of their analogues abroad, and pursued different solutions to the problems which they faced. But despite those differences, the Greenberg approach can be quite helpful in telling us where to look for the explanation of specific outcomes in race relations in each country. And though this is not a goal which I will pursue in this book, ultimately it can enable us to identify and explain both the salient similarities and the salient differences among patterns of race relations in different countries. It is therefore the general approach which I will follow in subsequent chapters, modified in only one important respect.

In explaining the rise and fall of "racial orders," Greenberg focuses almost entirely on "tensions and divisions within the white social structure." Surprisingly little attention is paid to the role of the subordinate racial group, perhaps on the grounds that it is whites who create and maintain racial hierarchy. But as a rich and growing historical literature makes clear, the dominated always participate in that process of creation, and not just as helpless victims and objects. Even when they act from a position of weakness and disadvantage, their actions and decisions play a central role in determining the course of historical change.[25] Therefore, in addition to including class divisions and conflict within the white population as important explanatory variables, I will attempt to do the same with the black population as well.

This will require us to look at a variety of social groups, depending on the particular historical moment we are examining, and at the interactions among them. During the final years of slavery, the discussion focuses on slaves, masters, and that portion of the free population involved in the abolitionist movement (chapter 2). During the half century after emancipation, I examine black and white workers and their employers (chapters 3–4), and members of the would-be "black elite" (chapter 5). And for the years since World War II, most of my attention goes to members of the black and white middle classes (chapters 6–7).

Inevitably information is easier to find for some of these groups than for others. While members of the black middle class have left abundant evidence of their individual and collective concerns, slaves and workers, most of them illiterate, have left little or no documentary record of their lives and times. Insofar as these latter groups can be "seen" at all through written evidence, it is almost always through the eyes of others: masters, employers, the police, journalists, foreign visitors. These are the usual difficulties which social historians encounter in writing "the history of the inarticulate," and I have dealt with them in the conventional way: combing newspapers and other sources for bits and pieces of evidence, trying to tap previously unutilized sources (chapter 4), and using the existing secondary literature produced by Brazilian and foreign scholars. I leave it to the reader to judge the results.

As we examine these various groups, much of the behavior we will be looking at will be social and economic in character—for example, employers' decisions concerning whom to hire and promote, social clubs' decisions about whom to admit as members and guests, individuals' decisions about whom to accept and reject as friends, neighbors, lovers. Much of it, however, will be political, and will take place within the contexts of state institutions and programs and of electoral and party politics. This will require us to consider an element frequently missing from social historical analysis: the question of politics, power, and the state.

A Political Perspective

When Brazilians, or those who study Brazil, use the term "racial democracy," they are describing Brazilian society and culture, or, to use the words of Gilberto Freyre, Brazilian civilization. It is curious that Freyre chose political terminology to express a social and cultural concept.[26] Over time, however, I have come to see the logic of his choice, which corresponds to the integral connection between race and politics in Brazil, and in particular between racial democracy and political democracy.

As chapter 5 will argue at greater length, the doctrine of racial democracy started to gel and take form at the turn of the century, during the period when Brazil was making the transition from monarchy to republic, and the country's planter elites were confronting the challenge of how to prevent the *povo*, the people, from taking part in, and by their sheer numbers coming to dominate, a system of electoral representation. Racial democracy thus formed part of a larger ideological effort to reconcile the republican ideals of equality and participation with the reality of social and political exclusion. It asserted that, because of the absence of racial barriers in Brazilian life, once slavery had been abolished black people were free to enter Brazilian society on terms of complete equality with whites, and indeed had done so in the years since 1888. Though such assertions found little support in empirical reality, they reassured those who would listen that even if Brazil had not yet achieved political democracy, it *had* achieved a form of social democracy, and the latter held within it the seeds of the former.[27]

Had I written this book fifteen years ago, I would probably have paid little or no attention to the theme of democracy. As a graduate student during the 1970s, insofar as I gave democracy any thought at all, I tended to dismiss it as a cynical exercise, a tool for the legitimation of bourgeois rule. By the 1980s, however, I had had the firsthand experience of watching an elected civilian government collapse in Argentina, and be overthrown and replaced by a brutal military regime. Seven years of military dictatorship in that country, and longer periods of similar governments in Brazil, Chile, and Uruguay, caused democracy as a form of government to rise considerably in my esteem. It was obviously preferable to military rule; and I had come to see how, far from automatically serving elite interests, the electoral political systems of the post–World War II period had in fact opened the door for popular movements in Latin America to push with considerable effectiveness for their collective interests, and to challenge the existing social and economic order. Indeed, it was the very success of those movements that had provoked conservative elites throughout the region to close down electoral politics in the 1960s, and replace them with the only form of regime capable of keeping those movements in check: military authoritarianism.[28]

But the dictatorships could not last forever. Having watched democracy die in Argentina in 1976, during the 1980s I had the opportunity to watch it being reborn in Brazil, amidst an outpouring of relief and rejoicing that I found profoundly moving. And the restoration of civilian rule was hardly unique to that country, or even to Latin America as a region. Throughout the capitalist and Communist world alike, the 1980s were the decade of democracy, as Latin Americans, Eastern Europeans, Russians, Chinese, Filipinos, Koreans, and Pakistanis mobilized against the dictatorships under which they had lived for decades, and demanded an expanded role in governance.[29]

This global trend, combined with my own experiences in Latin America, forcibly focused my attention on questions of democracy and mass-based political participation. It also reinforced my growing sense of the need to add a political dimension to the social history that I had originally set out to study and write. During my years as a graduate student, I had been inspired by the promise of "history from the bottom up," and by the challenge of bringing back into the historical record the workers, slaves, women, and other groups who had been quietly passed over in the traditional chronicles of wars, politics, and great men. I continue to believe in the validity, and indeed the necessity, of this enterprise. But I no longer see social history as, in the words of one of its early practitioners, "history . . . with the politics left out."[30] Throughout human history, and certainly in Latin America, the lives of common people have been powerfully affected by politics and the decisions taken by governments. Neglecting this political dimension of historical change not only narrows our understanding of those lives, but also deprives us of the opportunity to see how the actions of common people can have direct and powerful consequences for the political systems in which they live—as vividly evidenced by the startling collapse of the dictatorships of the 1980s. Historical analysis and narrative which fails to take into account the realities of politics, power, and the state will completely miss these interactions between state and society, and will ultimately be unable to explain or even adequately describe the historical experiences of the people who are its subject.[31]

The problem of course lies in how to identify, document, and explain these interactions—in the words of a recent successful practitioner of this art, in how "to fuse history from above with history from below."[32] This problem is particularly vexing in the case of Brazilian racial inequality. As I have already indicated, Brazil is not South Africa or the United States. Since the abolition of slavery in 1888, the Brazilian state has for the most part refrained from designing or implementing explicitly "racial" programs and policies comparable to segregation, or apartheid, or the more recent (in the United States) programs of affirmative action and equal opportunity. Thus the relationship between government action (or, equally important, inaction) and patterns of racial inequality is not nearly so visible or apparent as in other countries. Perhaps as a result, notes political scientist Pierre-Michel Fontaine, works proposing to deal with that relationship in Brazil "have one thing in common: they do not deal with political institutions, behavior, or attitudes, or with elections, electoral behavior, or political parties, or even public policy. . . . In fact, in some cases, such as that of Freyre, they do not deal with politics at all. Those that do, do so in a broad sense, at an abstract level of conflict and power imprecisely defined."[33]

One way to avoid the vagueness and abstractness which Fontaine describes is to do what he suggests no one has done: focus on specific institutions, and try to identify the ways they have influenced and determined patterns of race relations over time. This book presents a number of instances in which policies and actions taken by state institutions (legislative bodies, executive agencies, the courts) or institutions closely tied to the state (political parties, the Church, labor unions) have had significant impacts on Brazilian race relations. In addition to looking at official and semiofficial institutions, the book also looks at the other side of the state-society dialectic, examining the organizations and movements through which Afro-Brazilians have mobilized to take part in politics and combat racial inequality (chapters 2, 5, 7). In so doing, it attempts to illuminate the interactive, reciprocal relationship which has existed between those popular movements and the institutions of the state. The character of the political regime in power at any given historical moment and the policies which it puts into effect have a direct impact on the ways in which black people organize themselves and press for political change. And those black movements in turn have played a direct role in driving forward Brazil's repeated transitions from one type of regime to another—from monarchy (1822–1889) to oligarchic republic (1889–1930) to corporatist dictatorship (1937–1945) to populist republic (1946–1964) to military dictatorship (1964–1985) to the Third Republic—and the halting, uneven, but inexorable democratization of Brazilian politics.

A Regional Perspective

Let us briefly review what this book is about. First, it seeks to document some of the basic patterns of racial inequality which have existed in Brazil since the abolition of slavery, and to explain how and why those patterns have evolved over time. In trying to construct that explanation, it will attempt to link the history of race relations and racial inequality to larger patterns of economic, social, and political development. It will pay particular attention to the role of race in economic competition and class struggle. And it will also try to integrate politics and the state into the story, in an effort to show how developments in the political sphere helped determine the course of black-white race relations, and were themselves determined, at least in part, by those social relations.

Map of Brazil, with inset of São Paulo State

Obviously this is a lot to accomplish, and would be even more if one were to attempt such analysis for the country as a whole. In an effort to make the task more feasible, I have chosen to limit myself to the region where Florestan Fernandes carried out his pathbreaking research: the state of São Paulo.[34]

An area of secondary importance during Brazil's colonial period, in the 1800s São Paulo embarked on a gradually accelerating process of economic and demographic growth which eventually led to its present preeminent position within the Brazilian federation. That growth started in the early 1800s with the beginnings of coffee cultivation in the province. By 1900, fueled by European immigration, São Paulo's population was growing at a rate almost double that of the nation as a whole. As of 1920 São Paulo had the second largest population in the country, surpassed only by its neighbor, Minas Gerais; by the next national census, in 1940, São Paulo was the most populous state in Brazil, and it has continued to increase its dominance to the point where it now contains over one-fifth of the national population.[35]

Though São Paulo's economic and demographic growth was based initially on coffee, over the course of the twentieth century the state's economy has become increasingly industrial in character. Fueled by the investment capital and the local demand generated by coffee earnings, São Paulo's industrial economy overtook its competitors in other states by 1920 and is now responsible for over half the nation's industrial output.[36] Along with industrialization went urbanization. From a sleepy town of 35,000 souls in 1880, the state capital exploded to some 600,000 by 1920, and 2.2 million in 1950. By 1980 over half the state's population lived in Greater São Paulo, making it the third largest city in the world (after Mexico City and Tokyo).[37]

Of Brazil's various regions, São Paulo has been the one most affected by industrialization, urbanization, and modern capitalist development. If one is interested in examining how the heritage of plantation slavery in that country has been altered and transformed by twentieth-century conditions, São Paulo is clearly the most advanced case of such transformation. And as Brazil attempts to recapitulate the *paulista* experience of economic growth and development on a national scale, São Paulo's experience in the area of race becomes even more relevant as a possible forecast of things to come. As several observers have noted, Freyre's concept of "racial democracy" has at least some applicability to the plantation-based society and economy of northeastern Brazil, where Freyre was born and lived most of his life. Particularly at the time that he began writing, in the 1930s, that part of the country had experienced none of the wrenching changes which have taken place in São Paulo, and was still recognizable as one of Pierre van den Berghe's "traditional, paternalist" racial orders. But what is likely to happen to race relations in the Northeast as rural migrants stream into its cities, and if government efforts to promote industrial development in that region bear fruit? São Paulo provides an instructive example of how patterns of race relations inherited from the slave regime have responded to the stresses of modernization; our examination of its experience may shed light as well on the future direction of racial developments elsewhere in Brazil.

Finally, by focusing on São Paulo, we can follow through on the forecasts of Florestan Fernandes, and try to verify the degree to which capitalist modernization has in fact succeeded in breaking down the barriers of racial exclusion. Fernandes and his collaborators carried out their research in the late 1940s and early 1950s; as we return to the scene of their investigations some forty years later, how much progress do we find that the "bourgeois revolution" has made in obliterating the "legacy of the white race"?

Before arriving at the present, however, we must begin with the past, and with the transition from slavery to freedom.

1

WORKERS

2. Slavery and Emancipation, 1800–1890

For three hundred years, from the late 1500s through the late 1800s, plantation agriculture and African slavery formed the foundations of Brazilian society and economy. Planted and nurtured by Portuguese colonialism, these two related institutions sank roots deep into Brazilian soil, and played a determining role in defining the nation that Brazil would eventually become.[1] The destruction of Brazilian slavery was therefore a historical event of enormous importance, as well as a remarkable social and political achievement. What made it possible to bring slavery to an end in a country which had depended on it for so long? And once slavery had been abolished, how did former masters and former slaves go about constructing new arrangements and ways of life to replace those under which they had lived for generations?

Slavery

In comparison to northeastern Brazil, plantation agriculture and African slavery arrived in São Paulo relatively late. A string of sugar plantations had been established along the paulista coast at São Vicente, Portugal's first New World settlement, in the 1530s and 1540s. During the second half of the century, however, these initial efforts were superseded by newer and larger plantations in the northern captaincies[2] of Pernambuco and Bahia, which by the 1580s had emerged as the centers of Brazilian—and world—sugar production. Colonization efforts in São Paulo shifted to the cooler highlands looming over the coast, where in 1554 Jesuit missionaries had established the town of São Paulo de Piratininga. Turning their backs on plantation agriculture and commerce with Europe and Africa, the paulista colonists constructed an economy based on subsistence production, barter with the local Indian population, and periodic expeditions into the western wilderness in search of gold, diamonds, and Indian slaves. Forced labor in São Paulo thus remained predominantly Indian during the first two centuries of colonization.[3]

By the late 1700s, however, and with increasing intensity after 1800, plantation agriculture and African slavery penetrated this previously isolated colonial outpost. The first stage of that penetration was based on sugar, as landowners responded to the sugar price increases caused by the Anglo-French wars of the 1770s and 1790s and the Haitian Revolution.[4] But the second, more durable, and more dynamic stage of that penetration was based on coffee. Stimulated by increasing European demand for the crop, coffee cultivation had expanded rapidly in Rio de Janeiro between 1770 and 1830, by which point it had spread into adjoining areas of Minas Gerais and São Paulo provinces and had displaced sugar as the newly independent nation's most important export. Coffee's entry into São Paulo was particularly dramatic: by midcentury São Paulo's coffee plantations employed almost four times as many slaves as did sugar plantations, and by the 1860s the province had virtually ceased to export sugar and instead was basing its agricultural expansion entirely on coffee. As of 1850 Brazil was producing half the world's coffee supply; fifty years later, São Paulo State alone accounted for half the world supply, with the rest of Brazil contributing an additional quarter.[5]

As sugar and coffee spread through São Paulo, they brought slavery with them. By 1811 African and Afro-Brazilian slaves accounted for 23 percent of São Paulo's population, a proportion which rose to 28 percent by the 1830s and remained at that level through the 1850s before dropping to 19 percent in 1872. In absolute terms, São Paulo's slave population doubled in size between 1811 and 1836, from 38,542 to 78,858, and then doubled again by 1872, to 156,612 (see Appendix A). By the mid-1870s São Paulo housed the third largest slave population in the country, exceeded only by the neighboring provinces of Minas Gerais and Rio de Janeiro.[6]

Slavery had come to São Paulo, and with it came all the stresses and tensions associated with coerced labor. One of the more obvious such tensions was the grinding contradiction between the Christian principles on which Brazilian civilization professed to be based and the hideous realities of slavery in practice. Clerics, planters, slaves, and private citizens engaged in a ceaseless struggle to define the terms on which these two antithetical systems could coexist. One possible outcome of such struggles might have been that the teachings of Christianity would serve to alleviate the cruelty of slavery. In practice the reverse more often proved to be true: the demands of slavery and plantation agriculture worked to corrupt and erode Christian doctrine. Religion was enlisted as one of the primary bulwarks of the slave regime, one French observer of nineteenth-century plantation discipline noting that "it comprises two aspects: dogma and the whip, the priest and the overseer." Slaves were enjoined to serve their masters as they would serve God, so that they could receive their reward in the next world. Some priests even went so far as to propose an analogy between the suffering of the slaves and that of Christ himself, urging the slaves to be worthy of the honor of their Christly vocation. Apparently none pushed on to explore the role slaveowners would play in such an analogy. Nor did the slaveowners themselves, even the more compassionate of whom apparently saw no irony in convening their families, as did one paulista mistress, to recite a rosary so that their slave Francisco would not "feel too much the pain of his whipping."[7]

A second tension was that between slavery and the liberal principles used to justify Brazilian independence, which were subsequently enshrined in the Constitution of 1824. Brazilian elites had found liberal ideology most helpful in explaining to themselves and the world why they were entitled to overthrow Portuguese colonial rule and take charge of their own affairs. But, as throughout the Atlantic world, this then raised the awkward question of why liberal guarantees of freedom, juridical equality, and the rule of law should be suspended in the case of some 40 percent of the national population.[8]

For most slaveowners it was self-evident why the constitutional guarantees of citizenship did not extend to slaves, who, after all, were not citizens. Thus the Constitution's unequivocal outlawing of whippings, torture, branding, "and all other cruel punishments," and its declaration of freedom and equality as "inalienable rights of men," were simply understood not to apply to slaves.[9] Nevertheless, the contradictions between slavery and liberalism, between physical brutality and the rule of law, were blatant and undeniable, and as the century progressed, growing numbers of Brazilians found them harder and harder to ignore. This was particularly the case among those educated, middle- and upper-class reformers committed to the "modernization" of their country: those who wished to see Brazil follow the civilizing, progressive path trod by the constitutional monarchies and republics of western Europe and North America. These Brazilians could not help noticing that slavery did more than deprive a significant proportion of their country's inhabitants of basic legal rights and protections. In conjunction with the institution of the large plantation, it also formed the economic, social, and political basis of a system in which wealth and power were concentrated in the hands of a conservative agrarian oligarchy which was in a position to suspend legal guarantees not just for the slave population, but for much of the free population as well. Indeed, in a number of respects the concentration of wealth and power in the hands of planters and slaveowners looked strikingly similar to the aristocratic privileges which European liberalism had arisen to combat.[10]

Thus as the century progressed, those Brazilians committed to realizing the liberal promise of independence came to view slavery as one of the major obstacles to the realization of their hopes and aspirations. It was not until the second half of the century that elite and middle-class adherents to such a view became sufficiently numerous and mobilized to exercise much influence over Brazilian politics. While these liberal abolitionists were slowly growing in number, however, another group of Brazilians had perceived the contradiction between slavery and liberalism early on, and had increasingly proceeded to act on it. These Brazilians were the slaves themselves.

This raises a third, and perhaps the most powerful, tension inherent in forced labor: the unrelenting opposition and resistance of those subjected to it. One of the fundamental constants of New World slavery was that most slaves disliked forced servitude, and would go to considerable, and sometimes extreme, effort either to alter the conditions of their enslavement or to escape them entirely. There were as many ways to achieve these goals as there were slaves. Some sought to improve their lives by doing as little work as possible; others sought the same objective by working diligently and trying to attract their masters' favorable notice and approval. Some slaves sought to improve their diet by growing their own food on small subsistence plots; others concentrated their energies on earning money with which to buy food, freedom, or other goods; some stole, from either their masters or elsewhere; some did all three. Some slaves tried to escape slavery by fleeing their master's home or plantation; others concentrated on winning their owner's good will, in hopes of some-day obtaining a grant of freedom; others worked for money in their spare time and on holidays, and over the years accumulated enough to buy freedom for themselves or their children; the desperate ones sought freedom by killing either themselves or their masters.[11]

The struggle between owners seeking to derive maximum benefit from their property, and slaves seeking to improve their situation, or escape it entirely, made slavery an extremely tense and uneasy social system. As it spread into São Paulo, that tension became manifest in the province. As early as the 1770s and 1780s small *quilombos*, en-campments of runaway slaves, had appeared in the sugar-growing areas near Campinas, and by the 1810s plantation owners in those areas were expressing to royal officials "daily fears of assaults or invasions by our slaves." Such fears were aggravated in the 1830s by a wave of slave uprisings in Rio de Janeiro, Minas Gerais, and the northeastern provinces. The 1838 revolt of three hundred slaves on a Rio coffee plantation struck particularly close to home. It required the intervention of federal troops to put down, and, in the words of the Campinas planters, badly aggravated their "constant fright and fear of a sudden slave uprising." Such fears were by no means unrea-sonable, given that in 1830 and 1832 the Campinas authorities had uncovered rebellions being organized among slaves from a number of plantations. Similar uprisings of slaves along the coast, near Uba-tuba, were foiled in 1825 and 1831.[12]

Historians still know relatively little about the reasons for this intensification of slave uprisings in the 1830s.[13] Part of the explanation can doubtless be found in the generalized political turmoil of the decade. Facing increasing domestic opposition which culminated in a wave of urban riots in Rio de Janeiro, in 1831 Brazil's first emperor, Dom Pedro I, abdicated the throne in favor of his five-year-old son, Dom Pedro II. Until such time as the young crown prince reached the age of majority, executive power was vested in a three-man regency, elected by Parliament. Between 1831 and 1837, the regents and Parliament undertook a six-year "liberal experiment" aimed at decentralizing political authority and undoing the allegedly excessive concentration of power in the hands of the monarchy. Prominent among these reforms were the abolition of the emperor's Council of State, and the transfer of a number of administrative functions from the monarchy and Parliament to the newly created provincial assemblies.[14]

This weakening of the central government set the stage for a series of provincial rebellions which began in 1832 and continued into the 1840s. Slaves and free blacks were active participants in these uprisings, and also launched separate protests as well.[15] We may speculate that they were motivated not just by the crisis of central authority, which created unusual opportunities for collective action. There was also the jarring disparity between the liberal ideals of freedom and equality evoked first by independence, and now by the parliamentary reforms of the 1830s, and the continuing reality of forced servitude.

The first visible evidence of slaves and free blacks using liberal republican ideology as a weapon in the struggle against slavery and racial privilege had occurred in 1798 in the northeastern city of Salvador, where authorities uncovered a conspiracy to raise the black and poor white populations in a rebellion inspired by the French Revolution's calls for liberty, equality, and fraternity. In a Brazilian context (as in Haiti at the same time), such principles meant, not just the destruction of aristocratic privilege, but also the overturning of slavery and of all legal distinctions based on race.[16]

Prompt action by the authorities dismantled the plot before it came to fruition. It could not prevent the further dissemination of republicanism among members of the black population, however, many of whom by the 1810s were enthusiastic proponents of independence. Slaves and free blacks played a prominent role in the republican uprising of 1817 in Pernambuco; and in 1821 fifteen thousand slaves in Minas Gerais, responding to reports and rumors that independence was at hand and a new constitution was about to written, converged on the provincial capital to celebrate the freedom which they assumed this new charter would grant them, and to demand that blacks be declared juridically equal to whites.[17]

When independence came a year later, however, it was as the result of a fundamentally conservative movement that removed Portuguese rule but maintained intact virtually all the institutions created by colonialism. Slavery, the plantations, and even the monarchy all remained in place. Subsequent legislation sought to protect slaves in specific ways, stipulating limits of punishment beyond which masters were forbidden to go (for example, no more than fifty lashes of the whip per day), and decreeing the freedom of Africans introduced into the country after the outlawing of the slave trade in 1831. But such laws were routinely (and, in the case of the 1831 anti-slave-trade law, systematically) disobeyed. And additional postindependence legislation continued longstanding colonial restrictions on slaves, further confirming the absence of change. Slaves were forbidden to testify in court or bring complaints against their masters; they were forbidden to wear fine clothing, carry arms, or be outside their houses after dark unless they had permission from their masters; they were prohibited from gathering in groups for whatever purpose, unless with the prior permission of their masters and the authorities; and so on.[18]

The rebellions of the 1830s failed to modify any of these strictures, or to produce any significant change in slavery as an institution. To the contrary: they provoked sharp repression, and heightened fears by slaveowning elites throughout Brazil that, by weakening central authority, the liberal reforms of the 1830s had opened the door to social upheaval and political violence. Their response was the conservative *regresso* (return) of the 1840s, in which the liberal legislation of the 1830s was modified or overturned, and central authority was reconstituted under Dom Pedro II, crowned emperor in 1840. The regresso provoked a final wave of provincial rebellions (but no slave uprisings), which by 1850 had been definitively repressed.[19]

This consolidation and extension of state power intensified the conflicts inherent in the contradictory relationship among slaves, landowners, and the monarchy. Landowners saw no alternatives to a slave labor force, and demanded both expanded slave imports, and an expanded imperial presence to repress the growing slave population and keep it under control. But as the monarchy assumed the role of guarantor, enforcer, and mediator of the master-slave relationship, the terms of its mediation became increasingly unacceptable to the planters. Following its own modernizing program, and under pressure as well from the abolitionist movement, after 1850 the monarchy proved unexpectedly supportive of slave interests, and even adopted policies which called into question the very existence of slavery as an institution. Searching for new forms of resistance less risky than that of open rebellion, the slaves began to notice, and take advantage of, the opportunities created by the expanded state presence in the regulation of slavery, and the monarchy's ambivalent attitude toward the institution. The resulting convergence of interests among Crown, slaves, and abolitionists, which culminated in the complete abolition of slavery by the Golden Law of 1888, formed a direct threat to the planters, particularly those in that part of Brazil where plantation agriculture and the slave population had been growing most rapidly: the coffee-growing Southeast. Thus emancipation and the disgruntled planters of São Paulo would both play a major role in the destruction of the monarchy and the declaration of the Republic a mere eighteen months after the abolition of slavery.[20]

The Struggle for Emancipation[21]

The consolidation of monarchical authority in 1850 coincided with the first step in the destruction of Brazilian slavery: the effective ending of the Atlantic slave trade to Brazil. The 1831 antislaving treaty with Great Britain had never been enforced by the government, and had been flagrantly disregarded by buyers and sellers alike. In fact, between 1845 and 1850 the slave trade reached its all-time high, with an average of fifty-five thousand Africans arriving in the country each year.[22]

The very intensity of the trade, however, proved to be its undoing. The unprecedented volume of slave imports during the 1840s gave rise to fears that Brazil was being inundated by a potentially rebellious African population which might cause a repetition of the uprisings of the 1830s. It also provoked increased British diplomatic pressure to bring the trade to an end, and armed interventions in 1849 and 1850 by British warships in several Brazilian ports. In an effort to repel the invasion of Brazil both by African slaves and by British cruisers, the emperor's Council of State proposed the termination of the slave trade, which was promptly approved by the Chamber of Deputies and the Senate. Subsequent enforcement by imperial authorities (including the armed forces and the police) proved effective: imports dropped from 54,061 in 1849 to 22,856 the following year, and to 3,287 in 1851. By 1853 they had ceased entirely.[23]

Given the consistent excess of deaths over births in the Brazilian slave population, and the resulting inability of that population to sustain itself, the ending of the slave trade spelled slavery's eventual and inevitable demise. The key word here, however, is "eventual." In São Paulo, for example, the annual rate of decrease of the slave population, absent imports, was between 0.5 and 1.0 percent per year.[24] This meant that, even at maximum rates of decline, the slave population would still number more than fifty thousand by 1900, and more than thirty thousand by 1950.

The ending of the slave trade, therefore, was only the first step toward the elimination of slavery. The second came in 1871, when Dom Pedro's prime minister, Viscount Rio Branco, proposed the Law of the Free Womb, by which children born of slave mothers would be free upon reaching the age of majority. The bill also guaranteed slaves the right to buy their freedom (a right which they had long had in custom, but not in law), freed all slaves owned by the state, and created a state-administered fund to purchase the freedom of additional slaves not included in the 1871 legislation. After intense debate, the bill was approved by both houses of Parliament as the Rio Branco Law.

Why did legislators representing the agrarian interests of their various provinces agree to a bill which brought the abolition of slavery that much closer? Much of the explanation can be found in the regional redistribution of Brazilian slavery which had taken place over the course of the 1800s. The dramatic expansion of the coffee economy in southeastern Brazil had led to steady increases in the slave populations of those provinces. After the African slave trade was cut off in 1850, those increases were fueled, not by imports of Africans, but rather by a booming internal commerce which bought slaves in the economically stagnant Northeast and then transported them for sale to São Paulo, Rio, and Minas Gerais. In 1819, at the beginning of the coffee boom, half of Brazil's slaves had been located in the sugar-growing provinces of the Northeast, and only 37 percent in the coffee states. As a result of the interprovincial trade, by 1872 those proportions had neatly reversed themselves, with 32 percent of the nation's slaves now located in the Northeast, and 59 percent in the Southeast. Bahia's slave population had increased only marginally during that period; Pernambuco's was in full decline.[25]

Under pressure from both the government and the urban-based abolitionist movement, and seeing little future for slavery in their local economies, deputies from the northern states (which, because the Chamber of Deputies had not been reapportioned since 1824, were overrepresented in Parliament) reluctantly acquiesced in the bill. Not so the southern planters, who remained strongly committed to slavery as the only suitable form of labor for plantation agriculture, and who vigorously opposed the proposed legislation. That opposition was particularly intense in São Paulo, where landowners, angered in part by the emperor's appeals for the "reform" of slavery, had joined in 1870 to create the Republican Party, which called for the decentralization of the Brazilian state, and an end to imperial "Caesarism."[26]

The legislation of 1850 and 1871 constituted the most obvious and visible intervention by the monarchy in the affairs of masters and slaves. A less visible such intervention, initially unrelated to slavery, also had important impacts. This intervention was the legal procedural reform of 1841, which replaced locally elected justices of the peace with professional magistrates appointed by the Ministry of Justice.[27] Like the justices of the peace, imperial magistrates continued to be closely connected to local landowning elites, and responsive to their interests. But unlike the justices, professional judges were ultimately dependent not on the planters but rather on their superiors at the ministry. Most of the justices had been planters or businessmen with little knowledge of the law; the magistrates, by contrast, were law school graduates who formed part of a prestigious corps of professional administrators. And in the course of their legal training, many of them had come into contact with abolitionist literature and organizations; this was particularly the case among graduates of the law school in São Paulo, where by 1856 students had founded an active abolitionist society.[28]

The precise effects of the 1841 reform on local jurisprudence and administration remain to be studied. But recent research by Brazilian historians suggests that it had significant consequences for the slave population, and particularly for that population's ability to defend itself against the demands and impositions of slavery. For one, the new magistrates seem to have been less willing to ignore laws which conflicted with slaveowner interests. A prime example was the 1831 anti-slave-trade legislation, which, as we have seen, had simply been disregarded during the 1830s and 1840s. By the 1850s, Brazilian courts were routinely granting freedom to Africans who could prove that they had been brought into the country after 1831, and to the children of such Africans as well. In São Paulo Province specifically, one abolitionist lawyer, Afro-Brazilian Luis Gama, won freedom for several hundred slave clients during the 1860s and 1870s on the basis of the 1831 legislation.[29]

Further evidence suggesting a changed attitude on the part of the professional magistrates is the frequency with which slaves sought the protection of royal justice. Although large-scale slave rebellions had ceased by 1840, sporadic violence involving individuals or small groups of slaves continued. Following the judicial reform, planters and state officials in São Paulo noted that these crimes were taking on a new wrinkle: the usual pattern when slaves assaulted overseers or masters had been for them to try to escape into the forest and evade royal justice. Now, instead of running away, slaves were increasingly likely to turn themselves over to the police, confess their crimes, and demand the opportunity to have their cases heard in court.[30]

Some apparently did so in hopes of being sentenced either to prison or to the *galés* (literally, the "galleys"; hard labor on a chain gang), either of which they viewed as preferable to working on a plantation under a sadistic overseer or master.[31] Others, however, seem to have been relying on royal justice to judge their cases fairly, and to protect them from the cruelty of abusive masters and overseers. And it appears that this trust was not entirely misplaced. Both the formal and informal rules of Brazilian legal procedure continued to favor masters over slaves; but as the climate of public opinion, particularly among educated urban elites, turned against slavery,

judges now viewed with less tolerance the brutal excesses of plantation slavery, and proved more sympathetic to slaves seeking protection under the law.[32]

In their pleas and testimony, slaves responded to this opening by
trying to expand the boundaries of "justice" to include not just the
formal dictates of the law but also broader concepts of rights, customs, and obligations. In the cases referred to above, slaves in São
Paulo justified assaults, and even murder, as efforts to redress a
variety of grievances: their being sold to masters they did not wish to
work for; the sale of members of their families; demands by overseers
on leisure time to which slaves felt themselves entitled by custom; the
inadequate provision by masters of food or clothing; and so on. In
each of these cases slaves explained their actions in terms which
blended concepts of moral economy with liberal concepts of contract: when masters broke their implicit contracts with slaves, or
violated usages established by custom, slaves were entitled to seek
redress. And when masters denied them direct access to the courts or
the police, slaves had no choice but to take matters into their own
hands, and ensure by violent acts that they would finally be granted
access to the emperor's justice.[33]

In each of these cases, slaves were implicitly demanding the rights
accorded free men and women.[34] That demand became explicit in an
1871 murder case which sent shock waves running through the coffee
zones. When asked why he had killed his master, a slave in Rio Claro
replied that he had done so because "he did not know why he had to
work all his life for the exclusive benefit of a man who was his equal."
Seeking an explanation for how a plantation slave could ever imagine
that he was the equal of his master, a committee of 171 planters from
the Campinas region focused on the increasingly Brazilian character
of the slave population, and the slaves' greater familiarity with Brazilian life and customs.

These bondsmen, born and raised among us, and consequently sharing our
temperament and customs, and possessing an intellectual capacity that is
much more developed than that of their primitive forbears, tend to have
aspirations that are compatible with their development, and thus tend to
have freed themselves from that passive subservience characteristic of the
Africans. Their intimate communion with the free population in promis-

cuous relationships, and their mixed racial nature, has made them an intermediate type between the African and Latin races, and has given them an ability to debate the right of property which is imposed on them by the law, and to question the legitimacy and origin of that right.[35]

During the first half of the century the slaves brought to São Paulo had been newly arrived Africans. The termination of African imports in 1850 had marked a new phase in the slave trade, in which the coffee plantations would then be supplied by an internal slave trade that pulled slaves out of urban areas and nonplantation agriculture and dispatched them to the coffee zones. By the 1860s and 1870s the overwhelming majority of these new plantation workers were native-born Afro-Brazilians familiar with the language, customs, and laws of their country.[36] They were also aware of the growing opposition to slavery among free Brazilians, an opposition which was based in the urban areas from which many of them came, and where slavery was being gradually eliminated by the sale of slaves into the countryside. And even the Africans who were held on São Paulo's plantations and had now lived for a decade or more in Brazil were likely to know Portuguese, and were less set apart from each other by the differences in African origins and language which had divided the slaves along ethnic lines and made them more vulnerable to landowner control. Members of both these groups—native-born Brazilian slaves, and more acculturated Africans—were aware that slavery was in crisis, and that it was being seriously questioned by a growing body of Brazilian public opinion. Many were also aware that slavery as an institution directly contravened the religious and civic principles on which Brazilian life claimed to be based. Now they started to act on this knowledge, justifying their resistance and seeking legal redress by citing the inherent injustice of slavery and its denial, not only of God's laws, but of man's laws as well.

Such developments considerably sharpened the cutting edge of traditional forms of slave resistance. And as public and official support for slavery dwindled, the slaves were even emboldened to return to the rebellions of the 1820s and 1830s. In 1879 slaves rose up in Limeira, near Campinas; police uncovered several slave conspiracies in 1881; and bloody rebellions broke out on plantations near Cam-

pinas in 1882 and 1883. As in earlier cases involving individual
crimes, the slaves' vision of the police and the courts as defenders of
their rights emerges clearly. Having heard reports (false, as it turned
out) that emancipation had been decreed by Dom Pedro, the Campinas rebels had concluded that their masters were holding them in
servitude illegally. After taking over their plantations and killing
several whites, they then marched to town to turn themselves in to
the police, "telling all the facts with the most admirable sang-froid,"
as a Rio newspaper reported, and demanding that they be freed.[37]

These events amply confirmed a São Paulo assemblyman's observation in 1878 that, with respect to slavery, "there is no doubt that we
are on the edge of the abyss, treading on a volcano."[38] Yet even at this
late date, the province's planters remained firmly committed to slavery. Most had large sums invested in their slaves and did not care to
face the financial loss entailed by emancipation. Even those who
could absorb such losses found it difficult to see who would provide
the necessary labor for the coffee plantations if slavery were eliminated. They assumed that slaves would never work except under dire
compulsion, and they were deeply pessimistic about the free peasant
population as well, whose members for the most part displayed a
strong aversion to accepting regular employment on the plantations.
Seeing no real alternative to the labor system which had sustained
plantation agriculture in Brazil for centuries, the planters resolved to
stick to their guns and ride out the crisis as long as they could.[39]

The intransigence of the São Paulo planters left the abolitionist
movement in that province little recourse but to adopt a correspondingly radical stance and work outside the formal political system.
Following the death of Luis Gama in 1882, leadership of the movement in São Paulo was seized by Antônio Bento, a renegade member
of the landowning class who advocated the destruction of slavery by
any means necessary, including violence.[40] Basing his operations in
the black church of Nossa Senhora dos Remédios in the provincial
capital, Bento and his followers (many of whom were members of the
church's lay brotherhood) organized networks of *caifazes*, agents who
circulated through the countryside spreading news of the movement,
of the abolition of slavery elsewhere in Brazil (the provinces of Ama-
zonas and Ceará had outlawed slavery in 1884) and Latin America

(slavery was abolished in Cuba in 1886), and urging the slaves to rise up against their masters and flee.

Again slaves seized the opening created by political conflict among the free population. Aided and abetted by the abolitionists, by 1887 slaves were fleeing from São Paulo's plantations en masse. Imperial troops arrived to reinforce the police but, when faced with the impossible task of apprehending thousands of runaways, their officers formally petitioned the monarchy to be relieved of this assignment. If slaveowners were going to use force to hold on to their slaves, they would have to apply it themselves.[41]

It was at this point, and only at this point, that São Paulo's *fazendeiros* finally accepted the inevitability of emancipation. The impossibility of maintaining slavery in the face of massive slave resistance was clear, and in August and September of 1887 the province's Republican Party convened a series of meetings of planters in Campinas to discuss how to resolve the crisis. They sought to extend conditions of servitude a few more years by offering to free their slaves in return for the slaves' commitment to continue serving their masters—though now for wages—until 1890. But it was too late for such half measures. Faced with the prospect of the complete disintegration of slavery in the province, new meetings of planters were called for December in São Paulo City, at which the landowners abruptly changed course and launched a campaign of "planter emancipationism." During slavery's last year of existence, forty thousand slaves were freed by their masters in the coffee regions of central and western São Paulo, over a third of the state's total slave population. In February 1888 slavery was formally abolished in São Paulo City, and on March 13 the provincial Assembly unanimously petitioned Parliament to abolish slavery in Brazil.[42]

By May 13, 1888, when Princess Regent Isabel[43] signed the Lei Aurea, the Golden Law which definitively abolished slavery throughout Brazil, São Paulo's coffee planters were congratulating themselves on having anticipated the inevitable and ended slavery "through the spontaneous will of the masters, without the intervention of the authorities."[44] As we have seen, however, the masters' decision was hardly spontaneous, and there had in fact been considerable intervention by the imperial authorities, beginning with the abolition of the slave trade in 1850 and culminating in the army's refusal to stem the tide of slave flight during 1887 and 1888. There had also been substantial intervention on the part of the slaves, a point which was not lost on observers and participants at the time. A French visitor to São Paulo at the turn of the century was informed by his hosts that abolition took place because "the situation of such owners as had retained their slaves was becoming difficult; and discipline on the plantations was becoming impossible. The abolition law merely ratified the already profound disorganization of slave labour"—a disorganization produced, of course, by the slaves themselves.[45] An 1898 editorial commemorating the tenth anniversary of emancipation explained the event in almost identical terms.

Had the slaves not fled en masse from the plantations, rebelling against their masters . . . Had 20,000 of them not fled to the famous quilombo of Jabaquara [outside the port city of Santos, a center of abolitionist agitation], they might still be slaves today. . . . Slavery ended because the slave didn't wish to be a slave any longer, because the slave rebelled against his master and the law that enslaved him. . . . The May 13th law was no more than the legal sanctioning, so that public authority wouldn't be discredited, of an act that had already been consummated by the mass revolt of the slaves. . . . [46]

And even the previously cited report by São Paulo's provincial government, despite lauding the planters' "spontaneous decision," made clear the motives and forces behind that decision.

. . . toward the middle of 1887 . . . grave and unforeseen events precipitated the conclusion of slavery in the province. We refer to the flight en masse of slaves from a large number of agricultural establishments and the consequent abandonment of agriculture. These events, assuming ever more alarming proportions, partly because of the effects of the sudden withdrawal of workers from the plantations, partly because of the dangers posed to public security on the highways and in the towns through which the bands of fleeing slaves passed, could not fail to alarm the public spirit, inspiring apprehension and disquiet. . . . One could say, therefore, that by the end of 1887, if the emancipation of the slaves in all the province of São Paulo was not yet a reality, the hour of abolition was fast approaching.[47]

Though planters might try to claim credit for the achievement of emancipation, contemporary and subsequent observers acknowledged it as "a victory of the people and, we may add, a victory by the free blacks and slaves."[48] For the first time in Brazilian history, a mass-based movement had triumphed against oligarchical interests. Describing the abolition of slavery as "the most genuine popular conquest" in Brazilian history, the *Diário de Campinas* stated flatly that "the people made Abolition." "Quite rare in our land, the executive branch being the mere executor of a decree by the people," mused São Paulo's *Diário Popular* on May 14. And writing four years after the event, an editorialist in *O Estado de São Paulo* observed that popular opinion tended to attribute abolition to Princess Isabel and her decision to free the slaves, but that in fact it had been the first expression of democracy in the country's history. ". . . A mass-based movement, deeply and profoundly of the people, and spread over the entire vastness of our country, we have but one example in our history, and that is the movement that on May 13, 1888 achieved its glorious ratification, and its recognition by the government."[49]

The public response to that triumph was electrifying. The novelist Machado de Assis recalled that the celebrations following the passage of the Golden Law were "the only instance of popular delirium that I can remember ever having seen." One São Paulo newspaper described the crowds that gathered to celebrate: "To try to describe the splendor of that festival of joy, to tell everything that happened, falls beyond our abilities. . . . Never has this capital seen such multitudinous and unanimous enthusiasm. The common people, like children, forgot at times that they were celebrating the victory of their own beliefs, their own labors, their own sacrifices, and that they were glorifying those [the planters and legislators] who had submitted to the popular will." In later years another São Paulo journalist looked back to the fateful event to recall how "it was the first time in my entire life that I saw the common people, really the common people—carrying on like children, roaring with laughter, abandoning their work, scandalously displaying their joy. . . ."[50]

These quotations reveal several of the assumptions which undergirded Brazilian political culture in the nineteenth century (and which have survived, only slightly eroded, into the late twentieth century). Politics was an elite pursuit, one strictly off limits to the population at large. On this one occasion, therefore, when that population succeeded in imposing its will on national politics, it was recognized by all concerned as a unique and unprecedented moment.

Nor was it coincidental that several of these writers should independently concur in describing that population (*o povo*, the people) as children, since it was precisely the role of powerless, incompetent dependents that the great mass of the population was supposed to play in relation to the planter oligarchy. So when that *povo* uncharacteristically rose up to assert a role for itself in the setting of national policy, it might actually have seemed to the journalist quoted above that this was the first time in his life that he had seen the "common people." In fact he had seen them every day of his life, in the streets and squares of the city, and working as servants in private homes. But it was indeed the first time that he had seen them as active participants in politics—and, even more than active participants, as successful, victorious participants.

This had never happened before in Brazilian history, and the planters were determined that it never happen again. Accepting the Golden Law thrust on them by the society at large, São Paulo's planters now set about to structure postemancipation political, social, and economic arrangements in such a way as to ensure that their interests would never again be so directly challenged by popular forces.

The Aftermath of Emancipation

The political component of this restructuring centered on the overthrow of the monarchy, and its replacement by a decentralized Republic thoroughly controlled and dominated by provincial agrarian elites. The destruction of the monarchy occurred in November 1889, a year and a half after the Golden Law, and was engineered in large part by planters from São Paulo. During the 1870s and 1880s paulista landowners had increasingly come to feel that the institutions of the monarchy—particularly Parliament, which had not undergone reapportionment since the 1820s, and the upper house of which was appointed for life by the emperor—failed to give their state representation proportionate either to its population or to its financial contribution to the Empire. Leading the republican movement (which they had founded in 1870), and then conspiring in 1888 and 1889 with military officers who had also become dissatisfied with monarchical rule, the paulista Republicans "were the only group outside Rio de Janeiro to participate" in the overthrow of the monarchy. They then took a leading role in structuring the new Republic created by the Constitution of 1891.[51]

Characterized by a decentralized federal structure and extremely low levels of suffrage, the Republic proved to be the perfect vehicle for planter rule in São Paulo as throughout Brazil. "This system, directed by the president of the Republic and the governors of São Paulo and Minas Gerais, was an arrangement for the mutual support of incumbent elites at all levels of government."[52] Pierre Denis, a contemporary French observer, describes how it worked.

Brazil has, it is true, established universal suffrage; but the sovereign people, before delegating its sovereignty to its representatives, confides to the ruling class the duty of supervising its electoral functions. The large landed proprietors choose the candidates, and their instructions are usually obeyed. They form the structure, the framework, of all party politics; they are its strength, its very life; it is they who govern and administer Brazil.[53]

Denis erred in only one respect: the Constitution did not establish universal suffrage, but rather limited it to literate males, only a small minority of whom ever troubled to cast a vote.[54] Even more than the monarchy, the Republic was the ideal "planter state," one in which landowners held full sway over state and national politics.[55] The monarchy had at least maintained a multiparty electoral system in which Liberals, Conservatives, and, after 1870, Republicans competed against each other for power. Under the Republic, however, "interparty competition was almost meaningless and usually nonexistent." Political participation, as measured in suffrage, was more restricted than under the monarchy, and no "moderating power" now stood between the Brazilian masses and the landowners.[56]

Many of São Paulo's Afro-Brazilians, particularly those who had been born free, grown up in urban areas, and had some access to education, saluted the advent of the Republic with high hopes. Blacks meeting in Campinas two weeks after the fall of the monarchy voted to express their "complete solidarity" with the Republic, which they saw as "a guarantee to the colored class that, under the banner of this patriotic [Republican] party, distinctions of class and race will disappear; . . . [and] the present government will put into effect measures aimed at public education and the instruction of the *libertos.*"[57]

Other blacks, however, particularly the newly freed libertos, were not so sure. They knew the planters firsthand, and knew that those planters had no real interest in their former slaves' welfare. Nor were the planters about to give up the "distinctions of class and race" which set them apart from the great mass of Brazilians. Furthermore, many libertos saw the monarchy as the benevolent force which, within their lifetimes, had freed the children of slave mothers (1871), slaves over the age of 60 (1886), and, finally, the entire slave population (1888). Slaves had also come to see royal justice as an important resource that they could use in defending their rights, a frequently (if not always successfully) invoked protection against abusive, exploitative masters.[58]

For these Afro-Brazilians, the choice between the monarchy, which had brought slavery to an end, and a Republic headed by planters who had refused to accept emancipation until it had been forced on them by their slaves, was one weighted heavily toward monarchy, especially when the most prominent black abolitionists had publicly expressed their unhappiness with the Republican movement. Like his white counterpart Joaquim Nabuco, mulatto engineer André Rebouças had linked his appeals for abolition with demands for land reform and "rural democracy," and with fervent attacks on "latifundia, feudal barons, landlords, and Landocracy"—in other words, the planter class. An intimate of the royal family, Rebouças went into exile with them in 1889, and never returned to Brazil. Lawyer Luis Gama, an early and enthusiastic Republican, eventually resigned from the party in disgust over its failure to take a stand against slavery. Journalist José do Patrocínio, an original signer of the Republican Manifesto of 1870, took an even more radical path. In the months following abolition, as the monarchy entered its death throes, Patrocínio fought a desperate rearguard action by enlisting former slaves in the Black Guard, a paramilitary organization which he founded in Rio de Janeiro. Arguing that the Guard was necessary to protect the royal family from being overthrown by former slave-owners embittered by the Golden Law, he used it to disrupt and break up Republican lectures and meetings, sometimes with considerable attendant violence.[59]

Disturbed by these events in the nation's capital, São Paulo's Republicans sought to prevent the Black Guard from establishing any sort of foothold in the province. The Republican organ A *Província de São Paulo* reported on the Guard's attempts to organize units in the towns and cities of the province, and on how local Republicans and landowners were working to thwart such efforts, often in conjunction with black Republicans—though given the racial rhetoric employed against the Guard, one wonders how the Republicans succeeded in attracting any black supporters at all. *A Província* argued that the struggle "is not between monarchist libertos and Republican libertos; unfortunately it is between blacks and whites . . . whites for the Republic and blacks for the monarchy. . . ." "Every drop of white blood which is shed will be a blot on the face of the government. . . . This is no longer a question of Republican propaganda: our very civilization is at stake, the well-being of the population, the economic life of the country, and the moral supremacy of the white race."[60]

Because of the smaller black population in São Paulo, as compared with Rio, and the much greater strength of Republicanism in the province, the Black Guard never succeeded in establishing itself there. Nevertheless, monarchist sentiment was visible among the paulista black population. In Jundiaí monarchists forcibly ejected Republicans from the May 13 Club, an Afro-Brazilian social organization, leading to counterdemonstrations and fighting outside the club's headquarters. As late as 1930 the black papers published in São Paulo City were carrying news of monarchist clubs and social organizations in the black community; that same year the members of the Vai-Vai samba school, today one of the city's most important, opted to place a crown at the center of their flag, as homage to the monarchy.[61]

Former masters and former slaves differed, therefore, in their vision of the most appropriate political institutions for their new, postemancipation society. This disagreement in turn formed part of a larger disagreement, articulated both in action and in words, over the character and meaning of freedom itself. Not surprisingly, the libertos viewed freedom with hope and optimism; most landowners, by contrast, viewed the coming of freedom with deep disquiet, and a strong sense of uneasiness concerning the changes that it would bring in its wake.

Many landowners feared a continuation of the turmoil and violence which they had faced during the final years of slavery, and

particularly during 1887 and 1888. This fear expressed itself in a
variety of media, ranging from political debates to popular fiction. A
story published shortly after abolition in the *Correio Paulistano* recounted the gruesome tale of two former slaves who tried to heal a
sick white girl through *macumba* (witchcraft or sorcery). Having
failed in their efforts to save her life, they then baked her in a meat
pie which they served to the girl's unsuspecting mother. White people
got their revenge, however, in another short piece published in a
neighborhood newspaper in São Paulo, in which the author was
walking down a country lane when he was suddenly attacked by a
towering black man wielding a knife. He managed to pull out a gun
and blow his attacker's head off, leaving "fragments of his yellow
brain swimming in the blood and the mud."[62]

Both stories offered vivid images of the threat posed to white
people by perverse and savage black people. In both cases, however,
their authors readily admitted that they were utterly fictitious. At the
end of the second story, in fact, the author wakes to discover that he
has been dreaming, and that outside his window the sun is shining
and the birds are singing, "as if to drive away the final scenes of that
imaginary tragic drama, that horrible nightmare!" And indeed, even
under slavery, the "horrible nightmare" of black people rising up to
murder whites had flourished more in the imagination of the time
than in reality. Although the sensational episodes of slave attacks on
foremen and masters had dominated legislative debate and the front
pages of newspapers during the 1860s and 1870s, the fact was that
such violent forms of resistance were used by only a tiny minority of
slaves. Flight, which presented less immediate risk than open de-
fiance, remained the favored form of slave resistance through 1888. It
had been mass flight rather than armed rebellion which dealt slavery
its death blow, and as long as that flight was not obstructed, it usually
remained peaceful in form and intent. Francisco Lázaro Gonçalves,
the director of Minas Gerais's Association for the Promotion of Immigration, had visited São Paulo during the first months of 1888 to study
events there. While he could not condone the slaves' desertion of the
plantations, he felt compelled to report the facts as he had seen them.

Here let the truth be said, in justice to the slaves, whom the thirst for freedom
did not fascinate to the point of their using force on the plantations, or

committing robberies or disrespect against their former masters. No, the slaves abandoned the plantations either in small groups or en masse, making no show of the force that their numbers gave them, without discourtesies or unpleasantness. . . .[63]

The last year of slavery in the province had indeed been one of marked disorder, fear, and violence. But most observers concurred that relatively little of that violence could be laid to the slave population. Rather, most of it, and particularly the riots and confrontations that took place in the towns and cities, was the product of conflicts within the free population, among abolitionists, the police, and private slave-hunters hired by the planters. With freedom now in their grasp, few slaves were willing to risk it by engaging in violence. Instead, they had thrown themselves into a campaign of mass civil disobedience, one which Ruy Barbosa, a leading abolitionist from Bahia, would later characterize as "that glorious exodus of São Paulo's slaves, solemn, Biblical, as divine as the most beautiful episodes of the Scriptures."[64]

Once emancipation had taken place, and both slaves and abolitionists had achieved their goal of freedom, any remaining justification or rationale for further violence dissipated rapidly. Indeed, one of the motive forces behind the spread of "planter emancipationism" through the province had been the recognition that eliminating slavery would bring violence and the struggle against slavery to an end. Once emancipation had taken place, however, the second great uncertainty of freedom arose. What will happen, asked the *Província de São Paulo* in 1889, "when the libertos, with this education [of freedom] behind them, organize to impose salary conditions, hours of work, protection for their children?"[65]

The real danger posed by abolition was not so much physical violence as the empowering of Brazil's ex-slaves to join with the planters in negotiating the terms on which both parties would live and work together. Many planters were unable to imagine, let alone accept, the concept of bargaining with their former slaves. And those who were capable of either were deeply pessimistic about the likely outcomes of such a negotiation. Their pessimism was based on the assumption, the product of centuries of experience with slavery, that workers would not work unless forced to. The planters believed this to be true, not only of those Brazilians who had been born slaves, but those who had been born free as well. By the time of abolition such beliefs were being strongly reinforced by the currents of scientific racism sweeping the Atlantic world, which decreed the irredeemable inferiority of nonwhite and racially mixed peoples. Visiting French naturalist Louis Couty concisely summed up the application of such theories to Brazil in his declaration that "Brazil does not have people, or rather, the people that it was given by race mixture and by the freeing of the slaves do not play an active and useful role" in the country's development.[66] Such pessimistic evaluations of Brazil's racially mixed population struck a responsive chord among the nation's elite, who over the previous three centuries had been developing their own autochthonous *ideologia da vadiagem*, a firm and unshakable belief in the innate laziness and irresponsibility of the black and racially mixed Brazilian masses. Again, this belief was based on the harsh experience of plantation agriculture in Brazil. It was undeniably true that slaves did not want to work under such conditions; and it was equally true that free people did not either. Slaves had no choice in the matter; free people did, and used that power of choice to maintain as great a distance between themselves and plantation labor as possible. To the planters, the conclusion to be drawn from such a historical experience was obvious: slaves and free workers alike were *vadios*, bums and vagrants, who would not work except under the threat of extreme force—and often, not even then. Indeed, many planters had argued in response to the abolitionists that, with free workers of such abysmal quality, Brazil had no choice but to stick with slavery, since only under slavery could the plantations meet their labor needs.[67]

Even Brazilians opposed to the institution of slavery tended to share the *ideologia da vadiagem*, and accepted, either implicitly or explicitly, the notion that emancipation would not mean the end of coercion in the workplace. An 1845 proposal to replace slaves with free workers called for the creation of an "industrial army" of fifteen thousand young men, who would be drafted and subjected to military discipline during a five-year term of service. A later proposal to transform slaves gradually into free sharecroppers farming the same land they had worked as bondsmen summarized its ideas as "consisting simply of changing the denomination of *slaves* to *tenants*." By the

1880s the paulista abolitionist paper *A Redempção* felt that more should be changed than just the name, but agreed with the planters that most slaves were not adequately prepared for complete and absolute freedom. What was necessary was to "invent, under the title of contract laborer, a transitional status which [would have] nothing in common with slavery but which also would prevent the slave from supposing that he [had] the complete freedom to remain idle. . . ."[68]

The Rio Branco Law of 1871 had contained clauses prohibiting libertos from engaging in *vadiagem*, and obligating them to work. No such provisions were included in the Golden Law, however, and planters now found themselves facing the dreaded prospect of a labor force under no compulsion to work. Many planters refused at first to face the new realities, trying instead to retain as much of the old system as possible. Some of the initial efforts in this direction were extremely crude. Some *fazendeiros* sent hired gunmen to the local train station to meet trains, remove their black passengers at gunpoint, and force them into accepting employment. Other planters were slightly more subtle, working closely with local law enforcement officials to round up libertos, charge them under local vagrancy ordinances, and force them back to the plantations. Another tactic frequently denounced by libertos and abolitionists was the threat by local officials to draft libertos into the army or police, which they could escape only by signing a labor contract with a local landowner.[69]

Other planters, however, gradually came to realize that they could come to mutually agreeable arrangements with libertos without the use of strong-arm tactics. These planters recognized that emancipation had significantly altered the conditions under which work would be carried out on their plantations, and that in order to continue operating they would have to adapt to those new conditions. Thus began, in 1887 and 1888, a process of hard bargaining between the libertos and their former masters. What were the demands that the libertos presented? In comparison to the United States, where postemancipation bargaining is richly documented in plantation records, the archives of government agencies, and testimony by former slaves themselves, the historical record of such bargaining in Brazil is sparse and patchy. Nevertheless, those features of the negotiations that emerge in contemporary accounts offer clear similarities to the tug of war which took place in other slave societies following emancipation.[70]

While undeniably important, wages appear to have been almost a secondary consideration, pushed aside by the more pressing issue of working conditions. The libertos' overriding concern was to place as much distance as possible between themselves and their former status as slaves, and to ensure that their new conditions of employment bore as little resemblance as possible to their former servitude. For many freed men and women, this meant not accepting employment on plantations where they had been slaves. As one liberta declared in explaining why she was leaving the plantation where she had been born and raised, "I'm a slave and if I stay here, I'll remain a slave." "The idea of remaining in the house where he was a slave is repugnant to the liberto," one contemporary observer noted. Thus the mass flights from the plantations continued even after emancipation. Those who remained behind or sought work on other plantations demanded that the most noxious aspects of slavery be done away with. Foremen and overseers were to carry whips no longer, women and children were to be free of labor demands, and the locks were to be removed from the barracks in which the slaves had lived. Where possible, ex-slaves preferred to leave the barracks entirely and live in individual huts or shacks located far from the main house and free of direct supervision by the employer.[71]

Libertos were presenting these demands even before slavery was formally abolished. A Swiss visitor to São Paulo in late 1887 noted that the mass flights of that year had already started to transform the relationship between slave and master. The slaves' former passivity and sullen obedience had disappeared. "They raised their heads and began to speak aggressively to their masters; they imposed the conditions under which they wanted to continue to work, and at the smallest offense they threatened to leave." What is striking in this observation is not so much that slaves were demanding new conditions, which was only to be expected. Rather, it is that, when those demands were met, libertos *wanted* to continue to work. This observer's comment is corroborated by others. A letter by São Paulo planter Paula Souza, which appeared in *A Província de São Paulo* in April 1888, informed its readers that, despite their initial fears and misgivings, Souza and a number of his neighbors were having very positive experiences with their newly freed workers. The key to making new arrangements with one's workers, he reported, was to recognize that a "half-measure of freedom" would not do. The libertos "want to feel free, and to work under a new system, and with total responsibility." His willingness to concede "total, immediate, and unconditional freedom" to the libertos, and then to bargain with them in good faith, had led to his acquiring more than adequate supplies, not just of liberto workers, but of free peasant workers as well. This had been the experience of other planters in his region as well, "excluding proprietors with bad reputations. These, in fact, will be eliminated and replaced by the force of circumstances, and the agricultural system will not miss them."[72]

The previously quoted Lázaro Gonçalves, writing on his observations in the province in late 1887, seconded this point. In each of the plantations he visited, "the regime adopted by the ex-masters greatly influenced the behavior and decisions of the libertos." Those where planters had accepted the new situation continued to be staffed by "ex-slaves who had elected to stay, earning wages and still serving with the same obedience of former times, showing the greatest dedication to their ex-masters." Libertos needed jobs, and the planters needed the libertos, argued the *Diário de Campinas* in an editorial written three weeks after the passage of the Golden Law. Recent experience in the plantations around Campinas had shown that all that was required to work out mutually satisfactory arrangements between the two parties was for the planters to recognize that "the regime of slavery is over, and they will never find anyone to work for them unless they resolve to change their old habits acquired under slavery. . . . To a great degree a good employer produces a good employee, just as a bad employer produces a bad employee."[73]

The fact was that libertos trained in agricultural work and seeking employment in an overwhelmingly agrarian society had few alternative opportunities open to them. While some migrated to the cities, most remained in the countryside and were willing to accept work on the plantations, provided that it took place under conditions quite different from those which had characterized slavery. Where planters were willing to provide these new conditions, they had little difficulty attracting libertos back to work. As a result, the much-feared labor crisis which supposedly was destined to accompany emancipation simply failed to materialize. The harvests of 1888 and 1889 were brought in without disruption, and the plantations continued to function.[74]

Nevertheless, despite these positive outcomes, there was no denying that agriculture in São Paulo State, like all aspects of life in Brazil, had changed profoundly as a result of the Golden Law. The planters had dealt with their slaves for centuries from a position of unquestioned dominance. Emancipation had broken that dominance, even if only in part, and confronted the power of the planters with the massed power of the slaves and *o povo*. The implications of such an event were profoundly disturbing, as one of Minas Gerais's senators recognized at the time: "Slavery was abolished, in fact, by revolution."[75]

The Republic represented the planters' effort to contain and reverse the political, social, and economic consequences of that revolution. It would therefore prove to be a bitter disappointment to most of its black supporters. Far from doing away with "distinctions of class and race," as the black Republicans of Campinas had hoped, the Republic would cement landowner rule and then embark on a national campaign to "Europeanize" Brazil, a campaign in which the "whitening" of the national population, and the replacement of African racial heritage with European, would assume a prominent role. Intellectuals and policy makers developed a set of government programs aimed at transforming Brazil into a European society in the tropics. In a series of "urban reforms," downtown areas dominated by colonial-period buildings and architecture were torn down and rebuilt in European *belle époque* style. The Constitution of 1891 specifically banned African and Asian immigration into the country, and the national and state governments made the luring of European immigration into Brazil a priority of national development. And as the immigrants arrived, Brazilian sociologists and scientists busied themselves with research and writing which demonstrated to themselves and to the world how Brazil was rapidly transforming itself from a miscegenated backwater that looked "more like a corner of Africa than a nation of the New World" into a progressive Republic populated by Europeans and their descendants.[76]

Nowhere in Brazil was this effort to Europeanize the country more in force than in São Paulo, and nowhere in Brazil were its effects more strongly felt. A massive state program to subsidize European immigration into the state resulted in over half of the Europeans who came to Brazil during the Republic coming to São Paulo. Beyond the goal of Europeanizing the state, however, the program's primary purpose was to reverse the economic consequences of the "revolution" of emancipation, and to restore landowner control over the labor force. By the early 1890s its impacts were already evident, particularly among the recent beneficiaries of emancipation: the Afro-Brazilians.

3. Immigration, 1890–1930

During 1888 and 1889 former masters and former slaves in São Paulo began the unaccustomed exercise of bargaining and negotiating with each other over the conditions under which the latter would work for the former. Such negotiations continued into the 1890s, but were already being altered by the first rush of what would eventually prove to be a flood of European immigration into the state. In the forty years following emancipation São Paulo received over two million European immigrants, almost half of whom had their trans-Atlantic passages paid for by the state government.[1] Those immigrants had been brought to São Paulo to work, and work they did. In so doing, they systematically displaced and marginalized the state's Afro-Brazilian workers, in both the countryside and the cities. This chapter examines that displacement, focusing specifically on labor market competition between blacks and immigrants in the years after emancipation. What were the rules of that competition? Was the labor market a genuinely "free" one, or was it defined and structured in certain ways by the state, employers, workers acting through unions, or some combination thereof? If it was so defined, what were the consequences of a given labor market structure for the workers competing in that market, and for employers bidding for their services? In other words, how did the rules of the competition affect the outcome? And finally, what did black and immigrant workers bring to the competition, in terms of their skills, abilities, experience, and attitudes? And what sorts of bargains—among themselves, and with their employers and the state—were they willing to strike?

Structuring the Labor Market: The Planter State

Even prior to emancipation, free wage labor was not a complete anomaly on São Paulo's coffee plantations. As early as the 1850s a census of 2,600 coffee *fazendas* in the province showed that the labor force was over 10 percent free (versus 4 percent free on 667 sugar plantations canvased at the same time). Although most of these workers were native-born Brazilians, some of them were European immigrants who had come to the province in response to efforts by the imperial government and the provincial Assembly to promote European immigration to São Paulo and engage the immigrants in coffee cultivation. The results of these initial efforts were disappointing, from the point of view of both the immigrants and the planters. Accustomed to dealing mainly with slaves, planters tended to treat their immigrant employees in the same coercive manner; as the Swiss consul in Rio de Janeiro reported to his government, the objective of the Brazilian government seemed to be to substitute white slaves for black. One of the immigrants seconded this point, observing that, since immigrant workers had to contract heavy debts to pay the costs of their passage and supplies, there was little practical difference between a slave who had to pay two thousand milreis for his freedom, and an immigrant who owed his employer the same amount.[2]

Their initial experiences with immigrant labor left the planters dissatisfied as well. They were taken aback by the immigrants' resistance to the rigid plantation discipline, and then were aghast when the Europeans started to organize work stoppages and, in several cases, outright rebellion. By the 1860s immigrant labor had lost its attraction for the planters; seven thousand European settlers had arrived in the country between 1850 and 1860, but only sixteen hundred did so between 1860 and 1870.[3]

Europeans were not the only source of free labor available to the planters. São Paulo's free black, white, and *caboclo*[4] populations were available as well, in numbers exceeding the slave population. As we have seen, however, free Brazilians were reluctant to accept employment on coffee or sugar plantations. Like the immigrants, they found that planters tended to treat all their employees as slaves, even the free ones. Accepting plantation work thus put one uncomfortably close to slave status, especially if one were pardo or preto. As a result, free Brazilians and Africans preferred to remain in the subsistence sector, working their own plots of land and accepting plantation employment only on an occasional, sporadic basis. Even then they strongly preferred work which slaves did not do, such as clearing virgin land and building roads, both of which were considered too dangerous for owners to risk their slaves in.[5]

The perceived deficiencies of both free European and free Brazilian labor left São Paulo's planters little recourse but to continue buying slaves throughout the 1860s and 1870s, further cementing their dependence on slavery. As late as 1884, only one thousand families of free workers were employed on the province's coffee plantations.[6] Nevertheless, the ending of the slave trade in 1850 and the passage of the Rio Branco Law in 1871 were clear signs of slavery's eventual disappearance, and at least some of the province's planters were thinking about how they would deal with that eventual reality. Given the combined effects of scientific racism and the *ideologia da vadiagem*, the planters were deeply pessimistic about the prospect of making do with Brazilian workers. Debates in the provincial Assembly during the 1870s and 1880s on how to instill the "love of work" in the "national worker" invariably concluded with the judgment that, as one legislator elegantly put it, "they don't work because they're bums [*vadios*]." Another assemblyman rejected the notion of special programs or incentives to bring Brazilian workers to the plantations. "Either these individuals are workers or they're not. If they are workers, they don't need our help. And if they're not . . ."[7]

Such arguments were not applied to the Europeans, who suffered the liabilities of neither scientific racism (since they were white) nor the *ideologia da vadiagem* (since planters had not had enough experience with them to form strong fixed impressions). Thus in 1871 and 1872 São Paulo's Assembly set aside funds to underwrite costs incurred by planters wishing to bring immigrants from Europe to work on their plantations. Planters formed the Association to Aid Colonization and Immigration, which contracted to bring fifteen thousand workers to the province; unfortunately, by the conclusion of the contract in 1875 only 480 had arrived. Immigration picked up during the late 1870s, but "was still only a trickle compared to the growing labor demand in the coffee zone."[8]

Clearly more drastic action was required, and in 1884 the Assembly took it. In March of that year the provincial government appropriated 400,000 milreis to pay the travel costs of immigrants wishing to take up employment in agriculture, this amount to be funded by a new tax on slaves. Two years later, at the suggestion of the province's governor and supported by state funds, the private Society for the Promotion of Immigration was established to coordinate São Paulo's campaign to attract European workers. Responsible for informing European workers of employment opportunities available in São Paulo, paying their passage, overseeing their arrival in Brazil, and dispatching them to the coffee groves, the society carried out these functions until 1895, when they were taken over by the State Department of Agriculture (the Republican Constitution of 1891 having transformed São Paulo from a province into a state).[9]

European immigration to São Paulo did increase in response to these incentives, but not initially to levels sufficient to replace the slave labor force. Indeed, from the immigrants' point of view, this was precisely the problem: until the slave labor force *was* replaced, and free European workers no longer had to compete against coerced Africans and Afro-Brazilians, the immigrants were not inclined to come to Brazil, especially when they had the more attractive options of going to the United States or Argentina. To paraphrase Finley Peter Dunne, their fear was that employers who made slaves of black folks would make slaves of white folks too. And such fears were amply supported by widely publicized consular reports from European officials in São Paulo, who continued to describe working conditions for immigrants on São Paulo plantations as little better than slavery.[10]

Thus it was not until 1887, when the massive flights of slaves from the plantations foreshadowed the imminent demise of slavery, that annual European immigration into the province first broke the ten thousand mark. When it did, it jumped promptly to thirty-two thousand, more than the previous five years combined. Formal abolition in 1888 almost tripled that number, to ninety-two thousand—coincidentally, just slightly fewer than the number of slaves freed in the province that year by emancipation. Between 1890 and 1914 another

1.5 million Europeans would cross the Atlantic to São Paulo, the majority (63.6 percent) with their passages paid by the state government.[11]

From the planters' point of view, any benefits which these programs brought to the immigrants were purely incidental. Ever since the first discussions of subsidized immigration, the goal of such a program had been clear: to flood the labor market with workers, thus keeping the cost of labor low. The sponsor of the 1870 proposal to subsidize European immigration argued the desirability of creating a market situation in which "workers must search for landowners rather than landowners search for workers." Another supporter of the proposal noted the importance of "bringing in foreign workers, so that the cost of labor can go down. . . ." By the time the 1884 law was being debated, a growing number of planters had gotten the point: "It is impossible to have low salaries, without violence, if there are few workers and many people who wish to employ them." And by 1888: "It is evident that we need laborers . . . in order to increase the competition among them and in that way salaries will be lowered by means of the law of supply and demand." Yes, supply and demand would now replace the violence and coercion of slavery as a means of organizing production, argued Senator Antônio Prado, a member of one of the province's most prominent families, and an enthusiastic, if late, convert to "planter emancipationism." "Does the honorable opposition intend that the government should present to the legislature coercive means to force the libertos back to work? What might those means be? Might it not be that freedom is the most effective guarantee that the economic law of supply and demand will conveniently regulate conditions of labor?" And if the law of supply and demand did not happen to work to the planters' advantage, then a little market intervention, in the form of transportation subsidies to the immigrants, was perfectly permissible. After all, as Antônio Prado's brother Martinho cogently observed, "Immigrants with money are of no use to us."[12]

São Paulo's labor market in the years immediately following the abolition of slavery was one shaped by an unusual (in the context of the economic liberalism dominant in the turn-of-the-century Atlantic world, including Brazil) degree of state direction and intervention.[13] This was intervention seemingly devoid of any racial content, but in fact by choosing to invest funds in European workers, and refusing to make comparable investments in Brazilians, the province's planters, and the state apparatus which they controlled, had made their ethnic and racial preferences in workers crystal clear.[14] As emancipation drew closer, São Paulo's abolitionist newspaper, *A Redempção*, denounced the planters' apparent desire to "open the doors to the immigrants" and deny the libertos "the work that they [the planters] infamously extorted from the slaves." But by 1888 it indeed appeared that this was to be the meaning and result of abolition. The Europeans were being transported to São Paulo to compete with the libertos, and it was assumed at the outset that this would be a contest which the latter would lose. On the day after the signing of the Golden Law, São Paulo's *Diário Popular* reflected that the event was "a great good, not because of how it will benefit the black race, which, because of its backwardness, will continue to suffer almost as much as before. . . ." Rather, the beneficiaries will be those "appropriately educated and prepared to deal with the challenges posed by the new order of things. *The right man in the right place*, as the Americans say"—and that man clearly was not going to be black.[15]

Even more ominous was an article written a year after emancipation, entitled "The Segregation of the Liberto," which announced the virtual conclusion of the labor market competition and the definitive victory of the immigrants. Ignoring the substance of the earlier legislative debates, the article argued that no such competition had been intended or anticipated. "Nobody was thinking about a contest between the old laborers and the new. There was room for everyone." But the libertos' flight from the plantations, and their refusal to continue in their old positions, had left the planters no choice but to turn to the immigrants. "The Brazilian worker abandoned the position he had conquered, he made the immigrant replace him, he forced the landowner to opt for the latter." And now, "the gap left by the former laborer has been filled forever. . . . The liberto is segregated, rendered useless, lost to the productive life."[16]

One is startled by the rapidity with which the contest had run its course—it had been only a year since emancipation, and the vast majority of those Europeans who would enter São Paulo had yet to set foot on Brazilian shores—and by the rigid finality of its conclusion: not just defeat and displacement for the libertos, but segregation and exile, forever, from "the productive life."[17] One is struck as well by the assignment of blame for this tragic situation: it lay squarely on the shoulders of the ex-slaves themselves.

The material presented at the conclusion of the previous chapter suggests that these articles, and others like them, do not reflect actual conditions on São Paulo's plantations during the first two or three years immediately following emancipation. During 1887 and 1888 the slaves had indeed fled the plantations en masse; but in the weeks and months following May 13, deprived of any other means of support, most of them came back again to take up positions as wage laborers on the plantations. I would suggest that these articles should be read, not as empirical descriptions of what was happening in São Paulo at the time, but rather as expressions of what the state's elites hoped and indeed expected would come to pass: the displacement of black labor by white. White labor had been granted a privileged position over black, and was expected to take full advantage of it. But precisely how far would those privileges extend in practice? Would white workers in Brazil exploit their preferred position to create a racially exclusionary union movement and labor market, as their peers in other countries were doing at the same time?

Structuring the Labor Market: Organized Labor

The planters had brought Europeans to São Paulo to be workers. What they had not foreseen was that these workers would then proceed to form a workers' movement that, by the 1910s, formed a serious challenge to the established order.[18] Precise statistics on the membership of that movement are not available, but a study of 106 labor leaders in Brazil during this period found that fewer than a third of them were native-born; and of that third, only a handful lived and worked in São Paulo.[19] The immigrants' domination of the paulista labor movement, their insecurity in the face of the government's immigration policies and the resulting oversupply of labor, and the marginalization of Afro-Brazilian workers in São Paulo, might easily have led to outcomes like those in the United States and South Africa, where white workers demanded, and received, institutionalized barriers against black competition. Such was not the case, however. In searching for strategies with which to improve their position and confront their employers and the state, São Paulo's workers seem never even to have considered the possibility of the racial exclusion and segregation being pursued elsewhere. If anything, their approach was exactly the opposite. Acutely aware of the tactical opportunities which an ethnically and racially divided working class offered to employers and the state, and inspired by the egalitarian doctrines of socialism, anarchism, and anarchosyndicalism, labor organizers repeatedly invoked the goal of eliminating such divisions.

O Amigo do Povo spoke for the labor press as a whole when it denounced what it described as the government policy of "dividing in order to rule" by "pitting the foreign worker against the national worker. . . ." Organizers recognized that, by dividing the labor force into immigrant workers and Brazilians, and granting preference to the former, employers had produced a state of "latent warfare in the very heart of the working class" which could be fanned into flame at any time. A "heterogeneous population . . . separated by hatreds" was peculiarly vulnerable to such a strategy, and those hatreds were further exacerbated by the discontent and resentment of Brazilians locked out of the labor market. Urging its readers to renounce "false prejudices and false pride of race," the Italian-language paper *Avanti!* concluded that ethnic and national cleavages within the working class formed the single most important obstacle to the success of São Paulo's labor movement.[20]

Thus as they spoke to their immigrant and Brazilian readers, the labor papers repeatedly hammered home the message of equality: "We're not in the time of slavery any more—every individual, white or black, ugly or handsome, Brazilian or foreign, according to the laws of this country is a citizen, and as such, can take part in the affairs of the state and demand accounts from his oppressors." A more pessimistic approach was that black and white workers were equal not in their rights but in their common degradation, since all workers, regardless of race, remained enslaved and oppressed by capitalism. "Wages are the modern form of slavery"; "slavery died in name but not in fact." This implicit equalizing of blacks and whites occasionally became explicit, as in an article denouncing the twentieth anniversary of the Golden Law as "lies, hypocrisy, Jesuitisms, we say. . . . Between the *black slaves* who worked in their masters' fields, and the white slaves who labor in the factory . . . between the blacks from the Congo employed on the plantations prior to 1888 and the white workers from the most civilized countries of Europe who work *today* to enrich a gang of parasites, there is not, and there cannot be, any difference whatsoever."[21]

Employers first used the tactic of exploiting racial divisions within the labor force just three years after emancipation, during the 1891 dockworker strike in Santos. The Docas de Santos Company, which held monopoly control over the city's docks, brought in unemployed libertos who had fled to the city during 1887 and 1888, and used them as strikebreakers to defeat the predominantly immigrant strikers. The company used the same approach again in 1908, this time transferring to the docks black workers employed in Docas's gravel quarries, *fazendas*, and road-building crews. After the 1908 strike, the paper of the dockworkers' union devoted several articles to the company's campaign to promote "discord and racial struggle among the workers of Santos," and a recent study of these strikes concludes that the company was indeed "successful in presenting the conflict between strikers and strikebreakers as the result of 'color prejudice' among immigrant workers."[22]

Efforts to promote ethnic and racial antagonism within the labor force were particularly evident between 1917 and 1920, years of intense labor agitation in São Paulo. The successful general strike of 1917, and an abortive anarchist uprising in Rio de Janeiro the following year, provoked a wave of repression by employers and the state, and repeated attacks by public officials and the establishment press against subversive, traitorous foreign radicals. Newspapers which had rejoiced at the immigrants' arrival several years earlier now turned on them as importers of the alien, anti-Brazilian doctrines of anarchism and socialism, and employers who had welcomed the immigrants into their factories and plantations now denounced them as disloyal ingrates.[23]

Struggling to overcome these xenophobic appeals and forge a genuinely unified labor movement, São Paulo's unions stressed the principle of ethnic, national, and racial equality among all workers, and devoted particular attention to organizing and mobilizing the Brazilian population. A 1903 article attacked the practice of conducting meetings and public speeches in Italian, and urged that organizers do more of their proselytizing in Portuguese. The first issue of the *Jornal Operário* announced that it had come into existence to fill the need for a Portuguese-language workers' paper to speak directly to Brazilian workers.[24]

Appeals to the movement's Afro-Brazilian constituency took various forms. Organizers and labor newspapers invoked Zumbi of Palmares (see chapter 8) and other blacks who had fought against slavery as heroic examples of worker militance.[25] A 1908 article denounced as an outrage the practice among Catholic churches in Campinas of dividing white and black women into separate organizations and sisterhoods. A 1911 article on São Paulo's peasantry made clear that it was discussing Afro-Brazilians (it described their singing sambas and *cantigas de desafio*, the Brazilian answer-back song, in black dialect) and pointedly contrasted their innocent rural virtue with the corruption and viciousness of the urban bourgeoisie. The article went so far as to hold up this peasant idyll as a model for the future anarchist society: "The delicate sentiments of those good people are like the affectionate embrace that will someday unite free men on a free earth." And a 1919 article in the newspaper of the construction workers' union, written during the heat of the antiforeigner campaign in São Paulo, noted that the government's denunciations of immigrant agitators might make it look as though Brazilians were not involved in the labor movement. Nothing could be further from the truth, the author argued. Despite the fact that "we are descendants from a slave race, that our fathers died in the stocks or under the lash, while our mothers—as a foreigner put it—still have the marks of the master's whip on their buttocks," Brazilians were as actively involved in the struggle as any European.[26]

One does find bits of evidence which confirm Afro-Brazilian participation in, and even leadership of, the early paulista labor movement. Mulatto activist Eugênio Wansuit, a former abolitionist, was a prominent organizer of the 1912 dockworkers' strike in Santos, and was arrested and deported to Rio de Janeiro for his pains. In 1891 preto activist Salvador de Paula was one of the founders of the most successful mutual aid society of the Republican years, the Association of the Laboring Classes. And the black newspapers (see chapter 5) regularly ran stories and editorials encouraging their readers to take part in the labor movement, and to join in class solidarity with their white colleagues.[27]

But there is no denying that Afro-Brazilians were much less visible in the São Paulo labor movement, both as leaders and as members, than in Rio de Janeiro, Bahia, Recife, and elsewhere, and one must conclude by agreeing with Sheldon Maram's judgment that the early labor movement in the state was unsuccessful in achieving its goal of creating a racially and ethnically unified working class.[28] The immigrant response to the labor movement was far from overwhelming, and the Brazilian response weaker still. One reason for that weak response is hinted at in the laconic phrase "as a foreigner put it," seen in the quotation several paragraphs earlier. Despite their appeals for racial equality and working-class solidarity, many immigrant labor leaders could not break completely free of feelings of ethnic and racial superiority over their Brazilian colleagues. A 1903 article in O Amigo do Povo expressed despair at the idea of ever organizing the Brazilian povo, which lay vegetating in ignorance, sunk in poverty and lethargy. To make the revolution, the paper argued, would require "wills and characters that are stronger, physically and morally, than those possessed by the Brazilians, who are the product of a debilitated nation. . . ." Articles in the labor press sometimes took on explicitly racial overtones. A 1917 article criticizing recent repression of strikes argued that police had completely overstepped the bounds of Brazilian law and behaved like savages. Contrasting Brazil with the kingdom of Senegambia, "a vast region of blacks on the black continent," the paper argued that "this republic is not a Liberia, it's not a republic of blacks, of barely clad savages and primitive laws." No, Brazil was a cultured country, with the sole exception of its police. "The police are not, and never have been, Brazilian; the police are from Senegambia, they follow Senegambian laws, and their officers are Senegambians." A satirical play published in an anarchist monthly in 1905 presented a symbolic social scale running from nobleman to dog. A black butler ranks just above the dog and below a beggar, who expresses his humiliation at being removed from the mansion "by a well fed black." This effort was at least satirical; not so a 1918 article on the origin of black people, which recounted various racist folktales about how God had happened to give black people broad noses, kinky hair, and light-colored palms. The editor of the paper, which served the workers of the Sorocabana Railway Company (many of whom were black), described these legends "as most clever and well done."[29]

It was probably inevitable that the racial attitudes and tensions which characterized the society at large would emerge in the labor unions. But adding to the generalized racism of the time was the fact that the exclusion of black workers from industrial employment created a classic "reserve" labor force—an army of unemployed who could be called up at any time to break strikes, undermine efforts to unionize, and keep wages low. So limited were opportunities for black workers elsewhere in the economy that sufficient numbers could always be found to respond to employers' appeals for *furagreves*.[30] Many labor leaders understood how difficult it was for unemployed workers to refuse opportunities like these, but this did not stop them from voicing irritation with black strikebreakers, and particularly with those who signed on as thugs and hoodlums hired by employers to break up strikes and demonstrations. "What hurts and embitters is to see the sons of yesterday's slaves today replacing the old *capitães do mato* [hunters of runaway slaves] in the disgraceful mission of filling the ranks of those who beat up workers in search of their economic liberty and the improvement of their class through the only means at their disposal: the strike."[31]

It is important to note that the strikebreakers of this period were by no means exclusively black. A 1905 article portrayed many of them as "yokels" from Sicily and Venice—though, significantly, the piece was entitled "Slaves and Savages from Europe," implicitly equating strikebreaking with blackness. A 1904 article on the desperate condition of Portuguese immigrants in São Paulo noted that their situation was so bad that many of them, "in order that their families not die of hunger," had been driven to the ultimate betrayal of their fellow workers: enlisting in the police force.[32] Despite their preferred position, European workers proved no less vulnerable to the pressures of the labor market than their Afro-Brazilian peers—which explains, in part, the collapse of this first phase of the Brazilian labor movement during the early 1920s.

The anarchists and socialists had sought to bridge the gap between Brazilian and European workers, and had failed. Or rather, the degree to which they succeeded was not sufficient to produce a labor movement which could prevail against the forces of the Republican state. Certainly the labor movement was in no position to achieve its goal of introducing racial equality into the workplace. In the absence of such intervention, and as shaped by the immigration policies of the planter state, what were the outcomes of the labor market competition between São Paulo's black and white workers?

The Struggle for Jobs: Outcomes

In analyzing the results of black-white labor market competition, it is helpful to divide the discussion into rural and urban spheres. In the countryside, white workers, who were almost exclusively immigrants, quickly became concentrated in the most prosperous regions of the state, and in the most desirable jobs in those regions. Black and *caboclo* workers either retreated to more depressed parts of the state or held the least desirable jobs on the more profitable plantations. Planters in the badly eroded Paraíba Valley, for example, in the northeast section of the state, proved unable to provide wages and working conditions sufficiently desirable to attract the Europeans; for these planters, as well as for those in the neighboring coffee-growing areas of Rio de Janeiro and Minas Gerais states, as a contemporary observer put it, "white labour was a luxury which they could not maintain." As a result, by 1905 only 4 percent of the labor force in the Paraíba region was European.[33]

In the booming west-central region of the state, by contrast, the agricultural labor force was two-thirds European by the same date. Within that labor force, a clear system of racial preference prevailed. Warren Dean finds that "immigrants were generally preferred for *colono* contracts, undoubtedly the best positions on the plantation." Thomas Holloway agrees that "when the Paulistas decided to go to Europe for their workers, the Brazilian peasantry, including many ex-slaves and the native mixed-blood backwoodsmen, was relegated to a marginal position in the regional economy. . . . by the early twentieth century the die was cast, and work in the coffee fields of the west was universally identified with immigrants." When black and racially mixed Brazilians were hired at all, it was to perform "the seasonal, precarious jobs that were not sufficiently well paid to be attractive to the immigrants. They became *camaradas*, general laborers, who were paid by the month. When there was a local excess of immigrants, the freedmen might be further demoted to day laborer." Observing this situation, political scientist Paula Beiguelman

Table 3.1. Percentage Distribution of Brazilians and Immigrants in the Work Force in São Paulo City, 1920, by Selected Areas of the Economy

	Brazilians	Immigrants	N
Total economically active population	50.4	49.6	240,045
Industry	48.9	51.1	100,375
Commerce	37.5	62.5	30,580
Domestic service	63.1	36.9	15,467
Transportation	41.1	58.9	13,912
Armed forces, police, and firemen	90.7	9.3	5,783

Source: Directoria Geral de Estatística, *Recenseamento do Brasil realizado em 1º de setembro de 1920* (Rio de Janeiro, 1926), 4, pp. 170–173.

describes it as a two-tier, racially segmented labor market, with an upper level of "foreign wage-earners, who worked toward the eventual accumulation of cash savings; and a second, Brazilian, for the painful and difficult tasks rejected by the first."[34]

In the cities immigrants enjoyed the same preference in hiring that they experienced in the countryside. The 1893 census of São Paulo City showed that 72 percent of employees in commerce, 79 percent of factory workers, 81 percent of transport workers, and 86 percent of artisans were foreign-born. A 1902 source estimated the industrial labor force in the capital as more than 90 percent immigrant; in 1913 the *Correio Paulistano* estimated that 80 percent of the capital's construction workers were Italian; and a 1912 survey of the labor force in thirty-three textile factories in the state found that 80 percent of textile workers were foreign-born, the great majority of them Italian.[35]

By 1920 Brazilian workers had achieved relative parity in industrial employment, the largest area of the urban economy (see Table 3.1). They remained overrepresented, however, in the poorly paying areas of domestic service and the armed forces (over 90 percent of which consisted of notoriously underpaid enlisted men in the army and the police). Europeans retained a preferred position in commerce and transportation. And even in industrial employment, over half (51.6 percent) of the Brazilian-born factory workers were under the age of twenty-one, and scattered evidence, including the testimony of those who labored in São Paulo's factories at the time, indicates that many, if not most, of them were the children of immigrants.

Introduced to bosses and factory owners by their relatives, they frequently received preference in hiring, with the result that adult immigrants continued to dominate their segment of the industrial labor market (immigrant industrial workers aged twenty-one or older outnumbered their Brazilian counterparts by almost two to one), and their children dominated the younger age cohort as well.[36]

This continued preference for Europeans and Euro-Brazilians struck directly at the Afro-Brazilians. Florestan Fernandes has argued that by 1920 their position in the urban economy was even worse than it had been twenty or thirty years earlier, despite the phenomenal growth in industry, construction, and commerce that had taken place in the meantime. Blacks were almost completely barred from factory work, and black artisans had virtually disappeared from the city. Poor and working-class black people found their job opportunities restricted to domestic service and what today would be termed the informal sector.[37] Two Afro-Brazilians who lived through that period recall the conditions under which they worked.

There were almost as many blacks as Italians in those days, in São Paulo, [but] they lived in a state of total disintegration. . . . The immigrants were in the factories and in commerce. The only work left for the blacks was to clean houses and offices, cart wood, and other chores. We were all underemployed. You always used to see blacks pushing carts through the city and lining up in Quintino Bocaiuva Street, with their buckets and brushes, waiting for the call to clean a house here, scrub a floor there.

The blacks had to hustle, as they say today. They had to create various sources of work, as porters, gardeners, domestic servants, sweeping the sidewalks, washing cars. . . . All those jobs that didn't exist before, the blacks created—shoeshine boys, newspaper venders, day laborers, all those jobs they created for their subsistence, because the *fazendeiros* wouldn't hire blacks. . . .[38]

Some black men were able to find regular work laying track for the railroads or for the São Paulo Tramway, Light, and Power Company, which was building the city's tramway and electric systems at the time. And the exclusion of black workers from industrial employment was not absolute, since one does find occasional mention of factory workers in the social columns of the black press, as well as in employment records.[39] But clearly such opportunities were limited, and the great majority of black people found themselves forced into domestic service or the irregular, poorly paying jobs described above.

Outside the armed forces, domestic service was the one area of the manual labor market where Brazilians, both black and white, competed most effectively against the immigrants.[40] Not coincidentally, this also happened to be perhaps the least attractive area of the urban economy. Many features of domestic service under slavery survived more or less intact into the twentieth century. A native of São Paulo born in 1903, fifteen years after the abolition of slavery, recalls that, shortly after his birth, his father "sent for a slave to be rented" to nurse him. Dona Risoleta, an Afro-Brazilian woman who worked as a domestic servant during the 1910s and 1920s, recalls a workday that began at 4:00 A.M. and ran late into the night. Her employers' control over her life was almost total: "I could never keep up with the news, go to parties, or find out what was happening in the city. Six months would go by without my so much as leaving the house! There was always work to be done, and Saturday and Sunday were the worst; I had to make cookies, cakes, and candies because on Sunday the whole family would get together to visit."[41]

As we shall see shortly, liberto families were reluctant to have their women and children enter the wage labor market in the years following abolition, which led to an acute shortage of domestic servants in the state. The government responded in characteristic fashion, instructing its immigration agents in Europe to "promote the migration of persons who will dedicate themselves to domestic service."[42] But as employment opportunities for black men withered away over the course of the 1890s and early 1900s, black women had little recourse but to return to work as domestics. Employer preferences seem to have been evenly split between immigrants and Brazilians, to judge by the census statistics; while some considered European servants to be more chic, others valued Brazilians' command of Portuguese and knowledge of local mores and manners. Many of those willing to accept Brazilian employees expressed a preference, either in newspaper ads or in instructions to employment agencies, for white servants over black. Nevertheless, enough black women (and some black men) were able to obtain domestic work to make the black domestic servant a characteristic feature of life in São Paulo, as in other Brazilian cities.[43]

Black women's ability to obtain employment was almost literally a lifesaver to a community denied most other means of support. Afro-Brazilian informants who lived through that period recall that "the truth of the matter is that the ones who sustained the black family were the women, who, in my opinion, were great fighters. . . ." They had to be, to withstand the physical and emotional rigors of such a life. The typical black domestic "works like a titan," one of the black papers reported. "She washes, irons, cooks, polishes the floors, waits on table, and does the heaviest work imaginable, in contrast to her malnourished, exhausted physique. During her delicate times of month, she never has the proper rest. She has to work." The strength required to sustain such a struggle was sometimes more than a human could bear. Dona Risoleta credits the black Saint Benedict with having given her the strength to get up each morning at 4:00 A.M., and she recalls: "I called on God day and night not to let me go under. . . . I struggled on, alone, with God."[44]

The black women of those decades clearly deserve much, if not most, of the credit for having sustained the black community during a time when alternative opportunities of employment were almost nonexistent. But Afro-Brazilians never lost sight of the fact that domestic service and occasional day labor were the crumbs of an expanding urban economy. Dona Risoleta, for example, refused to allow her children to follow her into domestic service, telling her employer, "I will not sacrifice my daughter; she's not going to earn her living sacrificing herself the way I did." The black newspapers joined in urging their readers to do everything possible to prevent their daughters from entering the tyranny of domestic service, where they had to face excessive labor demands, the sexual advances of their employers, an absence of family life, and miserable wages to boot. "A maid is always worse off than a worker who works for eight hours at a set task, and can then go home."[45]

But jobs in the city's factories, workshops, and stores were not for the Afro-Brazilians. This was not the result of discriminatory legislation or decrees handed down from on high. Rather, it was the result of thousands—millions, over the years—of decisions made by individual employers concerning who they would hire and who they would not. While some proved willing to hire black workers during this period, most did not. Why? What did the European workers have that Afro-Brazilians did not? Why were the latter so consistently marginalized and pushed aside in the competition for jobs and advancement? Certainly that contest had been structured by state policy in such a way as to make it exceptionally rigorous; but did this mean that black people inevitably had to lose?

Explaining the Outcomes: The Fernandes Thesis

At this point we return to the pathbreaking and highly influential work of Florestan Fernandes, briefly introduced in chapter 1. Fernandes devoted much of his academic career to answering the questions posed above, and over time his writings, and those of his students, have become the most widely accepted and influential explanation of why black people were not integrated into paulista society (and into Brazilian society more generally) on terms of equality with white people.[46]

In explaining the reasons for racial inequality in Brazil, Fernandes viewed the immigrants and the Afro-Brazilians as products of two societies at quite different levels of economic and social development. The Europeans came from nations in the throes of capitalist growth and development, with functioning labor markets which had taught the immigrants work skills and the rigorous discipline of economic competition. The Brazilians, by contrast, had grown up in a society where labor relations based on slavery, coercion, and seigneurial domination of the labor force were still precapitalist in character. This experience of slavery posed a particular handicap to the Afro-Brazilians, in two ways. First, it left a strong inheritance of racism, which made whites unwilling to accept black people as equals, or to grant them opportunities for full integration into Brazilian society after emancipation. Even if such opportunities had been presented, however, Fernandes argued that most Afro-Brazilians would have been unable to take advantage of them because of the second aspect of the slave heritage: the ways in which slavery had crippled its victims intellectually, morally, socially, and economically. Slaves learned no marketable skills under slavery; quite the contrary, slavery had taught them to avoid work wherever and whenever possible. Slavery had not built up the black family; rather, it had undermined and destroyed it. And slavery had done nothing to instill a sense of community and self-worth in slaves; for reasons of security, it had sought to root out and destroy whatever instruments of solidarity and mutual support the slaves may have brought with them from Africa or tried to construct in the New World.

When, therefore, the Europeans arrived in São Paulo, and began to compete with black people in the rural and urban labor markets, there simply was no competition, argued Fernandes. Black people were "automatically" pushed aside by immigrants, who were more highly skilled, more imbued with a capitalist work ethic, and more effectively supported by family and community structures of solidarity. The resulting marginalization of São Paulo's black population was "a 'natural product' of their inability to feel, think, and act socially as free men." São Paulo did not reject the Afro-Brazilians, he concluded; rather, by their failure to assume the new, "modern" roles of citizen, employee, and wage-earner, the Afro-Brazilians in effect rejected the modernizing, capitalist society of twentieth-century São Paulo.[47]

Fernandes's work constitutes a courageous and at times brilliant effort to unmask the reality of Brazilian race relations, and to refute the notion of Brazil as a land of racial equality. However, his dichotomy of modern, progressive, highly skilled, hardworking Europeans, and anomic, irresponsible, sociopathic Afro-Brazilians finds little, if any, support in the evidence available.[48] Instead of a clear division between the two groups, we see a rather more ambiguous situation in which the black and immigrant populations actually resembled each other in striking and unexpected ways.[49]

We might begin by noting that, by the time of Brazil's first national census, in 1872, the majority of São Paulo's black and mulatto population was not slave but free.[50] Well before the abolition of slavery, and increasingly in the years leading up to 1888, most of the province's Afro-Brazilians had escaped slavery, and were at liberty to construct lives and careers of their own choosing. Far from floundering helplessly in the labor market, as Fernandes's argument would lead us to expect, many of these free pardos and pretos succeeded in establishing themselves as artisans and merchants, in São Paulo as throughout Brazil. It was only when the immigrants came, he noted, that these black craftsmen and entrepreneurs started to disappear from the urban scene.[51]

They simply didn't have the skills to face the Europeans, he argued—in skilled labor, commerce, or factory work. Certainly in the area of literacy, the immigrants possessed decided advantages over the Brazilian population in general, and over the Afro-Brazilian population specifically. The census of 1890 registered a literacy rate of only 12.5 percent among the state's native-born population, versus 41.7 percent among the foreign-born population.[52] The disparity between immigrants and blacks was probably even greater. The 1890 census did not break literacy rates down by race, but data from the 1940 census suggest that the literacy rate among native-born Brazilians at the turn of the century was approximately twice as high for Brazilian whites as for blacks.[53]

As suggested by the Fernandes thesis, black illiteracy was indeed a problem that had its roots in the recent experience of slavery. Few masters saw any point in investing in their slaves' education, and most probably preferred that their slaves be unable to read the newspapers and abolitionist propaganda circulating among São Paulo's plantations in the 1870s and 1880s.[54] The problem was further exacerbated after emancipation, however, by the educational policies of the Republic. The Constitution of 1891 departed from the imperial Constitution of 1824 in exempting the federal government from any obligation to sponsor public education, and simultaneously disenfranchising illiterates. Not until the early 1900s did the state of São Paulo start to construct the rudiments of an elementary school system; secondary schools did not become a significant item in the state budget until the 1920s.[55]

Faced with an almost complete lack of educational opportunity, and denied access to most private schools, the Afro-Brazilians responded by attempting to establish their own educational institutions. The most successful was the Colégio de São Benedito in Campinas, which functioned from 1901 to 1937. In the capital the Friends of the Nation mutual aid society, the Palmares Civic Center, and the Brazilian Black Front maintained elementary schools for varying periods between the 1910s and the 1930s.[56] But these scattered efforts, valiant though they were, could not compensate for the failure of the state to provide adequate instruction for its children, both black and white.

Thus it does appear that the immigrants offered their employers a higher rate of literacy than could the Brazilians, and particularly the Afro-Brazilians. But did higher literacy necessarily translate into better work performance and higher productivity? For members of a late twentieth-century society and economy, the answer is obvious: of course educated workers are more productive than uneducated workers. But in the factories and plantations of turn-of-the-century São Paulo, work skills did not necessarily revolve around literacy. And it is by no means obvious that the immigrants possessed clear advantages in these work-related skills. Fernandes's own informants recalled that, in the areas of carpentry and cabinetmaking, the "quality of the blacks' work was no worse than the whites." And while Fernandes asserted that the Europeans who came to the capital had more extensive experience with urban industrial work than did the Brazilians, either black or white, a number of historians take issue with him. Michael Hall argues that "most of those who came to the capital [São Paulo] appear, by all accounts, to have had no prior industrial or urban experience. While some artisans and other urban workers undoubtedly went to São Paulo, such immigration was not encouraged and it seems fairly clear that the overwhelming majority of the labor force was composed of men and women from the rural areas of Southern Europe." Looking specifically at Italian immigration, which accounted for almost half of the immigrants arriving in São Paulo, and studying it at its point of origin rather than its destination, Rudolph Bell found that between 1880 and 1910 "persons with skills useful in an urban or industrial setting tended to move to northern Europe, particularly Germany and Belgium," lured by higher salaries and low transportation costs; "they clearly failed to take advantage of any opportunities in North and South America."[57]

Since most factory workers in turn-of-the-century São Paulo learned their skills on the job, the question of previously acquired industrial skills may not even be relevant. This was particularly the case with minors, who constituted almost a third of the workers (3,152 out of 10,204) in the thirty-three textile factories surveyed by the State Department of Labor in 1912.[58] Brazilians, Africans, and Europeans all seem to have been equally capable of mastering the basic operations of factory work. The first national census, in 1872, indicated that 11.1 percent of the industrial work force was slaves, at a time when slaves represented 15.2 percent of the population as a whole.[59] And following abolition, Brazilians, among them sizable numbers of Afro-Brazilians, would form the majority of industrial laborers in Rio de Janeiro and other states which could not afford São Paulo's program of subsidized immigration.[60]

One is inclined to agree then with Lúcio Kowarick's judgment that "the use of foreigners in São Paulo's industry was not due to better qualifications on the part of immigrants, who only rarely brought with them any previous industrial experience in their counties of origin."[61] This was even more the case in the countryside, on the coffee plantations. I could find no instance of any planter ever arguing that the ex-slaves lacked the necessary skills to carry out plantation labor. Such an argument would have been patently absurd, given the fact that Afro-Brazilians and Africans had formed virtually the entire labor force in the coffee economy ever since the export boom began, in the early 1800s. Working with plantation records from the first decade of the century, Warren Dean concludes that there was no significant difference in productivity between Brazilian and immigrant plantation workers. Thus the preferred position granted to the immigrants "was partly founded upon discrimination against the national [Brazilian] workers, especially the blacks. Had they been paid equally on the basis of productivity without making distinctions of whiteness, the Italians might not have come at all."[62]

The reasons for the displacement of black labor, therefore, are not to be found in different levels of skill. Perhaps, then, they are to be found in the anomic social milieu which the black population allegedly created for itself, and to which Fernandes devoted extensive attention. Shattered family structure, alcoholism, crime, obsession with sex—all these characteristics combined to lock the black community in a state of anomie and "social pathology," which, when added to the low skill levels and aversion to work that were their inheritance from slavery, eliminated whatever hope the Afro-Brazilians might have had of competing successfully for jobs and opportunities in São Paulo's expanding economy.[63]

Certainly São Paulo's turn-of-the-century planter and urban elites would have recognized their black population in Fernandes's writings, since the anomic, irresponsible, shiftless black people pictured there are perfectly in keeping with the *ideologia da vadiagem*.[64] Indeed, an 1897 article in the *Diário de Campinas* observed (incorrectly) that in the nine years since emancipation the state's black population had virtually disappeared, and then it proceeded to explain the alleged disappearance in terms that could have been taken directly from Fernandes.

In reality the blacks were wiped out by the inheritance left them from their sad condition as slaves: vice, rooted in the constitution of their families; the little importance they gave to virginity; the brutalization of their intelligence owing to the animalistic lives they led, their constant drunkenness, the chronic alcoholism of their ancestors; and as the lamentable finishing touch, the bestial syphilis which they carried in their blood, [as punishment] for the violation of human laws. . . .[65]

Recent research, however, provides little support for this lurid image.[66] To begin with the question of marriage and the family, historians are finding that a nuclear family structure was more widespread in the Brazilian slave population than has previously been suspected.[67] After emancipation, Stanley Stein points to "an extraordinary number of marriages" among ex-slaves in the coffee zones, who were now at liberty to construct family units. Boris Fausto's work on turn-of-the-century São Paulo concurs in documenting "the value placed by 'black society' on rules followed by the society at large, including virginity and marriage, if possible with all the formal trappings."[68]

The censuses of 1890 and 1950 (the intervening censuses of 1920 and 1940 do not offer information on marriage rates by race) indicate that black people were only slightly less likely to marry than whites. When one compares the proportions of individuals in each racial group who had been married at some point in their lives (i.e., who were either married or widowed at the time of the census), the rate of marriage among Afro-Brazilians was 94.8 percent of that of whites in 1890, and 92.1 percent in 1950.[69]

Were the Fernandes thesis correct, we could expect black marriage rates to have been significantly lower than white in 1890, when the effects of slavery were still strongly felt, and then to converge with white rates over the course of the 1900s. These two censuses, however, show the divergences between black and white rates actually increasing over time. This finding is further reinforced by an examination of

Table 3.2. Percentage Distribution of Individuals Ever Married, 1950, by Race and Decade of Birth

	1871–1880	1881–1890	1891–1900	1901–1910	1911–1920	1921–1930
White	94.9	94.6	93.9	91.9	86.7	55.5
Pardo	91.3	91.7	91.8	90.0	83.9	53.4
Preto	91.4	91.3	90.2	87.8	81.0	49.8
Black/white[a]	96.2	96.6	96.5	96.2	94.3	91.5

Source: *Recenseamento, 1950: São Paulo*, table 7, pp. 6–7.
[a] Black marriage rate as a percentage of white marriage rate.

marriage rates among the various age cohorts included in the 1950 census (Table 3.2). The bottom line of that table expresses the black marriage rate as a percentage of the white rate. As we see, the relationship between the two rates holds quite steady for people born before 1910, and then starts to diverge. The greatest disparity is found among individuals born between 1921 and 1930, who started reaching marriageable age in the late 1930s, and who by the time of the 1950 census were aged between twenty and thirty. The racial disparity in marriage rates in that cohort may reflect the greater impact of the Great Depression on blacks than on whites; it may indicate a later marriage age for blacks than for whites; in light of earlier black cohorts' tendency to marry at rates close to those of the whites, however, it seems unlikely that it can be traced back to slavery.

These data do indicate a slightly lower tendency for Afro-Brazilians to marry and form family units. This was owing in substantial part to the difficulties which black men encountered in obtaining steady work at decent wages. Contemporary testimony suggests that black families tried to overcome these obstacles by constructing extended ties of support and solidarity among grandparents, relatives, godparents, and friends. Fernandes noted the existence of these networks, but concluded that, by draining savings from more prosperous black families to poor ones, they had a negative rather than a positive effect on the community's development. This "domestic solidarity," he argued, was thus a further "sociopathic" obstacle to the Afro-Brazilians' advancement. Curiously, however, he presented similar solidarity among the immigrant community as a positive feature of their family life, and a key element in their drive for upward mobility. There doubtless was a disparity in outcomes between the same strategy in different racial groups, which is in turn attributable to the disparity in earnings between whites and blacks. But to describe the same response to conditions of hardship and struggle as economic rationality for one group and social pathology for another seems questionable, to say the least.[70]

Recent research also leads one to question the notion of a black community sunk in criminality. Between 1880 and 1924 pretos and pardos were indeed arrested by police at a rate more than double that of their representation in the population as a whole (28.5 percent of all arrests in the state capital, where Afro-Brazilians were perhaps 11–12 percent of the total population). However, the number of black people actually brought to trial was much smaller, accounting for only 12.9 percent of total court cases during this period—a figure essentially the same as the proportion of Afro-Brazilians in the population at large. The discrepancy between the number of Afro-Brazilians arrested and those brought to trial reflects both the tendency of police to arrest black people even in the absence of sufficient evidence to prosecute and the relatively innocuous nature of their crimes. Blacks appeared infrequently in cases of violent crime, and when they did, it was usually as victim rather than aggressor, "suggesting the disparity between reality and the popular images of the 'disorderly, ruffian black.'" Newspaper reports on violent crime almost invariably focused on immigrants, "the majority of whom," according to a popular magazine article on the subject, "come from countries of violent, barbarous, and primitive criminality, such as Italy, Portugal, and Spain, nations where blood crimes comprise the largest category of crime. . . ."[71]

The failure of the black press during this period to devote even a single article to the problem of crime in the community further calls into question the alleged Afro-Brazilian tendency toward criminality. Other aspects of the community's "social disorganization" did weigh on the black papers' collective mind, however. Articles appeared regularly urging their readers to adopt "modern" morality: to abandon alcohol, gambling, and other vices, maintain public decorum, refrain from adultery and loose living, and to educate their children in a respectable trade or profession. "At every step we see black men living from vice, a large number of women lewd and unkempt, vagabond children roaming through the streets. . . ." Apparently the community was suffering from at least some of the anomie described by Fernandes.[72]

That anomie does not seem to have been the exclusive property of the black population, however. It is striking to find, when one turns to the labor or neighborhood newspapers aimed at the immigrants, perfect mirror images of those articles, bemoaning the same kind of "moral decay" that was allegedly affecting the blacks.[73] Clearly such laments reveal as much about the moralizing, middle-class outlook of the editors of these papers as they do about the black and immigrant workers being described. But what these articles suggest is that observers who held such values found as much to criticize among the immigrants as among the blacks. In fact, one of the earliest such papers, the Spanish-language *El Grito del Pueblo*, while noting clear disparities in employment patterns between Afro-Brazilians and immigrants, found no appreciable differences in their respective levels of anomie. The paper noted that Brazilian workers were always ready to turn out for the labor movement's parades or rallies, where they "applaud the orators, and cheer deliriously for Social Revolution. The next day, however, some go off to serve as fodder for the factories, others to the kitchen, others to clean the gardens and palaces of the bosses," and nothing changed. Why was this? Because "the Brazilian worker was only recently plucked from slavery, or he is the son or grandson of slaves. Because of this, his sense of civic responsibility is scarce, and he retains the meekness and brutishness instilled in him by the horrible torments of slavery." But the immigrants were no better. ". . . Owing to their sufferings in Europe, they are content with little salary, and settle into tenement slums and huts, housed like beasts, eating black bread and bananas. They live worse than pigs." The paper concluded that "these unhappy people differ little from the ex-slaves of Brazil. If the latter were prostituted by the lash of slavery, the former were overcome by the misery of their wages."[74]

The immigrant and labor press tended to concur in viewing modern industrial life, rather than slavery, as the cause of the social ills which afflicted the entire working class, white as well as black. "Modern industry, calling women to the factory, ruins the life of the family and the home. Children run in the streets, unprotected, uneducated save by an environment corrupted by poverty, and the father takes refuge in looking the other way." As for the father, "factory labor turns him into a brute . . . lured into pointless gossip, to the bars, to alcohol, to gambling, to cursing." Another labor paper replied to charges that workers use their holidays only to get drunk, gamble, and commit crimes. There may be some truth to this, the paper confessed, but if so it is the fault of the factory system, which brutalizes its victims, and forces children to work before they are old enough to get a decent education.[75]

The black and labor presses displayed striking agreement in their judgment of the moral challenges which their respective communities faced. Alcohol, which was no respecter of race or ethnicity, was clearly the worst. Closely tied to alcohol abuse were the dance halls and annual Carnaval celebrations in which "men, women and children, all in the senseless insanity of a disgusting libertinism, reveal a state of moral degeneracy that almost provokes nausea." The black press worried, too, about the excesses of these popular celebrations, but saw those excesses as just as likely to come from white celebrants as from black. The black paper O Alfinete (The Pin) warned its readers against a number of particularly notorious dance halls, where "most of the dancers are white women, and our black women also take part, to our shame, and our race's moral corruption."[76]

Illegitimate births and the absence of male providers were concerns frequently voiced in the black community, but they were perceived as problems among the immigrants as well. One paper ran a story urging its readers to stop giving charity to unmarried women who bear child after child. The specific case it cited was not a black woman but a young white one, "her face as white as a lily. . . ." The labor and black newspapers both recognized that domestic service posed one of the gravest risks to a young woman's honor (and to her future livelihood, if she became pregnant), and both published articles urging parents to send their daughters into any other occupation. Prostitution also received the attention of the labor press, which analyzed it, not as the result of social anomie or exaggerated sexuality, but rather in purely economic terms. "It is in order to earn her living that a woman, today, becomes a prostitute. As evidence for this observation, simply note that the immense majority of residents of brothels had a humble origin and, before their fall, suffered the most atrocious poverty. It is the enormous working class that keeps the whorehouses supplied."[77]

There is certainly evidence to indicate that, in the decades following emancipation, São Paulo's black community did suffer from the crime, poverty, and the "social disorganization" described by Fernandes, though perhaps not to the degree which he suggested. But crime, poverty, and anomie were not confined to black people. To the degree that the Fernandes thesis conforms to the *ideologia da vadiagem*—and at times it is difficult to detect much difference between the two—it applies to poor whites and immigrants as well as to blacks. In fact, we may infer from a 1917 article in the anarchist newspaper *A Plebe*, it would probably apply to almost the entire population of São Paulo. Employers and government officials had responded to the massive general strike of that year, and to workers' demands for wage increases, by claiming that if individuals in the state were suffering from poverty, it was because they were *vadios* who didn't want to work. If this were so, *A Plebe* caustically observed, then 90 percent of the state must indeed be *vadios*, because 90 percent of the state is poor.[78]

In the absence of evidence documenting that the immigrants possessed clear-cut advantages over black people in work skills or in adherence to conventional social norms, the Fernandes thesis in its original form is impossible to sustain. Besides its emphasis on black incapacity, however, the thesis points to some additional factors which may be more helpful in explaining the marginalization of São Paulo's black population. At this point we turn to the expectations, attitudes, and demands which employers, immigrants and Afro-Brazilians brought with them to the labor market.

Bargaining: Libertos, Immigrants, and Employers

Black anomie was not the only aspect of the slave heritage to figure in Fernandes's analysis. He also noted the importance of white racism, which he portrayed as widespread at all levels of Brazilian society.[79] Certainly it is difficult to argue with this point, which is amply confirmed by studies of Brazilian racial ideology during this period.[80] Racist attitudes were particularly strongly held at the elite level, and played a visible role in the decision of São Paulo's planters to invest state resources in promoting European immigration. It would be surprising, therefore, if such attitudes had not had a significant impact in excluding black workers from employment in post-emancipation São Paulo. Documenting that impact, however, and evaluating its relative importance in determining employers' preference for white workers over black is not as easy as might first appear, in large part because none of the thousands of employers who hired workers during this period was ever called on to record an explanation of why he favored one job applicant over another. Racism undoubtedly played a role in those decisions, but one which is difficult, if not impossible, to isolate and pin down.

In any case, racism alone is clearly insufficient to explain the apparent rejection of Afro-Brazilians by paulista employers after abolition. Racist attitudes were held throughout Brazil, yet did not impede the employment of Afro-Brazilians in other regions to nearly the same degree as they did in São Paulo. And during the 1840s and 1850s, planters' belief in the racial superiority of European workers did not prevent their prompt rejection of those workers as soon as the latter began to organize and actively resist the conditions of their employment on São Paulo's plantations.[81]

Before racism could exercise a determining influence on patterns of employment in São Paulo, labor market conditions had to change dramatically—as, by the 1890s, they indeed had, in two fundamental ways. First, black people were now free, and were using that freedom, as A Província de São Paulo had predicted, "to impose salary conditions, hours of work, [and] protection for their children." Some of the more enlightened planters could understand the libertos' motives, and how the experience of slavery had produced a deep determination among Afro-Brazilians to bring to an end the brutality and coercion of the old regime. But most landowners were equally determined to maintain the unquestioned dominance which they had long exercised over their laborers; and even observers sympathetic to the libertos' position tended to join in the general rejoicing over the coming of the immigrants, "which contributed greatly to rescue our *fazendeiros* from their dependence on the libertos, and from the just demands presented by the latter, after so many years of barbarous oppression."[82]

The second fundamental change in São Paulo's labor market was the key to the planters' ability to resist these demands. That change, obviously, was the subsidized immigration program, which undercut the bargaining position of the Afro-Brazilians in a number of ways. First, it flooded the São Paulo labor market with hundreds of thousands of workers who, in the absence of subsidies, would never have come to Brazil at all.[83] Second, it selected and brought to Brazil workers who would be particularly vulnerable to employer demands. Immigration subsidies attracted the poorest of European emigrants, those who lacked the earning capacity or savings to pay their own way to the United States or Argentina. They arrived in São Paulo "with little of capital or personal accomplishment," as a contemporary observer put it, and bargained with their new employers from a correspondingly weak position (as Martinho Prado had foreseen when he expressed his disinterest in "immigrants with money").[84]

Third, besides attracting the poorest of Europe's emigrants, it brought them to São Paulo in family units, seeking at all times "to reduce to a minimum the proportion of single men among those introduced at the public expense." Eighty percent of the people who passed through the immigrant hostel in São Paulo City came as families, averaging roughly five people per unit. Married men who sought work, therefore, had to worry not just about their own livelihood and survival but about that of their spouses and children as well. When added to the poverty of the subsidized immigrants, this produced a labor force which, during the early years of immigration, offered little resistance to employer demands.[85]

Finally, subsidizing the migration of entire families further weakened the immigrants' bargaining position by flooding the labor market with cheap and abundant child and female labor. Immigrant women and their children proved to be an indispensable part of both the plantation work force and the industrial work force.[86] Planters and industrialists insisted that they had no choice but to use female and child labor, since adult male wages were so high. But the real reason for the widespread use of women and minors in the São Paulo economy was more nearly the opposite: adult wages were so low that, in order to survive, families had little recourse but to send their women and children to work—which in turn drove wages lower still. In the plantation sector, reported the Italian consul in São Paulo in

1901, levels of remuneration were such that "only under the most ideal conditions can a single colono make enough to live on." And in the textile industry, the largest sector of São Paulo's industrial economy and one in which child and female labor accounted for over three-quarters of the work force, an adult male's wage bought less than half the minimum amount of food required to feed a family of four.[87] When faced with such conditions, most families opted to put their children to work, with the result that, noted a contemporary student of the Italian experience in São Paulo, "every child past toddling earns more than its current cost."[88]

The immigrants' willingness to send women and children into the labor market gave them a decided competitive advantage over the Afro-Brazilians. Following emancipation, the most intractable of the libertos' labor demands, and the most significant, as viewed both by the planters and by the ex-slaves themselves, was that women and children no longer be employed in field labor. Many black families went further and withdrew their women and children from wage labor altogether, leaving the fazendeiros and their wives to complain bitterly about having to do their own washing and prepare their own meals. "If the liberto does little, the liberta does absolutely nothing. They laze in the doorways of their houses, yawning and napping, whiling away the hours in sweet, happy, unconscious idleness."[89]

By insisting on freedom from violence and coercion in the workplace, and on the right to withdraw women and children from the labor market, the Afro-Brazilians had proposed new labor arrangements that the planters did not want to accept and, because of subsidized immigration, did not have to accept. Instead, the planters now hired European workers and put them to work, often under the control of overseers and hired gunmen who continued many of the brutal practices of the slave regime.[90] So bad were conditions in the countryside that in 1902, in response to persistent reports of the maltreatment of its nationals on São Paulo plantations, the Italian government forbade its citizens to accept subsidized passages to Brazil, a prohibition which remained in effect until the end of the subsidy program in 1927. This caused an immediate drop in subsidized immigrants, from 19,311 in 1902 to a mere 229 in 1903. The program soon recovered, however, extending its reach into other countries to bring in 26,015 immigrants in 1905, and a high of 53,719 in 1913.[91]

So lavish was the resulting supply of European labor that it fueled, not just the continued expansion of the coffee economy, but the growth of industry as well. This was hardly the goal which the planters had had in mind when they first designed the subsidy program, but the combination of coffee export earnings (which provided investment capital and the beginnings of a local market) and abundant labor turned São Paulo by the 1920s into the most important industrial center in Brazil, surpassing Rio de Janeiro.[92] And despite the demand for labor generated by this growth, according to the American consul in São Paulo in 1922, as a result of immigration "it is doubtful that there exists anywhere an industrial sector that offers better working conditions from the point of view of the employer. Workers in the various industries and workshops are abundant, hardworking, and they earn low salaries. The Portuguese workers in particular will do anything to preserve their jobs. . . ." The consul described the Italians and Spaniards as more "independent" in spirit, but executives at the Canadian-owned São Paulo Tramway, Light, and Power Company found Italian workers just as tractable as the Portuguese: speaking of their motormen and conductors, they noted that "a large majority of these men are Italians who would do anything rather than lose their daily pay. . . ."[93]

Restructuring the Labor Market:
The Immigrants Lose Their Preference

The desperation of these relatively privileged white workers is perhaps the most convincing proof of the efficacy of the state's labor policies. The planter state had sought policies which would keep labor cheap and insecure, and it found them. Such victories are never permanent, however. In the short run or in the long, they produce resistance and response. In the case of the immigrants, that response took various forms. One was the simple act of leaving Brazil for their countries of origin, or to pursue more promising opportunities in Argentina or the United States. Another was to shop about from plantation to plantation, or from factory to factory, in search of marginally better wages or working conditions, much as the libertos had done after abolition. A third was to pursue individual goals of upward mobility, pooling the combined earnings of family members to buy a small farm in the countryside or open a small business in the city. And a final response was collective: joining the labor movement and taking part in strike actions in both the cities and the countryside during the early decades of the century.[94]

These efforts by the immigrants to strengthen their bargaining position led to a gradual cooling of the paulista elites' initial rejoicing over immigration. As early as 1900 articles in the planters' *Revista Agrícola* were complaining about the immigrants' "inconstancy" and "ingratitude" in terms much the same as those applied to the libertos in the 1890s: "Nothing ties them to the soil; . . . they readily change their employers after each harvest. No more nomadic people could be imagined; they change incessantly from *fazenda* to *fazenda.*" Particularly galling was the purchase by immigrant workers of their own small farms and homesteads, a phenomenon which began in the late 1910s and which led the labor newspaper *O Combate* to comment that "certain *fazendeiros* have come to detest land sale agents today in the same way that those of yesteryear detested the abolitionists." Just as the abolitionists had lured slaves away from the plantations by inciting them to flight, so by the late 1910s and 1920s real estate agents were luring workers away by offering to sell them their own homesteads.[95]

As employers' enthusiasm for the immigrants waned, so too did the state's, or at least that arm of the state responsible for labor policy. As early as the mid-1890s the Secretariat of Agriculture was already warning of the social and even economic dangers of flooding the state with hundreds of thousands of immigrants. These dangers were examined in detail in a series of articles published in the State Department of Labor's *Boletim* during the 1910s, which analyzed the consequences of São Paulo's chronic situation of labor glut. While an oversupply of labor clearly redounded to employers' short-term advantage, it also promoted criminality, "vagabondage," hunger, and generalized social tension. As wages fell in the countryside, the *Boletim* argued, the result was an inflow of poverty-stricken immigrants into the capital, where they lived "as parasites, as beggars, as invalids, feeding themselves on charity, by hustling, and by crime. . . ." By 1917, department staffers were advancing the heretical notion that "to organize the labor market is to make it so that there will be no unemployed," and during the hiatus of European immigration caused by World War I, they even began to rethink some of the negative consequences of "the privilege conferred on foreign immigration to supply workers for agriculture," the result of which had been to marginalize (one article used the word "segregated") São Paulo's black and *caboclo* workers in the land of their birth. Articles published in the *Boletim* during the war years urged employers to reconsider the many virtues and abilities which Brazilian workers brought with them to the workplace—foremost among which, they noted, was the Brazilian worker's well-known disinclination to join unions or strike.[96]

São Paulo's elites still had considerable financial and ideological capital invested in the notion of the superiority of immigrant labor, and after the war ended Governor Washington Luis, in his 1921 "state of the state" address, announced his administration's intention to continue São Paulo's longstanding policy of maintaining "the cheapness of labor, and particularly agricultural labor, by the introduction on a large scale of honest, hardworking immigrants." The Department of Labor promptly took its cue, reporting in 1922 that "only through subsidized immigration will it be possible to keep [the plantations] supplied with labor." But as the 1920s continued, and more immigrants either bought their way out of the wage labor market or continued to engage in hard bargaining with employers, the aura surrounding foreign-born workers darkened and faded away. A poll of paulista coffee planters in 1925 found a majority of them now willing to employ Brazilian labor, and two years later the program of subsidized European immigration was finally terminated.[97]

The impact on labor relations in the state was immediate. In 1928, for the first time since records had been kept, Brazilian migrants into São Paulo outnumbered European immigrants. In 1927 Europeans had accounted for 61 percent of all *colono* labor contracts; in 1928 their representation in the *colono* labor force dropped to 27 percent, the difference being made up by native-born Brazilians.[98] The following year one of the black newspapers in São Paulo City reported on the turn-around in labor conditions in the countryside.

. . . The men of color of our *hinterland*, those whose labor consists of the cultivation of the soil and the business of agriculture, are in excellent

conditions as workers, enjoying the same advantages and benefits as the
other men of the soil. Black workers are as highly valued as the Italians, who
are São Paulo's agricultural workers *par excellence*. Which is to say that the
black of the *hinterland*, the contract laborer or day laborer of color, has
succeeded, more rapidly than the blacks of the city, in establishing himself
vis-à-vis his peers, obliging them to recognize his value and worth.[99]

The dominance of European workers would last longer in the
cities, but by the 1930s Afro-Brazilians were entering factory employment as well, coming to form part of São Paulo's industrial proletariat (chapter 4). As a white worker who lived through this period
suggests, their entry into the urban workplace was owing to the same
factor as their earlier exclusion: state policy governing the labor
market. If immigration had not been reduced and "there hadn't been
a shortage of manpower, the blacks would never have managed to get
into the factories. Everything would have stayed the way it was. If
the immigrants had continued to come the bosses would have given
them the preference, leaving the Brazilian worker behind."[100]

Conclusions

This rather lengthy chapter has sought to stress how evolving
interactions among employers, workers (both black and white), and
the Republican state explain the displacement of Afro-Brazilian
workers in São Paulo's postemancipation economy and society. Clearly the inheritance of slavery helped shape this process, by producing
both employers unaccustomed and unwilling to bargain with their
workers and an ex-slave population with very specific demands concerning the conditions under which its members would work as free
men and women. But that inheritance applied throughout most of
Brazil; yet "in no other place in the country [besides São Paulo] were
white immigrants so clearly the 'winners' and blacks the 'losers' [in
the process] of economic development and prosperity."[101]

The explanation for São Paulo's uniqueness is not to be found in
the superior abilities of its immigrant workers. Rather, it is to be
found in state policy which undercut Afro-Brazilians' bargaining
position by flooding the labor market with Europeans. In addition to
keeping wages low and weakening a labor movement committed to

racial equality and interracial solidarity, this policy enabled employers to turn their backs on those workers who sought to drive the hardest and most demanding bargains. Those workers were initially the ex-slave libertos; but by the 1910s and 1920s, the immigrants and their children had become more aggressive and effective in the pursuit of their individual and collective interests, and were making demands that, as we shall see in chapter 5, both the paulista elite and the native-born middle class found increasingly objectionable. The result was the redefinition of state policy in the mid-1920s to end the official preference given to Europeans, and the subsequent gradual restoration of Afro-Brazilians to a competitive, if subordinate, position in the market for manual labor.

This forty-year hiatus from the labor market was extremely damaging to the Afro-Brazilians, as emerges both in testimony from the period and in the marked disparities between São Paulo's black and white populations documented in the censuses of 1940 and 1950 (chapter 6). By depriving Afro-Brazilians of work experience and income, and reinforcing racist assumptions concerning the unemployability of black people, the hiatus would make much more difficult their struggle in subsequent years to play a full and equal role in the life of their state and nation. Nevertheless, an important first step in that struggle took place during the 1920s and 1930s, when black people entered the industrial proletariat.

4. Working, 1920–1960

At the moment that slavery was abolished, and during the early years of the First Republic, Brazil's economy was almost exclusively agrarian. The industrial census of 1907 recorded fewer than three thousand industrial enterprises in the entire country, 90 percent of which employed four or fewer workers. These firms marked the beginning, however, of a process of industrial expansion which has continued, at varying rates of intensity, to the present. Between 1907 and 1920 industrial output almost quintupled in Brazil; between 1920 and 1940 it increased by another 7,800 percent, by which point Brazil possessed over seventy thousand industrial firms employing a total of 1.4 million workers. Industrial output continued to grow at an average annual rate of 9 percent per year between 1946 and the early 1980s, and to diversify out of such traditional areas as textiles and food-processing into steel, autos, chemicals, and electrical machinery. During the 1970s industrial exports overtook agricultural commodities as Brazil's primary source of foreign exchange (manufactured goods made up almost 40 percent of Brazilian exports in 1975, while coffee accounted for less than 10 percent of export earnings), and by 1980 Brazil boasted the seventh largest industrial output in the capitalist world, surpassed only by the United States, Japan, and four Western European countries.[1]

São Paulo was in the forefront of this process, though its eventual emergence as Brazil's premier industrial state was by no means preordained. Of the hundred largest industrial firms operating in Brazil in 1907, only fifteen were based in the state of São Paulo, as compared with thirty-three in Rio de Janeiro, and twenty-six in Rio Grande do Sul. As a result, São Paulo accounted for a mere 16 percent of Brazil's industrial production that year. In subsequent decades, however, paulista entrepreneurs exploited the advantages provided by coffee export revenues (which provided capital) and state-subsidized immigration (which provided low-cost labor and a growing internal market) to pull ahead of their rivals elsewhere in Brazil. By 1920 São Paulo's share of national industrial output had doubled, to 32 percent, and then to 43 percent by 1940. By 1960 the state accounted for the majority of Brazil's industrial production, and was the most important industrial center, not just of Brazil, but of all South America.[2]

What were the effects of this industrial expansion on race relations in the state? Most observers agree that the initial effects (i.e., during the period 1900–1940) were for the most part negative. Industrialization, and the urbanization which accompanied it, generated job and other opportunities which, in the eyes of most Brazilian and European workers, were superior to those available in the countryside. But as we have seen, those opportunities were exploited almost entirely by white workers, and disproportionately by European immigrants. Both contemporary and present-day explanations for the exclusion of Afro-Brazilians from the industrial labor market stressed their incapacity to work in a disciplined factory setting. This incapacity does not seem to have extended to Rio de Janeiro, however, where Afro-Brazilians formed a sizable component of the industrial workforce. The exclusion of black workers from the first stage of paulista industrialization therefore seems to have had less to do with alleged black incapacity than with state policy which worked to flood the labor market with European workers, thus weakening the bargaining position of black and white workers alike, and enabling employers to indulge their preference for the latter.

But what would happen when state-promoted immigration came to an end, and white workers became scarcer? Would employers at that point prove more amenable to hiring black workers? If so, would black workers enter at levels comparable to those of their white peers? Or would laziness, incompetence, and incapacity continue to form obstacles to black employment and advancement, as they supposedly had in the decades immediately after abolition?

A Study of Two Firms

One way to answer such questions is to utilize the personnel records of industrial firms themselves.[3] This chapter makes use of such records from two major firms: the Jafet textile factory (Fiação, Tecelagem, e Estamparia Ypiranga Jafet), and the capital city's electrical and trolley utility, São Paulo Tramway, Light, and Power. Each company played a leading role in the industrialization of São Paulo.

In Brazil as in other nations, the textile industry spearheaded early industrialization. The inaugural issue of the State Labor Department's *Boletim* (1912) included an extended article on the state's textile industry which surveyed thirty-one factories in São Paulo City, an additional factory in the suburb of São Bernardo, and one more in the port city of Santos. By 1920, of the nine industrial establishments in São Paulo employing one thousand workers or more, seven were textile firms, and the textile industry as a whole employed over 40 percent of the state's industrial labor force.[4]

The textile industry in the state capital began with workshops and small factories in the downtown neighborhood of Bom Retiro, and then expanded during the 1890s and early 1900s into larger, more modern facilities in the then-outlying areas of Bras, Mooca, and Ipiranga. It was in this last neighborhood (coincidentally the site of the declaration of Brazilian independence in 1822) that the Jafet brothers, Lebanese immigrants who had prospered as importers and wholesalers of textiles during the 1890s, established their factory in 1906.[5] Like other entrepreneurs who opened factories there, they came to Ipiranga in response to low land prices, and the opportunity to invest in real estate as well as in industrial development. In so doing, they transformed the area virtually overnight. Lilian Elliott reported on her visit in the mid-1910s to

the windy upland flats of Ipiranga. A year or two ago much of this area was red clay swamp, with a cottage here and there and a few Italian market gardens producing vegetables for the city dwellers, and land could be bought for ten milreis an acre or less; today it is worth from two hundred to five hundred milreis; the wet lands have been filled in, an enormous undertaking, rows of workmen's houses extend for miles to the crest of the hill where the Monument stands commemorating the Declaration of Independence, and from its summit one has a view that is mottled with factory smoke and punctuated with tall chimneys. To see this and to watch the crowds of pretty chattering Italian girls pouring out of Braz and Mooca factories at noon or evening is to obtain a revelation of the newer South America.[6]

In calling her readers' attention to the "pretty chattering Italian girls" working in the textile factories, Elliott captured one of the distinctive characteristics of this "newer South America." The Labor Department's 1912 study of the textile industry in São Paulo found that almost three-quarters (72.0 percent) of textile workers were females, a third of whom were aged sixteen or under.[7] While the report dutifully cited employers' justifications for the use of child labor (shortage of adult workers, and the desire of parents to put their children to productive use and avoid their roaming unsupervised through the streets), its author could not refrain from expressing the "disagreeable impression caused in the visitor by the excessive number of children at work": "skeletal, rickety, some of them."[8]

Completely different in composition was the second company under examination, the São Paulo Tramway, Light, and Power Company. Established in 1899 by a consortium of Canadian and British engineers and investors, São Paulo Light, as it came to be known, by the 1930s had become the most important utility in Brazil and one of the largest companies in São Paulo State. It was responsible for all aspects of providing electrical power and urban transport to the state capital, and, over time, to a growing number of other cities in the state as it bought up their local utilities. Its monthly payroll, which hovered around seven thousand by the late 1920s, dropped below that level during the Great Depression but then rebounded during World War II and its aftermath, in response to the expansion of manufacturing activity which took place at that time. By 1949, even after ownership of its tramway system had been transferred to the municipality of São Paulo, its labor force exceeded nine thousand.[9]

In contrast to the Jafet firm, the work force at São Paulo Light was composed almost entirely of adult males, and thus provides a direct counterpoint to the female workers of the textile industry. Looking comparatively at these two firms thus provides a more comprehensive vision of the industrial proletariat, in gender terms, than looking at either firm in isolation.

Black and White Workers

In light of previous chapters' discussion of the exclusion of black workers from industrial employment, the first question to ask is, when, if at all, did Afro-Brazilians succeed in entering these companies in significant numbers? Because of the deficiencies in the records, this question is not easy to answer. Records on employees hired before 1920 are few in number, and usually provide no information on race. They become more numerous after 1920, but not until the 1930s (1932 in the case of São Paulo Light, 1935 in the case of Jafet), when the government imposed new recordkeeping requirements on Brazilian industry as part of the creation of the Social Security system, do personnel records routinely include information on race. However, the pre-1935 records do provide information on birthplace, which at least enables us to look at the relative representation of Brazilian and foreign-born workers in each firm. (For a discussion of the employee records generated by each company, and the sampling procedures employed in this research, see Appendix C.)

The pre–Social Security records suggest that Jafet turned to native-born labor somewhat earlier than did São Paulo Light. The pre-1920 data are too sparse to support firm conclusions, but suggest a labor force more or less evenly divided between Brazilians and immigrants at both firms. Between 1920 and 1930, however, by which point data are much more abundant, native-born Brazilians accounted for almost two-thirds (65.3 percent) of workers hired at Jafet (see Table 4.1), but only one-third (35.1 percent) of workers hired at São Paulo Light.[10]

The larger number of Brazilians hired at Jafet is doubtless owing to the previously discussed tendency of many textile factories to hire the native-born children of their immigrant employees.[11] At the same time, however, the growing number of Brazilians employed by the Jafet plant during the 1920s cannot be explained solely in terms of the offspring of immigrant workers. Unlike pre-1935 records at São Paulo Light, pre-1935 personnel forms at Jafet included an entry for race, and by the 1920s Jafet's personnel department was recording this information fairly regularly. When combined with the data yielded by the post-1935 Social Security records, the pre-1935 records provide a clear picture of the entry of Afro-Brazilian workers into the firm.

Table 4.1. Percentage Distribution of Workers Hired at Jafet, 1920–1960, by Race

	1921–1930	1931–1940	1941–1950	1951–1960
White	*92.4*	*89.3*	*86.7*	*73.7*
Immigrants	33.5	24.0	7.7	5.1
Brazilians	58.9	65.3	79.0	68.6
Amarelo	*0.0*	*0.0*	*0.2*	*0.0*
Black	*7.6*	*10.7*	*13.0*	*26.3*
Morenos[a]	1.0	1.9	0.6	0.2
Pardos	3.6	3.6	5.5	14.8
Pretos	3.0	5.2	6.9	11.3
N[b]	1,249	1,304		
		111	237	245

Note: In this and subsequent tables, columns may not add to the exact total of 100.0 because of rounding.

[a]On the *moreno* racial label, see Appendix B.

[b]First row is pre-1935 sample; second row is post-1935 sample (see Appendix C). Percentages for 1931–1940 represent an average of the two samples.

These figures indicate slow but steady growth in the proportion of black employees at the firm from the 1920s through the 1940s, followed by a rapid increase in black employment in the 1950s, during which Afro-Brazilian workers more than doubled their representation in the firm's work force. How does this compare with the figures for São Paulo Light? Here the picture is clouded by the absence of racial information in the early records. When the company instituted its new recordkeeping system in 1932, however, it prepared files not only for new employees but also for those hired in earlier years who were still with the firm in 1932. As a result, the Social Security records include a number of workers hired during the 1910s and 1920s. Analysis of those records shows a rather different pattern of black entry into São Paulo Light (see Table 4.2). By the 1920s a much higher proportion of the company's employees was black than was the case at Jafet: fully a fifth of the total labor force at São Paulo Light versus 7.6 percent at the textile company. In subsequent decades, however, that proportion remained more or less constant, dropping slightly in the 1930s, returning to the one-fifth level in the 1940s, and then rising slightly in the 1950s, to a proportion slightly below the proportion of black workers at Jafet.

While the pre-1932 records showed almost two-thirds of São Paulo

Table 4.2. Percentage Distribution of Workers Hired at São Paulo Light, 1921–1960, by Race

	1921–1930	1931–1940	1941–1950	1951–1960
White	79.0	81.8	79.7	76.4
Immigrants	27.4	15.7	9.3	5.3
Brazilians	51.6	66.1	70.4	71.1
Black	20.9	18.2	20.3	23.5
Morenos	0.4	2.7	1.0	0.4
Pardos	2.0	4.8	11.9	13.3
Pretos	1.6	8.3	7.3	9.8
Unspecified Afro-Brazilian[a]	16.9	2.4	0.1	0.0
N	101	227	327	96

[a]See Appendix C.

Light workers hired during the 1920s to have been foreign-born, the Social Security records indicate that only about a quarter of the workers hired there during the 1920s were immigrants. How does one explain this discrepancy? The most likely explanation is that the earlier recordkeeping system did not cover the transitory jobs in construction and day labor that Brazilians, and Afro-Brazilians in particular, were more likely to fill. The individuals recorded in the pre-1932 documents tended to be conductors and motormen for the trolley system, positions which at that time were dominated by Europeans. In later years black men managed to break the racial barriers and compete for those jobs; but previously cited contemporary testimony suggests that during the 1920s most black employees remained restricted to relatively unskilled construction work.[12] This impression is borne out by the Social Security records, which show that half of the black workers (48.6 percent) taken on by São Paulo Light before 1930 were hired as common laborers, versus only 18.6 percent of white workers. These unskilled workers seem to have come and gone through the firm in a fairly casual manner, and records kept on them were minimal up until the inauguration of the Social Security system. Nevertheless, they represented a significant part of the work force, as evidenced both by the post-1932 records and by surviving personnel records from one of São Paulo Light's subsidiaries, the Companhia Brasileira de Administração de Serviços Técnicos (COBAST).

Table 4.3. Percentage Distribution of Workers Hired at COBAST,
1921–1950, by Race

	1921–1930	1931–1940	1941–1950
White	*57.6*	*66.9*	*62.1*
Immigrants	28.8	20.2	4.9
Brazilians	28.8	46.7	57.2
Black	*42.3*	*33.2*	*37.9*
Morenos	0.0	4.6	3.9
Pardos	20.3	16.6	17.9
Pretos	22.0	12.0	16.1
N	59	392	285

COBAST functioned as part of the construction and engineering
wing of São Paulo Light, and a large proportion—perhaps the majority—of its employees were construction workers. A tabulation of
5 percent of its personnel records, which are maintained in the São
Paulo Light archives and which do provide information on race,
indicates that black workers formed a much larger proportion of
COBAST's work force, and immigrants a much smaller proportion,
than of the work force documented in the São Paulo Light records
(see Table 4.3).

Like the São Paulo Light records, the COBAST records indicate a
decrease in the representation of black workers over the course of the
1930s, followed by a recovery in the 1940s. This is in direct contrast to
white Brazilians, who between 1930 and 1940 increased their representation in the labor force by 28 percent at São Paulo Light, and 62
percent at COBAST. At these two companies white Brazilians were
clearly the principal beneficiaries of the changes in labor policy
during this period: the 1927 decision by the São Paulo State government to terminate the subsidized immigration program, and the
Nationalization of Labor Law handed down by the federal government in 1931, which required urban employers to maintain work
forces that were at least two-thirds native-born.[13] White Brazilians
increased their representation at Jafet as well during the 1930s, but at
a rate considerably slower than that of black workers. During the
1930s the proportion of native-born whites working at the factory
was 11 percent greater than it had been during the 1920s, but the
proportion of Afro-Brazilians was 41 percent greater.

Table 4.4. Percentage Distribution of Brazilian-born Workers Hired by Jafet and São Paulo Light, 1930–1960, by Birthplace

	1931–1940			1941–1950			1951–1960		
	White	Black	Total	White	Black	Total	White	Black	Total
	Jafet								
São Paulo State	77.9	10.5	88.4	77.6	9.8	87.4	37.7	8.1	45.8
Minas Gerais	4.5	1.9	6.4	5.1	2.2	7.3	10.8	5.4	16.2
Northeast	1.5	0.4	1.9	3.2	1.4	4.6	23.8	13.7	37.5
Rest of Brazil	3.0	0.4	3.4	0.6	0.0	0.6	0.0	0.6	0.6
Total	86.9	13.2	100.1	86.5	13.4	99.9	72.3	27.8	100.1
N		93			219			238	
	São Paulo Light								
São Paulo State	68.3	14.0	82.3	49.9	9.3	59.2	58.8	9.5	68.3
Minas Gerais	7.4	4.1	11.5	8.8	4.8	13.6	1.9	3.8	5.7
Northeast	2.5	1.2	3.7	17.0	7.4	24.4	9.5	9.5	19.0
Rest of Brazil	0.8	1.6	2.4	2.2	0.5	2.7	5.7	1.4	7.1
Total	79.0	20.9	99.9	77.9	22.0	99.9	75.9	24.2	100.1
N		198			303			91	

The post-1930 increase in black employment at Jafet, however, also reflects the smaller numbers of Afro-Brazilians working at the factory during the 1920s, as compared with São Paulo Light. The proportion of Afro-Brazilians working at the two companies prior to 1930 was almost three times greater at São Paulo Light than at Jafet; not until the 1950s, in fact, would Jafet employ as large a proportion of black workers as São Paulo Light had already hired in the 1920s. These data confirm contemporary testimony of the utility's unusual receptivity, in the context of the 1920s, toward hiring black workers. Some black observers attributed that receptivity to the company's constant need for construction workers to build its dams, power grids, and trolley lines. Others focused on the strike of 1919, during which black workers were brought into the firm as strikebreakers and then kept on when their competence and willingness to work became manifest.[14]

Dissimilarities between São Paulo Light and Jafet also appear when one looks more closely at the composition of the Brazilian workers who were displacing the immigrants (see Table 4.4). At Jafet such workers, regardless of whether they were black or white, were overwhelmingly paulistas until the 1950s, when the proportion of paulistas hired dropped by almost half and the firm was swamped by a wave of in-migrants, both black and white, from the Northeast and Minas Gerais. At São Paulo Light, by contrast, this wave had already broken in the 1940s and appears to have been receding by the 1950s.

At both firms a rise in the proportion of in-migrants translated into a rise in the proportion of black workers hired. Depending on the company and the decade, black workers composed between a sixth and a ninth of paulista workers hired; of workers from Minas Gerais and the Northeast, by contrast, blacks accounted for between a quarter and a half. As a result, the decade in which the Jafet company drew more than half its employees from Minas and the Northeast is also the decade in which black employment in the company more than doubled.

The displacement of paulista workers by in-migrants at Jafet during the 1950s was caused by the rapid pace of continuing industrialization in São Paulo. The state's explosive economic growth during and after World War II generated an ever-increasing demand for labor, which in turn exerted upward pressure on wages. In an effort to hold labor costs down, and perhaps in conscious imitation of the planters' earlier labor practices, the Jafet company sent recruiting agents into the rural areas of São Paulo and Minas Gerais, in search of peasants and farmworkers willing to come to the big city.[15] Such recruiting almost doubled the proportion of *mineiros* (natives of Minas Gerais) employed at the factory, but did little to staunch the decline of paulistas in the work force. This was because, by the 1950s, the "traditional" industries which had led the first wave of industrialization—textiles, clothing, food and beverages—were being overshadowed by a second wave of more highly capitalized, technologically advanced industries: autos, metalworking, electrical goods, chemicals. These industries, particularly the auto and metal industries, offered better wages and working conditions than those available in the textile sector. Paulistas therefore exited the textile industry to take advantage of opportunities available elsewhere.[16] This process is quite visible at Jafet, where, over the course of the 1950s, white paulistas dropped to only a third of the labor force, to be replaced by an almost equal number of black and white northeasterners.

Since São Paulo Light's wages and working conditions were supe-

rior to those of the textile industry, and closer to those offered by the
newer industries, it experienced no such exodus in the 1950s. To the contrary: paulistas actually increased their representation in the firm's
work force. But one wonders why mineiros were already an important part of the labor force by the 1930s, and northeasterners were
being hired in large numbers by the 1940s, ten years before similar
developments at Jafet. This difference is best explained in terms of the
gender composition of the two firms' work forces, and of the migrant
streams to São Paulo. The census of 1950 indicates a ratio of 152 males
to 100 females among northeastern-born residents of São Paulo State.
Since São Paulo Light hired males almost exclusively, and Jafet mainly females, it is hardly surprising to find a larger northeastern con-
tingent being hired during the 1940s at the former firm. By 1960,
however, more women were coming from the Northeast, with the
result that the male-female ratio among migrants from that region
had declined to 125 males to 100 females, and the potential pool of
northeastern textile workers had expanded accordingly.[17]

Regardless of the differences in timing between the two firms'
hiring patterns, we should not lose sight of the fact that, with the
exception of the Jafet factory during the 1920s, both firms consistently hired a proportion of black workers either equal to or greater
than the proportion of black people in the population as a whole. In
1940 Afro-Brazilians accounted for 9.0 percent of the population of
São Paulo City; during the 1931–1940 period, they made up 10.7
percent of the workers hired at Jafet, and 18.2 percent of workers
hired at São Paulo Light. In 1950, Afro-Brazilians accounted for 10.2
percent of the population of São Paulo City; during the 1941–1950
period, they made up 13.0 percent of workers hired at Jafet, and 20.3
of workers hired at São Paulo Light.[18] After 1930 the Jafet company
consistently hired a proportion of black workers higher than the
proportion in the population as a whole, and São Paulo Light hired a
proportion of black workers twice as high as their representation in
the population as a whole.

These are only two firms out of the thousands that operated in São
Paulo during this period. But statistical data gathered at the state
level confirm their evidence of growing black participation in the
industrial labor force. The census of 1940 indicated that Afro-Brazilians composed 9.5 percent of the employees of industrial firms in

the state, at a time when they made up 12.0 percent of the population as a whole (and a somewhat smaller proportion of the urban population, where factories were concentrated—as previously mentioned, they made up only 9.0 percent of the population of the capital, the state's most prosperous and dynamic city). By 1950 (by which time industrial employment in the state had almost doubled), the employment of Afro-Brazilians was at a par with their representation in the population: they composed 11.2 percent of the state population, and 11.3 percent of its industrial labor force.[19]

This is not to say that all was well with the black population. As we will see later in this chapter and in chapters 5 and 6, Afro-Brazilians were almost entirely excluded from middle-class, white-collar positions during this period. And even within the working class, as of 1940 almost twice as many Afro-Brazilians were working in domestic service, the informal sector, or were unemployed, as were working in industry.[20] This ratio was reduced considerably during the 1940s, however, when more and more Afro-Brazilians entered the industrial sector. Between 1940 and 1950 the number of pardos and pretos employed in industry in the state more than doubled, to 85,344. These workers were still heavily outnumbered by the 129,117 Afro-Brazilians working in domestic service or categorized by the census as "inactive," but the disparity between the two groups had declined substantially, in favor of industrial employment.[21]

Even more encouraging, the number of black industrial workers had grown at a rate exceeding that of white workers during the same period.[22] Given this growth in the black proletariat, and the continuing upturn in black hiring at both Jafet and São Paulo Light during the 1950s, it is clear that the situation of black exclusion from the industrial labor force was a pre-1930 phenomenon which had largely come to an end by 1940. One of the black magazines of the 1930s, *Evolução*, seemed to be saying as much when it featured as one of its covers a drawing of two black men—a farmer holding a plow, and an urban worker standing next to a factory—shaking hands in front of a background of modern apartment or office buildings. In conjunction with the magazine's title, the cover suggests black people's transition from being rural peasants to becoming urban wage laborers, while underlining the continued community of interest between the two groups on the basis of race.[23] The transition would not be an easy one; reports of industrial firms which have refused to hire blacks continue to appear in the São Paulo press to the present.[24] But for the most part São Paulo's industrial employers have accepted black workers, and in fact by 1980 were hiring them in numbers well in excess of their representation in the population as a whole (see chapter 6, Table 6.2).

Such a finding is by no means new; indeed, it lay at the core of Florestan Fernandes's optimism concerning the future path of race relations in Brazil. The inherent rationality of the capitalist marketplace, argued Fernandes, and the unwillingness of employers to continue excluding black workers after the state was no longer subsidizing the importation of cheap European labor, would eventually result in the full integration of Afro-Brazilians into the urban labor force. And as black people became further removed in time from the damaging experience of slavery, they would gradually acquire the psychological and attitudinal characteristics necessary to compete successfully in the marketplace. Urbanization and industrialization would create a "new Negro" capable of taking part in capitalist growth and development.

The data presented thus far do indicate that by the 1930s and 1940s Afro-Brazilians were obtaining industrial employment in sizable numbers. What do those data tell us about the terms on which white and black people entered the industrial proletariat during those years, and their respective experiences in the factories?

Before trying to answer that question, it would be helpful to have an idea of what the Jafet and São Paulo Light work forces looked like in general terms. As already noted, they were quite different in gender composition. Women composed the majority (61.9 percent of the white racial group, and 70.5 percent of blacks) of the workers at Jafet, but only 11 (all of whom were white clerical workers) of the 671 workers in the São Paulo Light sample. Despite this difference in gender composition, racially the two groups look quite similar, with whites composing a narrow majority of both samples (53.6 percent of the Jafet sample, and 51.3 percent of the São Paulo Light sample).[25] Within the black racial group, pardos and morenos (on the "moreno" racial label, see Appendix B) outnumbered pretos at both companies, by a ratio of 1.1:1 at Jafet, and 1.5:1 at São Paulo Light.[26]

Given that the preto population of São Paulo City was almost half again as large as the pardo population in 1940, and over three times larger in 1950, clearly pardos were overrepresented in both companies in relation to pretos, and enjoyed a substantial preference in hiring.[27] In extending such preference, however, these firms were not representative of São Paulo's industrial sector as a whole. In 1940 pardos had held a slight advantage over pretos in industrial employment in the state, when pardos constituted 38.7 percent of the working-age (ten or over) Afro-Brazilian population, and 40.0 percent of Afro-Brazilian industrial workers. But that advantage had disappeared by 1950, when pardos accounted for 28.0 percent of working-age Afro-Brazilians, and 27.8 percent of black industrial workers.[28]

Not coincidentally, pardo workers were most overrepresented in relation to pretos during those decades in which the largest numbers of northeasterners entered the two firms: the 1940s in the case of São Paulo Light, and the 1950s in the case of Jafet. Like the white workers, three-quarters of whom were native-born paulistas, most pretos (58.6 percent at Jafet, and 62.5 percent at São Paulo Light) hired at the two firms had been born in São Paulo State. Pardos, by contrast, were more likely to have migrated from the Northeast.[29]

White workers entered both firms at an earlier age than black workers did, though the difference was more pronounced at Jafet, where the median age of entry was 19.9 for white workers, and 22.1 for blacks; at São Paulo Light, it was 24.5 for white workers, 25.4 for blacks. The higher median age for both races at São Paulo Light doubtless corresponded to the greater skill requirements of many of the jobs to be filled there, and the more extensive experience required of black and white workers alike. Relatively less skill was demanded of workers entering a textile plant, with the result that workers could begin employment there at an earlier age.[30]

Lower skill requirements at Jafet, however, do not explain the higher age at entry among black workers. These data may indicate black families' continuing reluctance, mentioned earlier in chapter 3, to send their women and children into the labor market. The difference in ages at entry between black and white workers is accounted for almost entirely by differences in ages at entry among female workers. Black and white males entered at essentially the same ages (21.9 and 21.6, respectively), whereas white females entered at 19.3, and black females at 22.1. One out of seven white women hired by Jafet entered the factory at the age of fourteen or younger, versus only one out of fourteen black women. The reluctance of black families to send women and children to work may also help account for the disparity between employment patterns at Jafet and São Paulo Light. While black families may have held their women and minors back from factory employment, no such reluctance was attached to black men, who therefore entered São Paulo Light earlier in the century, and in larger numbers than their counterparts at Jafet. This is only supposition, since neither firm maintained information on workers who applied for jobs but were turned down. It is therefore impossible to know whether young black women were presenting themselves for jobs and being rejected, or simply not presenting themselves. What we do know is that black workers hired at Jafet were more likely to be adults, whereas most of the white workers were still teenagers.

Since much of the Fernandes thesis concerning the unemployability of black workers centered on the anomic quality of black family life, it is worth focusing for a moment on whatever data the samples may include on that score. Not surprisingly, all employees of both races knew their mother's name. When it came to their fathers, 2.1 percent of white workers at São Paulo Light, and 3.7 percent of black workers (6.6 percent of pardos, 0.9 percent of pretos), indicated that they did not know who their fathers were. At Jafet, the proportions were higher: 3.5 percent of white workers, and 9.8 percent of black workers. Nevertheless, when Jafet workers were asked to indicate the person or persons who would receive their back pay and benefits in case of death or accident at work, white and black workers provided similar responses, as indicated in Table 4.5. Black and white workers were most likely to designate their parents and siblings as their combined beneficiaries, followed by their spouse and children combined, and then their parents alone (one or both). One gets little sense here of anomic family life, or of sharp differences between the two racial groups.

The same is true when we turn to statistics on civil status, and on the rate at which workers at the two firms were constructing family units. Marriage was slightly more common among black workers at Jafet than among white workers, though this is probably accounted for by the older median age of black workers. At the time they were

Table 4.5. Numerical and Percentage Distributions of Beneficiaries Designated by Jafet Workers, by Race

	White		Black	
	N	%	N	%
Parent(s)	38	12.0	22	8.4
Parent(s) and sibling(s)	179	56.5	145	55.1
Sibling(s)	15	4.7	20	7.6
Spouse	22	6.9	19	7.2
Spouse and child(ren)	61	19.2	46	17.5
Child(ren)	2	0.6	7	2.7
Others	0	0.0	4	1.5
Total	317	99.9	263	100.0
No information	12		4	

hired, 77.0 percent of white workers at Jafet were single compared with 73.7 percent of black workers. At São Paulo Light, by contrast, white workers were more likely to be married than were blacks: 61.5 percent of white workers there were single at the time they were hired, versus 69.5 percent of black workers.

Racial differentials in literacy varied quite a bit between the two firms. At Jafet there was virtually no differential, with 86.0 percent of whites and 85.2 percent of blacks claiming literacy. There was also no racial differential *within* gender groups, though there was considerable variation *between* those groups: 95.4 percent of white males and 94.4 percent of black males claimed literacy, versus 80.2 percent of white females and 81.3 percent of black females. At São Paulo Light, by contrast, 95.0 percent of whites claimed literacy, versus only 78.4 percent of blacks (72.9 percent of pardos, 82.1 percent of pretos). Given that literacy was seldom a job requirement at Jafet, and that would-be literates could more easily bluff their way through, one is inclined to put more faith in the São Paulo Light figures.[31]

In addition to the biographical information which we have just examined, São Paulo Light recordkeepers gathered data on an additional variable: workers' profession or occupation prior to entering the firm. The occupational distributions of the two racial groups show clear differences (Table 4.6). Black workers were twice as likely as white workers to have come from the agricultural sector; conversely, whites were much more likely than blacks to have worked in supervisory and white-collar positions. But the bulk of the white and

Table 4.6. Percentage Distribution of São Paulo Light Workers' Previous Occupation and First Job Assignment at the Company, by Race

	White		Black	
	Previous Occupation	First Job at Company	Previous Occupation	First Job at Company
Managerial/				
professional	1.7	1.0	0.6	0.0
Clerical	6.8	5.4	0.9	0.8
Foreman	1.1	0.3	0.0	0.0
Skilled and semi-				
skilled trades	26.8	20.6	23.3	17.8
Apprentice/helper	8.2	14.1	12.5	9.8
Commercial/service	20.1	32.4	15.2	19.1
Factory worker	15.3	0.0	18.2	0.0
Common laborer	7.6	26.2	11.0	52.5
Agriculture	7.9	0.0	16.4	0.0
Other	4.5	0.0	1.8	0.0
Total	100.0	100.0	99.9	100.0
N	354	389	335	377
No information	42	7	46	4

black racial groups actually look fairly similar: slightly more than a third (35.0 percent of whites, 35.8 percent of blacks) having worked in the skilled trades, either as full-fledged workers or as apprentices and helpers in training, and another 40–45 percent (43.0 percent of whites, 44.4 percent of blacks) having worked in the commercial/ service sector, in factories, or as common laborers.[32]

Black and White Careers

Given these similarities in the two racial groups' backgrounds, the disparities in their initial job assignments within São Paulo Light are striking. More than half of black entrants were assigned to the pool of common laborers, but only a quarter of whites. Of those whites who had worked either as factory workers or as common laborers before entering São Paulo Light, fewer than half (42.6 percent of white factory workers, 46.2 of white common laborers) became common laborers at the company. Among black workers with these backgrounds, three-quarters were assigned to common labor (72.1 percent of black factory workers, 73.0 percent of black common laborers). Perhaps most striking, black workers who entered São Paulo Light with a background in the skilled trades, both at the master and apprentice levels, were more likely to be assigned to the pool of common laborers than to any other job category (37.5 percent of black skilled and semiskilled workers were assigned to common labor, and 64.3 percent of black apprentice/helpers).

Obviously a substantial proportion of white workers also were hired as common laborers. Whites who had worked in agriculture, in factories, or as common laborers, were all more likely to be assigned to the common labor pool than to any other job category. But an even more substantial proportion of whites managed to avoid common labor and instead become conductors, meter readers, messengers, or chauffeurs—service occupations, which paid better and conferred higher status than unskilled labor. Service occupations are also the one area of employment at São Paulo Light where pardos received clear preference over pretos and occupied a genuinely intermediate position halfway between whites and pretos. Of white workers 32.4 percent were hired for service jobs, versus 23.8 percent of pardos, and 11.3 percent of pretos. This preference is particularly striking in light of the pardos' lower literacy rate in comparison to preto employees.[33]

Black workers thus entered São Paulo Light in a position of marked disadvantage in relation to their white counterparts. Such does not seem to have been the case at Jafet, where the relative paucity of positions requiring either frequent contact with the public or a high level of technical skill produced a "flatter," less differentiated vocational structure. Former employees of the firm concurred that the position of weaver (which accounted for almost a third of all workers hired at Jafet) was probably the most desirable job in the factory, for reasons summed up by a study of textile factories in the southern United States during this period. "In an industry that had relentlessly stripped most jobs of initiative and skill, weavers remained more independent and better paid than most other textile workers." Furthermore, "weaving was the one job in the mill where men and women worked under more or less equal conditions."[34] Given the relative desirability of weaving, it is somewhat surprising to find that black workers enjoyed some measure of preference here: 27.2 percent of white workers were hired as weavers, versus 37.5 percent of black workers.

What about workers' experiences once they had entered their respective firms? We might begin with the question of worker discipline. Florestan Fernandes and others have argued that the primary obstacle impeding black entry into the labor force during the first decades of the century had been Afro-Brazilians' refusal, or inability, to accept the discipline required of workers in modern industrial enterprises. These two companies' records do indicate that, even in the 1930–1960 period, black workers experienced considerable difficulty in adjusting to, and meeting, their employers' demands. But the records also indicate that white workers faced similar problems, and in many respects performed at the same level as, or only marginally better than, their black counterparts.

At São Paulo Light, written warnings of poor job performance or other violations were issued to essentially the same proportions of black and white workers: 2.9 percent of blacks and 3.3 percent of whites received such warnings. White and black workers also received the more serious sanction of suspensions without pay in similar numbers: 10.0 percent of black workers received such suspensions, and 9.1 percent of white workers. White workers were more likely than blacks to suffer multiple suspensions, however, with the result that, when one calculates the number of suspensions per person-years worked, the white rate (0.05 suspensions per year) proves to be slightly higher than the black (0.04)—though again, the numbers are so close as to indicate very similar levels of job performance.[35]

At Jafet, warnings seem to have been verbal rather than written, since only six were encountered in the entire sample. The overall rate of suspensions was comparable to São Paulo Light, however, but was almost twice as high for blacks as for whites: 6.1 percent of white workers suffered suspensions, as compared with 10.9 percent of blacks. This disparity was caused by the much higher likelihood for black men, and particularly preto men, to have received suspensions. While relatively similar proportions of all white workers and black female workers received this disciplinary sanction (5.6 percent of white women, 7.5 percent of white men, and 8.0 percent of black women), the proportion of black men penalized in this way, 17.1 percent (11.9 percent of pardos, 23.5 percent of pretos), was more than double that of their white male and black female counterparts. As a result, the rate of suspensions per person-year worked was three times higher for black workers than for white: 0.12 per year for blacks, 0.04 for whites.

At São Paulo Light, white workers were suspended most frequently for negligence on the job and for schedule violations (coming to work late, leaving early, taking excessive breaks). Among black workers, insubordination and "disrespect for authorities" led the list of offenses, followed by negligence. At Jafet, black and white workers were both suspended frequently for insubordination and "disrespect"; but while such offenses were the most frequent cause of white suspensions at Jafet, black workers were suspended in even larger numbers for schedule infractions. Black workers were penalized for such acts at a rate 4.5 times that of white workers; indeed, schedule violations accounted for the majority of suspensions of black workers at Jafet.

Black workers at São Paulo Light were apparently more successful in adjusting to the demands of the workplace than black workers at Jafet. This impression is reinforced when we turn to the issue of how long workers were able to put up with those demands and remain in the two firms' work forces. In both firms black and white workers tended to leave after a year or less of employment, for reasons to be discussed shortly. Black workers, however, tended to leave after shorter periods of employment than whites. At São Paulo Light the median period of time a white worker remained with the firm was 12.0 months, whereas for black workers it was 10.0 months. A two-month differential also held at Jafet, though that differential is larger in relation to the amount of time worked: white workers spent a median period of 8.3 months in the firm, whereas black workers worked 6.3 months. The differential also applies exclusively to the *pardo* workers, who resigned after a median period of 5.3 months. *Preto* employees worked a median period of 8.3 months, the same length of time as white workers.

Did black workers leave their jobs because they chose to, or because they had to? In other words, did they leave voluntarily, by quitting, or were they fired? And if the latter, were they being fired "for just cause" *(com justa causa)*, in response to demonstrated shortcomings in their work performance? Or were they being fired "without just cause" *(sem justa causa)*, as part of efforts by employers to reduce the labor force during periods of economic contraction, or to restructure it for greater efficiency?

Some caution in responding to these queries is in order. As anyone who has ever held a paying position is well aware, the distinction between quitting a job and being fired from it is sometimes a fine one. And in the case of the workers we are looking at, that distinction was further muddied as a consequence of the national labor code (Consolidação das Leis do Trabalho) of 1943, which stipulated a series of rights and guarantees for workers who remained with their firms for one year or more. Workers who quit their jobs or were fired during the first year of employment had no right to severance pay of any kind. Once workers had completed the one-year probationary period, they were entitled to an *indenização* of one month's pay for every year worked at the firm, regardless of whether they quit or were fired. Workers fired without just cause were also entitled to one month's notice *(aviso prévio)*; if that notice was not given, they were entitled to one month's pay. Workers who were fired for just cause, or who resigned, forfeited their right to the *aviso prévio* but were still entitled to the *indenização*.[36]

Such laws motivated employers to keep two principles in mind. First, employers had an obvious interest in removing employees before the year of probation was over. This emerges clearly in the data on firings, which tended to take place at both firms, and in both racial groups, within the first year of employment.[37] Second, when workers completed the year of probation and acquired the rights accruing to "stable" workers, the costs of firing them without just cause, for purposes of work force reduction, rose significantly. Employers therefore sought to avoid such firings, and to disguise them instead as voluntary resignations.

Material contained in the Jafet personnel files suggests one way in which this has been done. Workers at Brazilian firms resign by means of a "request for release" *(pedido de demissão)* form, in which the worker inserts his or her name and reason for resigning. Many of the Jafet files contain blank forms of this type which had already been signed by the employee. Former workers at the firm informed me that employees were often asked to sign such forms when they were hired, which the company could then use later to discharge workers without incurring the costs and possible legal complications of firing.

No such tactics were used at São Paulo Light, but a careful reading of the files indicates that not every resignation or retirement from the company was completely voluntary. A 1943 evaluation of pardo electrician Onofre C., for example, described him as a "very bad element . . . constantly involved in fights and disputes with other employees." Onofre, who at that time had worked for the company for eight years, resigned his position the day after the evaluation was written, citing as his reason for doing so "the constant admonishments that he received for his work." In a 1952 case, four employees negotiated an agreement with the company by which they would resign from the firm "in return for the payment of a bonus corresponding to what they would be entitled to if they were fired." And in 1969, the company persuaded long-time employee Luiz M. to retire despite his explicitly stated desire to continue working. As in the 1952 case, he was persuaded to do so through the payment of a retirement bonus.[38]

In each of these cases, workers resigned or retired, but they did not do so at their own initiative. Rather, they left their positions under pressure from their employer, either coercive, as in the case of Onofre C., or persuasive, as in the other five cases. Having concluded that it no longer wished to have these individuals on the payroll, São Paulo Light took steps to remove them that stopped short of firing, but that made their departure from the firm not entirely voluntary.

In evaluating workers' performance, therefore, one would wish to distinguish between those resignations that were the result of worker initiative and those that took place in response to efforts by the firm to remove workers from the payroll. Such a distinction is generally impossible to draw on the basis of the São Paulo Light documents. In the case of that firm, we should simply keep in mind that the number of resignations recorded represents the outside limit of the number of workers leaving the firm of their own free will, and that the proportion of workers actually doing so was probably somewhat smaller.

In the case of Jafet, it is possible to arrive at a closer estimate of the proportion of "voluntary" to "involuntary" resignations. Firings for just cause required no advance notice, and could be done on the spot. Firings without just cause required a month's *aviso prévio*, during which workers could look for alternative employment. A number of workers at Jafet, upon receiving that advance notice, opted to resign rather than wait to be fired; in return, the firm agreed to pay them immediately a stipulated portion, usually one-half to three-quarters, of the benefits to which they would be entitled as compensation for being fired. The workers' reason for accepting such a bargain is that the payments guaranteed them by law were often delayed for several months or more because of bureaucratic red tape, the company's contesting the worker's claim, or other reasons. In the inflationary climate of the 1940s, 1950s, and 1960s, such delays significantly reduced the value of whatever money the worker eventually received.[39] Rather than contend with these uncertainties, many workers who had been informed that they were going to be fired opted to resign their positions in return for an immediate cash payment.[40] In cases in which these arrangements were recorded in their files, I assigned these individuals to a category of workers who resigned their positions involuntarily, in anticipation of being fired. Additional workers were also dismissed through the use of the presigned resignation forms, but it is impossible to isolate those cases through the written documentation alone. Thus, the documented cases of involuntary resignation represent a *minimum* estimate of the proportion of workers forced to resign against their will.

Even including these data on involuntary resignations, the majority of black and white workers at both firms are recorded as having left their jobs of their own free will (Table 4.7). At both firms, black workers resigned less frequently than white, but this is in part a function of their being fired more frequently, which deprived them of the opportunity to resign. Was this higher incidence of black dismissals owing to deficient job performance? Not at São Paulo Light (Table 4.8). While members of both racial groups were likely to be dismissed for cheating on fare collections and for failing to come to work, the most frequent cause of dismissal for black workers was work force reduction.[41] In light of previously cited evidence indicating a preference for pardos in hiring and job assignment, it is curious to note that dismissals for this purpose struck most heavily at pardos. Of those workers fired, 16.8 percent of whites, 18.0 percent of pretos, and 37.5 percent of pardos were let go *sem justa causa*, in order to reduce the work force.

At Jafet the racial distribution of forced departures from the firm was the reverse, with pardos receiving clear preference and pretos being most adversely affected. In order to make the data on forcible discharges at Jafet comparable to the data from São Paulo Light,

Table 4.7. Numerical and Percentage Distributions of São Paulo Light and Jafet Workers, by Manner of Leaving Firm

	White		Black	
	N	%	N	%
São Paulo Light Workers				
Resigned	198	50.5	166	44.1
Fired	121	30.9	138	36.7
Transferred to CMTC[a]	23	5.9	24	6.4
Retired	38	9.7	29	7.7
Deceased	12	3.1	19	5.1
Total	392	100.1	376	100.0
No information	4		5	
Jafet Workers[42]				
Fired	35	12.9	41	16.8
"Voluntarily" resigned	208	76.8	164	67.2
"Involuntarily" resigned	27	10.0	38	15.6
Deceased	1	0.4	1	0.4
Total	271	100.1	244	100.0
No information	58		23	

[a]In 1947 São Paulo Light's trolley system was purchased by the municipality of São Paulo and became the Companhia Metropolitana de Transportes Coletivos. All employees of the transport wing of the company therefore left São Paulo Light at that time and became city employees.

Table 4.8. Numerical and Percentage Distributions of São Paulo Light Workers, by Reason for Dismissal

	White		Black	
	N	%	N	%
Work force reduction	20	16.8	35	27.6
Irregularities in fare collections	32	26.9	27	21.3
Failing to come to work *(abandono)*	28	23.5	29	22.8
Generally unsatisfactory performance	25	21.0	16	12.6
Insubordination	9	7.6	13	10.2
Miscellaneous misdeeds	5	4.2	7	5.5
Total	119	100.0	127	100.0
No information	2		11	

Table 4.9. Numerical and Percentage Distributions of Jafet Workers, by Reason for Dismissal or Involuntary Resignation

	White		Black	
	N	%	N	%
Work force reduction (involuntary resignation)	27	45.8	38	49.4
Failing to come to work (abandono)	10	16.9	16	20.8
Generally unsatisfactory performance	9	15.3	18	23.4
Health or disability	6	10.2	1	1.3
Theft	4	6.8	0	0.0
Fighting	0	0.0	4	5.2
Activism	3	5.1	0	0.0
Total	59	100.1	77	100.1
No information	3		2	

Table 4.9 includes cases of involuntary resignations, considering them to be the equivalent of firing for purposes of work force reduction. It shows that, as a result of the firm's efforts during the late 1950s to reduce labor costs, dismissals for such purposes formed a much higher proportion of forcible discharges at Jafet than at São Paulo Light.[43] The proportions of black and white workers let go in this way were essentially the same, but there was considerable variation within the black racial group. Of those workers either fired with cause or compelled to resign involuntarily, 37.8 percent of pardos, 45.8 percent of whites, and 57.1 percent of pretos fell into the latter category. Most pardos and whites who left Jafet involuntarily did so as the result of dismissals with cause; most pretos who left Jafet involuntarily did so, not because of work-related shortcomings, but rather for purposes of work force reduction.

Table 4.10 sums up our findings on the forcible discharge of black and white workers at the two firms. At both firms blacks were more likely than whites to be discharged against their will. The disparity is more marked at Jafet, and is explained in equal part by dismissals with and without cause, to both of which blacks were more vulnerable than whites. At São Paulo Light, by contrast, blacks and whites were fired with cause in the same proportions. The difference between black and white rates of dismissal is thus explained by the greater vulnerability of black workers to being fired *without* cause.

Table 4.10. Percentage Distribution of Workers Forcibly
Discharged, by Workplace and Race

	White	Black
São Paulo Light		
Percentage fired	*30.9*	*36.7*
With just cause	25.3	24.5
Without just cause	5.1	9.3
Unknown	0.5	2.9
Jafet		
Percentage fired and resigned		
involuntarily	*22.9*	*32.4*
Fired	12.9	16.8
Resigned involuntarily	10.0	15.6

When ordered to trim their work force, and dismiss workers whose records were presumably satisfactory (otherwise they would have been fired already), supervisors at São Paulo Light apparently chose to dismiss black workers—and within the black group, mainly pardos—before they dismissed whites.

What about those workers who, at least according to their files, resigned their jobs voluntarily? We have already seen that they constituted the largest category of employees at both firms, and the overwhelming majority at Jafet. They also reached their decision to leave after relatively short periods of time in the firm. Black workers tended to leave sooner than whites, resigning after median periods of employment of 4.2 months at São Paulo Light, and 4.4 months (pardos after 3.1 months, pretos after 5.8 months) at Jafet. White workers stuck it out for a median period of 6.9 months at São Paulo Light, and 5.8 months at Jafet.

Why did workers decide to quit? It is impossible to know for certain, at least on the basis of the information provided in these files. São Paulo Light officials were punctilious about recording their reasons for firing workers, but they seem to have been relatively indifferent to workers' motives for resigning. Almost half of those workers who quit left no statement at all as to why they had done so; and of those who did provide such a statement, half stated simply that it was their "free will" to do so—though here we are probably encountering the company's efforts to establish documentary proof that workers had resigned voluntarily, and not under compulsion. The remaining

Table 4.11. Numerical and Percentage Distributions of Jafet Workers,
by Reason for Resigning

	White		Black	
	N	%	N	%
"Free will"	35	25.9	26	23.0
To move	35	25.9	29	25.7
Dislike of work conditions and/or salary	28	20.7	29	25.7
To stay at home	10	7.4	12	10.6
Plans to work elsewhere	17	12.6	9	8.0
Health problems	10	7.4	8	7.1
Total	135	99.9	113	100.1
No information	76		52	

Note: Sum of "no information" and total exceeds number of resignations (Table 4.9) because some workers gave multiple reasons for resigning.

quarter is too small a sample to permit meaningful patterns to emerge. The reason most frequently cited is moving, often back to the homes which these men had left to come to São Paulo; a handful complained about low pay and bad conditions of work; another handful expressed their intention to move to another company, or into another line of work. But in the face of the silence of the overwhelming majority of these men, there is little that we can say for certain about why they opted to leave the company.

The workers at Jafet were more communicative than those at São Paulo Light. Two-thirds indicated a reason for resigning, and of that two-thirds, over three-quarters indicated a reason more specific than "free will" or "personal interest" (see Table 4.11). Blacks and whites gave very similar reasons for leaving the firm: as at São Paulo Light, moving was the most frequently cited reason for resigning, followed by worker dissatisfaction with salary and working conditions. Certainly there were good reasons to resign a position at Jafet. Built at the turn of the century, the plant was never modernized, so that working conditions remained primitive at best. Workers who labored in factories of that vintage recalled how

deafening noise throughout the 13-hour workday made it difficult for workers to concentrate. . . . The ventilators used in the textile factories dispersed thick dust and tufts of cotton that made it difficult to breathe and to see. . . . In the underventilated weaving preparation rooms, chemical products emitted noxious odors, and 30 to 40 workers would work there 11 or more hours a day. Attention had to be given to the fabric, to the weave, to the speed of the shuttles; workers had to be careful not to let the spools fall on the floor. By the end of the day, their sweat mingled with the stench of the lubricants and acids, and there were never enough ventilators.[44]

Difficult physical conditions were only part of the problem, however. The process of manufacturing textiles involves a number of discrete steps and operations, each of which has to be carefully coordinated with the others in order to ensure the smooth flow of production. This resulted in a highly regimented workplace, in which supervisors were constantly after workers to maintain the rhythm of production and never waver in their concentration on their work. "Finding and tying threads broken by the spindles required absolute attention and a trained eye; watching the warp beams and smoothing out defects in fabrics by hand, requires infinite and careful attention." Workers were under relentless pressure to maintain that level of attention, and could be fined or punished for so much as talking to their neighbors, which supervisors denounced as being "jabbery." "The factory was like a prison," recalls a former Jafet employee.[45]

Many workers found such a level of control intolerable, and refused to accept the status of a small cog in a massive machine. Most summed up this feeling in their *pedidos de demissão* with the formulaic "can't get used to the work" *(não acostumar—se com o serviço),* though some, such as parda Etalvina M. de J., who quit her job after a five-day apprenticeship in 1953, were more specific. She was quitting, she informed the company, because of her "incompatibility with her fellow workers" and her "not being accustomed to receive orders."[46]

Because of the more decentralized nature of the work at São Paulo Light, supervision seems to have been less pervasive and all-encompassing, at least to judge by the lower incidence of suspensions. Working for São Paulo Light had its nasty and even dangerous side, however, particularly for the construction workers hired to build the company's dams, trolley lines, and electrical grids. A 1929 memo on the building of a power line in the neighborhood of Mooca reported "on the digging out of the holes for the tower footings. . . . The men in these holes are at times up to their hips in water and sometimes come out of the holes covered with slime and clay from their heads downwards, as I saw yesterday. To hurry up this job whilst the good weather last, we brought from São Bernardo 15 men of another gang, 3 of whom refused to work in the holes under the existing conditions of pay and came for their discharge," that is, resigned.[50]

Working as a trolley conductor, the second-largest job category at the firm after unskilled laborers, also had its drawbacks, primary among which was the high rate of accidents. Conductors working their way around the outside of the trolley (either to collect fares from passengers clinging to the sides of the cars, or to avoid the crush inside the car) collided with signal posts, passing trolleys, and other track-side obstructions. Conductors also got into fights with customers who felt that they were being overcharged or otherwise mistreated, were caught in moving parts, and suffered injuries in derailments and track-jumpings. José Basílio P., a conductor who joined the firm in 1941, had nine accidents in the ensuing four years, and resigned in 1945 after suffering severe injuries to his right arm, back, and abdomen in a trolley derailment. Following each of these incidents the company conducted its customary inquiry, and in each case it found that José Basílio was following prescribed company safety procedures at the time of the mishap. This was also the case in virtually every other accident involving a conductor that I encountered in this sample—which clearly indicates the hazardous nature of this particular line of work.[51]

In addition to the unappealing and even dangerous working conditions, and the low pay, there was another good reason as well for workers to quit these jobs: the fact that they tended to lead nowhere. This was particularly the case at Jafet, where only 2.3 percent of the workers recorded in the sample experienced any sort of promotion or change in job responsibilities.[52] Workers experienced more frequent promotion at São Paulo Light, but even so, over three-quarters of the workers hired by the firm (77.0 percent of whites, and 80.8 percent of blacks) left the company holding the same jobs they had been assigned at the time they entered. In the case of black workers, this meant that the majority of them were hired as common laborers and left the firm as common laborers. In the case of white workers, the largest category of employees (32.4 percent) was hired as service workers and left the firm in that position; another quarter were hired as common laborers and, again, left the firm in that position.

Still, over a fifth of São Paulo Light's workers experienced some measure of upward mobility during their time with the firm, and we should not pass over such advancements lightly—especially when we find that black workers achieved promotion at almost the same rate as whites. Most of these upwardly mobile Afro-Brazilians did not start from a strong position within the firm; among black workers who experienced promotion, over half (58.3 percent) began their service with the company as common laborers. Many of these men, however, had worked at higher-level occupations before entering São Paulo Light, and, over the course of their years of employment at the company, succeeded in returning to their original line of work. Of those black common laborers who were able to stick it out until their first promotion, half succeeded in advancing eventually to the level either of skilled worker within the firm or, even more impressively, of foreman.[53] Still, these promotions were not fast in coming: the median length of time that a black worker spent with São Paulo Light before receiving a promotion was 40.5 months, almost 3.5 years. Since this was far beyond the length of time which most workers, either black or white, spent with the firm, most black laborers—as indeed most workers, black or white—left the firm in the same position at which they entered.

Promotions came on the average a year earlier for white workers, who experienced a move upward after a median period of 28.5 months. In addition to coming sooner, they also tended to take white workers higher than they took black ones. The best that a black worker could realistically hope for was to rise to the level of foreman. Only two black workers in this sample experienced promotion to white-collar office jobs, and none was ever offered a professional or managerial position. Such positions were available to white workers, however. Not in large numbers, of course; of the 363 white workers hired to fill manual positions, only 11 rose to be managers, and 9 to clerical positions. Most of the company's white-collar jobs were filled by employees who were hired at those levels to begin with. But those twenty individuals indicate a rate of advancement from blue-collar to white-collar positions ten times higher for white workers than for black.

Conclusions

Having relied heavily on immigrant labor during their first decades of existence, by the 1920s both São Paulo Light and Jafet had opened their doors to Afro-Brazilians. Whatever perceived advantages the immigrants may have had in the turn-of-the-century competition for jobs had disappeared by the late 1920s, when the state government and private employers both withdrew their preference for immigrant workers and turned to native-born Brazilian workers to fill São Paulo's workplaces.

Both of the firms we have examined preferred to hire pardo workers over pretos, and São Paulo Light also showed preference in job assignments for pardo workers. With the exception of the high rate of suspensions for preto males at the Jafet company, however, pardo job performance was not superior in any measurable way to that of the pretos. On at least one important indicator, in fact, that of persistence and the willingness to stick with a job for a given period of time before giving up on it and resigning, preto workers at Jafet performed significantly better than pardos, and at the same level as whites.

Just as pardo job performance was essentially equal to that of pretos, so was black job performance essentially equal to that of whites. With the exception, again, of the high rate of suspension for black men at Jafet, black workers were disciplined and fired for inadequate job performance at the same rate as white workers. Nevertheless, when forced by economic downturn or contraction to dismiss workers who were doing their jobs satisfactorily but now had to be let go, both firms tended to dismiss black workers (primarily pardos at São Paulo Light, and pretos at Jafet) before whites. This doubtless had an alienating and discouraging effect among those black workers left behind, and may partly explain the tendency of black workers at São Paulo Light and pardo workers at Jafet to resign their jobs after shorter periods of service than whites. But although they quit their jobs earlier, black workers also quit their jobs in fewer numbers than whites. And in a company like São Paulo Light, which did offer opportunities for advancement into more skilled and better paying occupations, those Afro-Brazilians workers who managed to stay with the firm ended up experiencing upward mobility at rates comparable to those of white workers.

That upward mobility did have one iron limitation, however: the barrier between blue-collar and white-collar positions, a barrier which applied forcefully to white workers but which applied absolutely, and virtually without exception, to blacks. This barrier was in effect not just at São Paulo Light, but in paulista society as a whole, as we shall see when we turn our attention from the black working class to the upwardly striving *negros em ascensão*.

2

THE MIDDLE CLASS

5. Living in a Racial Democracy, 1900–1940

The previous two chapters have focused on the most visible social consequences of São Paulo's economic development, and those which affected the greatest number of people. These were, in the countryside, the transformation of the agricultural work force from slaves to free workers, and in the cities, the creation of an industrial proletariat. But at the same time that Europeans and Brazilians were going to work on São Paulo's plantations and in its factories, many were striving as well to escape the world of manual labor and move upward into the nascent middle class. Economic growth provided the conditions which made such upward mobility possible. In the agricultural sector, the break-up of older estates in regions of declining productivity, and the aggressive marketing of smaller properties on the western frontier by land-development companies, created a class of small- and medium-holders who, by 1934, owned over 40 percent of the producing coffee trees in the state.[1] In the cities, urban growth generated demand for goods and services provided by an expanding class of professionals, and by thousands of small and medium-sized businesses owned and operated by local entrepreneurs. Industries required managers and office workers; so did the financial and commercial sectors, and the federal, state, and municipal bureaucracies.

The result of these developments was the formation of a small but growing middle class, which by the 1920s was increasingly asserting itself in the political life of the Republic.[2] In São Paulo, as might be expected, this middle class was overwhelmingly white in composition. During the nineteenth century free pardos and pretos had composed a substantial proportion, perhaps the majority, of skilled artisans and craftsmen, many of whom owned their own small businesses. And some Afro-Brazilians had managed to rise beyond that level into government bureaucracy, white-collar employment, and the liberal professions.[3] Such opportunities for black people had always been more restricted in São Paulo than in Rio de Janeiro and the Northeast, however, and with the arrival of the immigrants they shrank even further. Denied access to broad-based public education, and already marginalized in blue-collar employment, São Paulo's black population was very poorly positioned to struggle for admission into this new white-collar class.

The censuses of 1900 and 1920 reveal nothing of that struggle; the 1940 census, however, indicates how far black people had come in the fifty years since the abolition of slavery, and how far they had yet to go (Table 5.1). Afro-Brazilians lagged well behind the white population in all areas, and particularly in the primarily urban sectors of the professions, and in ownership of industrial and commercial enterprises. In the entire state, out of a black population of 862,255, only 623 Afro-Brazilians owned nonagricultural businesses employing one or more workers. In the professions, Afro-Brazilians accounted for only 3.2 percent of all professionals, in a state where black people represented 12.2 percent of the working-age (ten or over) population. In the countryside black farmers appear at first glance to have done somewhat better. When one takes into account, however, that the agricultural sector in 1940 was disproportionately black in composition, the underrepresentation of black agricultural proprietors is comparable to that of black urban professionals. Pardos and pretos composed 15.0 percent of the total agricultural labor force in São Paulo, but only 5.5 percent of the owners of agricultural enterprises which employed outside labor.

The census suggests that the only area of middle-class employment in which Afro-Brazilians began to approach parity with their representation in the population as a whole was in the public sector.[4] Most of these state-sector jobs, however, fell well short of middle class status. They included such menial jobs as street sweepers, construc-

Table 5.1. Professionals, Entrepreneurs, and Public Employees in São Paulo State, 1940

	White	Pardo	Preto
Professionals	30,873	602	428
Owners of enterprises	58,578	1,267	1,369
Agricultural	30,795	1,036	977
Industry/transport	11,006	78	99
Commercial/service	16,777	153	293
Public employees	64,541	2,638	3,573

Source: IBGE, *Recenseamento geral de 1940. Censo demográfico: Estado de São Paulo* (Rio de Janeiro, 1950), table 30, pp. 24–25.

tion workers, and janitors, and poorly paid office jobs as messengers and orderlies. As at São Paulo Light (chapter 4), itself a semi-official utility closely tied to the state, promotion of black men to managerial or executive positions was rare, with the result that, as the black newspaper *Getulino* commented in 1923, "in this blessed state of São Paulo, one can count on one's fingers the number of black functionaries, by which I mean [public] employees with any real responsibility."[5] And the same racial barriers that prevailed in the private sector could assert themselves in public employment as well, as suggested by a 1915 case in which the labor newspaper *O Combate* charged that a highly qualified candidate for a teaching job in the public school at Itapetininga had been denied the position because of race. His "not being a paulista, and having skin a little darker than that of our political bosses, were the real reasons" behind his rejection, and the school board's decision to hire a white applicant.[6]

Nevertheless, when compared with the extremely limited job opportunities available to black men in São Paulo's private sector, public employment formed the most likely route for ambitious Afro-Brazilians looking to escape the stigma of manual labor and move upward into the white-collar world. Under both the Empire and the Republic, political patronage, and the provision of government jobs to deserving clients, was one of the central concerns of Brazilian politics.[7] The census data suggest that Afro-Brazilians received less than their share of such jobs; however, they were not excluded from the division of spoils entirely, and the social columns of the black newspapers make clear the importance of federal, state, and municipal employment in providing the economic base for a would-be black elite. Whenever the occupations of such individuals are mentioned, as often as not they were teachers in the public schools, or clerks and low-level officials in the postal service, the state tax office, municipal government, or such semiofficial agencies as the telephone company.[8] As a contributor to one of those papers recalled in later years, to qualify for membership in the black middle class "one didn't have to have a college degree. It was enough to be a public functionary or have some other relatively stable job."[9]

The black newspapers reveal not only the economic basis of São Paulo's black elite but the concerns and preoccupations of that elite as well. The state's black workers left virtually no written record of their experiences in the decades following abolition, with the result that the historian must try to piece together their story through the scattered observations of the planters, travelers, journalists, and state bureaucrats who viewed them, for the most part, from afar. When we turn to the pre-1940 black middle class, however, we confront abundant documentation, in the form of more than twenty weekly and monthly newspapers produced by and for that black elite.[10] Some of these publications were ephemeral, putting out only a handful of issues. Others ran for periods of several years or more; the longest-lived, *O Clarim da Alvorada* (The Clarion of Dawn), edited by José Correia Leite and Jayme de Aguiar, appeared regularly from 1924 to 1932, printing between one thousand and two thousand copies of each issue. *A Voz da Raça* (The Voice of the Race), the official publication of the Brazilian Black Front, which published from 1933 to 1937, occasionally printed as many as five thousand.[11] *O Clarim* and *A Voz* both hammered heavily at the message of social uplift and economic advancement for the black population as a whole; other papers, particularly those published by the social clubs, preferred to focus on the dances and parties of the black elite, and did their best to ignore troublesome racial, social, and political issues. Inevitably, however, such issues intruded on the lives of upwardly mobile and ambitious blacks, forcing even the society papers into printing editorials, opinion pieces, and letters to the editor, which constitute a rich record of the collective concerns of that black elite. And while the opinions expressed in the papers ranged over a variety of specific topics, those topics tended to converge in a larger debate on one of the basic ideological foundations of twentieth-century Brazilian life: the concept of racial democracy.

Racial Democracy

As we saw in chapter 1, the concept of racial democracy asserts that Brazil is a land entirely free of legal and institutional impediments to racial equality, and largely (particularly in comparison to countries like the United States) free of informal racial prejudice and discrimination as well. The nation offers all its citizens, black, brown, or white, virtually complete equality of opportunity in all areas of public life: education, politics, jobs, housing. Thus Afro-Brazilians enjoy opportunities to better themselves, and the freedom to compete against their fellow citizens in the contest for public and private goods, to a degree unknown in any other multiracial society in the world.[12]

The concept of racial democracy received its fullest and most coherent exposition in the writings of Gilberto Freyre, beginning in the 1930s. It was visibly taking form during the early decades of the 1900s, however, and its roots run well back into the nineteenth century. Over the course of the 1800s, racial strictures dating from Portuguese colonial rule were either explicitly outlawed or fell quietly into disuse, permitting a visible proportion of the free preto and pardo populations to experience significant upward mobility in Brazilian society. Foreign observers in particular were struck by the apparent freedom of black people to rise as high as their talents would take them.

In Brazil the liberto enters on an equal footing a society in which he is promptly treated as an equal. . . . Not only does prejudice not exist, and frequent unions among members of different races produce a large and important racially mixed population; even more, these free blacks and mulattoes mix freely and completely with the white population. . . . Not just at table, in the theater, in the salons, in all public places; also in the army, in the government, in the schools, in the legislative assemblies, one finds all colors mixed together on a basis of equality and the most complete familiarity. . . . [13]

Such observations may have overstated the opportunities for advancement actually available to black people in nineteenth-century

Brazil.[14] But they do suggest that Brazil during the Empire was a society of much greater racial equality than its northern counterpart, the United States, a point confirmed by former President Theodore Roosevelt following a visit to Brazil in 1914. "If I were asked to name one point in which there is a complete difference between the Brazilians and ourselves, I should say it was in the attitude to the black man. . . . [In Brazil] any Negro or mulatto who shows himself fit is without question given the place to which his abilities entitle him."[15]

Still, an awkward fact remained: by the 1870s and 1880s, Brazil was the only independent nation in the Americas whose citizens continued to hold slaves. Trying to justify the continuation of the institution, Brazilian masters argued that their slaves were treated far better than slaves elsewhere, and that, in comparison to other New World societies, bondage in their country was relatively mild and easygoing. Brazilian abolitionists, and many foreign observers as well, flatly rejected such assertions. Writing in the 1830s, F.L.C. Burlemaque curtly dismissed claims that "we are the best of masters. If we are the most merciful, what must others be!" Fifty years later, Joaquim Nabuco reported reading in the Brazilian press

frequent declarations that slavery among us is a very mild and pleasant condition for the slave, better for him, in fact, than for the master, a situation so fortunate, according to these descriptions, that one begins to suspect that, if slaves were asked, they would be bound to prefer slavery to freedom; which merely proves that newspapers and articles are not written by slaves or by persons who for one moment have imagined themselves in their condition.[16]

Despite its obvious contradiction of reality, the myth of benevolent Brazilian slavery was widely accepted at the time, and has proven quite durable in the years since.[17] Its utility while slavery was in existence is readily apparent. It served to salve the conscience of slaveowners (nominally Christians all), at the same time defending the institution against its Brazilian and foreign critics. The more interesting question is, why did it persist after slavery was abolished? Part of the reason was simple ideological inertia: the tendency of an established social myth to remain in place unless acted on by some external force. As it turned out, those forces in operation during the years after abolition tended to reinforce the myth rather than overturn it. In order to reduce the racial discord and strife that became a potential (and to some degree an actual) reality in the years after emancipation, former slaveowners, and Brazilian whites in general, had to maintain that the injuries and injustices of slavery, while objectionable, were not nearly as bad as they could have been.

This argument is presented in fairly pure form in an 1889 article by Lívio de Castro (himself a mulatto), published in *A Província de São Paulo*. Slavery, he admitted, "was not like voluntary labor, it was forced labor, and force breeds more force. Still, through a natural democratic impulse which reduced prejudices, and by the cumulative influence of habit, the plantation developed without any struggle between the races, thus avoiding the creation of a caste system like those of the ancient autocracies, of the Oriental nations, or of the North American confederation." Blacks and whites lived in peace together on the plantation, "granting to the master the majority of the rights and to the slave a portion of his affection." Thus began "the formation of a people who inherited the vices and virtues of the past, and are loyal to that past from which they sprang, in which they find their reason for being." And that plantation past, with its "democratic spirit," has made racial conflict impossible in Brazil. "Where is race hatred? In Brazil there are not two races, there is not even one: those which existed have lost their distinctive characteristics [through miscegenation]; that which will exist [in the future] is still in the process of formation."[18]

Such an argument, in which one sees the features of racial democracy starting to take form, not only reassured slaveowners that they had nothing to fear from their former slaves; it also undercut the proposals advanced by some abolitionists that the nation owed the libertos reparation for the exploitation and suffering which they had endured under slavery.[19] Still, one suspects that, once emancipation had taken place, few Brazilians felt completely comfortable arguing the relative mildness of the former slave regime. The evidence against it was too clear, and the memories too fresh.[20] It was more reassuring to focus on the future of black-white relations in Brazil than the past; and if one looked at the past at all, it was more encouraging to focus, not on the experience of slavery, but rather on the relative openness of nineteenth-century Brazilian society to free pardos and pretos. Now that Afro-Brazilians had left slavery and could take part in national life as free men and women, the exponents of racial democracy argued, they would all enjoy the same kinds of opportunities for advancement in the twentieth century that their free ancestors had enjoyed in the nineteenth.

Thus it was that Brazil, the last country in Christendom to abolish slavery, became the first to proclaim itself a racial democracy: a society which offered genuine equality of opportunity to all its citizens, and had delivered itself from racial tension, discrimination, and conflict.[21] Such hopes and promises coincided not only with the transition from slavery to freedom but with the transition from monarchy to republic as well, and with a corresponding vision of a more inclusive, participatory political system. Thus from its very outset racial democracy was closely associated with the ideal of political democracy, and was presumed to form part of a liberal, progressive political order.

The question, of course, is, to what degree did these visions of Brazil's current situation and future prospects correspond to reality? Brazilian historians and social scientists argue that in fact they did reflect the conditions of the time, but in a paradoxical, inverted way in which reality was the reverse of the vision. All societies expend enormous amounts of intellectual and emotional energy trying to resolve the contradictions between ideals and fact.[22] This struggle to reconcile myth with history, to paraphrase Emília Viotti da Costa, has been particularly intense in Brazil.[23] This was so because the liberal principles on which nineteenth-century Brazilian elites chose to build their national experiment, first under the monarchy and then under the Republic, were at such odds with the social and political realities which those principles sought to explain and organize.

In Europe, liberalism was the expression of a rising bourgeoisie and urban middle class struggling against the power of a landed aristocracy. When liberalism was imported into Brazil, however, it was seized by the landed elites, the Brazilian analogue of the European nobility, who used its denunciations of privilege and monopoly to justify the removal of Portuguese colonial control over Brazilian politics and economy. The civil libertarian aspects of liberalism, and its insistence on juridical equality and the rights of citizenship, were of much less interest to the landowners, who saw the great mass of the Brazilian population (and certainly of the Afro-Brazilian population) as utterly unfit to have a voice in the affairs of the newly independent polity. Unable to jettison the libertarian component of liberalism, Brazilian elites embarked on a search for political and ideological formulas which would permit the exclusion of the overwhelming majority of the population from full political and economic participation while formally maintaining the principles of citizenship and justice.

The result, under the Republic, was oligarchical, authoritarian rule masquerading as republican democracy. Political participation, in terms of voter turnout, declined sharply from the 1870s, when it had consisted of about 10 percent of the adult population, to between 1 and 3 percent under the Republic. Party competition ceased, and elections were openly fraudulent. As historian José Murilo de Carvalho has observed, the result was a complete reversal of the Republic's frequently voiced aspirations: criminals and gangsters policed elections, while upright citizens stayed home. "Under these conditions legal norms and social hierarchies gradually eroded. . . . There was a clear awareness that the real was hiding under the formal. The people knew that the formal was not serious. There was no way to participate, the Republic was not for real."[24]

Writing in the 1930s, following the fall of the Republic, historian Sérgio Buarque de Holanda summed up the Republican experience by observing that "democracy in Brazil was always a lamentable misunderstanding. A rural and semi-feudal aristocracy imported it and tried to accommodate it, wherever possible, to their rights and privileges." This attempted accommodation in turn produced what political scientist Francisco Weffort describes as a "legacy of equivocation," in which hierarchy and privilege were defended in the name of democracy and equality.[25]

The concept of racial democracy both reflects that "legacy of equivocation" and forms an integral part of it. The Republic asserted the ideal of democratic political participation while denying it in practice; racial democracy played a similar role with respect to racial hierarchy, justifying and defending the reality of racial inequality by invoking its opposite. It was clear to all that black people continued to occupy a depressed, subordinate position in Brazilian society. But by proclaiming that, even during slavery, Brazil had been moving toward racial equality, and with emancipation in 1888 had achieved it, the doctrine of racial democracy exempted state policy or informal racism from any further blame for the situation of the black population, and instead placed that blame squarely on the shoulders of the Afro-Brazilians themselves. If black people had failed to move upward in Brazilian society, clearly it was their own fault, since that society did not repress or hinder their progress in any way. The continuing reality of black poverty and marginalization was seen not as refutation of the idea of racial democracy, but rather as confirmation of the laziness, ignorance, stupidity, incapacity, and so on, which prevented black people from taking advantage of the opportunities offered them by Brazilian society—in short, a restatement of the *ideologia da vadiagem.*

Such incapacity was usually ascribed to the black population's recent experience of slavery. During this age of social Darwinism and scientific racism, however, such explanations tended to merge subtly, and sometimes not so subtly, into assertions of black incapacity based on racial inheritance. Those Afro-Brazilians who questioned the notion of racial democracy therefore ran the risk of being confronted with a detailed analysis of the deficiencies of the racial group to which they belonged—an analysis which, under the best of circumstances, would be painful and embarrassing to hear, and under the worst, would reflect directly on them as individuals and as members of the black racial group.

Faced with this disheartening prospect, most middle-class Afro-Brazilians in São Paulo declined to question the concept publicly, and some actively endorsed it. "In Brazil race prejudice does not exist, as some of our countrymen maintain; the nation is not to blame for the state of Brazilian blacks." While admitting that occasional acts of discrimination did occur, defenders of the status quo argued that such incidents did not constitute evidence of systematic discrimination against black people. "There are many blacks who affirm the existence of a little prejudice in our country! This is untrue, my fellow countrymen of color. There are some loutish, jealous individuals who always try to obstruct the advancement of some of our colored people, on behalf of their own candidates. This always happens, and is bound to happen, what with all the classes and individuals in search of advancement these days." Such incidents should be seen not as prejudice, but rather as "envy." "One cannot speak, in the strict sense, of race prejudice in Brazil. The situation of yesterday's slaves is not such as to require a public campaign in defense of their rights."[26]

The racial situation in Brazil looked particularly good, its defenders argued, when contrasted to that of the United States. "In North America, where prejudice is a fact, the blacks have their life, and the whites have theirs, but not here; everything in Brazil is ours, except for some minor incidents which one couldn't really call prejudice."[27] As a result, if blacks failed to make good in this land of racial equality, then clearly "the blame is not the whites'—it is ours!"[28] This was a painful and deeply wounding conclusion to have to draw, but the logic of racial democracy left its proponents no recourse. If they accepted Brazil as a land of equality, then Afro-Brazilians' failure within that land could be ascribed only to their own deficiencies. And while those deficiencies were readily explainable in terms of the recent experience of slavery, there would always be the suspicion, constantly reinforced by the dictates of scientific racism, that they were genetic rather than historical in nature, and were black people's ineradicable racial inheritance.

We will not discuss the scientific origins of the backwardness of our strong and heroic race. . . . Just because we are representatives of an inferior race, must we be condemned by the force of social prejudice? What blame do we have for our lamentable condition? . . . The blame isn't ours; look at the four hundred years of our enslavement, look at the miserable regime of ignorance under which we were brought up, look at the laws of biological regression and heredity. . . .[29]

The only way out for black people afflicted with this fear was to embrace the "whitening thesis" developed by turn-of-the-century Brazilian intellectuals as a response to European scientific racism.[30] Doctrinaire scientific racists viewed race mixture as a regressive process, in which European racial ancestry was weakened and diluted by being mixed with that of nonwhite peoples. Some Brazilian intellectuals accepted this doctrine, and its implicit bleak forecast for countries in which miscegenation was widespread. Others, however, devised a highly creative response which in effect took scientific racism a step further. Arguing that European theorists had too little faith in their own racial inheritance, Brazilian thinkers such as João Baptista de Lacerda and F. J. Oliveira Viana maintained that, when white people mixed their genes (or, in the language of the time, their blood) with those of nonwhites, it was the white racial heritage, and white racial attributes, which tended to dominate in the products of such unions. Over time, therefore, and assuming the continued arrival of European immigrants in the country, race mixture would gradually "breed out" African and Indian racial characteristics, and produce the eventual "whitening" *(branqueamento)* of Brazil.[31]

Aspiring to join the mainstream of Brazilian society, and seeing whitening as the most likely way to achieve that goal, some members of the Afro-Brazilian middle class endorsed the whitening thesis and the national project of replacing Brazil's African racial heritage with European. "Let us not seek to perpetuate our race, but, yes, to infiltrate ourselves into the bosom of the privileged race, the white race, because, we repeat, we are not Africans but rather purely Brazilian." Proposals in the early 1920s to bring Afro-American migrants from the United States to live and work in Brazil were strongly opposed by São Paulo's black press, which argued that such migration would pose "the greatest obstacle to the solution of Brazil's black problem." Why? Because "the migration of North American blacks will be the death blow to the mathematical process of the disappearance of the black race of Brazil." If anything, the black press argued, policy makers should be working on ways to "speed up the fusion of races in our country," not slow it down.[32]

Not all black observers, however, were convinced that whitening, and racial democracy Brazilian style, were necessarily the most advantageous arrangements for people of color. Some objected strenuously to how "the disappearance of the blacks through race mixture, through that famous Aryanization," had been made into a national priority, "letting a whole people perish, because they have to be replaced, because they're *mestiços*, because they're black and they must be made white, no matter what the cost. . . ."[33] Others were not even so certain that Brazil offered clear advantages over the United States in the area of race. No one denied the brutality of United States–style race relations. But that very brutality, and the Afro-Americans' need to defend themselves against the persecutions of white Americans, had generated a very different kind of Afro-American consciousness, one that some Afro-Brazilians envied. "Prejudice is a fact in the United States, the odious separation of races; and it was that prejudice that made the North American black a proud and haughty man. . . . He walks erect, facing down his terrible enemies, his own white countrymen. And in this way, the North American black always triumphs." Surveying the black-owned businesses, black colleges, churches, civic organizations, and other Afro-American institutions that had no counterpart in Brazil, one Afro-Brazilian observer speculated that perhaps "blatant, open prejudice is a stimulus to black competence and ability."[34]

The 1923 visit to Brazil by Robert Abbott, publisher of the Afro-American newspaper *The Chicago Defender*, prompted further debate on the United States–Brazil comparison. Abbott gave a series of lectures in Rio and São Paulo contrasting the racial situations in the two countries, and arguing the absence of race prejudice in Brazil. A number of his listeners begged to differ. "Asserting that there is no race prejudice in Brazil is like denying the defeat of Germany. . . . Dr. Abbott's coming to tell us about the situation of blacks in Brazil is like trying to teach the priest his rosary!" An even stronger reaction came from an unexpected source: Abílio Rodrigues, president of the elite black social club Kosmos, which normally maintained a discrete distance from controversial questions of any sort, most of all those concerning race. On this occasion, however, Rodrigues could not contain himself and, instead of his usual homily on bourgeois manners and morals, wrote an article dismissing Abbott's vision of Brazilian race relations as "a fantasy." Citing evidence of systematic discrimination against black job seekers in Brazil, he argued that Abbott had been deceived by the presence of a few pretos and pardos in the higher echelons of national life. "The doors of society only open [to these men] reluctantly, forced open by their indomitable intellectual abilities." Afro-Brazilians of more modest endowments are consistently marginalized and discriminated against, he argued, as in fact Abbott himself was when he came to São Paulo. Rodrigues reported that the black publisher had reserved a room at the Palace Hotel, but upon arriving, was told that the room was already occupied—standard treatment for black people in the city's hotels. "Is this the equality characteristic of true Brazilian democracy? . . . Illusion, pure illusion."[35]

Rodrigues's citing of job discrimination as one of the most difficult and frustrating aspects of black life in São Paulo was hardly accidental. The black newspapers returned to this theme time and again, denouncing the refusal of white employers to hire Afro-Brazilians. The black man seeking work "goes to the factories, but they don't hire him, often they won't even let him speak to the boss. He looks for ads in the papers, he hurries to where they're looking for workers, and even though he arrives ahead of everyone else, because he is colored he is put aside and then refused. . . . This is a well known social phenomenon in São Paulo, not just in the capital but in the cities of the interior, a phenomenon which grows from day to day. . . ." Indeed, this observer noted, the situation in São Paulo reminded him strongly of United States–style racial segregation, so much so in fact that "if things continue in this way, one of these days we will have here the terrible masked monsters of the famous secret society Ku Klux Klan! . . . Just wait. . . ."[36]

Less damaging economically, but deeply humiliating and aggravating, was racial discrimination in public services and accommodations. Black commentators concurred that such discrimination was particularly pronounced in the smaller towns and cities of the western coffee zones, where the continuing control by planters of local life and the massive influx of immigrants combined to create a "well defined and notorious color line," as one black paper put it. "Few are the cities in the interior of São Paulo where color prejudice is not a ruling fact. . . ."[37] Black papers in the capital regularly noted incidents of blacks being refused service in bars, hotels, restaurants, and barbershops in the state's smaller cities. An occasional source of conflict was the question of black access to public parks and squares, where residents gathered for their evening and Sunday-afternoon strolls, or "footings" (the English word was used). Blacks were permitted to hold such gatherings as long as they kept to a specified area of the park or plaza. In a 1924 case in which several blacks attempted to enter a part of the public square traditionally reserved for whites, the mayor admitted that Afro-Brazilians had the legal right to use any part of the square, but in practice "custom makes the law." He thereupon ordered the Afro-Brazilians back to their section of the square, with the exception of those who had failed to vote for him in the most recent election, who were banished from the *praça* altogether![38]

This incident nicely sums up the prevailing realities both of Republican democracy, in which civil rights and legality were routinely violated, and of racial democracy. By the 1920s a growing number of Afro-Brazilians were no longer willing to accept the glaring discrepancy between image and fact, between myth and history. In 1918 *O Alfinete* became the first of the black papers to suggest that "the equality and fraternity of peoples, . . . which the Republic implanted as a symbol of our democracy, is, as concerns the blacks, a fiction and a lie which until today have not been placed into practice." During the next decade most of the black papers accepted this analysis; only one, *O Clarim da Alvorada*, clung to the position that "here [in Brazil] it goes without saying: there is no prejudice whatsoever for us to fight against. We live in perfect harmony, not just with white Brazilians, but with the foreign element as well." By 1930, however, even *O Clarim* had conceded, now reluctantly agreeing that "in Brazil, racial equality is a lie."[39]

As far as the black elite was concerned—or that portion of it which contributed to the black press—racial democracy was dead. Or rather, the *myth* of racial democracy was dead. The *desire* for racial democracy was still very much alive: the hope that, through political action, Brazil might actually be transformed into the country that it claimed to be, a land of equal opportunity for all. Over the course of the 1920s, Afro-Brazilians set to work to turn this dream into reality.[40]

Getting Organized

The history of black associational life in Brazil is extremely rich, and stretches back well into the colonial period. Even as slaves Africans and Afro-Brazilians had found ways to come together in association with their peers. Some of the organizational forms they employed, such as *capoeira* or *candomblé*, were secret and surreptitious; others, such as religious brotherhoods organized under the aegis of the Catholic church, were open and public, and condoned by the society at large. All had as their goal meeting the cultural, religious, economic, and human needs of a people living and laboring under conditions of extreme exploitation.[41]

Emancipation left some of those needs in place, and created additional new ones. Emancipation also opened to black people the possibility of organizing under conditions different from those of slavery, with significantly expanded degrees of freedom. Given their previous history of organizational life, it is hardly surprising that the Afro-Brazilians promptly proceeded to respond to those new needs, and to exploit those new possibilities.

One organizational form which survived abolition intact was that of the religious brotherhoods. The most important black brotherhoods in São Paulo City were the Irmandade da Nossa Senhora do Rosário, founded in 1711, and the Irmandade da Nossa Senhora dos Remédios, founded in 1836. The Irmandade dos Remédios played a key role in the struggle for abolition in São Paulo, providing a headquarters for Antônio Bento and his *caifazes*, a number of whom were members of the brotherhood. The Irmandade do Rosário played no comparable role in the abolitionist movement, but did emerge briefly into public view during the early 1900s, when its members engaged in a legal battle with the municipality to prevent the latter from expropriating their church and tearing it down as part of the Belle Époque–inspired reconstruction of the central city. Ultimately the brothers were unsuccessful, and in 1906 they moved to a new church, which they built in the nearby Largo do Paissandu, and which remains a center of black life in São Paulo to the present.[42]

One distinctive aspect of churches maintained by Afro-Brazilian brotherhoods was the public dances held on their grounds, or in the street outside. These events created considerable tension between the brotherhoods and the Catholic hierarchy, who regarded African and Afro-Brazilian music and dancing as noisy public nuisances which demeaned the dignity of the Church. Following emancipation, therefore, Afro-Brazilians seized on their new freedom to start creating new organizations, independent of the Church, through which to hold their dances and gatherings. These organizations varied considerably in character and orientation, depending on the class background and social aspirations of their members. Some were informal aggregations of poor and working-class blacks who met on a regular basis to play music, dance, and socialize. Out of such gatherings grew the "Carnaval groups," the forerunners of today's samba schools. The first such group, the Grupo Carnavalesco Barra Funda (today Camisa Verde) was founded in 1914, the second, Campos Elíseos, in 1917, and the third, Vai-Vai, gradually took form during the 1920s and formally incorporated in 1930. The high points of their activities were the annual drumming, dancing, and marching competitions which took place during Carnaval, in February, and at the festival of Bom Jesus de Pirapora, in the small town of that name, in August. The groups remained active through the year, however, holding fundraisers, dances, trips to the beach in Santos, and other activities.[43]

The membership of the Carnaval groups tended to be working-class in character, and Afro-Brazilians aspiring to middle-class status felt that their ambitions were not particularly well served by belonging to such "popular" organizations. Upwardly mobile black people were rigorously barred, however, from white social clubs and dancing societies, a situation which continues largely in force in São Paulo to the present. Afro-Brazilians wishing to set themselves apart from the black *povo* therefore established their own social clubs, which proliferated in the capital, and in the major towns of the interior, during the early 1900s. Luvas Pretas (Black Gloves) was the first such society, established in 1904, and it was soon joined by others: Kosmos, founded in 1908, the Elite Club, the Smart Club, and so on. The orientation of these organizations and the hopes and aspirations of their members emerge clearly, and often poignantly, in the newspapers and social columns that they left behind as a record of their activities. The very names of their organizations indicate how they saw themselves, or wished to see themselves: the elite, the smart set. But at the same time they were a group systematically excluded from the larger society of which they formed part. Rejecting those whom they regarded as their social inferiors, and in turn rejected by their white peers, their response was to construct a social world which would simultaneously protect them from the hurts inflicted on them by white society and from social contamination by the black masses below them. The newspaper of the Kosmos club, for example, described the organization as "a miniature nation, of which we are valiant inhabitants and ardent patriots"; implicitly invoking the monarchy, and rejecting the notion of both racial democracy and the Republic, the club's anthem expressed its members' desire to construct "the perfect, ideal kingdom" for themselves, free of the harshness of daily life.

> Kosmos proudly follows
> Its path toward the glorious future,
> A boat on the immense Ocean,
> Gliding over tranquil seas.

Kosmos is the immensity,
The perfect, ideal kingdom,
Which endures in eternity
Like the lily and the crystal lamp.[44]

In real life, Kosmos proved to be neither immense nor eternal. Its annual reports reveal a struggling organization with a membership chronically unable or unwilling to pay its dues. In 1923, 143 new members joined the club while 121 were ejected, mainly for failure to pay dues; in 1924, 107 new members joined, and 117 were thrown out.[45] This revolving-door membership in turn reflected the precarious financial condition of the would-be Afro-Brazilian "smart set": although aspiring to upward mobility and middle-class status, only rarely did they actually command the jobs and incomes on which such status was based. As a result, none of the middle-class dancing societies achieved anything approaching the longevity of the more humble Carnaval groups, a number of which still exist today.

If music and dancing were one leisure activity highly valued by the Afro-Brazilians, sport was another. Here too, as with social clubs and dancing societies, white athletic clubs practiced rigorous exclusion of pretos and pardos. And again, the Afro-Brazilians' response to this situation was the creation of black clubs, several of which achieved considerable renown in the city for the high quality of their soccer teams. Best known were the São Geraldo Athletic Association, established around 1910, and the Cravos Vermelhos (Red Cloves) Club, founded in 1916, which later became the Club Athlético Brasil. Still, the ambition of most black soccer players was to play for the better-known white teams, and when the segregation of the São Paulo teams began to weaken in the 1930s (in grudging response to the hiring of black players by the Rio de Janeiro clubs in the 1920s, and the corresponding strengthening of those teams), the better players departed the black clubs to play for their white counterparts. Even at this point, however, Afro-Brazilians were denied membership in the white organizations, which, in addition to fielding professional teams, functioned as social and athletic clubs. Instead, they were admitted as paid employees, with none of the rights of members.[46]

With the exception of the religious brotherhoods, all the organizations we have looked at thus far centered their activities on leisure and recreation. Although they came into existence in response to racial discrimination and segregation, they were not created with the purpose of actively combatting such discrimination. A number of them have left evidence in their records and their newspapers of unhappiness and uneasiness among their membership concerning racial inequality and color bars in São Paulo; but none of them seem to have undertaken any collective efforts to protest, reduce, or eliminate those evils. This situation began to change during the 1920s, in response to developments both within the black community and within paulista and Brazilian society more generally.

It is not by chance that the moments of most intense Afro-Brazilian collective organization and action have coincided with moments of major political crisis and regime change in Brazilian history. Sometimes, as in 1887–1889, black collective action has contributed to those crises and helped provoke the breakdown of one kind of political regime and its replacement with another. More commonly, however, political debate and activity within the black community has intensified in response to the forces and pressures already producing crisis and uncertainty in the society at large.

Throughout Brazil, and particularly in São Paulo, the decade of the 1920s witnessed a deepening sense of public alienation from the Republic, which had been created with such high hopes in 1889. As urban working and middle classes had grown and expanded in São Paulo, Rio de Janeiro, and the southern states, they had increasingly come to resent the Republic's severe restrictions on popular political participation, and the way in which its institutions concentrated power in the hands of the planter class. And paradoxical though it may seem, by the 1920s a significant portion of the nation's agricultural elites was disenchanted with the Republic as well. While the Republic allowed those elites substantial control over local political life, it clearly favored the coffee interests of the Southeast over competing agricultural interests in the northern and southern sections of the country. And even the coffee planters were growing uneasy about the Republican state's gradual accumulation of more and more power in its hands as it went about carrying out the functions of a twentieth-century national state: in the area of the economy, manipulating currency rates and export policy, guaranteeing Brazil's credit-worthiness, intervening in the international coffee economy, and in the internal economy as well; in the social arena, debating and acting on labor policy and "the social question"; and in the area of politics, creating national armed forces capable of overcoming the state militias. Even the coffee planters, the godfathers and patrons of the Republican state, now feared that the policy makers and administrators of that state might be drifting out of their control and developing unacceptable levels of independence and autonomy.[47]

The early years of the Republic had witnessed several violent uprisings by poor and working-class Brazilians opposed to the policies of the planter state.[48] Mass-based unrest continued into the 1910s with the naval mutiny of 1910 in Rio, the Contestado Rebellion in Santa Catarina (1912–1916), the general strike of 1917, the anarchist uprising of 1918, and continued strike activity in 1919 and 1920.[49] And the 1920s witnessed a further broadening of the opposition to the Republic, when young army officers disgusted with the corruption and stagnation of the planter state formed a new political movement, *tenentismo* (the movement of the lieutenants), which launched military uprisings in 1922 in Rio, and in 1924 in São Paulo.

Like the labor unrest, these revolts were eventually put down by the government.[50] But by revealing the existence of deep dissatisfaction within the ranks of the military, they emboldened upper- and middle-class opponents of the regime to start creating a genuine political opposition. In São Paulo this movement took the form of the Democratic Party, founded in 1926. An "alliance of the middle classes of São Paulo with discontented elements of the agrarian sector," the Democrats were the first serious electoral opposition which the Paulista Republican Party had faced since it came to power in the early 1890s. Given the electoral and political structure of the Republic, which afforded the incumbent party broad powers to manipulate and control the electoral process, the Democratic Party stood little chance of putting its candidates into office. Nevertheless, coming as it did on the heels of the labor unrest and the *tenente* revolts, it signaled the presence of antagonism to the Republic which went far beyond workers and poor people to embrace the middle class and some sectors of the agrarian elite as well.[51]

Black people formed part of this rising tide of political organization and ferment. The Republic, after all, had treated them particularly badly. It began by depriving most of them of the right to participate in politics through its denial of suffrage to illiterates. Blacks in São Paulo had watched the state government invest millions of dollars in foreign immigrants while declining to spend anything on native-born black workers. Public education, the consistent demand of black people, was severely limited. Voting for the Republican party (as black—and white—electors in São Paulo consistently did, following mulatto Republican Francisco Glicério's sage advice that "to join the opposition in this country is an act of downright insanity") had not even brought black people their fair share of patronage jobs.[52]

As resistance to the Republic asserted itself during the 1920s, therefore, similar currents started to stir in the black community as well. In a more racially open society, such currents might have swept Afro-Brazilians into the labor movement, the *tenentes*, or the Democratic Party. But the same pattern which applied in the religious brotherhoods, the social clubs, and the athletic clubs applied in politics as well. Black men were largely barred from entering the officer corps, so they could not form part of *tenentismo*. The labor movement in São Paulo remained dominated by immigrant leadership; and the middle-class and elite members of both the Republican and Democratic parties had no interest whatsoever in seeing Afro-Brazilians take an active role in party politics.[53] As a result, as black people looked for ways to join the mounting opposition to the Republic, they began to think in terms of forming their own Afro-Brazilian political organization.

By 1925 *O Clarim da Alvorada* was calling for the creation of the Congress of Black Youth, "a big political party comprised exclusively of colored men." Such calls produced no immediate results, but were doubtless part of the impulse behind the founding in 1927 of the Palmares Civic Center. Named after the seventeenth-century *quilombo* of Palmares, the center was originally intended to provide a cooperative lending library for the black community. The organization soon progressed to holding meetings and lectures on issues of public interest, and in 1928 it launched a campaign to overturn a government decree forbidding blacks to enlist in the state militia, the Civil Guard. The center successfully petitioned Governor Júlio Prestes to void the decree, and then prevailed on him to overturn a similar ban barring black children from a contest run by the State Sanitary Service to find the most "robust" and eugenically desirable infant in the state.[54]

These initial forays into politics were sufficiently encouraging to lead *O Clarim* to raise the question, "Should the black be a politician?" Absolutely, was their response. "We have no knowledge of a single Governor who in his political platform has included a single line of interest to black people, so that they will receive benefits other than those which are only distributed at the time of elections"— namely, the purchase of their votes. "If we could put together a voting bloc, then the black would see his position change, without having to bow down at every step to the will and commandments of others."[55]

The elections of 1930 seemed to offer such an opportunity, but the immobilization of the Palmares Civic Center in late 1929, owing, ironically, to a disputed presidential election within the organization, deprived the black population of the institutional vehicle to forge a voting bloc. In any case, the election itself proved to be moot. It was won as usual by the Republican Party, but in October a third *tenente* uprising, supported this time by landowning elites from Rio Grande do Sul, Minas Gerais, and the northeastern states, voided the results of the election and overthrew the Republic. Getúlio Vargas, the governor of Rio Grande do Sul and the opposition presidential candidate in the recent elections, assumed the presidency, an office which he would occupy until 1945. A new era in Brazilian politics had begun.

The Brazilian Black Front

The Republic had collapsed; the rule of the planters was over. But what would now replace it? Between 1930 and 1937 a welter of competing political and economic interests—agrarian elites, labor unions, industrialists, military officers, the urban middle class, Communists, Fascists, unregenerate Republicans—struggled bitterly to define the new political order, resorting on more than one occasion to armed violence. Over the course of the decade these struggles became sufficiently intense that by 1937 President Vargas and his advisors used them as justification (or pretext, depending on one's point of view) for their decision to close down the political process, abolish political parties, and impose the dictatorial, Fascist-inspired Estado Novo (the New State) on the country.[56]

But in 1930 all this was yet to come, and those who had been badly served by the Republic and its false democracy had nothing but applause for the "revolution." Many Afro-Brazilians felt that they had particular reason to support it.

With no consul[ar protection]—a foreigner in my own country—I waited, trusting in the words and the actions of those who one day would have to rebel against all the ignominy, all the scorn heaped on the dignity of our race. . . . If the Brazilian Revolution hadn't broken down the doors of that decrepit mansion wherein cowered the slavish Republic, I believe that its institutions and its men would have fallen on their own, like rotting fruit which falls from the branch. At last, however, the hour of Brazil has arrived.[57]

Vargas did not disappoint his black supporters. After only a month in office he created the new Ministry of Labor and instructed its officials to begin work on a package of programs and reforms aimed at improving the position of Brazilian workers. One of the first products of this planning was the Law of the Nationalization of Labor, handed down in 1931, which aimed to "defend the Brazilian worker from competition by immigrants" by requiring industrial and commercial enterprises to maintain a workforce that was at least two-thirds Brazilian-born. Vargas also took steps to reduce immigration quotas, and spoke out on the need to guard against the formation of "cysts of foreign influence" on Brazilian soil.[58]

Such talk was music to the ears of São Paulo's black population. Acclaiming Vargas as the "father of the poor," Afro-Brazilians flocked to support him, as they would continue to do until his death in 1954.[59] They also moved to take advantage of the political opening created by the destruction of the Republican order, creating "the legion of black men" that *O Clarim da Alvorada* had first invoked in 1925.[60]

One of the prominent participants in black civic life in São Paulo during the 1920s, and a frequent contributor to the black press, was Arlindo Veiga dos Santos, a migrant from Bahia who worked as a secretary at the Law School, and as a part-time journalist. Dos Santos had worked with José Correia Leite and Jayme Aguiar in their efforts to organize the Congress of Black Youth, and had also served as president of the Palmares Civic Center. In September and October of 1931 dos Santos convened a series of public meetings to discuss the creation of a new, explicitly political, black organization to complement the work of Palmares. Both the attendance and the sentiments expressed at those meetings made clear that there was substantial public support for such a move, and the Frente Negra Brasileira, the Brazilian Black Front, was officially inaugurated on October 12.[61]

Several factors combined to produce this outpouring of support. One was undoubtedly the economic hardship of the depression. Perhaps even more important than economic pressures, however, were the political changes taking place in Brazil. The presumption that politics was exclusively an elite affair, from which the *povo* was rigorously excluded, had been seriously questioned during the 1910s and 1920s and now seemed to have been overturned by the revolution of 1930. Along with white workers and the white middle class, black people clamored to be included in the broader political participation which that revolution seemed to portend. A report in one of the mainstream white newspapers on the Front's organizing meetings noted the palpable atmosphere of hope and expectation. "Last night's meeting was truly noteworthy, both in terms of attendance, which was enormous, and of the speeches given. . . . One visibly feels the awakening of a national consciousness among the black Brazilians, driving them toward more direct participation in the social and political life of the country. . . ." Recalling those meetings years later, one who took part in them stressed the same theme: "The blacks wanted to participate because they felt themselves to be the greatest beneficiaries of the revolution [of 1930]. The slavocracy had been deposed from power, the men who always scorned and despised the blacks. Now it was time for the blacks to take part." Even relatively conservative black papers, such as *Progresso*, which had spent the 1920s trying to downplay the extent of discrimination and racism in the city, and urging moderation and accommodation on its readers, could not resist the excitement. "In the hour in which Brazil prepares to convene its Constitutional Assembly [1933], setting the tone for the new Brazil, the men and women of the black race must prepare to fight so that in that Assembly black people are represented by their legitimate racial brothers. . . . Men and women of the black race, struggle bravely so that in the highest councils of the nation the voice of the blacks will lift like a clarion, imposing on Brazil the splendors of Justice for our race."[62]

The public reaction to the Front's establishment exceeded any of its organizers' expectations. The organization expanded rapidly throughout São Paulo State, and into southern Minas Gerais and Espírito Santo; independent fronts were created in Bahia and Rio Grande do Sul as well.[63] In later years, former leaders of the Front recalled their amazement at this unprecedented outpouring of enthusiasm in the community, and their uncertainty as to how best to proceed in the face of such a response. Francisco Lucrécio, who joined the organization in his early twenties, recalls how "we were exhausted, we used to come out of [Front headquarters] sick because we were dedicated, we were fanatics. I didn't do anything else: just study, go home, and go to the Front. I never went to the movies, never went to the theater." São Paulo papers covering the organization's first political campaign (in 1933 Arlindo Veiga dos Santos ran for the city council) interviewed youths who had been working for forty-eight hours without rest, covering the city with posters for their candidate.[64]

Comparable levels of effort went into a variety of programs aimed at improving the situation of São Paulo's black population. The Front sponsored literacy and vocational courses for adults, and established an elementary school. It created a clinic which offered free or reduced-rate dental and medical care, and its legal department provided assistance to members embroiled in disputes with landlords or employers. It also offered mutual aid benefits, and established a credit union as part of a "buy your own home" campaign aimed at helping Afro-Brazilians to escape the fetid basement apartments of the center city by purchasing lots and houses in the then-outlying suburbs of Jabaquara, Saude, and Casa Verde. This campaign seems to have met with some success, judging from contemporary observations concerning the movement of black people into those newer sections of the city.[65]

These programs, and the Front's general message of the moral uplift and material advancement of the black race, attracted a substantial membership, though its precise size is difficult to determine. The São Paulo organization's claim of a hundred thousand members spread throughout Brazil is clearly exaggerated; even Michael Mitchell's estimate of six thousand members in São Paulo City, two thousand more in Santos, and an undetermined number in chapters around the state, may be high.[66] While most of the members seem to have been of poor and working-class origins, only those who had moved upward into white-collar or professional employment could aspire to join the leadership.[67] This class exclusivity was resented by poorer Afro-Brazilians, and by the mid-1930s was posing serious problems to the continued expansion of the organization. A 1935 article in A Voz da Raça reported resistance from blacks who refused to become members because of their feeling that "more and more there exists in the Front a bloc of conceited black men and women, who think that they're better than we are." The article unwittingly confirmed the accuracy of those impressions by going on to dismiss the individuals quoted as "unsophisticated, uncultured, and sunk in ignorance."[68]

Whatever its size, the Front's membership was apparently too small to exert any impact on electoral politics in the state. Despite a long-term campaign to register its members as voters, the Front does not seem to have elected a single candidate during its seven-year existence, and even experienced some difficulty in being registered as a political party. The court empowered to grant registration (the Tribunal Superior de Justiça Eleitoral) split in its reaction to the Front's petition, one of its members arguing that the proposed party "contravenes the public order . . . [because] it intends to demand rights already guaranteed by the Constitution," that is, the rights of full equality before the law. Another judge responded that, since those rights were in fact guaranteed by the Constitution, there should be no objection to a party adopting them as its platform. The third magistrate concurred, noting that "confusion arises from the fact that the goals of the society are written in the language of 'the new black' [preto novo], which is in no way illegal or unconstitutional." On the basis of this two-to-one vote, the Front was permitted to register as an accredited party in 1936.[69]

Despite its electoral failings, the Front did achieve some success as a pressure group and lobby on issues involving racial discrimination. It managed to eliminate whites-only admission policies at the city's roller-skating rinks and other places of public entertainment. It also took up again the matter of black entry into the Civil Guard, which the Palmares Civic Center had tried to resolve in the 1920s. Though no laws were on the books barring entry to blacks, informal discrimination continued to form an obstacle to black applicants. (This might have been predicted from the reaction of the Guard's commander to the 1928 decree: "Now that blacks can enter, we can open the door to lepers and cripples."[70]) Blaming "the internal administration of São Paulo's Civil Guard, which is composed, in its majority, of foreigners," the Front appealed directly to President Vargas, who, after receiving a delegation of the Front leadership, ordered the Guard to enlist immediately two hundred black recruits. Over the course of the 1930s some five hundred Afro-Brazilians entered the state militia, one of whom rose to be a full colonel.[71]

The reference to foreign domination of the Guard represents a recurring element in the Front's discourse: a xenophobic anti-immigrant orientation, which was in turn linked to an authoritarian ideology and practice which borrowed heavily from Fascism. Xenophobia was by no means unique to the Front during this period. During the Republic the government had worked to destroy the labor movement by denouncing its leaders as seditious aliens and having them deported. In the 1920s the Democratic Party brought similar charges against the Republicans, noting the substantial number of foreign-born entrepreneurs in the industrial wing of the Republican Party, and the Republicans' fraudulent manipulation of Italian *colonos'* "votes" in the countryside. This resulted, according to the Democrats, in "the obvious fact" that under Republican rule "São Paulo is denationalizing itself, thanks to the cohabitation of the dominant party with these ignoble alien elements."[72]

This rising tide of nativism was a direct response to the Republic's efforts to remake Brazil in the image of Europe, efforts which had not worked out precisely as planned. The Brazilian elites had imagined a "tropical Belle Époque" created in the image of bourgeois France and Great Britain. Instead, what they got was a "plague" of peasants and laborers from southern and eastern Europe who, to the planters' horror, proved to be just as illiterate, unwashed, crime-ridden, and averse to honest labor as their own racially mixed *povo*—and, to add injury to insult, a good deal politically more radical.[73]

The Brazilian middle class perceived a different threat posed by the immigrants, that of economic competition. During the 1890s Brazilian-born shopkeepers, clerks, and artisans in Rio de Janeiro had organized a nativist "Jacobin" movement to protest immigrant inroads in skilled trades and small businesses. No such movement developed at that time in São Paulo, though in 1896 the city suffered four days of anti-immigrant rioting set off by public complaints of Italian domination of skilled trades and petty commerce. But by the 1920s and 1930s, São Paulo had surpassed Rio in the depth and strength of its anti-immigrant sentiment. Such feelings were most solidly rooted in the state's economically embattled middle class, squeezed between the growing crisis (and, as of 1929, collapse) of the coffee economy, and the relentless competition with the immigrants and their children for jobs, education, and social position. It was no accident that Brazil's Fascist-inspired Integralist movement was born in São Paulo (in 1932), that "white-collar workers, disgruntled bureaucrats and professionals, career military men of the lower ranks, and small-town tradesmen dominated Integralist cell membership," and that anti-immigrant feeling formed one of the movement's dominant themes. The budding nativism of the 1920s burst into full flower in the politically charged, hothouse atmosphere of the 1930s, and extreme nationalism formed a constant theme in the political discourse of those years, particularly on the Right. The Integralists routinely denounced the control of Brazil's economy by foreign bankers and capitalists, published anti-Semitic literature so scurrilous that it attracted the favorable attention of the German Nazi newspaper *Der Stürmer*, and promoted a program of strident economic and cultural nationalism.[74]

If elites and the white middle class had succumbed to anti-immigrant feelings, it is hardly surprising to find the Afro-Brazilians doing so as well. More than any other group in São Paulo, they were the ones who had borne the brunt of immigration, and who had been most jarringly shunted aside as the state was "Europeanized." While many black people accepted the proposition that the Europeans had displaced the Afro-Brazilians because of their greater energy and willingness to work hard, others argued that Europeans were receiving the benefits of racial discrimination, and, worse yet, were developing a taste for it. During the 1920s the black papers ran repeated denunciations of discrimination by immigrants against blacks, primarily in the areas of employment and public services, on occasion concluding them with the fond hope that the immigrants "go look for other countries, and send themselves to other countries where there are no blacks, no backward, imbecilic, ignorant people of the sort that are found here on such a grand scale. Leave us ignorant and in peace; go to the great civilized centers. . . ." Or, as another black paper put it, if the immigrants didn't care to be around black people, there were boats leaving for Italy every week.[75]

The year 1928 marked the formerly optimistic *O Clarim da Alvorada's* last assertion that "we live in perfect harmony, not just with white Brazilians, but with the foreign element as well." By 1930 its editor had reversed course to denounce "the colonies of foreigners, who organize themselves and discriminate, permitting non-black Brazilians to join them and fearlessly proclaim our inferiority." *Progresso* concurred in noting a rising tide of racism in São Paulo: "These facts are always disagreeable, and particularly when the intolerance comes from elements who are not even in their own house"—that is, the immigrants.[76]

Given this deepening anger against the immigrants, and the xenophobic currents running strongly in São Paulo at the time, it was virtually inevitable that the Black Front would embrace nativism from the outset. Its statutes provided for an organization which would be "rigorously Brazilian" in character, and its publications and speeches consistently denounced foreign domination of Brazilian life, as personified by foreign capitalists, foreign landlords, and "the pro-foreigner policies which marked the ominous dominion of the Paulista Republican Party." Its leaders called for "a hard nationalist campaign, against the foreign or semi-foreign slime that engineers divisions, Bolshevism, Socialism, and other vile and infamous things," and urged the Vargas regime to "close the doors of Brazil [to foreigners] for twenty years or more" so that black people could reconquer their rightful position in the country.[77]

The parallels between the Front's anti-immigrant orientation and that of the Integralist movement are striking, as are other commonalities between the two movements. Both shared a contemptuous disdain for liberal democracy and, despite their rejection of foreign political philosophies, an open admiration for European Fascism. In a 1933 editorial saluting Adolf Hitler's rise to power, Arlindo Veiga dos Santos congratulated him for having rescued Germany from the hands of "Jewish cosmopolitanism" and "the narcotic opiate of fourteen years of liberal-democratic republicanism." *A Voz da Raça* reported admiringly on the achievements of Nazism and Fascism in instilling discipline and patriotism in their people. This admiration for authoritarianism extended to the Front's own system of internal governance: officers were chosen not by election but rather by incumbent officeholders, and the organization as a whole was policed by a "militia" modeled on the Integralists' Green Shirts and commanded by Pedro Paulo Barbosa, a dedicated anti-Communist and admirer of Mussolini.[78]

Allying itself ever more closely with Fascism and Integralism (the organization even adopted as its own the Integralists' motto of "for family, for country, and for God," modifying it slightly by adding "for race"), over the course of the 1930s the Front progressively alienated moderate and left-wing support within the black community, driving dissenters in the capital to create the competing Black Club of Social Culture and a small Black Socialist Front. The Santos chapter eventually cut ties with the central organization to enter into an electoral alliance with the Socialist Party (which, characteristically, the São Paulo headquarters dismissed as "a horde of undesirables from other countries"). In A Voz da Raça, dos Santos responded to such dissidents with vicious attacks on the "Judases to their race" and by sending the Brazilian Black Front militia to wreck the offices of a black newspaper critical of dos Santos's administration.[79]

These bitter divisions, when combined with the small size of the black vote, prevented the Front from ever achieving its goal of becoming a significant political force in São Paulo. If anything, one of the striking features of A Voz da Raça by the mid-1930s is the absence of specific, concrete political commentary on the events of the day. There is much denunciation of international Bolshevism and anonymous "traitors" and "enemies," but virtually no references to candidates, parties, or politics in São Paulo City or the state. An editorial on the congressional elections of June 1937 offered no specific endorsements, but simply expressed confidence that blacks would vote for those candidates who would best serve their interests.[80]

Getúlio Vargas dealt the Front its coup de grâce in December 1937, when he banned all political parties and closed down electoral politics in Brazil. Even at this point the Front sought to strike a bargain, offering black support for the Vargas dictatorship in exchange for the concessions it had unsuccessfully sought through electoral politics. Hailing the New State as the reaffirmation of Brazil's national identity and the essence of brasilidade, A Voz da Raça went on to express "our certainty that the legislators, conscious of their lofty responsibilities, will not let pass unperceived at the margins the blacks who have offered, and will continue to offer, such benefits to the Country."[81]

But the Front's leaders were mistaken. There were to be no legislators under the New State. The years from 1937 to 1945 constituted a highwater mark of authoritarian rule in Brazil, a period during which political and intellectual freedoms were severely circumscribed, and no institutional avenues existed for the expression of political dissent and opposition. Those mass-based organizations capable of posing a threat to the government were either repressed (the eventual fate of the Integralist movement) or brought firmly under state control (the fate of the labor unions). Those organizations too small or divided to threaten the government were permitted to die a natural death, which came for the Brazilian Black Front in May 1938, just days after the abortive Integralist uprising in Rio de Janeiro and, ironically, the fiftieth anniversary of emancipation.

It is easy to fault the Front for any number of failings: its authoritarianism, its extreme right-wing chauvinism, its failure to mobilize a following sufficiently large and organized to become a political force—and ultimately, its failure to improve significantly the social, economic, and political position of São Paulo's black population. It is also easy to blame those failings, in accord with the Fernandes thesis, on the ignorance, apathy, and confusion of the Afro-Brazilian population that the Front sought to unify and lead.[82] But to do so is to neglect the fact that the Front fell victim to essentially the same conflicts as those convulsing the political system more generally. Middle-class blacks and whites in São Paulo proved equally vulnerable to the lure of xenophobic nationalism and political authoritarianism. Ripped apart by the resulting polarization between a Fascist-inspired right wing, and a weaker, labor-based left wing, the Front thus replicated in microcosm the trajectory of paulista and Brazilian politics as a whole during the 1930s.[83]

If poverty, ignorance, and confusion had prevented the Afro-Brazilians from achieving their political goals, so had they prevented the entire nation from realizing 1930's apparent promise of broadened participation and genuine democracy, both racial and political. But even if the causes of the Black Front's failings transcended the black population, and affected all Brazilian society, the experience was none the less bitter for those who had taken part in it. As a result, when the dictatorship fell in 1945 and Brazil embarked on a new experiment in democracy, the Second Republic, members of the black middle class rejected proposals for a revived black political organization, and instead devoted themselves to capitalizing on the opportunities presented by São Paulo's accelerating economic growth.[84]

6. Blacks Ascending, 1940–1988

The years between 1940 and 1980 witnessed profound transformations in the social and economic character of São Paulo State. In 1940 the population had been 7.1 million, 1.3 million of whom lived in the state capital. Only two other cities (Campinas and Santos) had populations over a hundred thousand, and half of the state's workforce was employed in agriculture. By 1980 the population had more than tripled, to twenty-five million, and more people now lived in the capital than had lived in the entire state in 1940. Almost 90 percent of the population was urban, most of it (12.6 million) living in São Paulo City and its industrial suburbs. While the number of people employed in the agricultural sector had declined from 1.5 million to 1.1 million, and now represented only a tenth of the labor force, those employed in industry had increased from 428,000 to 2.8 million.[1]

In addition to promoting the growth of an urban working class, urbanization and economic development provided the basis for a phenomenal rate of increase in the middle class. The "administrative" sector (entrepreneurs, executives, and white-collar office workers), which had not even constituted a separate vocational category in the census of 1940, now employed 1.7 million paulistas, and formed the second-largest area of the labor market, exceeded only by industrial workers. Spearheaded by increases in education, medicine, and the field of accounting, the ranks of professionals had grown from 1940's level of 32,345 to almost three-quarters of a million (734,753). When added together, these two areas of white-collar employment (administration and professionals) now accounted for almost a quarter (23.8 percent) of the total work force (Table 6.2).[2]

To what degree, and under what conditions, did Afro-Brazilians participate in this expansion of the paulista middle class?

Afro-Brazilians and White-Collar Employment in São Paulo

We may begin by looking at education. During the first half of the century relatively few paulistas had been able even to complete high school, let alone college. This was the case partly because of the limited number of schools at either level in the state, and partly because most families needed to send their children into the labor force relatively early, often before they had finished primary school. As a result, in 1940 less than 2 percent of São Paulo's population had graduated from either high school or college.[3]

Both of these conditions began to change during the 1940s and 1950s. Middle- and working-class families who had profited from the state's economic growth now had the financial means to keep some or all of their children out of the labor market and in school. And by the 1940s, those families had access to a more developed educational infrastructure. The state government had started to expand the system of secondary schools in the 1920s, and in 1934 it established the University of São Paulo, which almost immediately became Brazil's foremost institution of higher learning. Educational opportunity continued to expand under the Second Republic (1946–1964) as well as under the military dictatorship of 1964–1985. Between 1970 and 1975 college enrollments in Brazil more than doubled, reflecting the military government's emphasis on upgrading Brazil's university system. It was also during the 1970s that São Paulo acquired a new federal university (the Federal University of São Carlos) and two new state universities (the State University of Campinas and the State University of São Paulo). Expansion was even more rapid among the private *faculdades* which sprang into existence to meet the demand for higher education among students unable to win admission to the more prestigious state and federal universities.[4]

As a result of this growth in São Paulo's system of higher education, by 1980 9.0 percent of the state's population had graduated from either high school or college.[5] The rate of increase was even more rapid among Afro-Brazilians, though such a rate is inflated by the shockingly low base of black educational achievement as of 1940: the census of that year indicated that only 344 Afro-Brazilians, out of a total black population of 862,255, had graduated from college; 1,717 had graduated from high school. By 1950 the situation had improved somewhat at the high school level, where the number of black graduates had doubled, to 3,538. The number of white high school graduates had almost tripled during the same period, however, from 101,617 to 297,653; and while the number of white college graduates had increased by over half (from 28,882 to 44,562), the number of Afro-Brazilian college graduates had actually declined, to 265. In 1940 approximately 1 of every 2,500 Afro-Brazilians living in the state was a college graduate; by 1950 that ratio dropped to 1 out of every 3,850.[6]

Racial differentials in higher education were nothing new in the São Paulo of the 1940s. As early as the 1880s, José Rubino de Oliveira, a black professor at the Law School, had pointed to the different levels of performance demanded of black and white students: "To win a diploma a Negro must show talent and knowledge; otherwise he won't pass here. As for the whites, any donkey can pass; I myself will open the gate for him." The point was reiterated by the headmistress of a Catholic girls school in the early 1950s. "We demand more of a black girl than of a white before we accept her. The situation is very delicate, and a colored girl, in order to be respected, must offer qualifications superior to those of the whites."[7]

Well aware of the special obstacles facing blacks who sought higher education, the National Convention of Brazilian Blacks held in São Paulo in November 1945, a month after the overthrow of the Vargas dictatorship, decided to concentrate its efforts on achieving two goals in the upcoming Constituent Assembly, which would convene in 1946 to write the charter for Brazil's Second Republic. The first goal was to have racial prejudice and discrimination declared to be criminal offenses; and the second was the enactment of a special program of federal scholarships for black students at high schools, universities, and the service academies.[8] As it turned out, neither provision was incorporated into the Constitution, with the result that black students at both the high school and college levels had to struggle along as best they could on their own and their families' resources. By 1980, however (census data on race were not published in 1960, and not collected in 1970), it was clear that, even without direct government support, Afro-Brazilians had made considerable progress. According to the census of that year, 125,050 of the state's Afro-Brazilian residents had completed eleven years (the number required to graduate from high school) or more of education. Of those high-school graduates, 39,946 had gone on to university study; of these, 16,344 had completed an additional four years or more, and thus presumably had obtained a university degree.[9]

The rate at which Afro-Brazilians were graduating from high school and college still lagged far behind the rate for whites.[10] However, since 1950 that rate had increased much more rapidly among the black population than among the white, and the number of black high school and college graduates was now large enough in absolute terms to constitute a numerically significant group of nonwhite competitors for entry into the paulista middle class.

As we saw in Part 1, the first phase of interracial competition in twentieth-century São Paulo took place at the level of the working class, and resulted in the resounding victory of white immigrant workers over Afro-Brazilians. With the ending of mass immigration in the late 1920s, however, Afro-Brazilians were able to make their way back into the manual labor force from which they had been displaced by the immigrants.

During the second half of the 1900s a second phase of racial competition began in São Paulo, as the children of black workers and of the pre-1940 black "elite" acquired the education that would enable them to compete for further upward mobility and admission into the ranks of white-collar employment. When they went out into the world to obtain such employment, however, they found themselves running into barriers almost as harsh and excluding as those which their grandparents had faced at the working-class level at the turn of the century. We first encountered evidence of systematic discrimination at the middle-class level in chapter 4, which showed the racial differences in upward mobility for workers at São Paulo Light: while black and white workers experienced job promotions in comparable proportions, such promotions for black workers consistently stopped short of white-collar or managerial positions. Those data relate only to one firm, however. More comprehensive evidence is available from several sources.

The first consists of testimony from personnel administrators in São Paulo. Staff members at private employment agencies and the São Paulo office of the National Job Service report that the majority of companies which file requests for employees routinely indicate that they will not accept Afro-Brazilians. Some agencies facilitate this practice by specifically asking companies whether they will accept black job applicants and then screening out such applicants if the company says no. Most personnel administrators, both at the employment agencies and in the firms themselves, express unhappiness and regret about this practice, but argue that they have no choice, since the executives who have final authority over hiring decisions consistently refuse to hire, or even seriously consider, black applicants for white-collar jobs.[11]

Such exclusion operates in a particularly poignant way at the lowest levels of office work, that of the young "office boys" (the English term is often used) who run errands, do odd jobs, and hope eventually to work their way up into the white-collar world. These are the most sought-after jobs for teenage workers in São Paulo, with roughly ten job seekers for each position available. As a result, employers are able to enforce strict standards of acceptability for those they will hire. What do they look for in an office boy? "Education— generally a high school student—good appearance, healthy, living near the workplace, prior work experience, able to work the eight hours demanded of an adult, even if he is still in school. And he must be white." This immediately rules out the majority of applicants for such positions, who are "thin, under-nourished, generally blacks or mulattoes, with bad teeth and poorly dressed."[12]

The specification in the above quotation that job applicants must be white is actually redundant, since most Brazilians would recognize "good appearance" *(boa aparência)*, a formula which appears frequently in Brazilian want ads, as a euphemism for white.[13] "Good appearance" is almost always specified as a requirement for any job involving direct contact with consumers or the public, who, paulista employers assume, do not care to be attended by black people. As a result, jobs as receptionists, salespeople, and even waiters in better restaurants, are closed off to Afro-Brazilians. In this sense racial discrimination in Brazil is even harsher and more excluding than South African apartheid, concludes the Brazilian newsweekly *Veja*.

"In Johannesburg, all the customers in the best restaurants are white—and all the waiters are black. In the best Brazilian restaurants, all the customers are white—and the waiters too."[14]

Restrictions on Afro-Brazilians dealing directly with the public extend to the professions as well. Even in journalism, generally recognized as one of the fields most open to black initiative, Afro-Brazilian writer Muniz Sodré finds that, while blacks are relatively free to enter the profession, "there does exist a line of segregation . . . [which is that] the colored journalist is assigned to internal work (copy-editing, the archive, etc.) where there is no direct contact with the public, or else toward areas considered to be of low prestige (sports, police reporting). In areas such as politics, or general reporting, it is very rare to find blacks. . . ."[15]

If executives do not wish to have Afro-Brazilians representing their company to the public, one would expect to find some of the most stringent restrictions of all in the area of public relations and advertising. Black artists, photographers, and technicians are employed by the industry, but the line is drawn at blacks appearing in television advertisements or on the printed page.[16] Black models complain about the extreme difficulty of finding work in Brazil, and a number of the most successful have chosen to pursue careers abroad, often in Europe, in preference to struggling along in their native country.[17]

An advertising executive explains why black people cannot be models in Brazil.

To understand this matter it's necessary to understand what the word "model" means. Literally, model means that which one wishes to imitate, or which serves as an example. Who in Brazil wants to imitate blacks? Middle-class whites are going to want to have a black person presented to them as an example? . . . Blacks are the poorest and most backward part of the population, and this is why our white society only accepts blacks in certain positions. And this is why advertising discriminates, because advertising has to reflect society, including its prejudices.[18]

The effects of those prejudices go considerably beyond their impact on the modeling profession, and are visible in a second body of evidence documenting racial discrimination at the middle-class level: data on salaries gathered by the federal government through the national census and the National Household Surveys of the 1970s and 1980s. The earliest such data come from a 1.27 percent sample of the 1960 census, in which information on race was gathered by census takers. The relationships among race, salary, education, and occupation revealed in those data provided little support for assertions of racial equality in the Brazilian job market. After controlling for type of job held, whether one worked in an urban (where salaries tend to be higher) or rural area, number of years on the job, education, and other relevant factors documented by the census, there remained a strong differential between black and white salaries which, economist Nelson do Valle Silva concluded, could be explained only by racial discrimination. This differential proved to be smallest among workers with little or no education, and then increased markedly as one moved up the educational ladder. "Not only [do] whites have higher initial returns to schooling, but the white-nonwhite relative difference actually increase[s] as schooling level increases. Thus, while for individuals with no schooling the average white income is about 19 percent larger than nonwhite incomes, the corresponding figure for those completing Junior High School . . . is 33 percent." On the basis of these data, Silva concluded that "discrimination against non-whites seems to increase as the general standing of the occupations also increases. Some of the largest coefficients of discrimination are to be found among white collar occupations, the very top of the occupational hierarchy."[19]

These 1960 findings have been corroborated by subsequent studies using data from the 1976 and 1982 household surveys, and from the 1980 national census, all of which show worsening salary inequality as one moves up the educational and occupational scale.[20] Using data from the 1980 census, Table 6.1 indicates the monthly median income of workers in various sectors of São Paulo's economy, expressed as a multiple of the official *salário mínimo*, the monthly minimum wage.[21] The final column of that table calculates the ratio between white and black (combined pardo and preto) median incomes, and indicates the percentage by which white incomes exceed black. (For example, the ratio of white to black median income for the economically active population as a whole is 1.39; median white income in São Paulo is therefore 39 percent higher than median black income.)

Nowhere in São Paulo's economy do black salaries equal white.

Table 6.1. Median Earnings[a] of Workers in Selected Areas of the Economy, São Paulo State, 1980

	Whites	Pardos	Pretos	White/Black[b]
Total economically active population	2.3	1.7	1.5	1.39
Areas Showing Above-average Inequality				
Professions	4.7	3.0	2.9	1.58
Commerce	2.6	1.7	1.6	1.54
Administration[c]	3.8	2.6	2.5	1.47
Areas Showing Below-average Inequality				
Miscellaneous and unclassified	1.9	1.7	1.6	1.13
Industry and construction	2.1	1.9	1.8	1.12
Service	1.1	1.0	1.0	1.10
Agriculture	1.1	1.0	1.0	1.10
Transport and communications	3.1	2.9	2.8	1.08

Source: Data provided to the author by the Departamento de Estudos e Indicadores Sociais (DEISO), IBGE.

[a]Median earnings expressed as a multiple of the monthly *salário mínimo;* see note 21.

[b]Figures indicate the ratios between white and black median incomes.

[c]Includes owners of enterprises, executives, managers, and office workers.

However, the levels of inequality vary substantially across different sectors of the labor market. If we divide the economy into those sectors where salary inequality falls above the average for the economically active population as a whole, and those where it falls below, we find that such inequality is most severe in the professions, commerce, and administration, and is least severe in transport and communications, agriculture, service occupations, industry and construction, and the miscellaneous category. Obviously the former are predominantly white-collar, middle-class areas of the labor market, while the latter are composed of blue-collar, working-class positions. As a result, the former tend to be much better paying than the latter, with two exceptions. The first is that of jobs in commerce, which are dominated by poorly paid positions in retail sales. Nevertheless, while black employees in this sector earn less on average than those in industry and construction, white employees earn considerably more. The second exception is that of transport and communications,

Table 6.2. Percentage Distribution of the Work Force in Selected Areas of the Economy, São Paulo State, 1980, by Race

	Whites	Pardos	Pretos	N
Total economically active population	73.1	19.2	5.3	10,411,726
Professions	86.6	6.7	2.1	734,753
Commerce	79.9	13.2	2.3	894,371
Administration	85.0	9.2	1.9	1,747,025
Miscellaneous and unclassified	66.3	24.4	6.4	844,752
Industry and construction	67.9	24.7	6.2	2,862,239
Service	62.3	26.9	9.7	1,403,273
Agriculture	70.9	20.3	6.6	1,071,072
Transport and communications	75.5	18.8	4.2	544,901

Source: See Table 6.1.

which is dominated by relatively well-paid (in relation to other blue-collar jobs) truck and bus drivers. Afro-Brazilians who work in this area of the economy earn almost as much as black professionals. Racial barriers to entering transport jobs also seem to be fairly low, since black workers fill these positions at rates quite close to their participation in the labor force as a whole (Table 6.2). Clearly transportation constitutes the most promising area of the paulista economy for black job seekers.

Transport and communications is also, however, the smallest area of the paulista job market, which is dominated by industry and construction, administration, service occupations, and agriculture. As we survey those sectors, we find that those areas of the economy which display the greatest salary inequality are also those in which barriers to black entry are greatest, and in which black participation is significantly lower than black participation in the economy as a whole. White workers clearly dominate these areas of the economy, and are significantly overrepresented in them. Conversely, areas of relatively low salary inequality tend to be those in which black workers are overrepresented, and white workers underrepresented (with the exception, again, of transport and communications, and, to a lesser degree, agriculture).

Racial Solidarity: Keeping the Middle Class White

Black people are hired for middle-class positions at rates much lower than those for whites, and once in those positions, they are paid much less. In previous years employers and others would have argued that such differentials were explained by lower levels of education and job experience among black job applicants, factors which admittedly are not taken into account in the above tables. However, as previously indicated, researchers who have controlled for those variables find that salary and job differentials are only partly explained by differences in qualifications, and that racial differences in salary actually tend to increase as black workers acquire higher levels of education. Black aspirants to middle-class positions have been excluded as much in spite of their educational achievements as because of their educational shortcomings.[22]

This raises the central question of this section of the chapter: Why do Brazilian employers discriminate at the middle-class level of the labor market far more than at the working-class level? Any answer to this question will be almost impossible to prove or verify. If asked, most Brazilian employers would steadfastly deny that they discriminate against black job seekers, since such an act would be a cardinal sin in a racial democracy. However, while in São Paulo in 1984–1985, I had the opportunity to look for a moment beneath the surface of Brazilian hiring practices, and to hear from an expert how the system really operates and what considerations motivate the men who make hiring decisions in São Paulo corporations. This individual was a former president of the São Paulo Association of Personnel Administrators, who had been asked by the administration of Governor Franco Montoro to gather information on racial hiring practices in the state. He met with me on November 27, 1984, to talk about his findings, based on interviews with fifty-eight personnel administrators in Greater São Paulo.[23]

Of the human resources professionals interviewed by my informant, some denied that discrimination took place in their firms, but then went on to express traditional negative racial stereotypes which would create formidable obstacles to blacks seeking jobs or promotions. Others said that no formally discriminatory procedures were in place at their companies, but acknowledged that they routinely favored white applicants over black. One frequently cited reason for doing so was they did not want to give their company a "bad" public image by placing blacks in visible positions. Another was that they wanted to avoid friction in the workplace, where there would be considerable resistance among white workers against working with black colleagues. This was particularly so, the personnel administrators reported, in the area of promotions; a black employee being placed in a supervisory position over white workers was a situation which they all regarded as quite problematic. Finally, a third group of administrators admitted that their companies had formally discriminatory procedures, which usually consisted of secret coded notations on job applications, and that they automatically screened out black applicants. A number of these administrators expressed regrets about these policies, but argued that the racial attitudes of top management in their companies, who strongly resist hiring Afro-Brazilians for middle- or upper-level jobs, left them no recourse.

It is interesting to note that, while most of these executives acknowledged practicing some degree of discrimination, very few would accept responsibility for such practices. Instead, they blamed their actions on the refusal of the "public," or workers in the firm, or upper management, or some combination thereof, to accept Afro-Brazilians in middle-class positions.[24] In the absence of any research on these alleged constituencies for racial discrimination, it is hard to know how much each group contributes to the exclusion of black workers from opportunities for upward mobility. Middle-class whites with whom I spoke repeatedly affirmed their willingness to work alongside qualified black colleagues, and such responses are supported by the results of a 1984 survey conducted among the white population of São Paulo, in which the overwhelming majority (88 percent) said they would have no problem working under a black supervisor. (The figure was slightly lower for middle-class respondents: 85 percent.) However, as anthropologist João Baptista Borges Pereira observed in commenting on these findings, these individuals were responding to a hypothetical situation which, given the realities of promotion in Brazilian firms, they are very unlikely ever to have to face. And given the value placed by Brazilian society on the principles of racial equality and democracy, he noted, very few respondents would be willing to admit to any racist feelings they might have, though they are willing to acknowledge them in others. This is a constant in surveys of racial attitudes in São Paulo, in which most white respondents express the opinion that whites are indeed prejudiced against blacks, but only a tiny minority will admit to holding such prejudices themselves.[25]

The absence of further research on these questions, and the desire of white Brazilians to blame anyone but themselves for racial discrimination, leads to considerable vagueness and uncertainty about where, why, how, how often, and by whom, such acts are committed. Reporting on the racial climate in São Paulo in the early 1950s, U.S. historian Richard Morse noted that "there exists an insidious, not easily assailed discriminatory attitude, in some ways comparable to anti-Jewish sentiment in the United States." He also noted that a significant number of white paulistas had given thought to the idea of elevating discriminatory practices from the level of an informal "gentlemen's agreement" to the more formal, institutionalized practices of United States–style segregation. "My experience in São Paulo suggests that America's much-publicized Jim-Crowism attracts certain middle-class Paulistas (mildly, to be sure) as a guaranty for status and security."[26] French sociologist Roger Bastide was not so sure that the attraction was mild. Carrying out his research in the 1940s and early 1950s, he observed a growing uneasiness among middle-class paulista whites concerning the possibilities for black advancement created by increased industrial employment and expanded opportunities for public education.

The whites have begun to feel threatened. . . . They are going to react, and that reaction, aimed at keeping blacks at the bottom of the social scale, is going to intensify and sharpen color prejudice; at the same time, segregation is going to appear at all levels of society. . . . A type of racial solidarity will establish itself among the various white ethnic groups in a policy of self-defense, embracing the Brazilian whose family has been here for four hundred years, the descendant of the immigrant, and the foreign capitalist.[27]

Bastide's prediction of generalized segregation in São Paulo failed to materialize, at least in the Jim Crow sense suggested by Morse. His prediction of a vaguer "racial solidarity," however, proved closer to the mark. This solidarity remains latent most of the time, and is activated only in situations in which upwardly mobile Afro-Brazilians enter into direct competition with whites. As black actress

Zezé Motta notes, "The majority of blacks only perceive that racism exists when they have the chance to compete with whites. . . . they only perceive this when they're moving up in the world." Another black informant agrees. "If you just remain among the masses, you won't feel any prejudice, because you're in your own setting. But as soon as you start to compete, then it gets tough, then you run into it head-on. . . . Then the prejudice begins."[28] The extensive research carried out by Florestan Fernandes further validates these observations.

When blacks and mulattoes show that they are not only capable of competing, but ready to compete, then the situation becomes more defined. It is at that point that one sees that there is a very large proportion of whites who behave in a genuinely democratic way and accept competition [with blacks]. But there is also another type of white, who, in this confrontation, assumes an attitude of panic, seeing a threat to himself and to civilization more generally. They say that "those people are coming up in the world, it's the end of Brazil!" It is not such a small group as is generally thought, and it creates serious problems for black and mulatto competition, finding various ways to disguise its resistance. . . .[29]

Even the mainstream conservative newspaper *O Estado de São Paulo* has recognized this aspect of race relations in São Paulo, while simultaneously trying to excuse it. "An example of this would be a case of competition for a job between two candidates, one of them colored. His color may, eventually, be used as a negative mark against the black, without this necessarily representing a racist ideology."[30] One might respond by paraphrasing the old punchline: with hiring and promotion practices like these, who needs racist ideology? But it is unlikely that such practices would exist independently of an ideology to support and justify them, particularly when they so sharply contradict the principles of racial democracy to which virtually all Brazilians swear allegiance. And in fact there *is* a racist ideology behind these actions—the "ideology of the whites," Octávio Ianni has labeled it—which is very much a part of life in the paulista middle class. It emerges quickly and often in conversations with members of that class, from which I infer that they do not consider it to be socially objectionable. This ideology, as described by Ianni and confirmed by my own experience, accepts the principles of racial democracy and formal equality, but then demands that blacks not test those principles by trying to push into positions where they are "not wanted," that is, seeking better education, jobs, housing, and so on. Such whites express a strong desire for racial harmony, but then insist that such harmony is best preserved by black people remaining in "their place," and not creating "disagreeable situations" of competition and challenge.[31]

This "ideology of the whites" also contains a powerful component of antiblack stereotyping which has its roots deep in Brazilian history, folklore, and culture, but which will sound painfully familiar to any citizen of the United States. Blacks are viewed as criminal, lazy, stupid, irresponsible, promiscuous, foul-smelling—the essence of the socially contaminating Other. To the degree that these negative images are accepted and believed in Brazil—and the degree is very high indeed, at all levels of society—one would expect to find staunch resistance to hiring black employees.[32]

But if these stereotypes operate so powerfully at the middle and upper levels of the labor market, why do they seem to lose their excluding force at the bottom levels of the work force? If Afro-Brazilians are being rejected for middle-class employment because of negative racial images, why are those images so readily suspended in the case of industrial employment, where lazy, stupid, irresponsible workers can foul up production schedules, endanger their fellow workers, and do thousands of dollars of damage to machines and materials? Even more telling, why are they suspended in the case of jobs in domestic service, which require the utmost honesty, responsibility, and reliability? Such images have never prevented white Brazilians from entrusting their cars, their homes, their children, and ultimately their lives to the care of black workers; why then have they so effectively excluded black people from parity in white-collar employment?

The excluding power of these racial stereotypes seems to vary in direct relation to the desirability of the job to be filled. During the early decades of the century, positions as factory workers and colonos were the most promising opportunities for the masses of unskilled workers competing for jobs in the paulista economy; at that time, those jobs were reserved for white workers. By the second half of the century, however, those jobs had been displaced in desirability by the white-collar, professional and commercial positions created by the state's continuing economic expansion. Upwardly mobile white families trained their sights on these new opportunities, and no longer offered themselves in sufficient numbers to meet the labor demands of the state's factories and plantations. As the program of subsidized immigration came to an end, and with it the constant infusions of newly arrived European workers, employers of industrial and agricultural labor had little choice but to open the doors to Afro-Brazilian job seekers.

At the middle-class level, however, the story was different. Here the rate of creation of new jobs, while impressive, has been insufficient to satisfy all the people, or even all the white people, who want them. An obvious part of the desirability of such positions is the relatively higher salaries which they command. Just as important, however, is the unequivocal way in which they distance their holders from the demeaning status of manual labor. Ever since the colonial period, in large part because of its close association with slavery, manual labor in Brazil has been considered to be a socially degrading and humiliating condition.[33] Household activities which are staples of domestic life in the United States—washing and ironing clothes, mowing the lawn, washing the car, carpentry and home repair—are regarded in Brazil as unseemly and inappropriate for middle-class people. Instead, such jobs—along with cooking and child care—are assigned to low-paid domestic servants or hired outside workers.

The central fact of middle-class life in Brazil is that it represents escape from the degraded, poverty-stricken world of manual labor, the world of the *povo*.[34] White-collar jobs thus carry psychological benefits that complement, and often even exceed, their financial benefits; and the competition to obtain and hold on to such jobs is correspondingly intense. Competitors for white-collar status use every resource available to them: education, personal and family connections, good looks—and racial status. At the turn of the century the immigrants were able to use such status to win preferred positions in the labor market; and in recent decades their descendants, the second- and third-generation Euro-Brazilians, have replicated this achievement, though now at the middle-class level.[35] As executives and employers, as workers, and as consumers of goods and services, white people in São Paulo have joined together to enforce the "racial solidarity" predicted by Bastide, and to reserve the most desirable areas of the paulista labor market for themselves.

This racial solidarity works quietly and effectively in the workplace.[36] It operates in a more blatant, visible manner in one of the most important Brazilian social institutions: the private social and athletic club.[37] These clubs are extremely important in Brazilian elite and middle-class life, for several reasons. One is the paucity of public parks, swimming pools, and recreational facilities in most cities, which means that middle-class and elite Brazilians must seek recreation in private facilities rather than public. Such an arrangement also enables them to avoid the kind of close contact with the *povo* that would take place in a more open, public setting. The clubs thus provide an environment in which middle-class Brazilians can distance themselves from the lower classes, and at the same time cultivate the friendships and social contacts that are so important in attaining, and keeping, higher social status in Brazil.

As numerous observers have noted, Brazilian life is based on personal relationships, exchanges, and favors, to a degree even greater than in the United States (where, of course, such interactions, many of which also take place in social clubs and civic organizations, are by no means insignificant). Anthropologists have described the extended social networks through which members of the Brazilian middle class maintain and cultivate the personal relations which are indispensable to making one's way in an intensely competitive, difficult environment. One of them, Roberto da Matta, contrasts the public "world of the street," where "life is a battle among strangers," to the private life of the home, where one lives in the security of close personal ties with family, relatives, and friends. When they must confront the hostile outside world, da Matta argues, Brazilians respond by building the same sort of web of friendships and relationships that shelters them in their homes. And as they extend the protections of private life into the public realm, the formal rules and regulations of public life are displaced by the private code of a "relational universe" in which "one can deny anything, save the request of a friend." For in Brazil, as literary critic Roberto Schwarz puts it, "the favor is our nearly universal mediation."[38]

It is through the social clubs that middle-class Brazilians forge bonds and cement ties with people who can do "favors" for each other: people who can inform each other of job opportunities, and can put in a good word for a friend, or a friend's child, when they go to apply for such jobs; people with friends at City Hall, who can help with a needed permit or a legal dispute; people who can help one's children get into a desired private school.[39] For the Brazilian middle and upper classes, the social clubs are one of the most important mechanisms of social integration and advancement available to them; and for those unable to gain admission, the clubs function as one of the most effective means of social and economic exclusion. As a result, the clubs have constituted one of the most difficult hurdles for Afro-Brazilians to get over. Black physician Edgard Santana noted in the early 1950s that they were the area of paulista life in which discrimination was most obvious, and came closest to United States–style segregation. "It is clear, defined prejudice, of the American type." Other reports from that period noted that some clubs did admit small numbers of black members but then restricted them to separate, black-only social events, and refused to allow them to use the pool and other facilities. A report from the 1940s suggested that "many whites do not wish to swim in the same water as people of color, whence the prohibitions and ingenious measures impeding darker persons from using the pools" at the clubs. Such measures remain in effect to the present, as indicated by a board member of the Tietê Boating Club: "If we were to accept a colored member and he entered the pool, within an hour one hundred members would quit the club."[40]

The exclusion of Afro-Brazilians from the clubs exacts a heavy price from them in at least two ways. The first is economic. "Because they are barred from close interpersonal contact with the lighter racial types who control access to these jobs and allocate them to racially lighter friends and relatives . . . [pretos and pardos] have little opportunity to exploit the social networks that could enable them to obtain higher level jobs."[41] The second price is psychological, and is paid in the coin of shattered self-esteem. Many middle-class blacks recall their ejections from white social clubs as among the most painful experiences of their lives. Actor Milton Gonçalves remembers going as a teenager with some white friends to a dance at the São Paulo Athletic Association to which they had bought tickets. His friends were allowed to enter, but he was stopped at the door and told he must wait outside for one of the club's directors. "I started sweating uncontrollably, my eyes filled with tears to the point where I could barely see. People kept going in, the line kept moving, and I stood there, off to one side, dying of shame." When the director arrived, Gonçalves threatened to go to the police and charge the club under the Afonso Arinos antidiscrimination law (see chapter 7). The director laughed and responded, "Do you really think the police are going to close this club on your account?" Years later Gonçalves recalled the incident as a turning point in his adolescence: "I woke up. No, of course they weren't going to close it. And the world fell in on my head. None of my friends came back to see what was going on. It was a profound and violent aggression [against me]. And it was collective. I could see that I couldn't count on anybody."[42]

The social clubs are the most visible form of a "racial solidarity" which maintains middle-class whites as an economically and socially privileged group in São Paulo. That solidarity is by no means absolute, however, even among middle-class whites, many of whom publicly and privately repudiate the practice of racial discrimination in their society. Nor does it operate in an automatic and unvarying way in every case of racial competition; the 1980 census shows the presence of tens of thousands of Afro-Brazilians in white-collar and professional employment in São Paulo. This reflects one of the distinctive aspects of Brazilian racism: its inconsistency and unpredictability, and its willingness to admit individual Afro-Brazilians to upward mobility while resolutely blocking such mobility for the Afro-Brazilian racial group as a whole.[43] This in turn has the effect of dividing the black population into the minority who have benefited from the Brazilian model of race relations, and the majority who have not. Within each group, attitudes and responses toward that model, and toward the question of what being a *negro em ascensão* means, vary enormously.

Blacks in a White World

We might begin by examining the effects of these racial barriers on those who fail to surmount them. The frequently cited Brazilian proverb that "here we don't have a racial problem; here the blacks know their place" has more than a grain of truth to it. One of the recurrent themes which emerge in interviews of Afro-Brazilians is that of the short but eloquent expression "*não adianta*" ("it won't get you anywhere"). Hard work, study, and effort don't result in advancement because "lugar do negro é lugar do negro mesmo" (the black's place is the black's place, period), and the obstacles which one has to overcome in order to leave that place are simply insuperable. Even among those who persist in struggling against those obstacles, the knowledge of the odds against them takes its toll, and leads many to lower their sights to a more "realistic" level. Opera star Maura Moreira, who found in Europe the professional opportunities which were denied her in Brazil, explains that "you develop an inferiority complex caused by all the insults, the slights, the discrimination that you suffer ever since infancy. Many, when confronted by an overt act of racism, try to explain it away, look for excuses, erase it—but its mark stays on you, influencing even the choice of a career, and of what places to go into and stay away from."[44]

By persuading Afro-Brazilians to lower their expectations in life, and not to create "disagreeable situations" by trying to push into places where they're not wanted (i.e., places which whites wish to reserve for themselves), the Brazilian model of race relations works very effectively to reduce racial tension and competition while maintaining blacks in a subordinate social and economic position. Indeed, the obstacles are seen as so formidable that those who continue to struggle against them feel that the only way they can triumph is by turning themselves into superhumans. A successful executive reports that he overcomes racial barriers by turning his anger into disciplined energy. "I give 150 percent in everything I do. . . . I overwhelm those people [who discriminate] with my competence."[45] Black psychiatrist Neusa Santos Souza discusses middle-class Afro-Brazilians' efforts to live up to this superhuman standard, and the consequent depression, melancholy, and feelings of inadequacy and defeat when they are unable to meet it.[46] A successful journalist seconds these points.

I'm sick of being the exception. It's tiring, you're always being watched and evaluated. Your work always has to be better than the others'. And while on one hand this can be good, because it leads you to constantly be better and improve yourself, on the other it's exhausting, and wears down your resistance. You want to be treated like a normal guy, with the right to make a mistake, but they won't let you. When you do well, everyone's astonished, and when you screw up, they massacre you. There comes a point where it's just too much, you're fed up.[47]

The rewards for being a "superblack" lag considerably behind the rewards for being a normal white. Salaries and possibilities for advancement are markedly inferior, and even those black paulistas who have enjoyed some success and advancement in life then find themselves hemmed in by racial restrictions on where they can live, what clubs they can join, what restaurants they can eat in, and what schools they can send their children to. Many middle-class blacks see little point in challenging these barriers, and try instead to work around them or avoid them entirely. This was a recurrent theme in the black newspapers of the 1920s, in which acts of racial discrimination often provoked editorial injunctions to readers to avoid the factory, dance hall, restaurant, and so on, where the incidents had taken place.[48] Such attitudes are common among today's black middle class as well. An engineer claims: "I live like a white person. . . . I've felt prejudice, but I don't take it seriously any more. If I can't go into one restaurant, I go into another." Former São Paulo City councilman Mário Américo Castro offers similar comments, explaining that he feels "no pressure whatsoever" from racial discrimination, because he carefully avoids potentially difficult situations. "I choose the places I go, and I don't insist on going where I don't fit. First I try to find out what kind of place it is, and what kind of person is likely to be present. . . . I'm not going to upset a situation that, for better or worse, is good."[49]

This last statement represents the attitude of many middle-class Afro-Brazilians, who, having expended tremendous effort to achieve some measure of success in Brazilian society, do not wish to endanger that success by confronting racism head-on.[50] Such confrontations are always risky and unpleasant, and, in the opinion of many blacks, are unlikely to improve the racial climate in Brazil in any significant way. If anything they may tend to aggravate it by provoking further white antagonism to black upward mobility. As a result, much of the black middle class, like the individuals quoted above, try to avoid situations in which they are likely to encounter white racism, and thus minimize its impacts on their daily life.

For many, this is apparently a successful approach. Of the middle-class blacks who I met in São Paulo, and of those interviewed in the newspapers, magazines, and books which I read while in Brazil, a sizable minority indicated that racial prejudice and discrimination had not affected their lives in any direct way.[51] These people readily acknowledged that racism is a serious force operating in the society at large, but then went on to declare that they had escaped its effects more or less unscathed. One must take such testimony seriously. But there is more than a hint in these declarations of the denial evident in white actress Arlete Salas's descriptions of her friends' attitudes toward her marriage with black singer Tony Torrado. "Nobody said anything [about the marriage]. Or if they said something, if they thought it was bad, I confess that I didn't hear it. Or I didn't pay attention. . . . We never had problems. It's true that many times I was hurt by malicious gossip, even concerning my children, but that's all over now." Nobody said anything; and if they did, she didn't hear it; and if she heard it, she didn't pay attention; and if sometimes the comments that nobody ever made, and that she never paid attention to, did hurt her, now they don't hurt anymore, because "that's all over."[52]

This reluctance to acknowledge the full extent and hurtfulness of race prejudice is a form of denial that one encounters not infrequently among black people in Brazil. A second, and perhaps even more basic, denial is the reluctance to acknowledge one's African racial ancestry, and accept the fact of one's blackness. From the first studies of upwardly mobile Afro-Brazilians to the most recent, one of the most powerful themes that emerges is that of whitening: the desire of pretos to be accepted as pardos, and of pardos to be accepted as white.[53]

Whitening is achieved through various means: through economic success, through cultivating white friends and acquaintances, through consciously adopting the norms and behavior of white middle-class life.[54] The most effective means of whitening, and one of the most sought-after, is to marry into a lighter (ideally, white) family and produce lighter (ideally, white) offspring. While statistical rates of intermarriage are not high in Brazil, they are certainly higher than in the United States, and are a visible phenomenon at the middle-class level.[55] Economist Nelson do Valle Silva notes that such intermarriage is partly explained by the extreme paucity of eligible black partners of either sex (but particularly women) at higher social levels.[56] Still, as a successful actor married to a white wife explains, the preference of many blacks for white partners is also the result of an upbringing which even the most consciously critical Afro-Brazilians are not able to erase completely. "We blacks over the age of 30 still carry with us an upbringing in which blacks were accustomed to underestimate themselves. All the [social] structure forced this on us. The teacher was white. The carpenter, the pharmacist. . . . This stayed with us, and still lies in the thoughts of each individual: among the whites, an aversion [to blacks], and among the blacks a spirit of submission, both sentiments almost unconscious." Whiteness is the ideal in marriage as in life more generally; the result is a strong interest among many Afro-Brazilians in contracting marriage with whites.[57]

It is very difficult for Afro-Brazilians to resist the pressures and temptations to shed their racial identity. "Blackness is the symbol of misery, of hunger. . . . I think that what always makes me flee from blackness is that image of poverty: poverty in all senses, from financial to intellectual." But to deny blackness is to deny a core part of one's identity—in the words of one of Haroldo Costa's informants, to "annihilate oneself," to "nullify oneself." To cease to be black is, in a way which is difficult but perhaps not impossible for whites to imagine, to cease to exist.[58]

Such pressures are felt most acutely by those Afro-Brazilians who have made visible progress toward becoming white: the mulattoes. In a vivid image of the kind of self-mutilation, usually psychological but occasionally physical, that whitening demands, one of Neuza Santos Souza's informants recalls how her mother tried to make her wear a clothespin on her nose during childhood to overcome its flatness. She goes on to describe the tensions of living somewhere between black and white. "I didn't know my place, but I knew that I wasn't black. Blacks were dirty, and I was clean; blacks were stupid, and I was intelligent; blacks lived in the slum, and I did not; and above all, blacks had thick noses and lips, and I didn't have them. I was a mulatta, I still had hopes of being saved."[59]

The notion that mulattoes can possibly be "saved" from their blackness, and enjoy a status above that of pretos, has generated considerable jealousy and antagonism between the two groups in Brazil. Part of black folklore in that country is that, in the words of Arlindo Veiga dos Santos, the founder of the Brazilian Black Front, "the greatest enemy of blacks is the white who is the grandson of blacks." In his research among São Paulo blacks, Roger Bastide found that "all our informants concur in emphasizing that the families most fiercely opposed to the pretos are those with a few drops of African blood in their veins."[60]

Although not all pardos seek to cut themselves off from the pretos, there is a visible tendency among the pardo racial group to emphasize its social superiority over darker Afro-Brazilians.[61] Such claims in turn form part of the larger effort by the black middle class to set itself apart from poor and working-class Afro-Brazilians, an effort which took visible form in a series of episodes in the 1940s centering on black "footings" in downtown São Paulo's Rua Direita.

Beginning in the late 1930s, poor and working-class blacks began going to the Rua Direita during evenings and Sunday afternoons to talk, meet, dance, and generally socialize. Even though the shops and banks were closed at those times, merchants in the district complained bitterly about the gatherings, concerned that "the foreigner or tourist passing through our metropolis will get the idea, if he takes a short evening walk along that street with its smart show-windows, that São Paulo is an Addis Ababa or a Havana owing to the large number of colored persons who infest that street and drive away families who might stroll there after the movies to admire the latest things on display." In 1944, the police began a campaign to clear the area of blacks, closing dance halls and barring Afro-Brazilians from going there, "as if we were in the middle of Dixie, in North America," in the words of one observer. Black organizations protested, and eventually worked out an arrangement which permitted black people to gather in the Rua Direita under police supervision.[62]

For poor and working-class blacks, the Rua Direita was a kind of free territory where they could socialize, dance, and relax from the rigors of the week. Actor Milton Gonçalves, who was a teenager during this period, recalls that it was the only place in the city where black people were permitted to gather publicly; everywhere else, "we lived constantly trying to avoid bothering the whites, asking permission for everything." Similar sentiments were expressed by a black character on a popular radio show of the late 1940s, who complained that the whites "want to fool me into thinking Rua Direita is theirs! No, it isn't. . . . the street is free. . . . I'm black, I'm Brazilian, and I'll walk on Rua Direita whenever I want!"[63]

For middle-class blacks, however, Rua Direita was a source of humiliation and embarrassment. During the 1930s the Black Front had denounced the gatherings there as painful public examples of "social corruption" and "moral degradation" among the city's black population. Ten years later similar comments appeared in the black press concerning the "ill-bred black dancers who, unhappily, and to our shame, use the Rua Direita for their choreographic exhibitions." The UNESCO researchers found that "the leaders of the colored organizations view those blacks who frequent the Rua Direita as the least reputable possible, and as having made that street 'a center of perdition,' and of cheap prostitution."[64]

Seeking to escape any possible association with these "disreputable" elements, middle-class blacks in São Paulo behaved in much the same way as their white counterparts. Withdrawing from the "world of the street"—or in this case, of Direita Street—they closed themselves off within the private world of their families, or in the somewhat larger, but still private, world of the exclusive Afro-Brazilian social clubs. The very names of these clubs—the Club dos Evoluidos (the Club of the Evolved Ones), the Aristocratic Club—express their members' vision of themselves as separate from, and above, the black masses.[65] Indeed, in retrospect it is clear that Florestan Fernandes's portrait of the anomic black people of the postemancipation years owes much to the attitudes held by his middle-class informants concerning the "animalized" black *lumpen*.[66]

Not all middle-class blacks have taken this road, however. Even in the 1930s and 1940s some of the members of this tiny class were willing to invest enormous energy and effort in trying to create broad-based organizations which would combat discrimination and try to improve the position of the black population as a whole. And by the 1970s and 1980s, the substantially expanded black middle class had spawned a new generation of leadership determined to confront racial discrimination directly rather than attempt to avoid it. Harking back to their predecessors in the abolitionist movement, the Black Front, and the Afro-Brazilian organizations of the 1940s and 1950s, these young militants sought to lead their people into a new phase of the century-long struggle to convert racial democracy from a myth to a reality.

7. Organizing, 1945–1988

The Second Republic, 1946–1964

The imposition of the Vargas dictatorship in 1937 had marked the end of a period of intensive political mobilization in the black community, as in Brazil more generally. Black organizations did not completely disappear under the dictatorship; dancing societies and social clubs continued to function, and the Vargas regime actively encouraged the development of the samba schools, though now under strict state control.[1] Civic organizations continued to operate as well, one of them, the José do Patrocínio Association, successfully petitioning President Vargas to ban racially discriminatory employment ads in São Paulo newspapers.[2]

The association's appeal to the dictatorship suggests some of the opportunities that Vargas's authoritarian populism created for non-elite groups to pursue their collective goals and interests. The Vargas administration was much more responsive than its Republican predecessors to the concerns of poor and working-class Brazilians, who soon learned how to exploit the openings created by the change in regime. At the same time, however, the goal of the New State's social and labor policies was to establish as effective control as possible over the nation's poor and working classes in order to use them as an essentially passive base of political support, as well as a source of cheap, quiescent labor for the expanding industrial economy. As a result, the New State did not form a particularly favorable setting for independent, mass-based political organization, either in the black community or in the society at large.[3]

The fall of the dictatorship in October 1945 therefore set off a wave of efforts to rejuvenate the black movement of the 1930s. The National Convention of Brazilian Blacks was held in the state capital in November with the goal of formulating a platform of demands to be presented to the upcoming Constituent Assembly, which would write the new constitution for the Second Republic. São Paulo's black press, defunct since 1937, promptly reappeared with the foundation of *Alvorada* (Dawn) in September 1945, *Senzala* (The Slave Quarters) in January 1946, and *O Novo Horizonte* (The New Horizon) in May 1946. The editor of *Alvorada*, José Correia Leite (editor of *O Clarim da Alvorada* during the 1920s and 1930s), hoped to use his publication as the means to form a new civic organization, the Association of Brazilian Blacks. His work in this area came to naught, however, as did efforts to run black candidates in the congressional elections of the early 1950s.[4]

These efforts by Afro-Brazilians in São Paulo and other states to organize along racial lines and take part in the newly established democracy excited considerable antagonism among whites. Attacks on the new black organizations appeared in the paulista press in 1947 and in Rio de Janeiro during the elections of 1950.

Black theaters, black newspapers, black clubs . . . Now they're even talking about black candidates for the October elections. Can one imagine a worse movement, or one more damaging to the unimpeachable spirit of our democracy? We had better fight it, without, of course, restricting the rights that the colored men claim and that have never been denied them. Otherwise, instead of white prejudice, we will have, paradoxically, black prejudice. We'll be taken to such extremes not by racism (which doesn't exist here), but by an ill-advised spirit of imitation [presumably of black movements in the United States], the most infamous consequence of which might be the establishment of a completely abominable system: individuals would become this or that, and be assigned to this or that post, not on the basis of their personal worth but by being, or not being, black. Pigmentation would serve as one's diploma.[5]

One is struck by the internal contradictions of this document. "Can one imagine a worse movement, or one more damaging to the unimpeachable spirit of our democracy," than blacks trying to get elected to office? If the unthinkable should come to pass, and blacks *are* elected to office, then we will have the "paradox" of black racism, white racism apparently being normal and nonparadoxical—except that it doesn't exist. And finally, the author expresses his outrage at the possibility that individuals might be selected to fill offices and positions on the basis of skin color rather than their abilities and qualifications. Yet this is essentially how job selection, especially for lucrative and influential positions, has historically tended to operate in Brazil: such jobs are automatically and unthinkingly reserved for whites; blacks need not apply.

What was bothering the critics of the black organizations was not that skin color might become a determining factor in the competition for upward mobility; this would have been nothing new in Brazilian society, and whites had learned to live with it quite comfortably. Rather, as the passage cited above makes clear, their fear was that a preference for whiteness might be replaced by a preference for blackness. Given the realities of life in Brazil, both past and present, this was, and is, an extremely remote possibility indeed. Nevertheless, the merest hint of such a development is enough to mobilize a sizable segment of the white population who then attempt to seize the moral high ground through pious denunciations of "reverse racism" among blacks.[6]

Such accusations reveal the deep uneasiness which black political mobilization provokes among the white population. This uneasiness stems from two sources. The first is that black mobilization forcibly reminds Brazilians that their country is not the racial democracy which it claims to be; if it were, Afro-Brazilians would have no specifically racial grievances to redress, and there would be no grounds for a black movement. But in fact much of the discourse of the black movement focuses on a graphic portrayal of the hurts and injuries which Afro-Brazilians have sustained over the centuries at the hands of their fellow countrymen. White people do not like to be confronted with this racial past, both because of the guilt that its memory might inspire, and because they fear the resentment and desire for vengeance which black people might reasonably be expected to harbor after generations of such treatment.

This in turn suggests the second source of white disquiet. Middle- and upper-class white people in Brazil are only too well aware that they sit atop a very tense society, one in which the majority of the population suffers the daily afflictions of poverty and race. These tensions are perhaps not so great as those of a slave society, because the inequalities which cause them are not so extreme as those of slavery. Nevertheless, as during the days of slavery, whites share the collective nightmare of what might happen if poor people or blacks ever get into a position of power from which they can avenge those hurts. Some argue that there is little likelihood of this ever happening, and that "even if among the blacks there is resentment and even hostility against whites, these feelings do not constitute forces sufficiently explosive to perturb the life of the state [of São Paulo]." Others, however, see more potential for violent confrontation, and decry those black militants and white academics who, by attacking the concept of racial democracy, "sow seeds capable, in the short term or the long, of confronting Brazil, which is already so tormented by such difficult social problems, with an even more explosive such problem, one which our people instinctively, and to their credit, marginalized."[7]

The principal effort to defuse such racial antagonism during the Second Republic was the Afonso Arinos Law of 1951, which outlawed racial discrimination in public services, education, and employment. Varying accounts of its genesis form a nice example of the longstanding tension in Brazilian race relations between myth and reality. Its author, Congressman Afonso Arinos de Melo Franco of Minas Gerais, has claimed that he introduced the bill in response to acts of discrimination which his black chauffeur had suffered at the hands of Spanish and other immigrants in Rio de Janeiro. "The agents of [racial] injustice are almost always *gringos* who are ignorant of our traditions and insensitive to our old customs of racial fraternity."[8] In fact, the role of foreigners in the origins of the bill was precisely the reverse. Franco introduced the bill to Congress following a widely publicized episode in which Afro-American dancer Katherine Dunham was refused admission to the Hotel Esplanada in São Paulo, and protested loudly and publicly about the incident—something that most Afro-Brazilians, "sensitive to our old customs of racial fraternity," would never do. In its graphic refutation of the myth of racial democracy, the incident was deeply embarrassing to the Brazilian elite, and moved Congress to pass the nation's first antidiscrimination law.[9]

The congressmen were moved by more than just embarrassment, however. In the congressional committee report endorsing the bill,

Congressman Plínio Barreto of São Paulo (a member of Franco's party, the conservative Democratic National Union) reminded his fellow legislators that events like the Dunham incident were distressingly common in Brazil, and could serve only to aggravate and bring into the open racial tensions which everyone wished to avoid. The bill should be passed, he argued,

as a means to transform the racist mentality one sees among us, principally in the upper social and political levels of the country, with grave and inevitable consequences for future social peace. . . . It is well known that certain civil careers, such as the diplomatic service, are closed to blacks; that the Navy and the Air Force create unjustifiable difficulties for blacks seeking to enter the officer corps; and that other restrictions exist in various sections of the [public] administration. . . . When the State, through its agents, offers such an example of hateful discrimination, which is banned by the Constitution, we should not be surprised when commercial establishments prevent blacks from entering their doors. . . . I urge you to put a stop to this state of affairs, the worsening of which will contribute to the establishment among us of a genuine battle between the races. . . .

Barreto went on to say that if such discrimination were not effectively outlawed, Brazil would go the way of the United States, with its "terrible problem" of racial antagonism—and, though he did not state this explicitly, its visible and assertive black movement.[10]

The Afonso Arinos Law proved singularly ineffective in reducing acts of discrimination in Brazil, as its author acknowledged in a 1980 interview. Despite the fact that numerous complaints had been made to the police under the law, Franco did not know of a single instance of conviction. "I would like it very much, and I really hope that someday there may be a judgment under the law, that a bar or restaurant [which had discriminated] might be closed, that a public official who had committed this crime might be fired. But nothing ever went that far."[11] In an effort to overcome the deficiencies of the law, during the 1980s black congressmen from São Paulo and Rio de Janeiro introduced a series of bills seeking to strengthen and extend its provisions. One was finally passed in 1988, when Carlos Alberto Oliveira and Benedita da Silva (both elected to Congress in 1986 from Rio de Janeiro) succeeded in getting a strengthened and broadened version of the Afonso Arinos Law, with greatly increased penalties for acts of discrimination, incorporated into the new Constitution.

Franco himself was still in Congress at this point, and vehemently opposed this effort to strengthen the law, for the same reasons which had motivated him some forty years before: fear of racial conflict. "I don't think it is good, it's inappropriate and inopportune. It might produce a situation of antagonism between blacks and whites."[12]

Black leaders in São Paulo, and in Brazil more generally, have historically been quite sensitive to these white fears of racial conflict, and have tried to avoid forms of political mobilization and action which whites might perceive as threatening.[13] During the 1880s pardo abolitionist André Rebouças promised slaveowners that he and his fellow abolitionists would scrupulously refrain from agitating and organizing among the slave population, since "addressing oneself to the victims [of slavery] provokes hatred and [the desire for] vengeance." Fifty years later the Brazilian Black Front informed the paulista public, through articles published in the mainstream press, that its members "have no desire to provoke racial conflict, but rather only wish to constitute a force capable of claiming a more honorable role within national life." In 1946 and 1947, the organizers of the abortive Association of Brazilian Blacks soon recognized that their denunciations of racism were winning them few friends in the white world; they therefore played down such protests, and reoriented their activities to focus on education, mutual aid, and self-help projects.[14]

Nevertheless, fears of black militance persisted, even during a period like the 1950s, when such militance remained very limited in scope and made virtually no impact on the Brazilian political system. The weakness of black movements at this time was partly the result of the bitter experience of the Black Front, which dissuaded many Afro-Brazilians from trying to mobilize the black population along racial lines. Perhaps even more important, however, was the orientation of the political institutions of the Second Republic, in particular the labor unions and the labor-based populist parties.

As Afro-Brazilians entered industrial employment, they automatically became part of the state-regulated labor movement created in the 1930s under Getúlio Vargas and maintained in place during the Second Republic. Although no figures are available on union membership by race, the frequent mention of union activities in the black press and the regularity with which black social and cultural organizations used union halls and facilities for their activities suggest that black workers, and even black organizations, received an unexpectedly (in light of Afro-Brazilians' previous experience with official Brazilian institutions) warm welcome in the union movement. This suggestion is further confirmed by the fact that by the mid-1950s individual Afro-Brazilians were starting to show up in positions of union leadership, a trend which became pronounced in the 1960s and 1970s.[15]

These unions formed the electoral base of support for the populist and left-wing political parties of the Second Republic: Getúlio Vargas's Brazilian Labor Party, the Brazilian Communist Party, and the Social Progressive Party, founded by São Paulo governor Adhemar de Barros. These parties competed vigorously for the working-class vote and were eager to bring black workers into the political system under their banners.[16] Afro-Brazilians did not emerge as a significant part of the leadership in any of them; but the willingness of both the unions and the labor-based parties to distribute significant material benefits to the rank and file in an essentially color-blind manner represented something quite new in Brazilian politics. Equally new, and equally appealing, was the populist parties' message that the day had finally come for workers and the poor to play a significant role in national politics, something which no previous party or regime had ever been willing to acknowledge. That role was to be played on terms defined and enforced by the union and party hierarchies, who ran their organizations in traditionally paternalistic, top-down fashion. But participation on such terms was clearly preferable to the complete lack of participation which had characterized the First Republic and the New State, and most black and white workers supported the populist parties in return for the benefits, both material and psychological, which those parties, particularly the Brazilian Labor Party, were able to provide.

Thus, a paradoxical but potent combination of, at the elite and middle-class levels, white hostility toward black political movements and, at the level of the working class and the poor, white receptiveness to black desires for inclusion in the political life of the Republic, effectively undercut the potential base of support for a racially defined, Afro-Brazilian political movement. When the populist parties offered black voters a place in the institutions of the Republic, most Afro-Brazilians turned their backs on the idea of racial mobilization, and instead threw their support either to Adhemar de Barros's Social Progressive Party or to "the Father of the Poor," Getúlio Vargas, and his Brazilian Labor Party.[17]

The Second Republic therefore proved to be a period during which São Paulo's black organizations avoided direct participation in politics and instead focused their energies on social and cultural activities and educational outreach. This orientation is apparent in the name of the most successful of these organizations, the Black Cultural Association, founded in 1954, which sponsored lectures, concerts, night courses, a youth division, and took a leading role in coordinating the city's commemorations of the seventieth anniversary of emancipation in 1958. Many of its activities were carried out in conjunction with two theater groups which also played a prominent part in black community life in São Paulo during this period: the Black Experimental Theater, and the Brazilian People's Theater. Originally based in the center of the city, the association moved to the outlying neighborhood of Casa Verde in 1969, where it functioned until its demise in the late 1970s.[18]

While all these groups invoked the principles of racial equality and the assumption by black people of their rightful place in Brazilian society, they proposed to achieve those goals through the slow, patient work of education (of both blacks and whites), and the reclaiming of an Afro-Brazilian cultural heritage which had been ignored and rejected by a society bent on whitening. None of them proposed an explicitly political program or organized political action, a tendency which was reinforced by the military coup of 1964 and the destruction of the Second Republic.

Military Rule, 1964–1985

Over the course of the 1950s and early 1960s the unions and the Brazilian Labor Party used their base of worker support to become an ever more potent presence in Brazilian politics. Their rise to power, which culminated in the assumption of the presidency in 1961 by João Goulart, former minister of labor under Vargas, provoked stiffening opposition among the elites and a substantial proportion of the middle class. Both groups felt directly threatened by the proposals and demands of the left-wing populists, who they held responsible for the runaway inflation and intensifying strike activity of the early 1960s. The heightening sense of economic crisis, and of polarization between left- and right-wing forces, further eroded the upper and middle classes' already tenuous commitment to the constitutional norms of the Republic, which had given so much power to the *povo* and its leaders. When the armed forces overthrew Goulart in March 1964, most upper- and middle-class Brazilians breathed a collective sigh of relief and pledged their support to the restructuring of Brazilian politics and society which the military now proposed: the replacement of the "irresponsible, corrupt" democracy of the Second Republic with a new authoritarian order controlled from above and immune to populist excesses.[19]

This orientation proved as inimical to mass-based political activities as had Getúlio Vargas's New State. During the first years of the dictatorship the military abolished the parties of the Second Republic, purged all political institutions, the military, and the labor movement of reported leftists, and arrested and imprisoned thousands of alleged "subversives," many of whom were tortured.[20] These policies of official repression were justified as part of the government's effort to save democracy by cleansing it of populist abuses (the first round of arrests and torture in 1964 took place under the code name Operation Clean-up) and restoring it to proper working order. By 1974 the military judged this cleansing process to be sufficiently advanced to permit the beginning of a second phase of military rule, a period of relaxation, "decompression" *(distensão)*, and political "opening" *(abertura)*, which would lead to a gradual transition back to civilian democracy.

Despite the officers' best efforts to control the timing and character of that transition, opposition forces succeeded in exploiting the "openings" created by *abertura* in surprising and unforeseen ways.[21] This was particularly the case in São Paulo, where opposition emerged from a variety of sources. Under the protection and leadership of Archbishop Dom Paulo Evaristo Arns, the progressive wing of the Catholic church organized poor people and workers into "Christian base communities" which, working in conjunction with other neighborhood and community organizations, proved unexpectedly effective in bringing political pressure to bear on local and state government for improvements in services, infrastructure and schools. In the area of labor relations, a militant "new union" movement appeared in the industrial belts around the state capital, launching a wave of successful wildcat strikes, which spread throughout south-central Brazil in 1978. In 1979 that movement formed the basis for the creation of the new Workers' Party, which by 1988 had won the mayoralty of São Paulo, the largest city in Brazil, and in 1989 came close to winning the presidency.[22] The rise of the Workers' Party was in turn part of a larger process by which the opposition parties successfully mobilized to overcome right-wing rule. Despite efforts by the military to define and control electoral procedures in such a way as virtually to guarantee government victories, the opposition parties swamped the government Democratic Social Party in the congressional and state elections of 1974 and 1982. The military's presidential candidate, Paulo Maluf (Democratic Social Party governor of São Paulo from 1979 to 1983) was then overwhelmingly defeated in the election of 1985, during which the government party splintered and collapsed as an effective political force.

The unexpected strength and resilience of the civilian opposition to military rule was a direct consequence of economic and other policies followed by the military regime. The period of military rule witnessed an unprecedented wave of economic growth between 1968 and 1974, the so-called Brazilian miracle, in which the gross national product grew by an annual rate of over 10 percent per year. Such growth was particularly pronounced in São Paulo State, where industrial and white-collar employment both grew apace, and the working and middle classes increased in size accordingly. However, these two classes enjoyed quite different levels of benefits from the "miracle." While many individual workers improved their standard of living by moving from low-wage agricultural or service labor into the industrial sector, industrial wages and workers' wages throughout the economy lagged further and further behind the rate of inflation. By the late 1970s the real value of the minimum wage set by the government was only two-thirds of what it had been at the beginning of the military regime in 1964, and only half of what it had been at its high point in 1957.[23]

White-collar workers and professionals fared much better during the miracle years. Even after the oil price increase of 1973 doubled inflation from an annual rate of 20 percent to 40 percent, economic growth continued to be strong, and the middle class continued to enjoy the benefits of such growth. Or at least *most* of the middle class. For, as we have seen from the previous chapter's analysis of wage and job data collected by the government during the late 1970s and early 1980s, Afro-Brazilian white-collar and professional workers did not profit from the miracle to nearly the same degree as their white counterparts. While black industrial, construction, service, and farm workers found themselves in much the same boat as their white peers, black professionals and office workers saw a substantial gulf separating them from their white counterparts, one which seemed only to widen as black job seekers improved their educational and job qualifications.

By the mid-1970s a growing number of black aspirants to middle-class status had become increasingly conscious of, and exasperated by, the racial barriers which were preventing them from receiving their fair share of the benefits of rapid economic growth. It was at this point that a new wave of black political mobilization began, as, in a movement which formed part of the broader process of *abertura*, these *negros em ascensão* began to debate and discuss among themselves the dilemmas posed by their position in a society which was neither a political democracy nor, they had come to conclude, a racial democracy.[24]

The New Black Movement and the Return to Democracy, 1978-1988

The first organized expressions of this black middle-class discontent took a form similar to those of the 1950s. In the state capital, a group of black artists and intellectuals formed the Center for Black Culture and Art in the downtown neighborhood of Bixiga in 1969. In 1972 another, unrelated group formed the Working Group of Black Professionals and University Graduates, which offered courses and lectures on Afro-Brazilian history and culture, as well as training for would-be black office boys, cashiers, draftsmen, and other Afro-Brazilians trying to break into low-level white-collar or commercial positions.[25] New black theater groups were founded in Campinas and São Paulo in 1974, and Black Art and Culture Week was held in the capital in 1975. The Center for Black Culture and Art was involved in all these activities, and in 1978 published the first in a series of annual collections of poetry by black authors, the *Cadernos Negros* (Black Notebooks), which continue to the present. In November 1978 the first Festival Comunitário Negro Zumbi (Zumbi Black Community Festival) was held in the city of Araraquara, in western São Paulo State, with concerts, plays, and other activities. Meanwhile, at the University of São Paulo, sociologist Eduardo de Oliveira e Oliveira, one of the founders of the Center for Black Culture and Art, had organized Black Fortnight during May 1977, which included lectures, public seminars, art exhibits, films, and a display at the São Paulo Municipal Library of black newspapers from the 1920s and 1930s.[26]

Over time these activities brought together a cohort of younger Afro-Brazilians who tended to be better educated than most black (or white) Brazilians, politically conscious, and deeply troubled about their status as black people in a racially stratified society. In addition to their interest in Afro-Brazilian history and culture, many of them were intrigued by what they saw as a surge in the "international black movement" worldwide: in particular, the independence movements in Portuguese Africa, and the civil rights and Black Power movements of the United States. These movements faced opponents which Afro-Brazilians saw as quite similar to those which they themselves confronted in Brazil: in the case of Africa, the modern legacy of Portuguese colonialism enforced by a right-wing authoritarian dictatorship; and in the case of the United States, a social order which had abolished plantation slavery but had left racial hierarchy very much intact. As both movements seemed to reach peaks of power and influence in the 1970s, with the independence of the Portuguese colonies and the enactment and implementation of equal opportunity and affirmative action legislation in the United States, young Afro-Brazilians began to wonder whether it might be possible to imitate their achievements in Brazil.[27]

By 1978 a number of factors were in place to motivate black political mobilization: a rising sense of frustration among middle-class blacks over the racial barriers which continued to bar their upward progress; a growing sense as well that an exclusively "cultural" approach was unlikely to produce immediate improvements in their situation; the concrete examples of black movements abroad which had experienced considerable success in achieving their objectives; and the mobilization and organization taking place in Brazilian society at large as a result of *abertura*. Capitalizing on the energy generated by the ninetieth anniversary of emancipation—May 13, 1978—some of these middle-class militants seized the moment and moved to create a new, 1970s version of the Brazilian Black Front. The immediate catalysts for their doing so were two events richly emblematic of the state of race relations in São Paulo. First, on April 28 a young black worker, Robson Silveira da Luz, died in police custody, apparently of torture, after having been held without charges for several days. The second event, two weeks later, was the summary ejection of four black youths from the Tietê Boating Club, where they were playing as part of a volleyball team.[28]

Neither of these occurrences was at all unique.[29] However, they received an unusual degree of public attention because of their coincidence with the ninetieth anniversary of emancipation, and their blatant denial of May 13's promise of racial equality and democracy. Activists who had participated in the black cultural organizations met on June 18 at the Center for Black Culture and Art to discuss a possible response. At that meeting they resolved to form the Unified Black Movement to Combat Racial Discrimination (later shortened to the Unified Black Movement, the MNU). A public meeting on the steps of the Municipal Theater, near the Rua Direita, on July 7 attracted several thousand supporters, and subsequent meetings in Rio de Janeiro, Minas Gerais, Bahia, and elsewhere spread the organization to black communities throughout Brazil.[30]

In its explicitly political orientation, the MNU marked a clear departure from the cultural organizations of the 1950s and 1970s. Organized around a cell structure (known as *centros de luta*, or "struggle centers"), the MNU sought to raise the consciousness of *(concientizar)* the black population concerning racial discrimination and inequality in Brazilian society, and to organize its members to struggle against such discrimination. Taking advantage of the opportunities presented by *abertura*, MNU activists hoped to put pressure on the Brazilian government, on the parties, and on other important organized interests in Brazilian life (academia, the bar, the Church) to combat racism within their own institutions and in the society at large, and to adopt policies which would lead to the expansion of economic, educational, health, and other opportunities for the black population as a whole.

Beyond these immediate goals of combatting racism and racial hierarchy, the MNU saw itself as pursuing a larger goal as well, that being the eradication of capitalism from Brazil. Its platform analyzed racism as an inevitable consequence of capitalist development, and argued that the only way to create genuine racial democracy in Brazil was to replace capitalism with socialism.[31] This orientation alienated many potential supporters from the outset, and a growing proportion of its membership as time went on.[32] However, even Afro-Brazilians who did not share the MNU's ideological posture responded favorably to its call to reach out to the black population at large, and to get its members involved in combatting racism.

This was a message that had caught the attention of the political parties as well. From 1965 to 1979 the military government had permitted only two parties to function in Brazil: the government party, the National Renovating Alliance, and the opposition party, the Brazilian Democratic Movement. In an effort to divide and weaken its opponents, in 1979 the government abandoned the two-party system and freed the opposition to dissolve into multiple competing parties. While the government party (now renamed the Democratic Social Party) remained intact, the opposition split into five new parties: the Party of the Brazilian Democratic Movement (PMDB); the Popular Party, which eventually merged with the Party of the Brazilian Democratic Movement; the Brazilian Labor Party; the Democratic Labor Party; and the Workers' Party.

Just at the moment that the black movement was showing unaccustomed signs of political assertiveness, during 1979 and 1980, each of the opposition parties was competing fiercely against the others for electoral support. Seeing a potential source of such support in this new black movement, all the opposition parties suddenly developed a newfound interest in the problem of racial discrimination and inequality. They all inserted antiracism planks in their platforms, and several created special commissions or working groups to examine the state of race relations in Brazil and formulate appropriate policy responses. The parties invited black activists to join their ranks, and, in São Paulo, nominated an unprecedented number of Afro-Brazilian candidates for federal, state, and municipal offices in the elections of

1982. Only the government party failed to insert antiracism language in its platform, in part because it didn't want to, and in part because it felt that it didn't need to, having persuaded all four of the state's most visible black officeholders to desert the opposition and join the ranks of the government.[33]

The elections of 1982 thus represented a test case for black political activism in São Paulo. As it turned out, the activists failed the test. In São Paulo as in the other large states of south-central Brazil, the elections were a resounding victory for the opposition parties. But of fifty-four Afro-Brazilian candidates who ran in São Paulo on major party tickets, only two—state assemblyman Benedito Cintra, and São Paulo City councilman José Maria Rodrigues Alves, both of the PMDB—won election. Even Adalberto Camargo, who had served as São Paulo's sole black congressman since 1966 and had formed a small political machine based largely on the black vote, went down to defeat.

As we shall see shortly, despite the failure of black candidates at the polls, the elections of 1982 and 1986 produced definite gains for the black movement in São Paulo politics. These gains were much smaller and more incremental than expected, however, and the rejection of black candidates by the electorate, both black and white, was a severe blow to the hopes of the black activists. The 1980s, therefore, formed a period of reflection for the black movement, and of efforts to analyze why it had failed in the electoral arena. Inevitably these reflections led to discussions of how an antiracism movement could most effectively be structured and led.

One of the first issues to be dealt with was the relationship of a black movement to the "white" political parties and political system. Some activists insisted on the need for a separate, autonomous black movement which, by pressuring and lobbying the parties from an independent, external position, could avoid being co-opted and corrupted by them. Such independence would also enable the black movement to escape the political divisions which had proved so ruinous to black movements in the past, and permit the movement to maintain some degree of internal unity.[34]

Other activists responded that the idea of an independent black movement above the party fray was attractive in principle, but unlikely to work in practice. As one or more parties proved more receptive to black lobbying and pressure, closer relationships would inevitably develop with those parties. Indeed, to the degree that the parties actually responded, in concrete ways, to black demands, a closer relationship of this type would be a positive development. For these militants, the question was which party or parties were most likely to serve black interests.

Few saw much benefit to be gained by an alliance with the Right, which historically had had little sympathy for popular causes in general, and tended to deny the existence of racial discrimination in Brazil. Many of the younger militants grouped in the MNU argued that the Left was a more logical candidate for black support. Others, however, were discomfited by the Left's tendency to dismiss racism as an "epiphenomenon" which would be resolved through socialism, and which in the meantime distracted activists from the "real" issues of capitalism and class inequality. These analysts saw the right- and left-wing parties as sharing in a "supra-ideological national pact" which argued that, as Brazil experienced ever greater economic and industrial development, the remnants of racial inequality and prejudice left over from the period of slavery would gradually disappear on their own.[35]

For these critics, the most likely political ally for the black movement was to be found in *trabalhismo*, the labor-based populism which Getúlio Vargas had bequeathed to Brazil as his political legacy. Black people were longstanding supporters of *trabalhismo*, the movement had a record of tangible achievement on behalf of all workers, both black and white, and it refused to be fettered by the political orthodoxies of either right-wing conservatism or left-wing radicalism. If anything, *trabalhismo* represented a flat-out rejection of the "national pact" in much the same way that the black movement itself did.[36] Such arguments seemed to be borne out by the close and successful association between black organizations and the Democratic Labor Party, based in Rio de Janeiro and headed by Leonel Brizola. Brizola, former governor of Rio Grande do Sul and a fiery populist congressman during the last years of the Second Republic, won the governorship of Rio de Janeiro in 1982 on a platform of *"socialismo moreno"* (literally, "brown socialism"). His party sent two black congressmen to Brasília—singer Timoteo Aguinaldo and writer Abdias do Nascimento—as well as Brazil's first Indian congressman,

Mário Juruna. Brizola also appointed Afro-Brazilians to direct three of the state's secretariats—Social Affairs, Labor and Housing, and the all-important Military Police—and launched a number of policy initiatives aimed at benefiting the poor and working-class population of Rio de Janeiro in general, and the black population specifically.[37]

However, any alliance between the black movement and political parties would ultimately depend on the ability of the movement to mobilize significant electoral support. While the black vote had turned out strongly for Brizola and the Democratic Labor Party in Rio de Janeiro, it had failed to play the same sort of role in São Paulo. As one paulista black activist put it, "A lot of people were bluffing: they said they had X number of votes, and then when the election came, it turned out that they didn't have any."[38] A survey of 540 black voters taken after the election suggests some of the reasons why. Of those polled, fewer than a quarter had voted for black candidates. However, those proportions varied substantially by class background. Among upper-middle-class blacks, 43 percent voted for black candidates; among white-collar office workers, 27 percent voted for black candidates; and among manual laborers (who formed the majority of voters polled), only 19 percent voted for black candidates.[39]

Black candidates seem to have appealed much more strongly to upwardly mobile blacks than to poor and working-class blacks. In part this may be a function of the difficulties which the candidates experienced in reaching the latter. In another survey of black voters taken prior to the elections, over 90 percent of low-income respondents were unable to name a single black candidate, or indeed *any* black political figure, either historical or contemporary.[40] Clearly neither the black movement nor the party organizations responsible for turning out the black vote had succeeded in making contact with these individuals. At the same time, however, these surveys also suggest that, even in cases in which movement or party activists did make contact with members of the black population, the results were not always positive. First, the surveys indicated a deep underlying skepticism concerning the likelihood of political solutions to the problem of racism. While three-quarters of respondents (and over 90 percent of well-educated, high-income respondents) said that racial prejudice existed in Brazil, when asked how that prejudice might best be combatted, *none* of the low-income voters, and only 10 percent of middle-income voters, proposed political action as the most likely solution. Furthermore, among those who had heard of the black movement and its programs (71 percent of informants), the majority expressed no opinion of it; among those who had an opinion, negative judgments outnumbered positive by a factor of almost two to one, and were most pronounced among high-income blacks, the group most familiar with the movement and its work.[41]

Clearly the black movement of the 1980s received only limited support from the population it tried to mobilize. While it found its strongest backing among upwardly mobile, better-educated blacks, it is among this group that it also encountered its most vehement critics, confirming findings by earlier researchers who describe the reluctance of middle-class blacks to engage in confrontational, organized movements which, by offending whites and "rocking the boat," could jeopardize the gains they have already made. Nor has the predominantly middle-class black movement been notably successful in generating interest and support among lower-class Afro-Brazilians. This is so for a number of reasons, not least of which are the obstacles standing in the way of any effort, racially based or not, to mobilize poor and working-class Brazilians.[42] Even when middle-class activists and poor blacks do make contact, they often end up talking past each other, and finding that they have little in common beyond the color of their skin. To unemployed blacks and those living on the fringes of the urban economy, racial discrimination seems the least of their worries. The differences between these people and the poverty-stricken whites and near-whites who live among them are negligible in comparison to those which divide middle-class blacks from their white counterparts. Food, housing, drinkable water, sewers, personal safety, a job—any of these immediate, concrete concerns ranks higher on poor blacks' list of priorities than the more elusive, abstract goal of racial equality.[43]

Nevertheless, while overt racism is perhaps less salient in the lives of poor and working-class blacks, most are conscious of its existence.[44] One of the components of the racial democracy myth is the proposition that, insofar as prejudice exists, it is confined to the elite classes, and is nonexistent among workers and the poor.[45] Recent research, however, has made clear the degree to which racial stereotypes and negative attitudes toward blacks are diffused among all

Brazilian social classes, including that majority of the population on the bottom.[46] Samuel Lowrie's research on race mixture in São Paulo during the early decades of the century led him to conclude that, even among the poorest levels of the population, such mixture, whether conducted within wedlock or outside it, was "for the most part, limited." Nelson do Valle Silva's later research on interracial marriage confirmed those findings, concluding that the tendency toward racial endogamy was strong among all social classes in Brazil, and strongest of all among the urban working class.[47] Black workers complain about the racial jokes and teasing directed at them by their colleagues, jokes which they are expected to laugh at and take in good part, but which many of them find wounding and offensive.[48] In their most extreme form, racist attitudes among white workers sometimes crystallize in the barring of black employees from dances, picnics, or other social activities organized by workers at a firm.[49]

Interpersonal and institutional racism are real problems for poor and working-class Afro-Brazilians. But their lives are afflicted by so many additional problems, and Brazilian racial ideology offers them such strong incentives to ignore a problem which rarely takes overt, physical form, that relatively few of them respond to the black activists' call for a movement to combat racism. As a result, in both 1982 and 1986, middle-class black candidates throughout Brazil consistently went down to defeat. Those few Afro-Brazilians who managed to win election tended to be people of working-class origin who gave class-based issues primacy over questions of race. "They presented themselves as *negros assumidos* [blacks who accept their racial identity rather than attempt to present themselves as white] who, precisely because of their racial identity, could better represent the interests of the population as a whole." This was clearly the case in São Paulo, where both of the black candidates elected to office enjoyed broad popularity among working-class and poor voters. City councilman José Maria Rodrigues Alves was widely known and respected as Zé Maria, a star player for the Corinthians soccer club; state assemblyman Benedito Cintra ran an intensive campaign in the factories and neighborhoods of the *periferia*, the lower-class bedroom communities surrounding the capital, and, in addition to his backing from the PMDB, won the support of the Communist Party for his stands on working-class issues.[50]

The conclusion to be drawn from the elections of the 1980s, as well as from those of the 1930s and 1950s, is that candidates who base their campaigns on racial issues stand virtually no chance of being elected. Such issues are of primary concern to a segment of the black middle class which possesses neither great voting power nor the ability to mobilize the votes of others. On the other hand, black candidates who can integrate racial issues into a platform responding to the social and economic concerns of poor and working-class whites *and* blacks stand a reasonable chance of being elected.

The most promising future for the antiracism movement in Brazil, therefore, would seem to lie in forming alliances with broader-based "popular" movements committed to combatting social and economic inequities in Brazilian society. The question, of course, is, are such movements interested in adding the issue of race to their other political concerns? During the *abertura* years, and the first years of the Third Republic, the answer has tended to be yes. The depth of those movements' commitment to combatting racism will become clear only with time. But the initial indications, particularly in light of Brazil's previous historical experience in the area of race, have been encouraging.

Much of the willingness of such mainstream institutions as the political parties, the Church, labor unions, and others to make common cause with the black movement is attributable to the short-term political goals and needs of those institutions (e.g., the parties' need for electoral support, or the Church's desire to make contact with, and have something to offer to, a substantial proportion of the poor population). At the same time, however, I believe that this new openness to the black movement is also a function of those institutions' recognition—or, more precisely, the recognition by selected individuals within them—of the integral relationship between racial inequality and the other multiple forms of social and economic inequality which pose such deep and fundamental obstacles to the construction of democracy in Brazil.[51]

Social and economic inequality impedes the creation of democracy in a number of ways, some obvious and some not so obvious. First, the poverty and minimal education of the mass of the Brazilian population make it difficult for them to take part in politics, and also make them extremely vulnerable to pressure and suasion from the elite groups who monopolize power and wealth. Despite these obstacles, over the course of the 1900s working-class and poor Brazilians have assumed an increasingly important and active role in national politics. Their very success in doing so, however, tends to trigger the second way in which social inequality impedes democracy: the determination which it engenders in elite classes to defend their privileged position against popular demands for social reform and a redistribution of wealth and power. As the populist Left became a more powerful political force in the Second Republic, elite groups, and much of the middle class as well, came to see one-person, one-vote democracy as a system which gave too much power to the *povo,* and enabled them to make "excessive" demands for increased wages and social benefits. This vision of democracy as a direct threat to elite and middle-class interests made possible the military coup of 1964, and the subsequent creation of the dictatorship.

On a deeper, ideological level, social and economic inequality also obstructs democracy in a third way, through the belief, invoked and cultivated by the elite for centuries, and now widespread among Brazilians of all social classes, that the *povo,* the masses, are basically incapable of running either their own immediate affairs or those of national politics. Ignorant, irresponsible, and childlike, the great mass of the Brazilian population is simply unable to exercise the maturity, care, and judgment required of citizens in a democratic polity. Such arguments, which are the direct lineal descendants of the colonial-period and nineteenth-century *ideologia da vadiagem,* can be used to justify the exclusion of the *povo* from the political process (most effectively, for example, by denying suffrage to illiterates), as well as the suspension of democratic institutions for extended periods (e.g., 1964–1985).

While these antidemocratic tendencies in Brazilian life often express themselves in terms of class inequality, they have a powerful racial component as well. Explanations of why the Brazilian *povo* are unsuited for political participation are often cast in racial terms; and the racial differentials documented in the censuses of 1940, 1950, and 1980 are just as striking as the class differentials. The black movements of the 1930s, 1940s, and 1950s had long pointed to the racial dimension of Brazilian inequality, and had argued that democracy could not truly be said to exist in Brazil until black people participated in national economic, political, and social life on equal terms with whites. With the UNESCO-sponsored studies of the 1950s such arguments began to be validated by white academics, some of whom, such as Florestan Fernandes, explicitly argued that understanding the nature of race relations in his country was fundamental to understanding, and determining, "the very destiny of democracy in Brazil."[52] Such arguments were further reinforced by the work of the young social scientists produced by the university "boom" of the 1970s, a number of whom took up the question of race as part of a broader critique of inequality in Brazilian society. The resulting alliance between social scientists (almost all of them white) and black activists was vividly symbolized, and further solidified, by the lobbying effort of the late 1970s to restore race as a category of information in the national census. The effort was coordinated by two organizations created in the mid-1970s: the Institute for Research on Black Cultures, based in Rio de Janeiro, and the National Association of Post-Graduate Education and Research in the Social Sciences.[53] The success of this campaign to get information on race back into the census in turn generated additional data which have made clear the degree of racial inequality in the country.

By the 1980s, therefore, a substantial number of individuals and organizations engaged in the struggle to push forward and widen the process of *abertura* had recognized the intimate and direct connection between political democracy and racial democracy, and the fact that in a highly unequal, racially stratified society like Brazil's, neither is likely to exist without the other. This recognition formed an integral part, for example, of the community-organizing and consciousness-raising work of the progressive wing of the Catholic church. This was a most unexpected development, given that ever since the days of slavery the church had been one of the firmest bulwarks of the traditional social order, and of racial privilege in particular. In its almost 500-year history, and despite the fact that it currently contains more Catholic bishoprics than any other nation in the world, the Brazilian church has had only two black bishops: Dom Silvério Pimenta (1840–1922), of Minas Gerais, and Dom José Maria Pires, current archbishop of the northeastern city of João Pessoa. As late as 1954 the statutes of the Franciscan order in Brazil specifically barred

blacks from entering the order; and even today, of some 12,700
Catholic priests in Brazil, only an estimated 200 are black.[54]

Nevertheless, as part of its work in opposing human rights abuses,
organizing poor people into Christian base communities, and pressing for a return to democracy, the "liberation" wing of the church
found itself being drawn closer to the black movement. Its work in
poor communities was almost invariably among populations that
were heavily nonwhite; and young blacks entering the priesthood
during the 1970s pushed hard for a redefinition of the church's traditional bland assurances concerning racial harmony and democracy in
Brazil. In 1978 the National Conference of Catholic Bishops (CNBB)
convened a series of meetings of black clergy which, two years later in
São Paulo, resulted in the creation of the Black Union and Consciousness Group, an organization of black religious and lay people
who saw themselves as simultaneously part of the black movement
and of the Catholic church. The bishops moved to create a special
ministry for black people, the Pastoral do Negro, and in 1986, overcoming considerable resistance from its more conservative members,
the CNBB decided to commemorate the centennial of abolition two
years later by making race relations the theme of its annual Brotherhood Campaign, an intensive, nationwide fundraising and educational campaign carried out during Lent. As part of that campaign
the bishops approved the publication of a *texto base* (a short booklet
aimed at a mass audience) which acknowledged past church com-
plicity in slavery and racial discrimination, and called for systematic
efforts to eliminate racial injustice in Brazil.[55]

The progressive priests' and bishops' willingness to embrace the
black cause was tremendously significant, both because of the church's
enormous visibility and prestige (which if anything had been en-
hanced during the period of military rule) and because of the access
which its network of base communities could provide to poor and
working-class Afro-Brazilians.[56] The relationship between the black
movement and the church, however, is by no means an easy and
comfortable one. Perhaps more than in any other nation, Brazilian
Catholicism has been riven by bitter struggle between its right and
left wings, a struggle in which race plays a significant role.[57] Many
black priests accuse conservative elements within the church hier-

archy of continuing to enforce racial privilege and discrimination within its ranks.[58] Others argue that one expects such attitudes and practices from the Right; what is exasperating is when even progressive clergy fail to recognize the specifically racial aspects of inequality in Brazil. A pardo priest complains that "white theologians, for all their talk about the context of oppression, have never come to terms with the simple, central fact that sixty per cent of the population of Brazil is black or has some black roots, and that 'context of oppression' is really a comfortable way of saying 'history of discrimination'."[59]

Black activists level similar charges at the political parties, even those officially supportive of the black movement and its goals.[60] In São Paulo State such criticism is most frequently directed at the Party of the Brazilian Democratic Movement, the opposition party formed in 1965 which swept into power in São Paulo in the 1982 elections, and retained power in the 1986 elections. Because of its role as the sole opposition party until 1979, the PMDB had included a broad spectrum of political factions from right to left, often functioning less as a unified political party than as a delicately balanced electoral coalition. During the early 1980s the reformist, progressive wing of the party—led by such figures as Governor Franco Montoro, São Paulo mayor Mário Covas, and Senator Fernando Henrique Cardoso—was dominant, and went to considerable lengths to welcome the black movement into the party. During the 1982 campaign Franco Montoro even promised that, if elected governor, he would appoint a black member to his cabinet. In light of the black candidates' poor showing that year, and the bitter struggle within the party over the first division of state administrative spoils in the PMDB's history, this promise went unfulfilled, as did black efforts to obtain a secretariat in the São Paulo city government.[61] In a compromise measure, however, the Montoro administration did take the step of creating a new state agency, the Council for the Participation and Development of the Black Community, encharged, in the words of the executive decree creating the agency, with "carrying out studies on the condition of the black community and proposing measures aimed at defending its rights, and eliminating the discrimination which affects it. . . ."[62] The Montoro administration also created the Advisory Group for Afro-Brazilian Affairs in the Secretariat of Culture. Its successor administration, that of Governor Orestes Quércia (also of the PMDB, elected in 1986[63]), created similar groups in the Secretariats of Labor and Education, and also carried through on Franco Montoro's earlier promise by appointing a black union activist, Osvaldo Ribeiro, to head the newly created Special Secretariat of Social Relations.[64]

Critics of the PMDB, and of the Afro-Brazilian activists tied to the party, were quick to denounce the creation of the Council for the Participation and Development of the Black Community, and of the black offices within the state secretariats, as a sop thrown to the party's black clientele, a purely cosmetic act with no real significance. Viewing these developments from a historical perspective, one must disagree. By acknowledging the existence of racial discrimination within Brazil, and then creating state agencies with the exclusive goal of documenting and combatting that discrimination, the PMDB in São Paulo had taken a step unprecedented in Brazilian history. Never before had an institution of the Brazilian state officially contradicted the long-standing myth of racial democracy. And never before had agencies of the state been charged with the express purpose of combatting racism.[65]

These agencies have no authority to enact executive decrees or new legislation. And, as their staffers are the first to admit, they are small, underfunded entities which occupy minute crannies in the organizational charts of the state government, and wield correspondingly limited political power. Nevertheless, one sees in these agencies, and in the decision to create them, a sort of *abertura* in Brazilian race relations, in at least two senses. First, as indicated above, the admission by the state government that racial democracy is not a reality in Brazil is itself a historic development which lends weight and legitimacy to the black movement's protests. Second, these agencies are themselves small openings through which black activists and politicians can insert themselves in the state apparatus and gain access to other state agencies, politicians, and administrators. Doubtless some will use this access primarily for personal advantage, exploiting their newfound position to further their own careers. Others, however, have already provided examples of how such access can be used to pursue broader goals. One such example is the creation of additional black offices in the individual state secretariats as a result of the original council's lobbying efforts. Another example is the requests by the council and the black offices in the Secretariats of Labor and Education for data from the state statistical service, SEADE, on black income, unemployment, and educational performance in the state of São Paulo. Such data had never been prepared before, and when SEADE began to release it, in a series of reports beginning in 1985, it received considerable publicity in the São Paulo media and had a marked impact in union and educational circles.[66]

This use of state resources to document and publicize racial inequality would never have occurred prior to the creation of the black agencies, nor would the outreach activities which they have undertaken. Although the agencies' budgets are miniscule in relation to the rest of the state apparatus, they provide levels of financial support and stability to which Afro-Brazilian organizations have very rarely, if ever, had access.[67] Each of these agencies has concluded that those resources are best used in publicizing racial issues, and provoking public debate and reflection on them—in short, in state-sponsored consciousness-raising. The council publishes a bimonthly newspaper (distributed free of charge in black neighborhoods and the central business district), inexpensive booklets on black history, black literature, and current racial issues, and has also produced a videotape on racial discrimination in hiring and employment. The black office in the Secretariat of Culture administers Project Zumbi, a month-long program of lectures, concerts, art exhibits, public debates, and TV and radio programs, which takes place each November. It sponsors other events as well, and in 1984 produced a facsimile edition of selected black newspapers of the 1920s and 1930s.[68] In 1988 the Secretariat of Education's Working Group on Afro-Brazilian Affairs produced 200,000 copies of a special magazine on the centennial of emancipation, which was distributed to students and teachers in the São Paulo public schools, and used as a basis for class discussions of the event.[69] In the Secretariat of Labor, the Group for Orientation and Intervention in Situations of Racial Discrimination in the Workplace is focusing its efforts on union leaders and personnel administrators in São Paulo firms, trying to enlist both groups in a campaign to eliminate discrimination in hiring and promotion.

The black agencies have thus divided their efforts between lobbying inside the state apparatus and lobbying outside the state apparatus, in civil society. They are trying, through a variety of initiatives in a variety of media, to put the issue of racial discrimination on the public agenda, to make it an issue that both blacks and whites are thinking about, and then to turn public awareness of the issue into tangible political pressure. This is painfully slow, long-term work carried out with minimal resources in a political environment that has historically been deeply resistant to change and innovation. Nevertheless, by the endpoint of our story, there is clear evidence that the black movement of the 1970s and 1980s has forced Brazilian society to reconsider its public and private attitudes on the question of race. As Brazilians gathered to celebrate the centennial of the abolition of slavery, they heard state officials, national celebrities, scholars, and citizens talking about racial democracy and Brazilian race relations in ways that would have been considered treasonous twenty years earlier. Let's listen to what they had to say.

3

PAST, PRESENT, FUTURE

8. One Hundred Years
of Freedom: May 13, 1988

Unlike the United States, where few citizens, black or white, can name the date on which the abolition of slavery took place,[1] in Brazil, May 13, 1888, is one of the country's most important historical milestones. This is hardly surprising in a nation so powerfully shaped and molded by the experience of slavery as was Brazil. When the Golden Law abolished slavery, it brought to an end the social, legal, and economic institution on which Brazilian life had been based for more than three hundred years. Slavery had been the heart and soul of Brazilian society; the day on which it ended could hardly go unmarked.[2]

For those twentieth-century Brazilians who never had any direct contact with slavery, perhaps even more important than what happened on May 13 are the interpretations that future generations imposed on it. The Brazilian Left and the Brazilian Right could both draw comfort from the event, and see in it an object lesson for their own times. Conservatives could cite the Golden Law as a case study in how best to resolve vexatious political issues: through judicious deliberations by established elites, followed by executive action by an enlightened head of state who holds the society's best interests at heart. Brazilians of a more populist or leftist orientation could argue that this may have been the appearance of the Golden Law, but the reality was that abolition was forced on the monarchy by mass-based political action. Emancipation was ultimately the product, not of decisions taken by the country's ruling elites, but rather of the first, and quite possibly the only, successful mass movement in Brazilian history.

Both because of the event which it commemorates and because of the political uses to which it has been put, over the last hundred years May 13 has become one of the most significant dates in Brazilian history, engraved in the memory of every Brazilian schoolchild, and celebrated each year as Abolition Day. Both its meaning and the forms which its observance has taken have varied substantially over time.

Celebrating May 13: 1888–1978

As we saw in chapter 2, the first May 13, in 1888, was a day of complete jubilation, when elite observers saw for the first time "the common people, really the common people" parading through the streets to celebrate their triumph. In the politically charged atmosphere of the following year, as the monarchy entered its death throes, São Paulo's authorities had no wish to see "the common people"—many of whom, especially among the black population, had strong monarchist sympathies—in the streets once again. Declaring a state of siege, and aided by cold, rainy weather on the day itself, they were able to keep popular observances to a minimum. Except for a small parade sponsored by the hatmakers' mutual aid society, and "the blacks' sambas near the house of Dr. Antônio Bento," the city's leading abolitionist, the day passed largely unmarked. Festivities elsewhere in the state were more lively, and reflected the tensions of the day. In Jundiaí a confrontation between monarchists and Republicans erupted into open fighting at a party organized by the black May 13 Club; and in Araraquara the chief of police refused to allow libertos to celebrate at all, arresting the organizers of the day's events and ordering back to their plantations those black workers who had come into town to take part.[3]

Official discouragement of May 13 observances seems to have intensified after the declaration of the Republic that November. Support for the monarchy continued to be widespread among the libertos, many of whom, rightly or wrongly, assigned the credit for emancipation to Princess Isabel and the royal family. The authorities of the newly constituted Republic therefore had little interest in promoting a holiday which could turn into an occasion for the expression of pro-monarchical sentiment. Nevertheless, celebration of the date never died out completely. Commenting in 1892 on the general absence of Abolition Day observances, *O Estado de São Paulo* let slip a revealing qualification: "except for the libertos' street dances in the Rua da Liberdade." Scattered references to those dances (usually referred to as sambas or *batuques*) indicate that they continued through the 1890s and into the twentieth century as the former slaves' homage to abolition.[4]

A second source of support for May 13 observances was the immigrant and labor organizations based in the capital and the major towns of the interior. These organizations did not always agree among themselves on the precise meaning of emancipation or how it should be commemorated. Some saw it as the elimination of the last barrier to European immigration, and the opening of the doors of opportunity for manual laborers in Brazil. More radical observers, particularly those in the anarchist movement, saw it as a snare and a delusion, an event which claimed to liberate Brazilian workers but in fact simply subjected them to a new form of servitude, that of wage slavery. Some of these militants argued that May 13 should be forgotten entirely, since it served only to distract workers from their *real* holiday, International Labor Day on May 1, which took place just two weeks earlier. Other radicals, while agreeing that emancipation left exploitation and inequality in Brazilian society largely intact, nevertheless saw the abolitionist movement, and the massive flights of the slave population from the plantations, as a heroic example of worker struggle, one fully deserving of annual commemoration.[5]

In the end, however, May 13 was saved as a civic holiday not by the labor or immigrant organizations, which as the years passed gradually lost interest in the date, but rather by the black civic and social organizations discussed in chapter 5. The street dances put on by the libertos and poor blacks served to mark the day, but could be shrugged off by the white elites as the spontaneous outbursts of a childish *povo*, which would seize on any opportunity for a party. Harder to dismiss in this way were the events sponsored each year by black social clubs around the state (many of them named in honor of May 13). These festivities usually centered on such "civilized" activities as speeches honoring emancipation (often by local political figures), poetry readings, music, and, in the evening, ballroom dances. By the late 1920s, observances in the state capital included a march by representatives of the various black organizations from center city to the tomb of black abolitionist Luis Gama in the Consolação cemetery. Following ceremonies at his grave, they would then visit the offices of newspapers and radio stations to impress on the media the importance of May 13 in Brazilian history.[6]

Another feature of May 13 during the 1920s was the annual black-white ("preto-branco") soccer game sponsored by black organizations and white athletic clubs in the capital. At this point in the history of Brazilian sport, segregation of soccer teams had only just begun to break down in Rio de Janeiro and was still firmly entrenched in São Paulo. The city's top black and white players were thus confined to separate leagues, with no opportunity to play each other save in informal scrimmages. In an effort to circumvent this segregation and give black players greater exposure, in 1927 several black leaders came up with the idea of an annual black-white game, to be played on Abolition Day. These games received extensive coverage in the local media, which were astonished to find the black players, who had been relegated to the "secondary" division of the local league, consistently victorious over the whites. In 1928, when the black team, "against all expectations," defeated the whites for the second time, A Gazeta noted that "the white team included the names most in evidence in the principal division [of the local league]. Among them were four players from last year's championship team; we don't understand how such a strong team was defeated." Part of the reason is suggested by the labor newspaper O Combate's coverage of the same game.

. . . from the first moments, facing the prospect of a titanic game, the great mass of spectators chose its favorite, which was the Black team, continually urging it onward in an uncontained desire to cheer. It seemed that the crowd's every effort was bent on seeing the black team win, and that it saw in that victory a question of honor. . . . It's been quite a while since our fans showed as much passion as they did yesterday, with such vibrant and spontaneous enthusiasm.[7]

Locked out of Brazilian life in so many ways, including athletics, Afro-Brazilians on this one day were permitted to compete with whites on, literally and figuratively, a level playing field. The players were not about to miss this rare opportunity, and neither were their fans, who, we may assume, were largely Afro-Brazilian themselves.[8] Perhaps in response to the use which black players were able to make of that opportunity, and the poor showing of the white teams, the black-white games seem to have been discontinued after 1930, and were then replaced by marathon races organized by the Black Club of Social Culture, in which only pardos and pretos took part.[9]

During the 1940s and 1950s, May 13 continued to be celebrated by the black organizations in much the same way as in the 1920s, with lectures, concerts, dances, and athletic events.[10] One new addition was the Bonequinha de Café (literally, "Little Coffee-Colored Doll") beauty contest. Given the virtual impossibility of Afro-Brazilian women winning beauty competitions at this time, the Renaissance Club, Rio de Janeiro's elite black social club, had established an annual contest to choose Miss Renaissance, thus enabling would-be black beauty queens to compete at least among themselves. Following this example, São Paulo's 220 Club launched the Bonequinha de Café contest in 1961. Even in this entirely black competition, white standards of beauty retained considerable weight, as suggested by a comment in Campinas's black newspaper that the winner of the 1963 contest, a young mulatta from Rio de Janeiro, was "a bit too light to hold the title of Bonequinha de Café. . . ."[11]

In addition to the Bonequinha contest, the 220 Club pioneered a second innovation in May 13 observances. Since early in the century, São Paulo's black organizations had venerated several mythic figures symbolizing black contributions to Brazilian history and the forging of the Brazilian nation. The most prominent of these figures was the Mãe Preta, the Black Mother, who represented the millions of slave and free black women who had nursed and cared for the children of white families during the years of slavery and after. The Black Mother was often cited in the black newspapers as a symbol, not just of the sacrifices that black people had made for Brazil, but also of the powerful ways in which Euro- and Afro-Brazilians were linked in a common destiny. And indeed, what could be more compelling than the symbol of mother's milk, in this case the milk of black mothers shared with white children?[12]

Up through the 1950s, Black Mother Day was celebrated on September 28, the date in 1871 on which the Law of the Free Womb had been passed. In 1955, the municipality erected a statue of the Black Mother next to the Church of the Rosary, São Paulo's oldest historically black congregation. Beginning sometime in the 1960s, the 220 Club, aided by some of São Paulo's *candomblé* cults, began celebrating Black Mother Day on May 13, with festivities held at the site of the statue. By 1970 the mayor and archbishop of São Paulo were both attending the annual event, and in 1972 the club succeeded in bringing President Emílio Garrastazu Médici to São Paulo for that year's celebration, thus insuring the attendance of every major politician in Greater São Paulo. In 1975, however, Médici's successor, President Ernesto Geisel, curtly rejected an invitation to take part in the May 13 festivities, denouncing "the exaltation of the Black Mother as [an act of] racial discrimination," and accusing the organization which had invited him, the Association of Colored Men, of practicing *racismo às avessas* (see chapter 7, note 6).[13]

Geisel's charges of racism in connection with this event appear particularly wrongheaded when one contrasts the placid, benign Black Mother with a competing mythic figure, the black warrior-king Zumbi (pronounced Zoom-BEE), who was making his way back into Brazilian popular consciousness during the 1970s. Zumbi was the monarch of the seventeenth-century *quilombo* of Palmares, a loose federation of villages in a remote part of northeastern Brazil populated by escaped slaves and other fugitives from Portuguese rule. Palmares succeeded in maintaining its independence for over seventy years, until its destruction in 1694; according to legend, Zumbi died fighting the final Portuguese offensive against the *quilombo*.[14]

While the Black Mother (and her male counterpart, Pai João, Father John) represented the submissive, accommodating black response to slavery, Zumbi symbolized fierce and umcompromising resistance to the slave regime. As such he was never completely forgotten by Afro-Brazilians, and would occasionally reemerge as a symbol during periods of particular militance in the black community.[15] For the reasons discussed in the previous chapter, the 1970s was such a time. The rapid economic growth of the Brazilian "miracle" benefited many middle-class Afro-Brazilians, but never as much as it benefited their white counterparts. And for the great majority of Afro-Brazilians, the affluence of the miracle years was hopelessly out of reach, cruelly taunting them from afar. The response to these disappointments and resentments was a resurgence of organization and militance among Afro-Brazilians, who now sought alternative heroes and heroines to replace the Black Mother and Father John. Some of those heroes, such as Amilcar Cabral, Martin Luther King, Jr., Bob Marley, and Malcolm X, came from abroad. But others were homegrown, and preeminent among them was Zumbi, who emerged as a powerful public symbol over the course of the 1970s. Pop singer Jorge Ben's hit song "Zumbi," released in 1974, was one of the first signs of that reemergence.

> I want to see what will happen.
> When Zumbi arrives.
> Zumbi is the Lord of war,
> Zumbi is the Lord of demands.
> When Zumbi arrives,
> It will be he who commands.[16]

In 1978 black artists and activists in São Paulo State began holding local "Zumbi festivals" (Festival Comunitário Negro Zumbi), with street theater, readings, concerts, and dances to mark the anniversary of Zumbi's death, November 20. Just as labor activists at the beginning of the century had rejected May 13 and invoked May 1 as the "real" worker holiday, now the black activists of the 1970s also rejected May 13, which, they argued, portrays black people as the passive recipients of Princess Isabel's kindness, subjects rather than agents of their own history. November 20, Zumbi Day, was the "real" black holiday, they proposed, one which symbolized the spirit and practice of steadfast black resistance to the oppression and exploitation of slavery.[17]

Though Zumbi was first and foremost a black hero, his visibility spread well beyond the Afro-Brazilian population. Opponents of the dictatorship seized on him as a symbol of resistance to authoritarian rule, the warrior-king who had never given up the struggle against the linked oppressions of colonialism and slavery. He had led his people in constructing their own way of life, free of interference from the landowning elite. Leftists described him as the leader of the first socialist society in the Americas, and invoked Palmares as an implicit critique of what modern Brazilian society had become. Cities like

São Paulo and Rio de Janeiro were now clogged, polluted, crime-ridden urban nightmares, but Palmares had been a pastoral idyll. Modern Brazil was ruled by "savage capitalism," but Palmares had been a "primitive communist" society to which all contributed according to their abilities, and all received according to their needs. And ultimately, of course, Palmares had offered a refuge to which the victims of authoritarian oppression could escape. Small wonder, then, that opponents of the dictatorship not infrequently invoked, in the words of composer Milton Nascimento, "the *quilombos* of yesterday, today, and tomorrow," and the hope of "making Palmares again."[18]

Even the military government acknowledged Zumbi's symbolic power. In 1980 the federal government created the Zumbi National Park in the state of Alagoas, on what is believed to be the site of Palmares. Civilian administrations elected in 1982 sought to capitalize on Zumbi as well. In Rio de Janeiro, the state Secretariat of Education initiated Project Zumbi with the goal of increasing instruction on Afro-Brazilian history and culture in the public schools. In São Paulo Project Zumbi became an annual month-long program of lectures, films, concerts, art exhibits, and other cultural activities centering on the black presence in Brazil. Sponsored by the state Secretariat of Culture, these events take place in November, in conjunction with Zumbi Day—now renamed the Day of Black Consciousness.[19]

The Centennial: May 13, 1988

Given Zumbi's success in displacing the Black Mother and, along with her, May 13 itself, I found myself wondering, as 1988 drew closer, how Brazilians would celebrate an event whose meaning and relevance were being called increasingly into question. Upon taking office in 1985, President José Sarney announced that the centennial of emancipation would be celebrated as a major national holiday. The Ministry of Culture was encharged with putting together a nation-wide program of concerts, art exhibits, public lectures and debates, scholarly conferences, and other activities; [20] and in the months prior to the centennial, it seemed as though every organized entity in Brazilian life was preparing to take part. State and municipal governments organized their own observances; universities convened international conferences to discuss the experiences of slavery and emancipation; newspapers and magazines prepared special issues and supplements to mark the day, and television and radio stations ran special programs; samba schools in Rio, São Paulo, and elsewhere based their 1988 Carnaval presentations on the theme of the centennial; the Catholic church focused its annual Brotherhood Campaign on the theme "Blacks and Brotherhood"; private firms and companies took out ads in honor of abolition; and of course the organizations of the black movement planned to mark the day in their own way.

As they prepared to celebrate abolition, Brazilians found themselves caught up in a national debate on what emancipation had really meant, and how it had changed (or failed to change) Brazilian life.[21] The first issue connected with May 13 was whether the date should even be celebrated at all. Many Afro-Brazilians, ranging from university-educated professionals and intellectuals through the working-class members of samba schools and *candomblé* cults, expressed strong skepticism, if not outright opposition.[22] The most widely diffused example of this attitude was the prize-winning samba, "One Hundred Years of Freedom: Reality or Illusion?", presented by the Mangueira samba school in the Rio de Janeiro Carnaval competition of 1988.

> Can it be . . .
> The dawn of liberty,
> Or was it all just illusion?
> Can it be . . .
> That the dreamed-of Golden Law,
> Signed so long ago,
> Was not the end of slavery?
> In the real world today,
> Where is freedom?
> Where is it? I don't see it.
>
> I dreamed . . .
> That Zumbi of Palmares returned.
> The blacks' misery ended;
> It was a new redemption.
>
> Lord . . .
> See the struggle of good against evil,
> In which so much blood was spilled
> To fight racial prejudice.[23]

For many of Brazil's black militants, abolition was a lie and a farce, two words used repeatedly during the commemorations.[24] The Golden Law was a decree which ended formal bondage but left in place the scourges of poverty, disease, illiteracy, and racism, from which black people continue to suffer to the present. To protest these realities, black organizations in Rio de Janeiro and Salvador formed a united front to boycott any festivities on May 13 itself, and instead sponsored marches prior to that day in opposition to the event. In Salvador the political pressure of the Carnaval blocs was sufficiently strong to persuade both the municipality and the state government to hold no activities at all on May 13. The only commemoration of abolition in the capital of Afro-Brazil, as Salvador has been called, was a march and public demonstration on May 12, the theme of which was "one hundred years without abolition" (a play on words in Portuguese: *cem anos sem abolição*), and at which the Princess Isabel was burned in effigy.[25]

A similar march in Rio on May 11 provoked a much more hostile reaction from the authorities. As part of its efforts to popularize and dramatize black history in Brazil, the Rio de Janeiro Commission of Black Religious, Seminarians, and Priests had issued a booklet in July 1987 attacking "false heroes who contributed to the massacre of blacks in Brazil." In addition to Princess Isabel and others, the pamphlet denounced the duke of Caxias, the commander of Brazilian forces during the Paraguayan War (1864–1870), and an honored hero of Brazilian military history. The commission also announced its intention to petition to change the name of Duque de Caxias, a poor and largely black suburb of Rio de Janeiro.[26]

When Rio's military police learned that the marchers' route would take them past the Pantheon, where lie the remains of the duke of Caxias, their commander informed the press that "a march is a normal, democratic event, and the black movement is a very nice movement, but the march is not going to pass" in front of the Pantheon. The city's civilian officials sought to work out some sort of compromise between the police and the marchers, but eventually withdrew and allowed the police free rein. Seven hundred fifty troops were sent into the streets to prevent five thousand marchers from proceeding past the Pantheon. The police seized banners that they interpreted as having political content, prevented the march's leaders from addressing the crowd, and arrested two union leaders who attempted to speak. The *Jornal do Brasil* described the police presence as "the greatest repressive apparatus seen [in downtown Rio de Janeiro] since the beginning of civilian rule in 1985."[27]

On May 13 itself, the public educational channel in Rio canceled, at the last minute, the debate "Abolition: Myth or Reality," sponsored by the Ministry of Culture. The circumstances of the cancellation remain unclear: some reports say that the decision was made by the ministry; others blame the TV station; and others say that the program's black participants withdrew after being informed that the debate would be broadcast to a smaller number of stations than originally planned. Whatever the reason, the cancellation contributed to the sense of discord and unease surrounding the holiday in Rio.[28]

Tension was also visible in Brasília, the national capital, where a session of Congress convened to pay homage to May 13 was interrupted by members of the Unified Black Movement chanting, "We want work, we want jobs! May 13 is not the day of the blacks!"[29] President Sarney treaded carefully in his radio address to the nation, seeking to satisfy all parties by combining the traditional interpretation of the events of 1888 with a more modern, critical perspective. This made for some confusion at times. Sarney opened his speech with the standard explanation of how Brazil had achieved emancipation in its own uniquely Brazilian way, peacefully and nonviolently, but then went on to pay homage to "the slaves who refused to accept submission, who resisted in the quilombos . . . and who lived the sacred revolt of liberty." He also invoked Zumbi, "the hero-symbol" of "courage, bravery, martyrdom, and resistance," reminded listeners of his administration's efforts on behalf of the Zumbi National Park, and announced the creation of the new state-sponsored Palmares Foundation, "to make possible a black presence in all the sectors of leadership in this country." Having reached out to the black movement, however, he then sought to reassure his conservative and military supporters by praising Princess Isabel, the duke of Caxias, and "the military men who accepted the argument that the Army could never be a slave-hunter, pursuing the fugitives from slavery." Having covered all the bases, Sarney concluded with the Delphic observation that "history does not rewrite itself. Perhaps another history is written. But truth remains, reposing in the silence of past times."[30]

Florestan Fernandes, by 1988 a congressman (on the Workers' Party ticket) and member of the national Constituent Assembly, took the occasion of the centennial to differ with the president, explicitly rejecting the notion of a single, knowable truth "reposing in the silence of past times." "Historical dates are not defined on their own terms, and once and for all. Human beings create them over time, and bring the past into the present and into struggles which are constantly being renewed." He went on to say that the purpose of the centennial, therefore, should not be just to remember the experience of slavery and abolition, but to reflect on the meaning of those events for present-day Brazilian society, and its continuing efforts to achieve justice and equality.[31]

Not all the celebrants of May 13 shared this interest in the contemporary situation. A number of governmental agencies, both in São Paulo and at the national level, chose to focus their activities exclusively on slavery. In São Paulo, for example, the State Archive commemorated the date with the public exhibit "Sources on the History of Slavery in São Paulo," and the University of São Paulo hosted the International Congress on Slavery, with hundreds of scholars from Brazil, the United States, Europe, and other Latin American countries. Such observances served the worthy purpose of reminding Brazilians of the three hundred–year experience of slavery in their country, and the profound ways in which that experience has shaped Brazilian society and civilization. Yet this focus on slavery often tended to divert attention from the contemporary scene.[32]

One can see this diversionary effect in the contrast between the two major São Paulo newspapers' coverage of the centennial. *O Estado de São Paulo*, the state's venerable "establishment" newspaper (founded in 1875 by a partnership of twenty of the state's leading landowners), commemorated the day with the special supplement *Abolition: One Hundred Years of Freedom*. The articles composing the supplement were written by respected and well-known historians, and focused entirely on slavery and the struggle for abolition. Both their subject matter and the fact that they were published apart from the main body of the paper presented May 13 as a date with little relevance or application to the present. The *Estado's* chief competitor, the *Folha de São Paulo*, also issued a special supplement for May 13, entitled *One Hundred Years of Abolition*. Like the *Estado* supplement, this one focused on the past, though it broadened its coverage beyond slavery to consider the treatment of Afro-Brazilians in nineteenth-century Brazilian literature and anthropology, the work of turn-of-the-century black writer Lima Barreto, and the period immediately after abolition. But in addition to this supplement, the *Folha* also ran a diverse set of articles in the main body of the newspaper over a period of several days leading up to May 13. These articles discussed the state of the black movement in Brazil, racial inequality in jobs and salaries, racial images in Brazilian advertising, interviews with middle-class black families in São Paulo, descriptions of the state of race relations in the United States and South Africa, and other contemporary topics concerning race.[33] Unlike *O Estado*, the *Folha* thus presented May 13 as a date which should stimulate not only historical reflection but careful examination of Brazil's current situation as well.

Other celebrants avoided discussion of present-day racial problems by taking a more "cultural" (or, in the terminology of the black movement, "folkloric") approach which concentrated on African contributions to Brazilian music, dance, and cuisine. Inspired by Gilberto Freyre and the works of Bahian novelist Jorge Amado, such an approach emphasized the special *alegria* (happiness, gaiety, mirth) which Africans brought with them to Brazil, and which is now considered so characteristic of Brazilian civilization.[34]

The concept of *alegria* posits that, despite the miserable conditions in which most of them live, Brazilians have an innate ability to rise above their poverty and be happy. Indeed, according to this notion, gaiety and good cheer, usually expressed by singing and dancing, are most evident and widespread among Brazil's poorest people. One cannot help but note the similarities between this notion and its earlier variants, in both Brazil and the United States, which asserted the happiness and contentment of slaves under slavery. Just as defenders of the institution argued that black people didn't really suffer from slavery the way white people would, so the proponents of *alegria* maintain that poor people don't really suffer from poverty in the way that rich or middle-class people would.

Like the larger concept of racial democracy, *alegria* seeks to defuse social tension in a country of tremendous inequality.[35] Its advocates, therefore, object strongly to any efforts to question or criticize the concept.[36] Minister of the Interior João Alves, former governor of the northeastern state of Sergipe and the only black cabinet minister, angrily denounced efforts by the black movement to orient the May 13 observances away from "folklore" and toward an examination of present-day racial hierarchy in Brazil. "The commemoration should be highlighting and valuing the importance of black contributions to music and dance and cooking in Brazil. Instead, they launch this unfortunate campaign [elsewhere in the interview Alves described it as "crazy" and "disgraceful"], creating problems which don't exist in Brazilian society, which in turn could produce negative consequences."[37]

But even official pressure of this sort proved unable to keep the question of present-day inequality off the May 13 agenda. If anything, what was most striking about the centennial was the way in which it stimulated a frank, open, and at times painful revision of one of Brazil's most deeply held self-images: that of racial democracy.

The Death of Racial Democracy

As we saw in chapter 5, even before its formulation by Gilberto Freyre in the 1930s, racial democracy had been subjected to a withering critique by black organizations and newspapers in São Paulo. Such criticisms continued after World War II, now validated by the findings of the UNESCO-sponsored research projects. And by the 1970s and 1980s such criticisms had intensified further, articulated both by Afro-Brazilian militants and by white social scientists using statistical data provided by the government itself.

Abertura, the end of the dictatorship, and the effort to build democracy further reinforced such criticisms. Chapter 7 argued that by the 1980s a growing number of Brazilian activists and intellectuals had come to see that racial inequality formed one of the primary obstacles to the establishment of democratic norms and institutions in Brazilian society. As the black press and civic organizations had been arguing since the 1920s, until the majority, or near-majority, of Brazil's population that was of pure or mixed African descent was accorded full participation in Brazilian life on terms of complete equality with whites, democracy in the larger sense simply could not be said to exist.

Proponents of political democracy had also come to see the concept of racial democracy as a cornerstone of the ideological apparatus with which the nation's conservative elites had sought to retain and justify their control over society. Racial democracy assured blacks that Brazil was a land of racial equality, when in fact it was not. Similarly, both the First and Second republics had claimed, against strong evidence to the contrary, to be participatory democracies.[38] If a major part of building democracy in the Third Republic was to expose such obfuscatory and deceptive rhetoric, attacking the aging and visibly false myth of racial democracy seemed a good place to begin.

Racial democracy also made an appealing target because of the way in which the military governments had sought to cloak themselves in the folds of the myth. Despite the resolve with which they seized power in 1964 and held it for the next two decades, the officers were never entirely comfortable with their role in doing away with democracy. They frequently reminded those who would listen that they had destroyed Brazilian democracy precisely in order to save it, and that their long-term goal was to clean up and restructure its institutions in such a way that a democratic polity would eventually be able to function free of the excesses and corruption that had plagued Brazilian politics in the past.[39] In the meantime, during the period in which Brazil was clearly not a political democracy, it was helpful for the dictatorship to be able to claim that it continued to be democratic in at least one sense: that of race. Officials of the dictatorship made this point repeatedly, and classified any criticism of the myth as an act of subversion.[40]

Thus by the time the military left power, in 1985, the notion of racial democracy had been discredited as much by its political associations with right-wing authoritarianism as by its questionable relationship with reality. Not only was it easy to make a convincing empirical case against the concept; for many Brazilians, it was also an act of political liberation, and an explicit rejection of the dictatorship, to do so. These factors all combined to make the centennial the perfect occasion on which to deal the myth its coup de grâce.

Unwilling to turn against his military and conservative allies, President Sarney remained silent on this issue, but his minister of culture, Celso Furtado, did not hesitate to speak out.[41] "The idea that there is racial democracy in Brazil is false as long as the overwhelming majority of the black population lives marginalized and in poverty." In an echo of United States affirmative action policies, Furtado proposed to start overcoming this situation by "guaranteeing" a minimum number of slots in Brazilian schools and universities for Afro-Brazilian students, a startling and unprecedented proposal in the Brazilian context (as of course it once was in the United States).[42]

The press was even more emphatic in its burying of racial democracy. The nation's two major newsweeklies (comparable to *Time* and *Newsweek* in the United States) joined in reading the last rites. "The myth of racial democracy appears to be definitively in its grave," observed *Istoé*, while *Veja* implicitly dismissed the notion of racial democracy by opening its cover story on May 13 with the observation that "one hundred years after Abolition, in Brazil there are two distinct citizenships—white and black." It then went on to discuss at length some of the racial inequities documented by the census of 1980.[43]

In São Paulo, the *Folha* opened with a lead editorial on "the perception, ever more widespread, that 'racial democracy,' in its official and semi-official versions, does not reflect Brazilian reality. . . ." In Rio, the *Jornal do Brasil* interviewed a series of intellectuals and public figures who were virtually unanimous in their repudiation of the concept. Historian Francisco Iglésias curtly dismissed it as "foolishness," and his colleague Décio Freitas turned the concept on its head by insisting that "racial discrimination is the basis of Brazilian culture." Octávio Ianni summed up prevailing opinion by observing that "more than anybody blacks know that racial democracy is a lie in a country in which there is no political democracy, much less racial democracy." Racial democracy even received a nail in its coffin from an unexpected quarter: *The Brasilians*, a generally apolitical newspaper published in New York by Brazilian emigrés, carried a lead editorial entitled "Another Myth Bites the Dust," which surveyed the results of the 1980 census, strongly condemned racial discrimination in Brazil, and saluted the "new and long overdue openness in dealing with racial issues" there.[44]

Still, while the myth is largely discredited, it would be premature to write it off completely. It is a concept that is deeply and widely diffused in Brazilian society, one which will not be overturned overnight. As might be expected, the centennial was also an opportunity for its believers to reaffirm their commitment, as the Rio newspaper *O Globo* did in its editorial "The True Discrimination." Faithfully recapitulating the racial democracy argument, *O Globo* argued that if discrimination existed in Brazil, it was discrimination against poor people, not against blacks. It therefore urged black people not to allow themselves to be "manipulated" (by whom was left unclear) into "an adversarial relationship, potentially violent, between whites and blacks. This would cause a repetition of the bloody events which took place in the United States during the 1960s." And the same *Jornal do Brasil* supplement which included the interviews condemning racial democracy contained another article, "The Mulatta and Dom Miguel," which saluted miscegenation between mulattas, "who can be anything except fragile," and their lusty Portuguese masters, "the best colonizer who ever existed." The overwhelming sexual attraction between these two groups "preceded and neutralized the prejudices and antagonisms that usually impede the mixture of two peoples," thus laying the groundwork for, in best Freyrean fashion, the creation of racial democracy in Brazil.[45]

The old ways die hard, and the myth of racial democracy is likely to be with us, even if waning in influence, for a while to come. But when the old ways do die, what do they leave behind? The myth worked for most of the twentieth century to damp down and contain racial tension and antagonism in Brazil. With this potent social control gone, and activists fanning black people's sense of injury and grievance, might those antagonisms burst into the open, and explode in violence?

This is the great fear in Brazil. During the days of slavery, Brazilians felt that they were living on the edge of the abyss: in the words of the nineteenth-century commentator Perdigão Malheiro, on the lip of "a volcano . . . a bomb ready to explode with the first spark." In the twentieth century such fear has transcended the institution of slavery, and now embraces the poverty-stricken *povo* as a whole. But since those poor people are disproportionately black, and since black people have a history of such particularly intense exploitation and oppression, this fear of the masses rising up to avenge themselves continues to express itself in racial terms.

This "rising up" could take various forms. One is the spontaneous, individualized action of crime, which by 1988 was epidemic in Brazilian cities. A magazine article commemorating May 13, 1986, described a growing state of "civil war" in Brazil with strong racial overtones, as "young unemployed blacks attack middle-class whites in the cities. For many whites in Rio de Janeiro, São Paulo, and Belo Horizonte, young blacks are synonymous with potential assailants." As a result, "racial division is growing apace."[46]

Less immediately threatening than black crime, but in some ways just as worrisome, is the possibility that blacks might organize to advance their collective interests and, perhaps, to settle present and past accounts with the society which has so oppressed them. As we saw in chapter 7, white fear of such a prospect is most evident during periods of black political and social mobilization; because the 1980s have been such a period, white uneasiness in the face of the resurgent black movement has been palpable. This uneasiness found expression in a report prepared in 1982 by an advisor to São Paulo governor Paulo Maluf. Its subject was the political threat posed by the black and pardo populations, which are growing at a rate faster than the white population. ". . . In the year 2000 the [national] population of pardos and *negros* will be in the neighborhood of 60 percent of the total, much larger than the white. By means of elections it will be able to dominate Brazilian politics and control all the top positions—unless we do as is done in Washington, DC, where, since the black population is about 63 percent of the total, there are no elections. . . ." In order to prevent a black takeover of Brazilian politics (the logical outcome of genuine racial democracy), the report proposed a statewide campaign of birth control for nonwhites, which would make for "a better Brazil."[47]

Such fears emerged as well on the occasion of the centennial. We have already mentioned *O Globo*'s forebodings of an "adversarial relationship, potentially violent" between blacks and whites in Brazil. Similar concerns appear to have motivated the suppression of the May 12 march in Rio de Janeiro, an action which the police justified by accusing the black movement of "distributing misinformation to the people with the unpatriotic intention of stimulating antagonism and even hatred among brothers of different races and colors. . . ." They were also voiced by the distinguished jurist and politician Afonso Arinos de Melo Franco, author of the 1951 antiracism law. When asked his opinion of the recently approved article of the new Brazilian Constitution, which extended his earlier law and greatly increased its penalties for discriminatory acts, he responded: "I don't approve of it, it's inopportune and inappropriate. It might give rise to antagonism between blacks and whites."[48]

As the myth of racial democracy withers and dies, many Brazilians fear that its passing will open the door to the racial strife and hatred that other countries have suffered and that Brazil has been blessedly free of. Other Brazilians, however, take a more hopeful and optimistic view. Only with the death of the myth, they argue, can the construction of the reality begin. Cleansing Brazilian life of its lies and deceptions concerning race is the necessary first step toward constructing a society based on genuine racial equality, the dream which has been the leitmotif of Afro-Brazilian protest since the 1920s.

The issue, of course, is whether white Brazilians share their black countrymen's hopes and aspirations. Black historian Joel Rufino dos Santos believes that many of them do. If the myth of racial democracy has had any positive impact at all, he argues, it lies in having instilled in the Brazilian mind the concept of racial equality as a positive good, as something to be valued and desired. "Brazilians have in their heads the belief that racial democracy exists in their country, which is false. But connected to that belief, and underlying it, is the burning desire for [real] racial democracy."[49] I have had occasion to see numerous expressions of that desire, perhaps the most public of which was a historic prime-time television series which ran in Brazil during 1984 and 1985. The first *telenovela* (prime-time evening soap opera) ever to pay serious attention to the problem of race in modern Brazil, "Corpo a corpo" (Body to Body) told the story of a love affair between an upwardly mobile black professional, Sônia (played by Zezé Motta, known to American audiences through her title role in the Brazilian film *Xica da Silva*), and Cláudio, son of an upper-class family headed by the racist patriarch Alfredo. Alfredo makes clear that he will never permit his son to marry Sônia, and, in a climactic scene, tells her that his blood and hers will never mix (i.e., she will not be the mother of his grandchildren). Shortly thereafter

Alfredo has a serious accident, and requires a blood transfusion. He has a rare blood type which the hospital cannot provide, but Sônia's blood turns out to be the same type, and she saves his life by offering him her blood—thus negating his prediction. When Alfredo recovers, he has a complete change of heart, admits the error of his racist ways, and welcomes Sônia into the family as his beloved daughter-in-law.

Like any soap opera, the story was sentimental and utterly improbable. It was also genuinely moving, and touched a deep chord in the Brazilian public, sparking a national debate on the meaning of this fable for modern Brazil. Many black viewers applauded the appearance for the first time on Brazilian television of a "normal," middle-class, black family. Others, however, maintained that Sônia's family was perhaps *too* normal, and, since white people set the norm in Brazil, acted not like a black family, but rather like a white family played by black actors. (And indeed, in one episode Cláudio laughingly tells Sônia that her family reminds him of the family on the U.S. television show "Father Knows Best.") Some went on to say that Sônia herself was too "white" a character. "I think they whitened that *negra* too much. . . . She's too good, she cries too much, she's too ideological. Just to give a black character the same importance as a white, they didn't have to make her such a jerk." From another perspective, Ruth de Souza, the actress who played Sônia's mother (and a veteran of the Black Experimental Theater of the 1950s—see chapter 7), said that she herself was unhappy with the series because of Alfredo's forthright and intense expressions of racism. ". . . The abuse he piled on Sônia really hurt the black community. The 16-year-old daughter of a friend of mine cried when she saw the strength of Alfredo's feelings. At that moment she really saw the force of racism. And for what? Nobody showed her a way out."[50]

White people too had their objections to the show, which they expressed in a stream of letters and telephone calls to the stars and producers protesting Sônia and Cláudio's interracial romance. Those letters provide further evidence, if any is needed, that significant numbers of white Brazilians remain committed to the continuation of racial inequality. Considering the concrete ways in which they benefit from such inequality, receiving clear preference in education, marriage, employment, and social status, this is hardly surprising.

Whether Euro-Brazilians want and will accept real racial democracy will depend on their willingness to forego these preferences and to share out such opportunities among all members, black and white, of the society at large. Most are unlikely to make this sacrifice voluntarily—unless, that is, they can be persuaded that they will receive in exchange something equal or superior in value to what they are giving up. This is just one, but perhaps the most basic, of the challenges facing Brazil's antiracism movement: to convince, persuade, or pressure white Brazilians into recognizing how they and their country would benefit by the ending of race prejudice and discrimination.

São Paulo: May 13

Where will such ideas, pressure, and suasion come from? At least initially, from the thousands of black and white Brazilians who paraded through the streets of São Paulo on May 13 to celebrate the centennial. The weather was beautiful and the mood festive as the marchers gathered in the Largo do Paissandu, site of the black Church of the Rosary, and the starting point of the March of Reflection and Struggle. The crowd was lively and diverse, including delegations from organizations ranging from labor unions to *capoeira* academies and samba schools. Young militants of the Unified Black Movement celebrated "ten years of struggle," while grizzled veterans of the Brazilian Black Front, now in their seventies and eighties, held their flag aloft and marched gamely down the avenue. As they do each May 13, *candomblé* priestesses in traditional Bahian dress sprinkled the statue of the Black Mother with perfumed water and distributed ceremonial popcorn to the crowd. This year, however, they did so beneath a banner which trumpeted, in Portuguese, that "the oppressor never gives freedom voluntarily; the oppressed must conquer it—Martin Luther King, Jr.—USA."[51]

The parade was sponsored by the state government, which in May 1988 was in the hands of the Party of the Brazilian Democratic Movement, the PMDB. Ever since the "party reform" of 1979 splintered the opposition into five competing parties, the PMDB in São Paulo had made a concerted effort to win the support of the state's Afro-Brazilian population; the May 13 parade, coordinated by the newly created Special Secretariat of Social Relations, was a particularly visible example of that effort. In reaching out for the black vote, however, the PMDB was competing directly with the Workers' Party, which had formed an informal coalition with the militants of the Unified Black Movement. Workers' Party and PMDB organizers clashed at the May 13 parade when a Workers' Party sound van tried to seize the lead position at the head of the procession. PMDB marshals managed to head the van off and relegate it to the rear of the parade, from where it broadcast a steady barrage of chanting and music which contrasted sharply with the exhortations of PMDB organizers to marchers to remember that May 13 was not a day to party, but rather "a day of reflection."[52]

Whether one chose to party or to reflect, there was no mistaking the marchers' high spirits. Here they were among their own, facing no jeering opposition, denouncing racism with full conviction and in full voice. It was a sparkling autumn day, and even the old *frentenegrinos* (members of the Black Front) marched with a spring in their step. As the marchers arrived at their destination, passing through the Rua Direita to arrive at the Praça da Sé in front of São Paulo's cathedral, their jubilation continued unabated. It was at this point, however, that the political divergences among the participants became even more visible—or, I should say, more audible. The parade's organizers had mounted a sound stage in front of the cathedral from which a succession of speakers was to address the crowd (with a large banner alongside, on behalf of the PMDB Group of Black Politicians, urging the crowd to "vote black in the coming elections"). As it entered the plaza, the Workers' Party van pulled up alongside the stage, turned its sound equipment up full blast, and engaged in a furious battle with the PMDB speakers to see who could drown each other out. My head aching, and no longer able to make out any words in the cacophonous barrage of sound, I left the plaza and headed for my bus stop. As I walked I reflected on the dark symbolism of the two parties trying to obliterate each other's messages with waves of sound. I thought as well about the ragged street children we had passed as we marched along, some of whom dodged in and out among the marchers, excited by the cheering and music, others of whom approached us with wan resignation, trying to sell us gum, fruit, razor blades. Had the day's events meant anything to these children, most of them black? Would the march make their lives better in any way?

As one hundred years before, on May 13 we celebrated emancipation, and wondered what May 14 would bring.

9. Looking Back, Looking Forward

This book concludes by returning to the questions with which it began. What has racial inequality looked like in São Paulo since the abolition of slavery? How much of it can be ascribed to impersonal, structural causes, and how much to purposeful racial discrimination? And how have patterns of racial hierarchy been affected by, and in turn contributed to, the political changes which have taken place in Brazil during the last one hundred years?

Racial Inequality

Racial inequality, like social inequality more generally, is one of the basic facts of Brazilian life.[1] What I have tried to emphasize in this book is how the character of that inequality has changed over time.

In the years and decades immediately following emancipation, pardo and preto workers in São Paulo were denied admission both to urban industrial employment and to the more desirable jobs in the agricultural sector. These color bars began to break down during the 1920s and 1930s, and by the 1940s were for the most part defunct. By 1980, as Table 6.2 indicates, black workers were overrepresented in industrial, construction, and agricultural employment, and were earning wages relatively close to, though still lower than, those received by their white counterparts.

By the second half of the century, however, factory work and *colono* contracts were no longer the best opportunities available to Brazilian wage earners. The São Paulo labor market had expanded, not just in terms of absolute size, but also in terms of the variety of opportunities available to job seekers. Jobs in commerce, the professions, and administration, which had accounted for only 10 percent of the labor force in 1920, composed almost a third (32.4 percent) of the labor force in 1980. As racial barriers weakened and eroded in blue-collar employment, they asserted themselves very strongly indeed at this middle-class level, producing a severe underrepresentation of black employees in these sectors of the economy, and high levels of salary inequality.

The conventional Brazilian explanation for these racial disparities in employment focuses on slavery and its double legacy of black incapacity and white prejudice. This book has argued that the exclusion of Afro-Brazilian workers from the São Paulo job market during the late 1800s and early 1900s cannot be ascribed to black incompetence, which is not supported by the evidence available, and which apparently formed no obstacle to the hiring of black workers in Rio de Janeiro and the Northeast. Instead I have emphasized the importance of state intervention in the labor market, which enabled employers to reject the new working conditions proposed by black workers and to make more favorable bargains with the Europeans. As the immigrants and their children became more aggressive and effective in pursuing their individual and collective interests, the state government reoriented its policies and abandoned the program of subsidized immigration in 1927. This promptly brought black workers back into the manual labor force in São Paulo, in which they have participated at high levels ever since.

Low educational and skill levels are often cited as the reasons for the underrepresentation of black workers in white-collar positions. Black educational attainment does indeed lag behind white.[2] But as recent research has indicated, disparities in income and job attainment between blacks and whites actually increase, in both relative and absolute terms, as one moves up the educational ladder: the more education that black job seekers obtain, the farther they fall behind their white peers in the competition for good jobs and salaries, and the greater an impediment discrimination seems to become.[3] Detecting the precise sources of that discrimination is difficult. Personnel administrators say that they are acting under orders from higher executives; executives say that they are responding to the preferences of the public and to the demands of their white employees, who do not wish to work alongside blacks. Members of that white public and work force, in turn, insist that they themselves are opposed to discrimination, but readily admit that most other whites they know are not quite so enlightened.

Whoever is enforcing and propagating it, the second legacy of slavery—white prejudice based on negative racial stereotypes—seems to emerge as one of the major motives behind discrimination. It is striking, however, to note how the power of these stereotypes seems to ebb and flow over time, and from one sector of the economy to another. During the early decades of the century, images of black laziness and incompetence served to justify planters' and industrialists' unwillingness to hire libertos and other Afro-Brazilians; but the excluding power of those images abruptly evaporated during the 1920s. And while they are frequently cited today as the reason why blacks are not hired for white-collar positions, negative stereotypes apparently pose no obstacle to the hiring of black people to fill service occupations of considerable trust and responsibility.

Clearly some historical conditions are favorable to the propagation and empowerment of racist stereotypes, and others are not. With the strength and resources of the planter state behind them, São Paulo's employers were free to invoke such images, and to act on them; with the ending of the immigration program, and the destruction of the planter state in 1930, the stereotypes lost their excluding power in the industrial and agricultural sectors of the economy. They remain alive and active in Brazilian consciousness, however, and in recent decades have been exploited by members of the white middle class to defend their hard-won and at times tenuous social superiority over the *povo*. In this more recent period, unlike during the First Republic, negative racial images do not have official state support.[4] As a result, as many observers have commented, their role in denying black people equality of opportunity is more elusive and subtle than in systems of comprehensive, state-mandated and enforced racial inequality. However, those very qualities give Brazilian racism a flexible, adaptive quality that, in the long run, provides more effective protection and support for racial hierarchy than do cruder and more overt systems of state-enforced discrimination.

Racial exclusion at the working-class level was overturned by two developments: the reversal of state labor policy, and a process of economic development which generated a new stratum of jobs more desirable and lucrative than those in industry and agriculture. Such positive effects did not extend to the white-collar sector of the labor market, where racial barriers remain firmly in place. Nor does economic growth offer the hope of breaking down such barriers in the future. Throughout the industrialized world, administration and the professions remain the most prestigious and highest-paying areas of the labor market; at least for the immediate future, there will be no new layers of even more desirable job opportunities to siphon off upwardly mobile white workers from the white-collar sector, and open it up to Afro-Brazilians. To the contrary: in light of the extended economic crisis which has afflicted Brazil during the 1980s, and the resultant slowdown in the expansion of employment opportunities at the white-collar level, competitive pressures in that part of the labor market may actually have increased over the last ten years, and the color bar in white-collar employment may have been strengthened.[5]

One finds it difficult, therefore, to concur with predictions that economic growth and development will eventually resolve the country's racial inequities. Democratic politics, and action by the state, appear to be the more likely forces to overturn racial hierarchy. As we have seen, racial hierarchy itself forms one of the most formidable obstacles to the establishment of democratic norms and institutions in Brazil. Nevertheless, significant progress has been made in both areas over the last hundred years.

Race and Politics

This book began with the struggle of black people to escape their state-enforced captivity. After roughly a forty-year period in which imperial policy and slave resistance gradually undermined slavery as an institution, the slaves' massive flights from the plantations in 1887 and 1888 finally forced their owners to enact the Golden Law and accept full emancipation. The very success of mass-based political action in destroying slavery, however, contributed directly to the alienation of planter support from the monarchy and its replacement by a planter-dominated Republic eighteen months later.

The ensuing period of Republican rule had catastrophic consequences for the black population, which, particularly in São Paulo State, suffered a triple exclusion from the mainstream of national life. The formal and informal practices of the Republic denied political participation to virtually the entire population. The effort to remake Brazil in the image of Europe, and the doctrine of whitening, pointedly excluded Afro-Brazilians from this new Republican society in the making. And the labor policies of the São Paulo State government barred Afro-Brazilians from participation in the rapidly growing economy.

When the Republic fell in 1930, therefore, Afro-Brazilians heartily applauded its demise, and moved to take advantage of the opportunities opened by the new regime. Such opportunities did not extend to inclusion by the mainstream political parties, so Afro-Brazilians responded by creating their own racially defined party, the Brazilian Black Front. The Front eventually fell victim to the same conflicts and polarization between Left and Right which were tearing apart the Brazilian political system more generally, and when Getúlio Vargas imposed the New State in 1937, the Black Front suffered the same dissolution as the other political parties of that era.

While it closed down electoral politics, Vargas's right-wing populism simultaneously opened up other avenues of participation for Afro-Brazilians, most notably in the expanding industrial labor force, and in the labor movement through which the New State sought to organize and control this new working class. The overthrow of Vargas in 1945, and the subsequent restoration of electoral politics in the Second Republic, provided the conditions for the expansion of labor-based and populist political parties which, unlike the parties of the First Republic and the 1930s, now included black people in their appeals to poor and working-class Brazilians. Blacks responded by throwing their support to those parties, thus removing the electoral base for the resurgence of a racially defined political movement comparable to the Black Front.

The military coup of 1964 brought this experiment in populist democracy to an end. Like the earlier dictatorship of 1937–1945, the military regime of 1964–1985 greatly restricted political participation while promoting a program of economic development which gave Afro-Brazilians the possibility of further economic advancement, now into the middle class. In pursuing those opportunities, however, upwardly mobile Afro-Brazilians found themselves running into the silent barriers of white racial solidarity; and in response to those barriers, a new black movement appeared in the 1970s. Inspired by black struggles for freedom and equality in Africa and the United States, and stimulated by the process of *abertura* under way at the time, the Unified Black Movement and other organizations adopted an explicitly political orientation, and sought to mobilize the black population to combat, through electoral and other means, racial discrimination and inequality in Brazilian society. The movement failed to generate significant support among poor and working-class blacks. But it did succeed in getting parties, the Catholic church, labor unions, and other organizations to start paying attention, for the first time ever, to issues of racial injustice in Brazilian society; and by the mid-1980s, state and federal governments were addressing those issues in ways unprecedented in Brazilian history.

The Future

We seem to have at least some reason, then, to accept Gilberto Freyre's and Florestan Fernandes's optimistic assessments of the long-term prospects of Brazilian race relations. But as I write these words, in mid-1990, optimism is decidedly out of vogue in Brazil.[6] Struggling against crushing foreign debt and an inflation rate of well over 1,000 percent in 1989, the country faces what may well be the most severe economic crisis of its history. That crisis finds expression in social indicators as well. In São Paulo City, the most prosperous urban area in Brazil, an estimated 50 percent of the population lives in *favela* slums. In Brazil as a whole, an estimated seven million people (roughly one out of every twenty Brazilians) are children who "have lost all or most ties to their families and live or work on the streets of São Paulo, Rio de Janeiro and other large cities." Of the more than half-million abandoned children cared for in state-supported orphanages, 90 percent are black. A similar proportion obtains among the juvenile criminal population. The president of the federal Foundation for the Welfare of Minors observes that in Brazil today "a child who is small, black, and poor is by definition thought to be dangerous."[7]

In São Paulo—again, the richest state in Brazil—the number of abandoned children is approximately equal to that of the number of children enrolled in the public school system. "What kind of future can one expect," asks a Brazilian commentator, "if half the population is comprised of marginals?"[8] Most of those children will live lives blighted and stunted by acute poverty; many of them will resort to crime; and some of them will return to the nightmare with which this book began: that of slavery and forced labor. Between 1970 and 1986 over nineteen thousand cases of enslavement were brought to the attention of the Brazilian authorities, most of them involving agricultural workers being held in prisonlike conditions on isolated plantations. Tens—perhaps hundreds—of thousands more such workers languished undetected, or ignored, by the police. In São Paulo State alone, the state secretary of labor estimated in 1987 that thirty-five thousand workers were being held by employers against their will, and were laboring under conditions reminiscent of nineteenth-century slavery. Many of the punishments used on these workers, in fact, are the same as those used on Brazilian plantations hundreds of years ago.[9]

Even in such a grim report, however, one notes at least two important changes since the days of African slavery. First, and most obviously, slavery is now illegal, with the result that workers who can get their cases brought to the attention of the authorities stand a good chance of winning their freedom. Second, modern-day Brazilian slavery is an equal opportunity employer, open to whites, yellows, and Indians as well as blacks. Is this an improvement over racially defined African slavery? Definitely. As long as slave status was restricted to Africans and Afro-Brazilians, it was possible for whites to avert their eyes and ignore the horrors of the slave regime. When those horrors directly threaten members of one's own race and, by extension, oneself, whites are correspondingly more likely to recognize them, and to insist that they be eliminated.

But even if forced labor in Brazil is no longer racially defined, what about the other barriers of racial exclusion which still remain in place? How likely is it that white Brazilians, and particularly middle-class white Brazilians, will agree to surrender their racial privileges and accept policies aimed at creating genuine racial equality between blacks and whites? What is their reaction likely to be to the sorts of equal opportunity and affirmative action programs, based on the United States experience of the 1970s, now being proposed by Afro-Brazilian politicians and activists?[10]

A quick comparison of the circumstances surrounding the enactment of civil rights and equal opportunity legislation in the United States in the 1960s, and those obtaining in Brazil today, suggests the unlikelihood of United States–style state action against racism replicating itself in Brazil. The United States of the 1960s had experienced two decades of strong economic growth, with the promise of more to come. The resulting mood of prosperity and expansion made it possible for white Americans to acquiesce in the broadening of opportunity to the nation's racial minorities, which at that time constituted less than an eighth of the national population.[11]

Nonwhites in Brazil, by contrast, compose almost half of the national population. And the Brazil of 1990, unlike the United States of the 1960s, has experienced a decade of profound economic crisis. The scope and magnitude of Brazilian poverty make it impossible to pretend that the end of racial discrimination would mean the end of suffering and privation in that country—the explicit goal of the United States' Great Society. Nor would it mean the end of violent crime, which for many white Brazilians is the most tangible negative consequence of Brazil's social and racial inequalities. Thus for most white Brazilians, proposals to open opportunities for education, jobs, and housing to that near-majority of the population which is of mixed or pure African ancestry promise only to deprive middle-class whites of their privileged position while bringing them no compensatory benefits.[12]

Continuing the comparison a bit further, and moving it to a different level, the United States' civil rights movement was able to persuade American society in the 1960s that the continuation of racial discrimination and inequality was wrong not just on pragmatic, practical grounds (since, for example, it bred poverty and crime) but on moral grounds as well. The civil rights legislation of the 1960s was made possible in large part by black leaders'—most notably Martin Luther King, Jr.—ability to seize the moral imagination of the country, and make Americans see that racial discrimination violated the basic teachings both of Christianity and of classical liberalism, the twin pillars on which the American experiment was built.

Since the Brazilian national experiment is based on these same two pillars, a similar appeal should be possible in that country as well. But here we come up against the debilitating effects of Brazilian elites' use of the principles and slogans of liberal democracy to disguise and legitimate authoritarian, exclusionary political regimes. As most Brazilians will readily acknowledge, one of the consequences of this political cognitive dissonance has been a deep and pervasive cynicism, particularly concerning high-flown political ideals and principles.[13] Public appeals based on such concepts as justice, equality, and the rights of citizenship tend to be dismissed as either hopelessly naive or the most cynical kind of demagoguery—and with good reason, since the history of Brazilian politics over the last hundred years provides abundant evidence of the emptiness of those concepts, and the folly of believing in them. This means that popular, mass-based campaigns aimed at realizing such ideals face the additional obstacle of first persuading their listeners that ideals deserve to be taken seriously, and that if put into practice, they might actually make for a better Brazil. The fact that organizers of such movements start with these principles working against them rather than for them is further indication of the effectiveness of elite strategies for preserving continued inequality in their country.

We could go on at length exploring additional obstacles to the construction of racial democracy in Brazil: the continuing faith of millions of Afro-Brazilians in "whitening" as a vehicle of social mobility, and their resulting reluctance to confront or question racism; the multitude of highly visible problems facing Brazil, many of which demand more immediate responses than the vaguer, underlying problem of racial inequality, and against which civil rights activists must compete for public attention; the reluctance of Brazilians, both black and white, to enflame possible racial antagonisms by pressing for equal rights for blacks; and, not least, the extreme poverty and illiteracy of the mass of the country's black population, which makes them difficult to reach and enlist in the campaign against racial inequality. All these circumstances lead one to the conclusion that the answer to this Brazilian dilemma, if and when it comes, will be quite different from the answer which the United States developed in the 1960s and 1970s.

Given the failure of the United States' equal opportunity and affirmative action programs to eradicate racial inequalities in this country, one's first impulse is to welcome such differences. But the fact is that affirmative action has had its most positive impacts in precisely the area of the labor market where present-day racial strictures in Brazil are harshest and most excluding: white-collar, middle-class employment. One fears as well a response to Brazil's racial dilemma which would be perfectly in keeping with longstanding political practice in that country: accepting and even invoking the ideal of a new, genuine racial democracy while quietly permitting deeply ingrained patterns of racial inequality to continue undisturbed. Echoing U.S. president Dwight Eisenhower's belief that men's hearts will never be changed by legislation, a columnist for one of São Paulo's leading newspapers argues that "in Brazil there are laws for everything, but there are laws that 'stick' and laws that don't stick. . . . In Brazil there is an aggressive, open racism which pays no heed to law or the authorities. . . . We are a nation of racists, pure and simple, and no [antiracism law] has ever been obeyed."[14] As a result, even those who strongly oppose racial injustice despair of ever eradicating it through laws and state action.

As I have said, optimism is in short supply in Brazil today. If one is to find it anywhere, perhaps it lies, paradoxically, in reading the record of the past, and witnessing the constantly renewed struggle of Brazilians, both black and white, to overcome and tear down the political, social, and economic barriers which preserve privilege for the few and deny opportunity to the many. These struggles, individual and collective, have produced breathtaking changes in Brazilian society in the last hundred years. Our story began in an agrarian society based on plantation slavery and ruled by monarchy, a society in which, even after slavery was abolished, black people were effectively barred from taking part in the economic and political life of their country. It concludes one hundred years later in an urban, industrial democracy in which black people and white people vote in open elections for those candidates and parties that they see as most likely to meet their individual and collective needs.

Whenever it has happened in Brazilian history, democratization of the political system has produced unanticipated consequences, and the advancement of popular struggles in surprising and unexpected ways.[15] If democracy is permitted to function in Brazil, it will produce more such outcomes in the years and decades to come; and perhaps one of those unexpected developments will be a collective decision on the part of Brazilian society to combat racial discrimination and inequality. There are good reasons for predicting that no such action will be forthcoming. But having valued the myth of racial democracy for so long, and now having had to renounce it, will Brazilians be willing to leave glaring racial injustice in place as its legacy? After decades of having derived enormous pride and prestige from their international image as the world's most harmonious multiracial society, will Brazilians accept a new place on the world stage as a "South Africa without apartheid"? I doubt it. Perhaps their response will be to try to construct a new myth of racial democracy to replace the old. But I prefer to think that some day in the future, just as the world looked to Brazil in the 1940s and 1950s for instruction in how to build racial democracy, so it will be looking to Brazil again for an object lesson in how a nation replaces myth with reality.

APPENDICES

GLOSSARY

NOTES

SELECTED BIBLIOGRAPHY

INDEX

Appendix A
Population of São Paulo State, 1800–1980

	Whites	Browns	Blacks	Yellows[a]	Unspecified	Total	Slaves
1797							
N	89,323	30,487	38,640	—	—	158,450	—
%	56.4	19.2	24.4				
1811							
N	87,624	44,692	33,152	—	—	165,468	38,542
%	53.0	27.0	20.0				23.3
1836							
N	148,984	61,906	72,120	—	740	283,750	78,858
%	52.5	21.8	25.4		0.3		27.8
1872							
N	433,432	235,923	167,999	—	—	837,354	156,612
%	51.8	28.2	20.1				18.7
1890							
N	873,423	331,804	179,526	—	—	1,384,753	
%	63.1	24.0	13.0				
1900	—	—	—	—	—	2,282,279	
1920	—	—	—	—	—	4,592,188	
1940							
N	6,097,862	337,814	524,441	214,848	5,351	7,180,316	
%	84.9	4.7	7.3	3.0	0.1		
1950							
N	7,823,111	292,669	727,789	276,851	14,003	9,134,423	
%	85.6	3.2	8.0	3.0	0.2		
1960							
N	10,605,624	1,076,113	763,625	357,239	21,205	12,823,806	
%	82.7	8.4	6.0	2.8	0.2		
1970	—	—	—	—	—	17,771,948	
1980							
N	18,712,885	4,613,762	1,152,215	474,901	88,311	25,042,074	
%	74.7	18.4	4.6	1.9	0.4		

Sources: 1797–1872, Samuel Harman Lowrie, "O elemento negro na população de São Paulo," *Revista do Arquivo Municipal de São Paulo* 4, 48 (1938), table 1, p. 12; 1872–1950, IBGE, *Recenseamento geral de 1950. Censo demográfico: Estado de São Paulo* (Rio de Janeiro, 1954), table 1, p. 1; 1960, IBGE, *Recenseamento geral de 1960. Censo demográfico: Estado de São Paulo* (Rio de Janeiro, n.d.), table 5, p. 10; 1970, IBGE, *Recenseamento geral de 1970. Censo demográfico: Brasil* (Rio de Janeiro, n.d.), table 40, p. 151; 1980, IBGE, *Recenseamento geral de 1980. Censo demográfico—dados gerais, migração, instrução, fecundidade, mortalidade—São Paulo* (Rio de Janeiro, 1983), table 1.4, pp. 10–11.

Note: The censuses for 1900, 1920, and 1970 did not provide a racial breakdown.
[a]People of Asian ancestry.

Appendix B
Brazilian Racial Terminology

It is well-known that Brazilians and North Americans have structured their multiracial societies in different ways. When citizens of the United States think about their fellow citizens of European and African descent, they assign such people to one of two dichotomous categories, "white" and "black." The black category is composed of people with any visible degree of African ancestry, regardless of whether such people also show evidence of European ancestry. The white category, by contrast, is composed of people who show no visible evidence of African or other non-European ancestry.[1]

The Brazilian system of racial categorization treats race mixture rather differently. While such mixture was in theory prohibited during the colonial period, laws to that effect went largely unobserved and unenforced, and extensive miscegenation took place in the colony. Colonial society distinguished between the products of such miscegenation *(pardos* or *mulatos)* and people of pure African ancestry *(pretos* or *negros)*, assigning higher legal and social status to the former. By the end of the colonial period, people of mixed racial ancestry outnumbered whites, and were "probably the most rapidly growing racial element in Brazil."[2]

The existence of this intermediate racial category has long been recognized as one of the fundamental differences between the United States and Brazilian systems of race relations; it formed the focal point, in fact, of Carl Degler's celebrated comparative treatment of race relations in the two countries, *Neither Black nor White.*[3] And as race mixture has continued into the twentieth century, it has generated a proliferation of racial labels which goes far beyond the initial three-category system. When asked to describe their color, Brazilians canvased in the 1980 census responded with 136 color and racial labels; when asked the same question in the National Household Survey of 1976, respondents provided interviewers with nearly 200 such terms.[4]

A number of social scientists, both Brazilian and foreign, have cited this proliferation of racial identities as one of the major factors preventing institutionalized racial discrimination in Brazil. After his informants used forty different racial labels to identify a series of photographs of individuals of varying color, anthropologist Marvin Harris concluded that if Brazilians "ever decided to become segregationists à la Mississippi or Capetown, they would have to build forty different kinds of schools rather than merely two." Harris and others go on to argue that these complexities also prevent informal discrimination in day-to-day life as well. "There are no subjectively meaningful Brazilian social groups based exclusively upon racial criteria. The terms Negro *(preto)* and white *(branco)* could denote clear-cut population segments for nobody but a physical anthropologist. In the actual dynamics of everyday life, superordinate-subordinate relationships are determined by the interplay between a variety of achieved and ascribed statuses, of which race is an important but not decisive element."[5]

We will return shortly to the issue of whether blacks (defined here, as in the rest of this book, as people of pure or mixed racial ancestry) and whites constitute "subjectively meaningful" social groups in Brazil. For the moment, let us consider whether blacks and whites constitute *objectively* meaningful social groups. The Brazilian censuses of 1940, 1950, and 1980, and the National Household Surveys of the 1970s and 1980s, all documented clear disparities between white and nonwhite Brazilians in the areas of health, income, and education. They also demonstrated that, although pardos do occupy a position in the Brazilian racial hierarchy between pretos and whites, the position is much closer to that of the preto racial group than to the whites.[6] These findings have led a number of social scientists to conclude that in Brazil "the 'color line' seems to be located between whites and nonwhites, and not between mulattoes and blacks, as it is sometimes believed to be." Thus "to consider Blacks and mulattoes as composing a homogeneous 'nonwhite' racial group does no violence to reality."[7]

On the basis of such arguments, as well as of its own analysis of the 1976 and 1980 data, the government agency responsible for collecting census and other demographic data, the Brazilian Institute of Geography and Statistics (IBGE— and more specifically, within IBGE, the Department of Social Studies and Indicators), decided in 1980 to begin analyzing and publishing racial data in dichotomous form, dividing the population into whites (brancos) and blacks (negros). This quiet, seemingly routine decision by a group of government researchers and technocrats was actually rather far-reaching in its implications. While not abandoning the traditional three-category concept of race (or four, if one includes the category of "yellows," *amarelos*, used for people of Asian ancestry), IBGE had moved toward an alternative conceptualization of Brazilian race relations, in which people of both pure and mixed African ancestry are seen as a single racial group—in short, a North American vision of race.[8]

In São Paulo, Rio de Janeiro, and the states of southern Brazil, this dichotomous vision of Brazilian racial hierarchy corresponds not just to "objective" statistical indicators but to subjective Brazilian perceptions of race as well.[9] In survey research carried out in the southern state of Santa Catarina in the late 1950s, sociologists Fernando Henrique Cardoso and Octávio Ianni found that "whites make a social and cultural distinction between their black and mulatto neighbors and themselves. Conversely, blacks and mulattoes distinguish themselves from whites in the same way. The dichotomy which exists is clear. . . . all non-white individuals are considered to be *negros*." On the basis of further research in the neighboring state of Paraná (which also borders on São Paulo), Ianni went on to argue that Brazilians tend to dichotomize their society into the racially superior white "us," and the racially inferior black, brown, and red "them." Following his own research in Rio Grande do Sul, Cardoso was ready to state flatly that "the mulatto is a *black*, and, therefore, an *inferior*, but, at the same time, he is a privileged black." Or, to reverse the order of this observation, the mulatto is a privileged black (though recent research calls into question the extent of those privileges), but still a black, and therefore an inferior.[10]

Historian Décio Freitas, responding to the question, who is a black?, argues that in Brazil "we consider as blacks all those who are dark-skinned, who possess a pigmentation which is neither white nor Indian. These 'pardos,' who according to IBGE constitute the majority of non-whites . . . are considered socially to be blacks."[11] Evidence in support of this proposition may be found in one of the archives which was most useful to me in my research: the clipping files of *O Estado de São Paulo*, the state's leading newspaper. *O Estado* maintains topical files on a variety of subjects, including "*Negros* in Brazil," and "Mulattoes in Brazil."[12] The file on *negros*, which goes back to the 1880s, contains three thick folders and hundreds of articles. As of mid-1988, the file on mulattoes contained eight articles. This reflects two facts: that São Paulo journalists writing about Afro-Brazilians during the last century have tended to group them under the heading of *negros;* and even when those journalists have distinguished between pretos and pardos, *O Estado's* archivists continue to group them into a single "black" category. The racial category of mulatto, supposedly so important in Brazil, seems barely to have figured in these people's consciousness.

Considerably more important than pardo, or mulatto, it would seem, is a racial category which has assumed increasing prominence in Brazil in recent years, that of *moreno* (literally, "tan" or "brunet"). Of the almost two hundred color denominations used by respondents in the 1976 National Household Survey, the two most frequent responses, accounting for over three-quarters of the individuals canvased, were white (42.4 percent) and moreno (34.8 percent).[13] Unlike "pardo" or "preto," "moreno" does not automatically connote African ancestry. However, students of race in Brazil disagree as to whether morenos are whites.[14] For anthropologist Maria Suely Kofes de Almeida, who did her research in São Paulo, "'moreno' is a subcategory of a broader category: white." A white informant in Rio de Janeiro agrees: "If you're morena, if you've got brownish skin, delicate features, and straight hair, you're considered to be within the norm, White. . . ."[15]

U.S. historian Carl Degler, by contrast, cites numerous instances in which "moreno" is used as a euphemism for "preto" or "mulatto," and is clearly distinguished from white.[16] In São Paulo, Bastide and Fernandes found the term frequently used to refer to "dark mulattoes and pretos" by those who wished to avoid offending them; it appears regularly in the social columns of São Paulo's black newspapers as an identifying label.[17] And when we follow through on the data from the 1976 survey, we find further evidence that the racial status of moreno is more closely associated with black racial status than with white. An initial question on the survey asked respondents to describe their own color, in response to which over three-quarters labeled themselves as white or moreno. A second question then asked respondents to assign themselves to one of the official IBGE racial categories: branco, pardo, preto, and amarelo. Of those who had identified themselves as moreno, 66.1 percent assigned themselves to the pardo category, and 8.3 percent to the preto category. Three-quarters of those who identified themselves as morenos were Afro-Brazilians—and perhaps more, since some Afro-Brazilian morenos may have chosen to assign themselves to the white category.[18]

Always alert to new developments on the Brazilian racial scene, in 1979 Gilberto Freyre commented on "the ever more generalized use, in Brazil, of the word moreno and the ever higher value, among Brazilians, of the condition or appearance of being moreno." Noting the large number of white people who tan themselves on Brazil's beaches in an effort to produce a moreno appearance, Freyre concluded that many Brazilians, when asked by the census takers in 1980 what their color was, would respond "moreno. And not white, nor black, nor yellow."[19]

Freyre had a number of reasons for calling his readers' attention to the rise of *morenidade* in Brazil. On a tactical level, he was combatting demands by black activists and white scholars that the government restore race as a category of information to the 1980 census (chapter 7). But in a larger, strategic sense, he was stressing the concept of *morenidade* because he saw it as a means by which Brazil would convert itself into a country "beyond race," in which racial inequalities and tensions no longer chafed and worried the country as they had in the past. Promoting the racial category of moreno (which, as he indicated in the article cited above, would free Brazilians from the old white-black-yellow racial labels) was thus part of Freyre's life work of attempting to diffuse and dispel the powerful tensions of Brazil's racial past and present. Ironically, however, Freyre's own treatment of *morenidade* tends to evoke the longstanding Brazilian dream of whitening. Noting that "the most expressive examples" of Brazilian feminine beauty are all morenas, he then cited three actresses, each of them white: Sônia Braga, Vera Fischer, and Bruna Lombardi. The society "beyond race" thus proves to be yet another repetition of the turn-of-the-century fantasy of a white Brazil—and with beautiful women to boot![20]

Census figures make clear that during the last fifty years Brazil has experienced a process not of whitening but of "browning." Between 1940 and 1980 the pardo population was the country's fastest growing racial group, rising from 21.2 percent to 38.8 percent of the national population. During the same period whites declined from 63.5 percent to 54.2 percent of the total, and pretos from 14.6 percent to 5.9 percent.[21] If upwardly mobile Afro-Brazilians have been moving out of the pardo category and into the white racial category, it has not been in numbers sufficient to reverse this trend; and indeed, recent research by demographer Charles Wood suggests that such movement is negligible.

Wood used data from the 1950 and 1980 censuses to test whether Afro-Brazilians were availing themselves of the "mulatto escape hatch" and "passing" in significant numbers from the black racial category into the white. Focusing on the 1950 population between the ages of ten and twenty-nine, he used life-table survival techniques to calculate how large each racial group should have been in 1980, by which point they would have aged to between forty and fifty-nine. He found that, while the total population was very close (99.0 percent) to the projected value, each racial group showed marked, and unexpected, variations. The preto racial group was 38.3 percent smaller than expected, the pardo racial group was 32.6 percent larger than expected, and the white racial group was 8.2 percent smaller. Wood concluded that over a third of those labeled as pretos in 1950 had changed their racial identity to pardos by 1980. However, very few, if any, pardos had transferred into the white category. If anything, movement from the white category into the pardo category appeared to be occurring more frequently than the reverse.[22]

These findings reinforce the picture of a dichotomous racial classification system, in which movement *within* the black racial category is common and widespread, but in which movement across the barrier separating the white and black racial groups is relatively rare. It is important to note, however, that Wood's data, and all the other evidence cited thus far, come from the second half of the 1900s. This leaves open the possibility that black-white dichotomy may be the result of modernization and economic development, and is a late twentieth-century phenomenon which has little applicability to earlier periods of Brazilian history. Gilberto Freyre, after all, devoted an entire chapter of his history of nineteenth-century Brazil to "the rise of the college graduate and the mulatto"; even if it no longer applies today, might the traditional three-tier racial hierarchy be an accurate depiction of turn-of-the-century Brazilian society?[23]

Freyre and other authors do provide suggestive evidence of mulatto upward mobility in nineteenth-century Brazil. But as Freyre himself makes clear in discussing such mobility, "naturally we refer to the light mulatto; barring special favorable circumstances, the situation of the darker ones was much the same as that of the Negro."[24] And most of this evidence is anecdotal, focusing on selected individuals; statistical data concerning the pardo and preto racial groups as a whole never figure in these assertions of the greater opportunities open to mulattoes.[25]

In their own anecdotal survey of conditions in nineteenth-century São Paulo, Bastide and Fernandes conclude that there was in fact a strong dividing line in paulista society between "*negros*" and "*mestiços*," on the one hand, and whites, on the other. And while finding scattered evidence of greater pardo advancement (in relation to pretos), they conclude that such advancement took place "to a much lesser degree" in São Paulo than in Rio de Janeiro or the Northeast.[26] Mary Karasch's analysis of the 1834 census of Rio de Janeiro convincingly demonstrates that pardos occupied a genuinely intermediate position between blacks and whites on the occupational scale. However, these data come from shortly after independence; by the turn of the century, Sam Adamo's analysis of demographic data from the city shows that "mortality for mulattoes equalled or surpassed that of blacks. Familial stability of the [mulatto] group was also inferior to that of their darker counterparts. The data suggest upward mobility was achieved by only a few of the mulattoes in Brazil, while the overwhelming majority languished along the fringe of society with blacks."[27]

As important as statistical studies in deciding whether turn-of-the-century Brazil was a three-tier or two-tier racial system are the attitudes and perceptions of those Brazilians alive at the time. Here it is revealing to consult interview material gathered by Gilberto Freyre himself from Brazilians who lived through the period of the First Republic (1889–1930). In discussing race relations in those years, most of Freyre's informants distinguished between pretos and pardos. Many of them, however, then went on to lump the two groups together as "people of color" and to express strong prejudice against them.[28] The one black person interviewed, a pardo, also grouped Afro-Brazilians together, and confirmed the prejudice which both groups confronted during the years of the Republic. "Being a mulatto, my feeling toward mulattos and Negroes has to be one of solidarity, because since childhood I have suffered the social inferiority of the colored man in my country."[29]

Freyre portrayed the Republic as a period of "considerable progress in ethnic democratization." As chapters 3 and 5 of this book indicate, however, and as Freyre readily conceded, these were also the years of the "whitening thesis," during which, like their European and North American counterparts, Brazil's elites were fascinated by the concept of white racial supremacy.[30] Freyre argued that the dream of whitening led Brazilian society to offer greater opportunities to those individuals who had mixed their African ancestry with European. But the evidence presented in this book suggests that that dream in fact led Brazilians to deny opportunity to individuals who had mixed their European ancestry with African. Freyre and his supporters could present only scattered anecdotal evidence that there were significant differences between pardo and preto "life chances" during the Republican period; and in fact a number of his anecdotes suggest the opposite. Meanwhile, the only systematic quantitative research done to date on black living conditions during those years (the Adamo study) finds little appreciable difference between pardos and pretos.

Ever since the colonial period Brazilians have drawn a distinction between pardos and pretos, who they see as two related but different groups. Hallowed by centuries of usage, and now deeply engrained in Brazilian culture and attitudes, the distinction is a real one, with concrete social consequences. I accept its reality, and try to identify individuals as pardos or pretos when I have the information to do so. At the same time, however, this historical distinction has tended to obscure the strong similarities between the pardo and preto racial groups, and the very similar obstacles to upward mobility which members of both groups face. It is true that pardos are more likely than pretos to achieve such mobility; but the benefits of racial preference and social advancement come to only a small proportion of the pardo racial group, most of whom continue to live and work in conditions indistinguishable from those of their preto countrymen. As a result, on most statistical indicators the pardo population as a whole ranks only slightly higher than the preto population, and does not come close to occupying the position midway between whites and pretos that has frequently been asserted. Thus, although I acknowledge the existence of significant differences between the pardo and preto racial groups, some of which I discuss in the course of this book, for the most part I have chosen to emphasize the commonalities between the two groups as well as the black-white racial dichotomy, which, I believe, accurately describes twentieth-century Brazilian society.

Notes for Appendix B

1. This dichotomous system of racial classification has been in effect in the United States since the early 1900s. On the role of the mulatto population (which was tabulated as a separate racial category in the U.S. census from 1850 through 1920) prior to (and since) 1900, see Joel Williamson, *New People: Miscegenation and Mulattoes in the United States* (New York, 1980).

2. Dauril Alden, "Late Colonial Brazil," in Leslie Bethell, ed., *Cambridge History of Latin America* (Cambridge and New York, 1984), 2, p. 608; in the same volume, see also Maria Luiza Marcílio, "The Population of Colonial Brazil," pp. 37–63.

3. Carl Degler, *Neither Black nor White: Slavery and Race Relations in Brazil and the United States* (New York, 1971). In that book Degler described Brazil's "mulatto escape hatch," asserting that racially mixed individuals enjoy opportunities for upward mobility that are generally denied to people of pure African ancestry, and posited that "the mulatto is the key" to understanding the differences in the two countries' racial histories.

4. Clóvis Moura, "A herança do cativeiro," *Retrato do Brasil* 1, 10 (1984), p. 112; Gláucio Ary Dillon Soares and Nelson do Valle Silva, "Urbanization, Race, and Class in Brazilian Politics," *Latin American Research Review* 22, 2 (1987), p. 167.

5. Marvin Harris, *Patterns of Race in the Americas* (New York, 1964), pp. 58–59.

6. See, for example, the salary data in Table 6.2. Or note the literacy rates of Brazil's black and white populations, as indicated in the censuses of 1940, 1950, and 1980. (The 1980 census provides no information on literacy by race, so I used the percentage of the population with one or more years of schooling as a surrogate indicator. For the population as a whole, this number [66,526,266] corresponds fairly closely to the number of literates [69,703,993].)

	1940	1950	1980
Whites	39.5	44.2	(78.1)
Pardos	21.5	22.2	(59.6)
Pretos	15.8	20.2	(58.2)

IBGE, *Recenseamento geral de 1940. Censo demográfico: Estados Unidos do Brasil* (Rio de Janeiro, 1950), table 17, pp. 28–29; IBGE, *Recenseamento geral de 1950. Censo demográfico: Estados Unidos do Brasil* (Rio de Janeiro, 1956), table 17, pp. 20–21; IBGE, *Recenseamento geral do Brasil—1980. Censo demográfico—dados gerais, migração, instrução, fecundidade, mortalidade—Brasil* (Rio de Janeiro, 1983), table 1.5, pp. 12–13; and table 3.1, pp. 114–115.

7. Nelson do Valle Silva, "Black-White Income Differentials in Brazil, 1960" (Ph.D. dissertation, University of Michigan, 1978), pp. 143–144; Nelson do Valle Silva, "Updating the Cost of Not Being White in Brazil," in Pierre-Michel Fontaine, ed., *Race, Class, and Power in Brazil* (Los Angeles, 1985), p. 43. See also Peggy Lovell's research on salary inequality documented in the 1980 census, which concludes that while "there were crucial differences between blacks and mulattoes" in the labor market, "the findings clearly show that . . . the major dividing line falls between whites and nonwhites (hence confirming Silva's findings)." Peggy A. Lovell, "Racial Inequality and the Brazilian Labor Market" (Ph.D. dissertation, University of Florida, 1989), pp. 152–153. For other authors who view pardos and pretos as a single

Appendix B

black category, see Amaury de Souza, "Raça e política no Brasil urbano," *Revista de Administração de Empresas* 11, 4 (1971), pp. 61–70; Carlos Hasenbalg, *Discriminação e desigualdades raciais no Brasil* (Rio de Janeiro, 1979), pp. 197–221; Carlos Hasenbalg, "Race and Socioeconomic Inequalities in Brazil," in Pierre-Michel Fontaine, *Race, Class and Power*, pp. 25–41; Fundação Carlos Chagas, *Diagnóstico sobre a situação educacional de negros (pardos e pretos) no Estado de São Paulo* (São Paulo, 1986); Charles H. Wood and José Alberto Magno de Carvalho, *The Demography of Inequality in Brazil* (Cambridge and New York, 1988), pp. 144, 269–270; and the studies cited in note 8.

8. For discussion of the IBGE decision to start grouping racial data in dichotomous categories, see Lúcia Elena Garcia de Oliveira et al., *O lugar do negro na força de trabalho* (Rio de Janeiro, 1985), pp. 11–12; see also Francisca Laíde de Oliveira et al., "Aspectos da situação sócio-econômica de brancos e negros no Brasil" (internal rpt., IBGE, Rio de Janeiro, 1981). IBGE's decision to group pardos and pretos into a single *negro* racial category was subsequently replicated by the São Paulo State statistical service, SEADE. See the two-part article "Os negros no mercado de trabalho na Grande São Paulo," *Pesquisa de Emprego e Desemprego na Grande São Paulo* 9 (1985), pp. 8–16, and 10 (1985), pp. 8–19; and Miguel W. Chaia, "Discriminação racial," *Revista Fundação SEADE* 2, 2–3 (1986), pp. 7–14.

9. Beginning with Gilberto Freyre, most of the research which stresses the importance of the intermediate mulatto racial category has been carried out in the Northeast. See Donald Pierson, *Negroes in Brazil: A Study of Race Contact in Bahia* (Chicago, 1942); Charles Wagley, ed., *Race and Class in Rural Brazil* (rpt., New York, 1963); Harris, *Patterns of Race*. Not having lived or conducted research in the Northeast, I cannot comment on the use of racial terminology in that region.

10. Octávio Ianni, *Raças e classes sociais no Brasil* (2nd edition, São Paulo, 1988), pp. 54, 83; Octávio Ianni, *As metamorfoses do escravo: Apogeu e crise da escravatura no Brasil meridional* (São Paulo, 1962), pp. 181, 244; Fernando Henrique Cardoso, *Capitalismo e escravidão no Brasil meridional: O negro na sociedade escravocrata do Rio Grande do Sul* (São Paulo, 1962), p. 301, emphasis in original.

11. Décio Freitas, "Que é um negro?" *Folha de São Paulo* (March 1, 1982), p. 3.

12. Arquivo de *O Estado de São Paulo*, file 6109, and file 50.690.

13. The other labels were: pardos (7.6 percent), pretos (4.5 percent), *moreno claro*, light moreno (2.8 percent), *claro*, light-skinned (2.5 percent); and all other responses combined (5.3 percent). Soares and Silva, "Urbanization, Race, and Class," p. 166.

14. See the various definitions of "moreno" in Thomas H. Stephens, *Dictionary of Latin American Racial and Ethnic Terminology* (Gainesville, 1989), p. 320, some of which categorize morenos as "socially white," but most of which do not.

15. Maria Suely Kofes de Almeida, "Entre nós, os pobres, eles, os negros" (*dissertação de mestrado*, Universidade Estadual de Campinas, 1976), p. 80; Daphne Patai, *Brazilian Women Speak: Contemporary Life Stories* (New Brunswick, 1988), p. 12.

16. Degler, *Neither Black nor White*, pp. 102, 103, 110, 142, 144, 201.

17. Roger Bastide and Florestan Fernandes, *Brancos e negros em São Paulo* (3rd edition, São Paulo, 1971), p. 136.

18. Soares and Silva, "Urbanization, Race, and Class," p. 166. In responding to the second question, 2.6 percent of those who had initially identified themselves as pardo,

and 2.0 percent of those who had identified themselves as preto, assigned themselves to the white racial category.

19. Gilberto Freyre, "Brasileiro—sua cor?" *Folha de São Paulo* (December 5, 1979).

20. Reading the meaning of *morenidade* rather differently was populist politician Leonel Brizola, whose program of *socialismo moreno* brought him to power as governor of Rio de Janeiro State in the elections of 1982, and made him a leading contender for the Brazilian presidency in the elections of 1989. See chapter 7.

21. Charles H. Wood, "Census Categories and Subjective Classifications of Race in Brazil: An Empirical Assessment" (unpublished paper presented at the Seminário Internacional sobre Desigualdade Racial no Brasil Contemporáneo, Belo Horizonte, March 1990), table 1.

22. Wood, "Census Categories."

23. Gilberto Freyre, *The Mansions and the Shanties: The Making of Modern Brazil* (New York, 1963), pp. 354–399. São Paulo historian Emília Viotti da Costa accepts the Freyre interpretation as well. "Whether in rural or urban areas, mulattos as a whole were more upwardly mobile than their darker-skinned brethren. The opportunities for social elevation increased in proportion to the lightness of a freedman's skin. And as the nineteenth century progressed, the situation of the mulatto improved." *The Brazilian Empire: Myths and Histories* (Chicago, 1985), p. 186.

24. Freyre, *Mansions and Shanties*, p. 410.

25. Such data are indeed hard to come by. But Freyre could have found at least some evidence of mulattoes' higher status in the 1872 census, which showed that 87.4 percent of the pardo population was free, as opposed to only 47.1 percent of the preto population. Directoria Geral de Estatística, *Recenseamento da população do Império do Brasil a que se procedeu no dia 1º de agosto de 1872. Quadros geraes* (Rio de Janeiro, 1873), table 1.

26. Bastide and Fernandes, *Brancos e negros*, pp. 85–86, 116.

27. Mary C. Karasch, *Slave Life in Rio de Janeiro, 1808–1850* (Princeton, 1987), p. 69; Sam C. Adamo, "The Broken Promise: Race, Health and Justice in Rio de Janeiro, 1890–1940" (Ph.D. dissertation, University of New Mexico, 1983), p. 271.

28. Some sample quotations from the white interviewees: "I have always been against the union of Negroes and mulattoes with whites." This same individual said he would have been "greatly displeased" if one of his children had tried to marry "a person of darker skin." Another informant felt that it was "undeniable" that there existed "a frank distinction between persons of color and the so-called whites of European origin, thus creating a perennial social inequality and an automatic separation of the races by voluntary choice." Júlio de Mesquita, publisher of *O Estado de São Paulo*, said, "I would never willingly accept the marriage of any member of my family with anyone who was clearly a person of color. This I say, because I cannot agree to bringing people into a world where they would be unfortunate, and in Brazil it is the Negro and mulatto who are increasingly, in every way, among the unfortunates." Another informant concurred, saying that if any of his female relatives "had chosen colored husbands, I should have considered them mad. If I could not prevent such a marriage, I would be most profoundly displeased, not because I am racially prejudiced, but simply because present realities make me fearful for the tranquility and happiness of a white person obliged to face for the rest of his life the results which

such a strange and unusual union would necessarily produce." Freyre reproduced this material virtually without comment, never acknowledging its direct refutation of his assertions of racial democracy. Gilberto Freyre, *Order and Progress: Brazil from Monarchy to Republic* (New York, 1970), pp. 203–218.

29. Freyre, *Order and Progress*, p. 204.

30. Freyre noted that, during the Campos Sales presidency (1898–1902), "there was much discussion of white supremacy," and that the baron of Rio Branco, foreign minister from 1902 to 1912, "allowed himself to be carried to Aryanist extremes." *Order and Progress*, pp. 178–179, 198, 202. For commentary in São Paulo's leading newspaper on "the moral supremacy of the white race," see "Loucos ou ineptos," *A Província de São Paulo* (May 9, 1889).

Appendix C
Personnel Records at the
Jafet and São Paulo Tramway,
Light, and Power Companies

At both the Jafet and São Paulo Light companies, personnel records are divided into two series of documents. The first, in use from the firms' foundings through the mid-1930s, is a short summary record, called *fichas pequenas* (small cards) at Jafet, and *records prontuários* at São Paulo Light. These were filled out at the time an individual was hired, and contain little or no information on that individual's subsequent career with the firm. A much more detailed document came into use in 1932 at São Paulo Light, and in 1935 at Jafet, to comply with the recordkeeping requirements of the new Social Security system. These later documents contain more biographical information on the employee than do the earlier records, and also keep a record (more complete at São Paulo Light than at Jafet) on the employee's work experience within the firm.

Given the differences in the two series of documents (pre- and post–Social Security), I decided to sample them differently. At Jafet I took a 20 percent sample of the *fichas pequenas*, simply tabulating the age (fifteen and under, sixteen and over), sex, race, and nationality (Brazilian or immigrant) of the individuals encountered. This produced a sample of 4,229 individuals hired by the firm between 1910 and 1935, the basic characteristics of which are shown in Table C.1.

Because of the wealth and detail of information contained in the second, post-1935 series of documents, it was not possible to take as large a sample of that material. In order to obtain a large enough number of Afro-Brazilian workers to ensure a statistically significant analysis, I took a racially stratified sample of this group of records: 1 percent of all white workers encountered, and 4 percent of nonwhites (*amarelos*, morenos, pardos, and pretos). The sample was obtained by simply counting sequentially through file drawers (which are organized alphabetically by first name, as is the custom in Brazil) and taking every nth record. This procedure produced a sample of 530 individuals, categorized in Table C.2.

I should emphasize that, since it is racially stratified, this sample as it stands is not representative of the Jafet work force as a whole, in which the proportion of

Table C.1. Sample of Workers at Jafet Plant, 1910–1935,
Using Pre-1935 Documentation

	Absolute Number	Percentage
Age		
6–15	1,151	27.2
16–	3,078	72.8
Sex		
Female	2,994	70.8
Male	1,235	29.2
Nationality		
Brazilian	2,850	67.4
Immigrants	1,379	32.6
Race[a]		
White	2,358	90.8
Moreno	43	1.7
Pardo	108	4.2
Preto	87	3.4
No race recorded	1,633[b]	—

[a]Percentages were calculated excluding workers of unknown race.

[b]Includes 643 immigrants who presumably were white.

whites would be four times greater than it is in Table C.2. This sample can be used to compare biographical and career information on black and white workers as separate groups; unless one corrects for the underrepresentation of white workers, however, it cannot be used to draw conclusions about the labor force as a whole.

I handled the São Paulo Light records similarly to the Jafet records. However, differences in recordkeeping practices at the two firms led me to make a couple of changes in the sampling procedure. First, none of the short, pre–Social Security *records prontuários* included information on race. Since this greatly reduced the utility of those records for my research, I decided to take only a 5 percent sample of these documents, just to get an idea of the immigrant-Brazilian ratio in the company's work force at that time. This produced a sample of 1,122 individuals who worked for São Paulo Light between 1905 and 1935. All but a handful (one woman, and four young men age fifteen or under) were adult males. Three hundred seventy-one were Brazilian-born, 606 were foreign-born (mainly Portuguese, eastern Europeans, Italians, and Spaniards, in that order), and 145 had no birthplace listed.

The second difference with Jafet arose when I moved on to the Social Security–era documents. Once the new recordkeeping arrangements went into effect at Jafet, the company's personnel administrators were punctilious about recording information on workers' race, simply making uniform a practice which they were already following in the *fichas pequenas* by the late 1920s. Recordkeepers at São Paulo Light, however, continued their earlier custom of

Table C.2. Sample of Workers at Jafet, 1935–1960,
Using Post-1935 Documentation

	Male	Female	Total
White	109	175	284
Amarelo	0	2	2
Moreno	1	8	9
Pardo	38	80	118
Preto	33	84	117
Total	181	349	530

neglecting to record information on race, even though the new personnel forms explicitly asked for it. Thus a substantial number of personnel documents recorded during the 1930s appear at first glance to contain no information on workers' race. This also affected those workers who had been hired by São Paulo Light during the 1910s and 1920s and were still on the payroll at the time that the Social Security legislation went into effect. Often neither their old *records prontuários* nor their new Social Security documentation provided any information on their race.

Obviously this posed a serious obstacle to my plan to take a racially stratified sample of the company's work force—again, as at Jafet, 1 percent of the white workers and 4 percent of the nonwhites. I resolved this problem by using an additional document which appeared in almost every worker's file: his or her photograph. Although I did encounter borderline cases which were difficult to assign to either the white or black category, most were fairly clearcut. What I was *not* able to do on the basis of photographs was to assign pardo or preto status to Afro-Brazilians, nor did I attempt to do so. Instead, these individuals were assigned to an "unspecified Afro-Brazilian" category. This category of identification disappears in the 1940s, when the company's recordkeepers became more attentive to the datum of race.

This procedure produced a sample of 671 individuals, categorized as indicated in Table C.3. Again, as with the Jafet count, this sample was designed to facilitate comparisons between the black and white racial groups. It underrepresents the proportion of white workers in São Paulo Light by a factor of four and therefore cannot be used to make general statements about the company's workforce without correcting for that underrepresentation.

I should note a further difference between the Jafet and São Paulo Light records, which arises from the history of the two firms. After attempting a modernization and labor force–reduction campaign in the late 1950s, the Jafet family decided to close the factory in 1960 and devote their energies and resources to other, more lucrative enterprises. The firm's employees therefore constitute a social group with a clearly defined endpoint in time.

São Paulo Light, by contrast, remains a functioning, dynamic entity (though in 1981 it was nationalized and now operates under state management as Eletricidade de São Paulo [Eletropaulo]). Its work force therefore has no fixed endpoint, and significant numbers of employees hired as far back as the 1940s

Table C.3. Sample of Workers at São Paulo Light, 1909–1960,
Using Post-1935 Documentation

	Male	Female	Total
White[a]	333	11	344
Moreno	22	0	22
Pardo	148	0	148
Preto	117	0	117
Unspecified Afro-Brazilian[b]	40	0	40
Total	660	11	671

[a]Includes fifty-seven individuals identified by photograph rather than
by written documentation.
[b]Identified by photograph rather than written documentation.

remained active in the firm at the time of my research. In order to protect the
privacy of its current employees and those recently in its employ, the company
granted me access only to the files of workers hired no later than 1960, and
discharged no later than 1970. As a result, workers hired in the 1950s represented
the largest decade-cohort in the Jafet sample but a relatively small one at São
Paulo Light (92 workers, versus 61 hired in the 1920s, 183 hired in the 1930s, and
319 hired in the 1940s).

Finally, a closing similarity between the two sets of documents: as might be
expected, a number of the individuals sampled were employed by their companies on more than one occasion. In the case of Jafet, for example, 476 of the 530
workers in the sample had only one experience of employment at the factory.
Another 54 workers, however, worked for Jafet, left their jobs, and then were
rehired at later dates. Of these 54 individuals, 46 were hired twice, 5 were hired
three times, 2 were hired four times, and 1 individual worked for the company on
five separate occasions. This sample of 530 workers therefore had a total of 596
experiences of employment with the firm. At São Paulo Light, the analogous
figure is 671 workers who had a total of 777 experiences of employment with the
firm. Analysis which looks at these workers as a social group (which examines,
e.g., their marital status, or birthplace, or median age upon entering the firm, or
education) uses the *individual* as the unit of analysis, and is based on information
recorded when that person was first hired. Analysis which looks at these workers'
experience within the firm (e.g., median period of time worked, disciplinary
record, promotions) takes the *experience of employment* as the unit of analysis,
and therefore uses the larger data sets of 596 (in the case of Jafet) and 777 cases (in
the case of São Paulo Light).

Glossary

amarelo—yellow; a person of Asian ancestry

abertura—opening; the process of phased transition from military dictatorship to civilian democracy during the 1970s and 1980s

aviso prévio—one month's notice that employers must provide to workers when firing them without just cause; or the payment of one month's salary if that notice is not given

boa aparência—good appearance; in want ads and job descriptions, a euphemism for white racial status

branco—white; a person of more or less unmixed European ancestry

branqueamento—whitening; the process of becoming white

caboclo—dark-skinned ruralite of indeterminate racial origin

caifazes—activist abolitionists who encouraged and assisted slaves to flee the plantations

caipira—peasant, backwoodsman

candomblé—Afro-Brazilian religion, based on West African deities and forms of worship

capanga—gunman or ruffian hired by plantation owner

capitão do mato—hunter of escaped slaves

capoeira—combination of dance and martial art, developed by slaves

colono—contract laborer on a coffee plantation, paid a set fee for tending a certain number of trees

concientizar—to raise the consciousness of

distensão—period of "decompression" during the mid-1970s, when the military dictatorship reduced its human rights violations, and relaxed restrictions on civilian political organizations

faculdade—institution of higher education; school within a university

favela—urban slum, usually composed of small houses built by the inhabitants

fazenda—plantation; large agricultural estate

fazendeiro—owner of a *fazenda*

furagreve—strikebreaker

galés—literally, the "galleys"; prison sentence of forced labor on a chain gang

263

indenização—severance pay of one month's salary for each year worked at the firm

liberto—a former slave, now free

mineiro—native of the state of Minas Gerais

moreno—brunet; a person with tan or light brown skin

mulato—mulatto; a person of mixed race

negro—black; originally, in the colonial period and nineteenth century, a person of unmixed African ancestry; while retaining its original meaning, over the course of the twentieth century *"negro"* has increasingly come to mean a person with any visible African ancestry, mixed or unmixed

negro assumido—black person who accepts and embraces his or her racial identity, and does not try to present himself or herself as white

negro em ascensão—upwardly mobile black person

pardo—brown; a person of mixed race

paulista—native of, or pertaining to, the state of São Paulo

periferia—poor suburban communities surrounding São Paulo

povo—the people, the masses

preto—a person of unmixed African ancestry

quilombo—settlement or encampment of escaped slaves

racismo às avessas—literally, reverse or upside-down racism; black racism against whites

regresso—reconsolidation of central monarchical authority during the 1840s

salário mínimo—minimum wage, expressed in terms of a monthly salary, and set by the federal government

tenentismo—radical movement of young army officers during the First Republic

trabalhismo—movement in support of Getúlio Vargas's policies concerning workers and organized labor

vadiagem—vagrancy, idleness, avoiding work

vadio—bum, vagrant, idle individual who refuses to work

Notes

Chapter 1. Introduction

1. "Black" is used here to refer to people of both pure and mixed African ancestry, referred to in Brazil as *pretos* (blacks) and *pardos* (browns, mulattoes). It will retain that sense throughout the book, and will be used interchangeably with "Afro-Brazilian." This corresponds to present-day Brazilian usage, which tends to group pardos and pretos together under the heading of *negros* (blacks). At the same time, however, Brazilians continue to distinguish between pardos and pretos, and I will use these more specific terms as well. For a fuller discussion of racial terminology in Brazil, see Appendix B.

2. According to the census of 1980, of Brazil's 119.0 million people, 53.3 million were Afro-Brazilians: 7.1 million pretos and 46.2 million pardos. Instituto Brasileiro de Geografia e Estatística (hereafter IBGE), *Recenseamento geral do Brasil—1980. Censo demográfico—dados gerais, migração, instrução, fecundidade, mortalidade—Brasil* (Rio de Janeiro, 1983), table 1.11, pp. 34–35. This was double the black population of the United States, which in 1980 was 26.7 million. United States Bureau of the Census, *Statistical Abstract of the United States, 1987* (Washington, D.C., 1986), p. 17. Nigeria, with an estimated 1980 population of 84.7 million, is the only country in the world with a larger black population than Brazil's.

3. For useful summaries of the literature on Brazilian race relations, see Emília Viotti da Costa's essay "The Myth of Racial Democracy: A Legacy of the Empire," in her *The Brazilian Empire: Myths and Histories* (Chicago, 1985); Thomas E. Skidmore, "Race and Class in Brazil: Historical Perspectives," in Pierre-Michel Fontaine, ed., *Race, Class, and Power in Brazil* (Los Angeles, 1985); and Pierre-Michel Fontaine, "Research in the Political Economy of Afro-Latin America," *Latin American Research Review* 12, 1 (1980), pp. 111–141. The work of the post-1970 generation of critics is discussed extensively in chapter 6.

Comparisons of Brazil's racial situation with that of South Africa seem to have originated, and are still most frequently heard, among the more militant of the post-1950 black activists, discussed in chapter 7. See, for example, Abdias do Nascimento's analysis of Brazilian "racial democracy" as "the South American version of South Africa. . . . Apartheid is a policy that is separate from, but equal to, 'racial democracy' in Brazil." *O genocídio do negro brasileiro: Processo de um racismo mascarado* (Rio de Janeiro, 1978), p. 87. In recent years, however, the Brazil–South Africa comparison has made its way into more mainstream political discourse, particularly on the Left. Political scientist Paulo Sérgio Pinheiro equates the two countries' racial systems in "Racismo à brasileira," *Folha de São Paulo* (December 12, 1984), p. 23; in "Joana e o paraiso da opressão," *Folha de São Paulo* (September 23, 1984); and in "Cem anos de solidão," *Caderno B, Jornal do Brasil* (May 8, 1988), p. 8, where he describes the Brazilian situation as "implicit apartheid" and "unwritten apartheid." Luis Inácio "Lula" da Silva, leader of the Workers' Party and recipient of 47 percent of the national vote in the presidential elections of 1989, also argues the similarities between apartheid and the Brazilian system of race relations: "It is not a legal apartheid, not a philosophical, juridical, socioeconomic institution, based on theoretical principles and on legislation. But it is a de facto apartheid, in the political sense, insofar as [it represents] the supremacy of a dominant white elite who see a direct correlation between skin color and possibilities of access to rights and power." Luis Inácio "Lula" da Silva, "A mistificação da democracia racial," *Folha de São Paulo* (February 16, 1988), p. 3.

4. See chapter 6.

5. The literature on Brazilian slavery is surveyed in Richard Graham, "Brazilian Slavery Re-examined: A Review Article," *Journal of Social History* 3, 4 (1970), pp. 431–453; Stuart B. Schwartz, "Recent Trends in the Study of Slavery in Brazil," *Luso-Brazilian Review* 25, 1 (1988), pp. 1–25; and Robert M. Levine, "'Turning on the Lights': Brazilian Slavery Reconsidered One Hundred Years after Abolition," *Latin American Research Review* 24, 2 (1989), pp. 201–217. For some of the more important monographs, see the works by Gilberto Freyre cited in note 9 below; Fernando Henrique Cardoso, *Capitalismo e escravidão no Brasil meridional: O negro na sociedade escravocrata do Rio Grande do Sul* (São Paulo, 1962); Robert E. Conrad, ed., *Children of God's Fire: A Documentary History of Black Slavery in Brazil* (Princeton, 1983); Jacob Gorender, *O escravismo colonial* (3rd edition, São Paulo, 1980); Octávio Ianni, *As metamorfoses do escravo: Apogeu e crise da escravatura no Brasil meridional* (São Paulo, 1962); Mary C. Karasch, *Slave Life in Rio de Janeiro, 1808–1850* (Princeton, 1987); Katia M. de Queirós Mattoso, *Ser escravo no Brasil* (São Paulo, 1982); Suely Robles Reis de Queiroz, *Escravidão negra em São Paulo: Um estudo das tensões provocadas pelo escravismo no século XIX* (Rio de Janeiro, 1977); Stuart B. Schwartz, *Sugar Plantations in the Formation of Brazilian Society: Bahia, 1550–1835* (Cambridge and New York, 1985); Robert Wayne Slenes, "The Demography and Economics of Brazilian Slavery, 1850–1888" (Ph.D. dissertation, Stanford University, 1976); Stanley J. Stein, *Vassouras: A Brazilian Coffee County, 1850–1900* (2nd edition, Princeton, 1985). In recent years there have been a number of books published on the final decades of Brazilian slavery, and the transition from slave labor to free labor. The earliest of these books—Emília

Viotti da Costa, *Da senzala à colônia* (2nd edition, São Paulo, 1982)—remains the best.

6. Philip Curtin estimates a total importation of 3.6 million Africans into Brazil versus 399,000 into the United States; Robert Conrad estimates that "probably more than 5,000,000 Africans" came to Brazil through the slave trade. Philip Curtin, *The Atlantic Slave Trade: A Census* (Madison, 1969), pp. 116, 268; Robert E. Conrad, *World of Sorrow: The African Slave Trade to Brazil* (Baton Rouge, 1986), p. 192. Estimates of the proportion of Brazil's population that was slave at the moment of independence vary from 30.8 percent (Marcílio) to 48.7 (Merrick and Graham); Dauril Alden proposes an intermediate figure of 38.1 percent. Maria Luiza Marcílio, "The Population of Colonial Brazil," in Leslie Bethell, ed., *Cambridge History of Latin America* (Cambridge and New York, 1984), 2, p. 63; Thomas W. Merrick and Douglas H. Graham, *Population and Economic Development in Brazil: 1800 to the Present* (Baltimore, 1979), p. 29; Dauril Alden, "Late Colonial Brazil," in Bethell, *Cambridge History of Latin America*, 2, p. 607. In the United States, by contrast, 17.8 percent of the population was counted as slave in the first national census, in 1790. United States Bureau of the Census, *Negro Population in the United States, 1790-1915* (Washington, D.C., 1918), p. 53. The 1790 census indicates that an additional 1.5 percent of the U.S. population was free black; in Brazil in 1819, the corresponding percentage was 27.8 percent. Alden, "Late Colonial Brazil," p. 607.

7. It is often asserted that most of the historical records concerning Brazilian slavery were destroyed by government decree at the time of emancipation, in 1888. The recent outpouring of research on slavery in that country demonstrates that this was not the case; see also Robert W. Slenes, "O que Rui Barbosa não queimou: Novas fontes para o estudo da escravidão no século XIX," *Estudos Econômicos* 13, 1 (1983), pp. 117-149.

8. A.J.R. Russell-Wood, *The Black Man in Slavery and Freedom in Colonial Brazil* (New York, 1982), p. 22. See also Laura de Mello e Souza's comments in *Desclassificados do ouro: A pobreza mineira no século XVIII* (Rio de Janeiro, 1982), p. 222, when she argues that in Brazil "free poor people have remained forgotten through the centuries," by their own society and by historians alike.

A recent example of a broader, more inclusive approach is Stuart Schwartz's previously cited *Sugar Plantations in the Formation of Brazilian Society*, which "is not so much about slavery per se as it is about the relationship between plantation production and the overall structure of society. In other words, although slavery lies at the core of the study, [he sees] it as a result of certain economic and cultural features that are themselves influenced by the dynamic relations between slave and master and between slavery and the larger society. In other words, slavery is viewed here as part of a larger structure of social and economic relations." P. xiv.

9. Much of Freyre's work is available in English translation. See in particular his three-volume history of Brazil, *The Masters and the Slaves: A Study in the Development of Brazilian Civilization* (New York, 1946; first Brazilian edition 1933); *The Mansions and the Shanties: The Making of Modern Brazil* (New York, 1963; first Brazilian edition 1936); and *Order and Progress: Brazil from Mon-*

archy to Republic (New York, 1970; first Brazilian edition 1959), all recently reissued by the University of California Press. See also his shorter works: *Brazil: An Interpretation* (New York, 1945); and *New World in the Tropics* (New York, 1961). For a balanced assessment of Freyre's career, see Thomas Skidmore, "Gilberto Freyre (1900–1987)," *Hispanic American Historical Review* 68, 4 (1988), pp. 803–805.

10. Freyre, *Masters and the Slaves*, pp. xii–xv.

11. Gilberto Freyre, "A propósito de preconceito de raça no Brasil," *O Estado de São Paulo* (June 25, 1969). The late 1960s and early 1970s were a period of intensive repression in Brazil, during which hundreds of students and academics suspected of leftist sympathies were arrested and tortured. Thomas Skidmore, *The Politics of Military Rule in Brazil, 1964–1985* (New York, 1988), pp. 125–135; Joan Dassin, ed., *Torture in Brazil* (New York, 1986). It was during this period, in 1969, that the Brazilian National Security Council singled out as a prime example of "leftist subversion" academic studies documenting "racial discrimination, which seek to provoke new sources of dissatisfaction with the regime, and with the duly constituted authorities." Thales de Azevedo, *Democracia racial* (Petrópolis, 1975), p. 53, fn. 27.

12. Fernandes's magnum opus, which touches only tangentially on matters of race, is *A revolução burguesa no Brasil* (São Paulo, 1974). His most important work on race relations is *A integração do negro na sociedade de classes*, 2 vols. (3rd edition, São Paulo, 1978), an abridged version of which is available in English as *The Negro in Brazilian Society* (New York, 1969). For other major titles, see his *O negro no mundo dos brancos* (São Paulo, 1972) and *Brancos e negros em São Paulo* (3rd edition, São Paulo, 1971), co-authored with Roger Bastide. He has published numerous articles in English; see "The Weight of the Past," in John Hope Franklin, ed., *Color and Race* (Boston, 1969); "Immigration and Race Relations in São Paulo," in Magnus Morner, ed., *Race and Class in Latin America* (New York, 1970); "Beyond Poverty: The Negro and the Mulatto in Brazil," in Robert Brent Toplin, ed., *Slavery and Race Relations in Latin America* (New York, 1974); and "The Negro in Brazilian Society: Twenty-five Years Later," in Maxine L. Margolis and William E. Carter, eds., *Brazil: Anthropological Perspectives* (New York, 1979). Of interest also is the work of Fernandes's students: Fernando Henrique Cardoso, *Capitalismo e escravidão;* and Ianni, *Metamorfoses do escravo;* Octávio Ianni, *Escravidão e racismo* (São Paulo, 1978); and Octávio Ianni, *Raças e classes sociais no Brasil* (2nd edition, São Paulo, 1988). See also Cardoso and Ianni's important jointly authored work, *Côr e mobilidade social em Florianópolis* (São Paulo, 1960).

13. Fernandes's arguments are examined in detail in chapter 3.

14. For examples of the influence which these two interpretations continue to exercise over Brazilian thought, see two of the editorials marking the centennial of the abolition of slavery: "A verdadeira discriminação," *O Globo* (May 13, 1988), p. 4, which is pure Freyre; and "Cem anos depois," *Folha de São Paulo* (May 13, 1988), p. 2, which is pure Fernandes.

15. In the absence of survey data on how Brazilians view and explain race relations in their country, this summary of Brazilian attitudes is based on my conversations with several hundred Brazilians over the last five years. Given my

own background, this "sample" is inevitably weighted toward members of the urban middle, professional, and academic classes, both black and white, in the cities of São Paulo and Rio de Janeiro. But I was also able to talk with a fair number of lower-level office workers, some service workers, and a handful of unskilled manual laborers at one of the warehouses where I did research.

16. However, observers of the country, myself included, noted a perceptible erosion in Brazilians' customary buoyancy when they were beaten down by the devastating economic crisis of the 1980s, touched off by the beginning of the international debt crisis in 1982. See, for example: "Growing Middle-Class Discontent," *Latin American Regional Reports: Brazil* (February 10, 1984), pp. 4–5; "Brazil's Political, Economic Confidence Falters," *Latin America Update* 12, 6 (November–December 1987), p. 3; "Unfamiliar Feelings of Pessimism Overtake Brazil's Politics and Economy," *New York Times* (November 10, 1988), p. 3; Alex Shoumatoff, "Rio: Is the Carnival Over?" *New York Times Sunday Magazine* (March 19, 1989), pp. 46–48, 94–97. A cartoon in Brazil's leading newsweekly, *Veja*, captures this unwonted spirit of pessimism. Two middle-class white men are talking. One asks the other, "So where do you think Brazil is headed?" The other replies, "Who knows? But one thing I do know: I don't want to be around when it gets there." "Distância," *Veja* (May 11, 1988), p. 13.

17. Freyre, *Mansions and Shanties*, p. 431; Gilberto Freyre, "Brasileiro—sua cor?" *Folha de São Paulo* (December 5, 1979). See also his "O fim das raças fixas?" *Folha de São Paulo* (August 3, 1979); and "O negro vai chegar à presidência da República antes da mulher," *Jornal do Brasil* (April 14, 1979). In *Mansions and Shanties*, originally published in 1936, Freyre had already forecast such a development, citing anthropologist Edgar Roquette-Pinto's observation that "pure Negroes" had virtually disappeared from Brazil: "By and large, the Negro of Brazil is the mulatto. The negroid. Among us the Negro problem has been simplified by the long process of miscegenation." P. 418.

18. Fernandes, *O negro no mundo dos brancos*, p. 30. See also the article by Fernandes's collaborator, French sociologist Roger Bastide, "The Development of Race Relations in Brazil," in Guy Hunter, ed., *Industrialisation and Race Relations: A Symposium* (London, 1965), which concludes on a similarly optimistic note: "Whereas it is the negative factors of industrialisation on racial relations which seem to dominate in the period we have just examined [1930–1950], . . . it is now [1960] the positive factors which are coming into play." P. 24.

19. Stanley Greenberg, *Race and State in Capitalist Development: Comparative Perspectives* (New Haven, 1980), p. 20. Carlos Hasenbalg, an Argentine sociologist trained in the United States and now resident in Brazil, makes a similar series of points in *Discriminação e desigualdades raciais no Brasil* (Rio de Janeiro, 1979), pp. 77–86. Indeed, the title of the dissertation on which his book is based nicely captures this point: Carlos Hasenbalg, "Race Relations in Post-Abolition Brazil: The Smooth Preservation of Racial Inequalities" (Ph.D. dissertation, University of California–Berkeley, 1978). For his critique of Fernandes's work in particular, see *Discriminação*, pp. 75–77.

Fernandes admits the possibility that capitalist development might tend to reinforce preexisting racial inequality rather than break it down: "It is possible that color prejudice will find in class society structural conditions favorable to its perpetuation. . . ." However, this caveat comes at the conclusion of a long passage which stresses the tendency of modern class inequalities to replace racial inequality. Bastide and Fernandes, *Brancos e negros*, pp. 143–146.

20. Pierre van den Berghe, *Race and Racism: A Comparative Perspective* (New York, 1967).

21. Greenberg, *Race and State*; John W. Cell, *The Highest Stage of White Supremacy: The Origins of Segregation in South Africa and the American South* (Cambridge and New York, 1982); George M. Fredrickson, *White Supremacy: A Study in American and South African History* (New York, 1981). For a comparative discussion of these three books, see George Reid Andrews, "Comparing the Comparers: White Supremacy in the United States and South Africa," *Journal of Social History* 20, 3 (1987), pp. 585–599. For an examination of the long-term evolution of racial inequality in the United States which is not explicitly comparative, but which is nevertheless very illuminating on a number of these questions, see William J. Wilson, *The Declining Significance of Race: Blacks and Changing American Institutions* (2nd edition, Chicago, 1980). And for an insightful examination of post–World War II racial inequality in the United States, see Michael Reich, *Racial Inequality: A Political-Economic Analysis* (Princeton, 1981).

22. On this "alliance of gold and maize" in South Africa, and the cooperative relationship between planters and industrialists in the American South, see also Cell, *Highest Stage*, pp. 63, 161–169.

23. On the racial policies of organized labor in the United States, see Greenberg, *Race and State*, pp. 311–355; Wilson, *Declining Significance*, pp. 42–87; Julius Jacobson, ed., *The Negro and the American Labor Movement* (Garden City, N.Y., 1968); William H. Harris, *The Harder We Run: Black Workers since the Civil War* (New York, 1982); Philip S. Foner and Ronald L. Lewis, eds., *Black Workers: A Documentary History from Colonial Times to the Present* (Philadelphia, 1988); Robert H. Zieger, ed., *Organized Labor in the Twentieth-Century South* (Knoxville, forthcoming 1991). On organized labor in South Africa, see Robert H. Davies, *Capital, State and White Labour in South Africa, 1900–1960* (Atlantic Highlands, N.J., 1979); Fredrick A. Johnstone, *Class, Race and Gold: A Study of Class Relations and Racial Discrimination in South Africa* (Lanham, Md., 1976); David Yudelman, *The Emergence of Modern South Africa: State, Capital and the Incorporation of Organized Labor in the South African Gold Fields* (Westport, Conn., 1983); and Jon Lewis, "South African Labor History: A Historiographical Assessment," *Radical History Review* 46–47 (1990), pp. 213–236.

24. For interesting recent comparisons of the American South and Brazil, see Richard Graham, "Slavery and Economic Development: Brazil and the United States South in the Nineteenth Century," *Comparative Studies in Society and History* 23, 4 (1981), pp. 620–655; Rebecca Scott, "The Meaning of Freedom: Postemancipation Society in Sugar-Producing Regions of Brazil, Cuba, and Louisiana" (unpublished paper presented to the Seminar on Social History and Theory, University of California–Irvine, March 1986); and Steve Hahn, "Class

and State in Postemancipation Societies: Southern Planters in Comparative Perspective," *American Historical Review* 95, 1 (1990), pp. 75–98.

25. This orientation forms the basis of much of the best work in social history, and particularly its subfields of labor, black, and women's history. It has been quite influential in Latin American history. See for example Florencia Mallon, *The Defense of Community in Peru's Central Highlands: Peasant Struggle and Capitalist Transition, 1860–1940* (Princeton, 1983); Steve J. Stern, *Peru's Indian Peoples and the Challenge of Spanish Conquest: Huamanga to 1640* (Madison, 1982); Peter Winn, *Weavers of Revolution: The Yarur Workers and Chile's Road to Socialism* (New York, 1986).

26. On occasion Freyre did differentiate between "social" and "political" democracy, but then promptly proceeded to blur the distinction: "It would, truly enough, be ridiculous to pretend that the long period, ever since colonial times, during which a large part of Brazil had lived under a system of feudal organization had predisposed people to the practice of political democracy. . . . It seems to me, meanwhile, that no student of Luso-American society can fail to recognize the fact that . . . what I have here called Brazilian feudalism was in reality a combination of aristocracy, democracy, and even anarchy. And this union of opposites would appear to be serving as the basis for the development in Brazil of a society that is democratic in its ethnic, social, and cultural composition. . . ." *Masters and Slaves,* pp. xiv–xv. See also note 27.

27. See Freyre's comments on "the democratic, democratizing, even anarchic elements always present in the amalgamation of races and cultures," and how such amalgamation would eventually break down the "recalcitrantly aristocratic" and "patriarchal" aspects of Brazilian life, replacing "subjects" with "citizens." *Mansions and Shanties,* pp. 231–232.

28. I develop these points at greater length in George Reid Andrews, "Latin American Workers," *Journal of Social History* 21, 2 (1987), pp. 311–326.

29. Given the absence of political representation for Africans in South Africa, I would also include the antiapartheid movement in that country as part of this transnational surge toward democracy.

30. G. M. Trevelyan, *English Social History* (London, 1944), p. 1.

31. For some criticisms of social history on these scores, and proposals to reintegrate it with political history, see Elizabeth Fox-Genovese and Eugene Genovese, "The Political Crisis of Social History: A Marxian Perspective," *Journal of Social History* 10, 2 (1976), pp. 205–220; Samuel Hays, "Society and Politics: Politics and Society," *Journal of Interdisciplinary History* 15, 3 (1985), pp. 481–499; Gertrude Himmelfarb, "Denigrating the Rule of Reason," *Harper's* (April 1984), pp. 84–90; Tony Judt, "A Clown in Regal Purple: Social History and the Social Historians," *History Workshop* 7 (1979), pp. 66–94; Theda Skocpol, "Bringing the State Back In," in Peter Evans, Dietrich Rueschemeyer, and Theda Skocpol, eds., *Bringing the State Back In* (Cambridge and New York, 1985); and Charles Tilly, "Retrieving European Lives," and William B. Taylor, "Between Global Process and Local Knowledge: An Inquiry into Early Latin American Social History, 1500–1900," both in Olivier Zunz, ed., *Reliving the Past: The Worlds of Social History* (Chapel Hill, 1985).

32. Winn, *Weavers of Revolution*, p. 8.

33. Fontaine, "Political Economy," p. 127.

34. During the colonial period São Paulo formed a "captaincy" administered by a governor. With independence in 1822 it became a province. And with the overthrow of the monarchy in 1889 and the declaration of the Republic, it became a "state." São Paulo is also the name of the capital city of the captaincy/province/state; I try to make clear in the text when I am referring to the state, and when to the city.

35. Of the 119 million Brazilians canvased in the 1980 census, 25 million lived in São Paulo State. The next largest states were São Paulo's neighbors, Minas Gerais (13.4 million) and Rio de Janeiro (11.3 million), and the northeastern state of Bahia (9.5 million). All other Brazilian states had populations less than 8 million. IBGE, *Recenseamento, 1980. Brasil*, table 1.11, p. 34.

36. On Brazilian industrialization, and the role of São Paulo in that industrialization, see John P. Dickenson, *Brazil* (Boulder, 1978).

37. IBGE, *Recenseamento geral do Brasil—1980. Censo demográfico—dados gerais, migração, instrução, fecundidade, mortalidade—São Paulo* (Rio de Janeiro, 1982), table 1.11, p. 106.

Chapter 2. Slavery and Emancipation, 1800–1890

1. The centrality of plantation agriculture in Brazilian history is suggested by the titles, and the content, of two admirable syntheses of the colonial period: James Lang, *Portuguese Brazil: The King's Plantation* (New York, 1979); and Stuart B. Schwartz, "Plantations and Peripheries," in Leslie Bethell, ed., *Cambridge History of Latin America* (Cambridge and New York, 1984), 1, pp. 423–499.

2. As indicated in chapter 1, a "captaincy" was a Portuguese administrative division, roughly equivalent in Brazil to nineteenth-century provinces and twentieth-century states.

3. On Indian slavery, see John M. Monteiro, "São Paulo in the Seventeenth Century: Society and Economy" (Ph.D. dissertation, University of Chicago, 1985).

4. On the rise of sugar cultivation, see Maria Thereza Schorer Petrone, *A lavoura canavieira em São Paulo* (São Paulo, 1968).

5. Figures from Rollie Poppino, *Brazil: The Land and the People* (New York, 1968), pp. 147–153; Emília Viotti da Costa, *Da senzala à colônia* (2nd edition, São Paulo, 1982), p. 7; Suely Robles Reis de Queiroz, *Escravidão negra em São Paulo: Um estudo das tensões provocadas pelo escravismo no século XIX* (Rio de Janeiro, 1977), p. 23; Thomas Holloway, *Immigrants on the Land: Coffee and Society in São Paulo, 1886–1934* (Chapel Hill, 1980), pp. 6–9, 175.

6. Samuel Harman Lowrie, "O elemento negro na população de São Paulo," *Revista do Arquivo Municipal de São Paulo* 4, 48 (1938), table 1, p. 12; Robert Conrad, *The Destruction of Brazilian Slavery, 1850–1888* (Berkeley, 1972), tables 2–5, pp. 284–287.

7. On the use of religion as a means of maintaining discipline on São Paulo plantations, see Costa, *Senzala a colônia*, pp. 237–241, 273; and Queiroz,

Escravidão negra, pp. 47–49. For Padre Antônio Vieira's famous sermon comparing slaves to Christ, and urging on them total obedience to their masters, see Robert Conrad, *Children of God's Fire: A Documentary History of Black Slavery in Brazil* (Princeton, 1983), pp. 163–174. The themes of this sermon appear in Tomás Gutiérrez Alea's brilliant film *La última cena* (The Last Supper, 1976), which examines the relationship between Christianity and slavery on a Cuban sugar plantation in the late 1700s.

8. David Brion Davis, *The Problem of Slavery in the Age of Revolution, 1770–1823* (Ithaca, 1975); David Brion Davis, *Slavery and Human Progress* (New York, 1984).

9. The contradictions between liberalism and slavery in Brazil are explored in the work of Emília Viotti da Costa. See her *Senzala à colônia,* pp. 325–343, and *The Brazilian Empire: Myths and Histories* (Chicago, 1985), pp. 53–77.

10. On the general problem of liberal reform in nineteenth-century Brazil, in addition to Costa, see Richard Graham, *Britain and the Onset of Modernization in Brazil, 1850–1914* (Cambridge and New York, 1968), pp. 252–276; Roberto Schwarz's essay "As idéias fora do lugar," in his *Ao vencedor as batatas* (São Paulo, 1977), pp. 13–28; and Thomas Flory, *Judge and Jury in Imperial Brazil, 1808–1871* (Austin, 1981), pp. 5–30.

11. The varieties of slave resistance are explored in the literature cited in chapter 1, note 5.

12. Clóvis Moura, *Rebeliões de senzala: Quilombos, insurreições, guerrilhas* (3rd edition, São Paulo, 1981), pp. 204–214; Queiroz, *Escravidão negra,* pp. 57–58, 163–165, 176–182.

13. For the only definitive study of such an uprising to date, see Jaime João Reis, *Rebelião escrava no Brasil: A história do levante dos malês (1835)* (São Paulo, 1986).

14. On the "liberal experiment" of this period, see Roderick J. Barman, *Brazil: The Forging of a Nation, 1798–1852* (Stanford, 1988), pp. 161–188. Another of the liberal reforms was to change the nature of the regency in 1834, reducing it to one individual elected, not by Parliament, but by the provincial electors at large.

15. On the provincial rebellions, and the participation in them of slaves and free blacks, see Leslie Bethell and José Murilo de Carvalho, "Brazil from Independence to the Middle of the Nineteenth Century," in Bethell, *Cambridge History of Latin America* (Cambridge and New York, 1985), 3, pp. 694–695, 702–709; Barman, *Brazil,* pp. 169, 182, 192, 195–197.

16. On similar conspiracies among slaves and free blacks in Argentina and Venezuela at the same time, see Boleslao Lewin, "La 'conspiración de los franceses' en Buenos Aires (1795)," *Anuario del Instituto de Investigaciones Históricas* 4 (Rosario, 1960), pp. 9–58; Pedro M. Arcaya U., *Insurrección de los negros de la serranía de Coro* (Caracas, 1949).

17. Costa, *Brazilian Empire,* pp. 10–12, 56, 140.

18. On the nineteenth-century laws governing slaves, see Queiroz, *Escravidão negra,* pp. 52–77; Costa, *Senzala á colônia,* pp. 273–288; Conrad, *Children of God's Fire,* pp. 251–259.

19. Barman, *Brazil,* pp. 217–243; Bethell and Carvalho, "Brazil," pp. 709–718.

20. "Abolition, understood as the combination of the public policies which gradually led to the extinction of slavery, constitutes a privileged vantage point from which to examine the relations between the government, i.e., the King and his bureaucrats, and the class of rural landowners. . . . At no other moment, and on no other issue, was the opposition between the motives and interests of the bureaucratic pole of power [the state] and the interests of the social and economic pole of power [the planters] so clear. If, in the frequently used expression of the period, slavery was the cancer which ate away at society, it was also the cancer which ate away at the bases of the Imperial state, and finally ended by destroying it." José Murilo de Carvalho, *Teatro de sombras: A política imperial* (São Paulo, 1988), p. 50.

21. The basic treatments of this topic are Conrad, *Destruction of Brazilian Slavery;* Costa, *Senzala à colônia,* and *A abolição* (São Paulo, 1982); and Robert Brent Toplin, *The Abolition of Slavery in Brazil* (New York, 1971). See also Seymour Drescher, "Brazilian Abolition in Comparative Perspective," *Hispanic American Historical Review* 68, 3 (1988), pp. 429–460.

22. Leslie Bethell, *The Abolition of the Brazilian Slave Trade* (Cambridge and New York, 1970), p. 390.

23. Bethell, *Abolition of the Brazilian Slave Trade,* pp. 327–359, 390.

24. Robert W. Slenes, "The Demography and Economics of Brazilian Slavery, 1850–1888" (Ph.D. dissertation, Stanford University, 1976), p. 365; on the inability of the slave population to sustain itself, see the same, pp. 297–365; and Robert E. Conrad, *World of Sorrow: The African Slave Trade to Brazil* (Baton Rouge, 1986), pp. 7–24.

25. Herbert Klein, *The Middle Passage: Comparative Studies in the Atlantic Slave Trade* (Princeton, 1978), pp. 95–120; Conrad, *World of Sorrow,* pp. 171–192.

26. Conrad, *Destruction of Brazilian Slavery,* pp. 91–95; Carvalho, *Teatro de sombras,* pp. 65–67. The continuing commitment of southeastern planters to slavery is clear, not just in their writings and speeches, but also in the prices they were willing to pay for slaves bought from the Northeast. On the disparity between slave prices in the North and the South during this period, see Slenes, "Demography and Economics," pp. 179–188.

27. The reform also sought to professionalize the provincial police forces by placing them under the control of the Ministry of Justice. Thomas Holloway, "The Brazilian 'Judicial Police' in Florianópolis, Santa Catarina, 1841–1871," *Journal of Social History* 20, 4 (1987), pp. 733–756.

28. The 1841 judicial reform and the differences between the justices of the peace and the professional magistrates are discussed in Flory, *Judge and Jury.* On the abolitionist movement at the São Paulo law school, see Richard M. Morse, "The Negro in São Paulo, Brazil," *Journal of Negro History* 38, 3 (1953), pp. 292–293.

29. Gama is an extraordinary historical figure. Born in Bahia in 1830 of a free African mother and a Portuguese father, he was illegally sold into slavery in 1840 by his father and sent south to São Paulo in the interprovincial slave trade. He fled his owner in 1848, served six years in the military police, and eventually became a lawyer. An accomplished writer and public speaker, by the time of his

death in 1882 he had became São Paulo's most prominent and best-known abolitionist. Sud Menucci, *O precursor do abolicionismo no Brasil: Luiz Gama* (São Paulo, 1938).

30. For interesting analyses of these new developments in slave criminality in São Paulo, see Célia Maria Marinho de Azevedo, *Onda negra, medo branco: O negro no imaginário das elites—século XIX* (Rio de Janeiro, 1987), pp. 180–199; Maria Helena P. T. Machado, *Crime e escravidão: Trabalho, luta, resistência nas lavouras paulistas, 1830–1888* (São Paulo, 1987), passim, but particularly pp. 68, 77.

31. The provincial chief of police observed in 1871 that "for the citizen, the *galés* are moral death; for the slave, they are liberty." Costa, *Senzala à colônia*, p. 288. As a result, São Paulo's governor noted later in the decade, slaves who had attacked their masters "neither hide nor try to conceal the proofs of their crime— placidly and tranquilly they seek out the authorities and offer themselves up to the vengeance of the law, dreaming of the shackles that for them are redemption." Queiroz, *Escravidão negra*, p. 155.

32. For evidence from São Paulo newspapers of this shift of opinion against slavery, and particularly against the torture and abuse of slaves, see Lília Moritz Schwarcz, *Retrato em branco e negro: Jornais, escravos, e cidadãos em São Paulo no final do século XIX* (São Paulo, 1987), pp. 207–215.

33. These cases are described and summarized in Machado, *Crime e escravidão*, pp. 114–123. A similar line of defense was used by Luis Gama, when he argued that slaves who attacked their masters were simply defending themselves against the assault and robbery inherent in slavery. This strategy does not seem to have resulted in the acquittal of any of his clients. Menucci, *Precursor*, pp. 148–153.

34. See Warren Dean's discussion of how, by the 1860s, slaves "had absorbed the rhetoric of egalitarianism and citizenship," and were using it to explain and justify their grievances. *Rio Claro: A Brazilian Plantation System, 1820–1920* (Stanford, 1976), p. 127.

35. Slenes, "Demography and Economics," p. 550; also quoted in Dean, *Rio Claro*, pp. 124–125.

36. As of 1872, 90.8 percent of the nation's 1.5 million slaves were native-born Afro-Brazilians. Directoria Geral de Estatística, *Recenseamento da população do Império do Brasil a que se procedeu no dia 1º de agosto de 1872. Quadros geraes* (Rio de Janeiro, 1873), table 1.

37. Conrad, *Destruction of Brazilian Slavery*, pp. 184–186; Costa, *Senzala à colônia*, 298–299; Azevedo, *Onda negra*, pp. 199–202; Machado, *Crime e escravidão*, p. 52; Dean, *Rio Claro*, p. 139.

38. Azevedo, *Onda negra*, p. 117. French naturalist Louis Couty, who visited São Paulo in 1883, shortly after the Campinas uprisings, recorded similar impressions, noting that the province seemed on the verge of violent revolution. Costa, *Senzala à colônia*, p. 298.

39. Even the province's most "progressive" planters, those who adhered to the recently founded Republican Party, badly disappointed the abolitionists by refusing to take a stand against slavery. Luis Gama, initially an enthusiastic Republican, resigned from the party in disgust over its failure to endorse aboli-

tion. Joseph L. Love, *São Paulo in the Brazilian Federation, 1889–1937* (Stanford, 1980), p. 104.

40. Bento's fellow abolitionist Joaquim Nabuco once described him as a Brazilian John Brown. Conrad, *Destruction of Brazilian Slavery*, p. 242.

41. For the tumultuous events of this period, see Conrad, *Destruction of Brazilian Slavery*, pp. 239–262; Toplin, *Abolition of Slavery*, pp. 194–224; Costa, *Senzala à colônia*, pp. 308–319.

42. Love, *São Paulo*, pp. 104–106; Conrad, *Destruction of Brazilian Slavery*, pp. 248–262; Thomas Holloway, "Immigration and Abolition: The Transition from Slave to Free Labor in the São Paulo Coffee Zone," in Dauril Alden and Warren Dean, eds., *Essays Concerning the Socioeconomic History of Brazil and Portuguese India* (Gainesville, 1977), p. 156; Costa, *Senzala à colônia*, p. 310–318; Azevedo, *Onda negra*, pp. 213–214. During March and April 1888, another twenty-five thousand slaves were freed in the coffee zones of neighboring Rio de Janeiro Province. Conrad, *Destruction of Brazilian Slavery*, p. 269.

43. Dom Pedro was traveling in Europe at this time; his daughter Isabel occupied the throne in his absence.

44. *Relatório apresentado ao Exm. Sr. Presidente da Província de São Paulo pela Comissão Central de Estatística* (São Paulo, 1888), p. 245.

45. Pierre Denis, *Brazil* (London, 1911), p. 183.

46. *Rebate* (June 3, 1898), p. 1.

47. *Relatório . . . pela Comissão Central da Estatística*, p. 245.

48. Costa, *Abolição*, p. 94.

49. Cleber da Silva Maciel, *Discriminações raciais: Negros em Campinas (1888–1921)* (Campinas, 1988), p. 86; "Liberdade, um compromisso assumido pelo 'Diário Popular'," in *Abolição: 100 anos*, special supplement of *Diário Popular* (May 12, 1988), p. 5; "Dia a dia," *O Estado de São Paulo* (May 13, 1892), p. 1. During the celebrations marking the centennial of Brazilian abolition, President José Sarney concurred, describing abolition as "the greatest civic campaign ever undertaken in this country." "Maestro acusa a Bossa Nova de racista," *Folha de São Paulo* (May 12, 1988), p. 14.

50. Costa, *Abolição*, p. 93; "As festas de hontem," *Diário Popular* (May 14, 1888), p. 2; "Diário do Rio," *O Estado de São Paulo* (May 16, 1898), p. 1. See also Conrad, *Destruction of Brazilian Slavery*, pp. 273–274.

51. Costa, *Brazilian Empire*, pp. 221–228; Love, *São Paulo*, p. 110.

52. Love, *São Paulo*, p. xv.

53. Denis, *Brazil*, pp. 21–22.

54. Brazil was 14.8 percent literate in 1890 and 24.5 percent literate in 1920; yet in only two presidential elections between 1890 and 1930 did voter turnout exceed 3 percent of the national population. Joseph L. Love, "Political Participation in Brazil, 1881–1969," *Luso-Brazilian Review* 7, 2 (1970), pp. 8–9.

55. "The empire of the planters . . . only begins in Brazil with the fall of the Empire." Sérgio Buarque de Holanda, quoted in Carvalho, *Teatro de sombras*, p. 21.

56. Love, *São Paulo*, p. 139. Prior to the electoral "reform" of 1881, 50.6 percent of the free male population was registered to vote. Richard Graham argues that the 1881 reform, which he estimates "reduced the number of those

who voted from over 1,000,000 to some 150,000," was passed by planter interests fearful of the dangers posed by an expanding electorate which they would find increasingly difficult to control. Richard Graham, *Patronage and Politics in Nineteenth-Century Brazil* (Stanford, 1990), pp. 108, 184. On the miniscule voter turnouts under the republic, see Love, "Political Participation"; and José Murilo de Carvalho, *Os bestializados: O Rio de Janeiro e a República que não foi* (São Paulo, 1987), pp. 66–90.

57. *A Província de São Paulo* (November 27, 1889); *Diário de Campinas* (November 27, 1889), quoted in Maciel, *Discriminações raciais*, p. 189.

58. These points are made by Brazilian historian Sidney Chalhoub in "Slaves, Freedmen and the Politics of Freedom in Brazil: The Experience of Blacks in the City of Rio," presented at the Conference on the Meaning of Freedom, Greensburg, Pa., August 1988. José Murilo de Carvalho also notes the "negative reaction of the black population to the Republic" and the fact that "the Monarchy fell as it was reaching its point of greatest popularity among these people [blacks and workers], in part as a result of the abolition of slavery." Carvalho, *Os bestializados*, p. 29. See also Gilberto Freyre, *Order and Progress: Brazil from Monarchy to Republic* (New York, 1970), pp. 8–10, 171.

59. On the disillusionment of black abolitionists with republicanism, see Love, *São Paulo*, p. 104; Conrad, *Destruction of Brazilian Slavery*, pp. 160–162. On José do Patrocinio and the Black Guard, see June Hahner, *Poverty and Politics: The Urban Poor in Brazil, 1870–1920* (Albuquerque, 1986), pp. 70–71.

60. "Os defensores da rainha," *A Província de São Paulo* (April 25, 1889); "Loucos ou ineptos," *A Província de São Paulo* (May 9, 1889). For further articles on the Guard, see "Santos, 13," *A Província de São Paulo* (January 15, 1889); "Guarda Negra," *A Província de São Paulo* (January 13, 1889); "Contra a Guarda Negra," *A Província de São Paulo* (January 30, 1889); "Cartas do interior," *Diário Popular* (May 22, 1889). For reports on the guard elsewhere, see "Cartas do Rio," *Diário Popular* (May 13, 1889).

61. "Jundiahy," *A Província de São Paulo* (May 15, 1889); "Jundiahy: Sociedade 13 de Maio," *A Província de São Paulo* (June 20, 1889); "Gentileza," *Progresso* (February 24, 1929), p. 2; "D. Pedro Henrique," *Progresso* (September 28, 1930), p. 1; "Símbolos do samba, sem orígem exata," *Folha de São Paulo* (January 20, 1985), p. 24. As late as the 1960s Arlindo Veiga dos Santos, a prominent black monarchist in São Paulo during the 1920s, and founder and president of the Brazilian Black Front in the 1930s, was still editing a monthly newspaper, *Monarquia*, and had not given up the cause.

62. "Tia Josepha," *Correio Paulistano* (July 27 and 28, 1888), quoted in Schwarcz, *Retrato em branco e negro*, pp. 237–239, and in Azevedo, *Onda negra*, pp. 17–18; "A floresta da morte," *Folha do Braz* (January 6, 1901).

63. Francisco de Paula Lázaro Gonçalves, *Relatório apresentado à Associação Promotora de Immigração em Minas* (Juiz de Fora, 1888), pp. 7–8. My thanks to Thomas Holloway for providing me with this citation. See also Conrad, *Destruction of Brazilian Slavery*, who argues that "some violence accompanied the liberation of more than a hundred thousand slaves in São Paulo, but the remarkable achievement was carried out with a high degree of good will and tolerance on all sides." P. 257.

64. Azevedo, *Onda negra*, p. 213, fn. 52.

65. "Tiram as consequências," *A Província de São Paulo* (November 15, 1889).

66. Louis Couty, *O Brasil em 1884: Esboços sociológicos* (Rio de Janeiro, 1984), p. 200. On the influence of scientific racism in Brazil, see Thomas Skidmore, *Black into White: Race and Nationality in Brazilian Thought* (New York, 1974), pp. 27–32, 48–53.

67. The colonial roots of the *ideologia da vadiagem* are laid out in Laura de Mello e Souza, *Desclassificados do ouro: A pobreza mineira no século XVIII* (Rio de Janeiro, 1982), especially pp. 64–72, 215–222. Lúcio Kowarick brings the story up through the early 1900s in *Trabalho e vadiagem: A origem do trabalho livre no Brasil* (São Paulo, 1987).

68. Azevedo, *Onda negra*, pp. 51, 227.

69. Maurício Lamberg, *O Brasil* (Rio de Janeiro, 1896), p. 341; João Pedro da Veiga Filho, *Estudo econômico e financeiro sobre o Estado de São Paulo* (São Paulo, 1896), p. 62; Schwarcz, *Retrato em branco e negro*, p. 179; Maciel, *Discriminações raciais*, pp. 138–146, 160; "O recrutamento," *A Província de São Paulo* (September 29, 1888); "Santos, 13," *A Província de São Paulo* (January 15, 1889); "Contra a Guarda Negra," *A Província de São Paulo* (January 30, 1889). As late as the 1920s, police in Campinas engaged in regular campaigns to round up black women in the poorer neighborhoods of the city and charge them under vagrancy statutes; the black newspaper *Getulino* denounced these actions as an effort to force black women into accepting employment as domestic servants. See the issues of *Getulino* for November 4, 11, and 25, 1923.

70. For careful analyses of such bargaining in the United States and Cuba, see Leon F. Litwack, *Been in the Storm So Long: The Aftermath of Slavery* (New York, 1979); Eric Foner, *Nothing But Freedom: Emancipation and Its Legacy* (Baton Rouge, 1983); and Rebecca J. Scott, *Slave Emancipation in Cuba: The Transition to Free Labor, 1860–1899* (Princeton, 1985), pp. 201–278. For a useful survey of the literature on postemancipation bargaining, see Rebecca Scott, "Comparing Emancipations: A Review Essay," *Journal of Social History* 20, 3 (1987), pp. 565–584.

71. Stanley J. Stein, *Vassouras: A Brazilian Coffee County, 1850–1900* (2nd edition, Princeton, 1985), pp. 256–274; Gonçalves, *Relatório*, pp. 10–12; Denis, *Brazil*, pp. 317–320; Lamberg, *Brasil*, pp. 342–344.

72. Lamberg, *Brasil*, p. 342; Conrad, *Children of God's Fire*, pp. 476–480.

73. Gonçalves, *Relatório*, pp. 24, 31, and 24–39 passim; *Diário de Campinas* (June 2, 1888), quoted in Maciel, *Discriminações raciais*, p. 126. For similar comments on planters' ability to retain liberto workers, see Azevedo, *Onda negra*, pp. 237–238; Florestan Fernandes, *A integração do negro na sociedade de classes* (3rd edition, São Paulo, 1978), 1, pp. 31–34; Conrad, *Destruction of Brazilian Slavery*, pp. 255–56; Toplin, *Abolition of Slavery*, pp. 260–61.

74. F. W. Daffert, *Coleção dos trabalhos agrícolas extraidos dos relatórios annuaes de 1888–1893, do Instituto Agronômico do Estado de S. Paulo (Brasil) em Campinas* (São Paulo, 1895), p. 34; Henrique Raffard, *Alguns dias na Pauliceia* (São Paulo, 1977), p. 33; Stein, *Vassouras*, p. 265.

75. Toplin, *Abolition of Slavery*, pp. 239, 245.

76. On the reconstruction of Rio de Janeiro and São Paulo during this period,

see Jeffrey D. Needell, "Making the Carioca *Belle Époque* Concrete: The Urban Reforms of Rio de Janeiro under Pereira Passos," *Journal of Urban History* 10, 4 (1984), pp. 383–422; Ernani Silva Bruno, *História e tradições da cidade de São Paulo*, Volume 3, *Metrópole do café (1872–1918)* (3rd edition, São Paulo, 1984). On the "whitening thesis" and the effort to change Brazil's racial composition from black to white, see Skidmore, *Black into White*. The reference to turn-of-the-century Brazil looking "more like a corner of Africa than a nation of the New World" is from Brazilian intellectual Luiz Edmundo, quoted in Needell, "Making the Carioca *Belle Époque*," p. 408.

Chapter 3. Immigration: 1890–1930

1. Between 1888 and 1928, 2.1 million Europeans entered the state. This figure was considerably larger than São Paulo's 1890 population of 1.4 million, and represented over half (57 percent) of total European migration to Brazil during those years. Thomas Holloway, *Immigrants on the Land: Coffee and Society in São Paulo, 1886–1934* (Chapel Hill, 1980), p. 179; Thomas W. Merrick and Douglas H. Graham, *Population and Economic Development in Brazil: 1800 to the Present* (Baltimore, 1979), p. 92. During the 1888–1928 period government records also show 960,000 emigrants leaving the state through the port of Santos. Others doubtless left São Paulo by overland transportation and subsequently departed Brazil through Rio de Janeiro and other ports. Holloway, *Immigrants on the Land*, p. 179.

2. Emília Viotti da Costa, *Da senzala à colônia* (2nd edition, São Paulo, 1982), pp. 7, 49–90; Warren Dean, *Rio Claro: A Brazilian Plantation System, 1820–1920* (Stanford, 1976), pp. 88–123; Verena Stolcke and Michael M. Hall, "The Introduction of Free Labour on the São Paulo Coffee Plantations," *Journal of Peasant Studies* 10, 2–3 (1983), pp. 170–200.

3. Costa, *Senzala à colônia*, p. 109.

4. "*Caboclo*" is usually defined as a "civilized Brazilian Indian of pure blood" or "a Brazilian half-breed (of white and Indian)." *Novo Michaelis dicionário ilustrado* (São Paulo, 1961), 2, p. 200; see also Holloway, *Immigrants on the Land*, p. 106. An 1893 article in the São Paulo press, however, differentiated between *caboclos* and *mamelucos* (Indian-white mestizos), and implied that the former are the product of a broader process of race mixture among Africans, Indians, and whites. "Colônias orphanológicas," *O Estado de São Paulo* (January 12, 1893). In practice, in São Paulo, "*caboclo*" seems to have meant a dark-skinned ruralite of indeterminate race, usually engaged in subsistence agriculture or day labor on the plantations, and forming part of the rural *caipira* (peasant, backwoodsman) culture. On *caipira* culture in the nineteenth century, see Maria Sylvia de Carvalho Franco, *Homens livres na ordem escravocrata* (São Paulo, 1969); in the twentieth century, see Antônio Cándido Mello e Souza, *Os parceiros do Rio Bonito* (2nd edition, São Paulo, 1979).

5. Lúcio Kowarick, *Trabalho e vadiagem: A origem do trabalho livre no Brasil* (São Paulo, 1987), pp. 65–69; Paula Beiguelman, *Formação do povo no complexo cafeeiro: Aspectos políticos* (2nd edition, São Paulo, 1977), pp. 105–109; Costa, *Senzala à colônia*, p. 13.

6. Holloway, *Immigrants on the Land*, p. 74.

7. Célia Maria Marinho de Azevedo, *Onda negra, medo branco: O negro no imaginário das elites—século XIX* (Rio de Janeiro, 1987), pp. 133–139.

8. Holloway, *Immigrants on the Land*, pp. 35–36.

9. Holloway, *Immigrants on the Land*, pp. 35–39; Chiara Vangelista, *Le braccia per la fazenda: Immigrati e "caipiras" nella formazione del mercato del lavoro paulista* (Milan, 1982), pp. 40–51.

10. Michael Hall, "The Origins of Mass Immigration in Brazil, 1871–1914" (Ph.D. dissertation, Columbia University, 1969), p. 90; Pierre Denis, *Brazil* (London, 1911), pp. 185–186.

11. Kowarick, *Trabalho e vadiagem*, p. 94, notes the coincidence between the 92,000 immigrants entering the state in 1888 and the estimated 107,000 slaves freed. The percentage of subsidized immigrants is calculated from data provided by Merrick and Graham, *Population*, p. 92; Vangelista, *Braccia per la fazenda*, pp. 83–84, sets the percentage of subsidized immigrants slightly lower, but provides no data for 1890–1899, when rates of immigration, and of subsidies for immigration, were at their highest.

12. For these various quotations, see Beiguelman, *Formação do povo*, p. 65; Azevedo, *Onda negra*, p. 138; Stolcke and Hall, "Introduction of Free Labour," p. 182; Florestan Fernandes, *A integração do negro na sociedade de classes* (3rd edition, São Paulo, 1978), 1, p. 37; Michael Hall, "Origins of Mass Immigration," p. 102. Similar arguments had been advanced earlier in the century in an 1814 petition from Bahian elites to the Crown requesting the king to promote migration to Brazil from Portugal's Atlantic islands. "Because of their poverty, these workers will seek employment and will be even more useful to the agriculture of this country than the blacks." Robert Conrad, *Children of God's Fire: A Documentary History of Black Slavery in Brazil* (Princeton, 1983), pp. 405–406.

13. Though for evidence suggesting that, in other areas besides immigration, "the [republican] state played a considerably more important part in the economy than has generally been recognized," see Steven Topik, *The Political Economy of the Brazilian State, 1889–1930* (Austin, 1987). P. 161.

14. An 1885 proposal to extend to Brazilian migrants the same privileges as those enjoyed by Europeans—paid maritime passages, and lodging at state expense at the immigrant hostel in São Paulo City—was rejected by the provincial Assembly. Proposals by abolitionist leaders that state funds should be expended on education and training to help the libertos compete in the labor market never even made it to the floor for debate. Azevedo, *Onda negra*, pp. 167–171. On the racial aspects of the debate over immigration, see the same, pp. 59–76, 139–174 passim.

15. Azevedo, *Onda negra*, pp. 231–234; "O que ganhamos," *Diário Popular* (May 14, 1888), p. 1.

16. "Questões e problemas: A segregação do liberto," *A Província de São Paulo* (May 22, 1889).

17. A segregationist tone can also be detected in an 1895 *Correio Paulistano* article commemorating May 13, Abolition Day, which says of "the African race" that, "incorporated into the Brazilian people, it does not bother us that they live with us apart [*vive conosco aparte*], feeling with us the same things that we

feel. . . ." Quoted in Lília Moritz Schwarcz, *Retrato em branco e negro: Jornais, escravos, e cidadãos em São Paulo no final do século XIX* (São Paulo, 1987), p. 196. This of course was also the period during which institutionalized segregation was taking form in the southern United States. See C. Vann Woodward, *The Strange Career of Jim Crow* (3rd edition, New York, 1974); John W. Cell, *The Highest Stage of White Supremacy: The Origins of Segregation in South Africa and the American South* (Cambridge and New York, 1982).

18. On the Brazilian labor movement during this period, see Paula Beiguelman, *Os companheiros de São Paulo* (São Paulo, 1977); Edgar Carone, *Movimento operário no Brasil, 1877–1944* (São Paulo, 1979); Boris Fausto, *Trabalho urbano e conflito social, 1890–1920* (São Paulo, 1977); Sheldon Leslie Maram, *Anarquistas, imigrantes, e o movimento operário brasileiro, 1890–1920* (Rio de Janeiro, 1979); Paulo Sérgio Pinheiro and Michael Hall, eds., *A classe operária no Brasil, 1889–1930. Documentos*, Volume 1, *O movimento operário* (São Paulo, 1979). For a comparative discussion of Brazilian labor during this period, see Thomas Skidmore, "Workers and Soldiers: Urban Labor Movements and Elite Responses in Twentieth-Century Latin America," in Virginia Bernhard, ed., *Elites, Masses and Modernization in Latin America, 1850–1930* (Austin, 1979).

19. Maram, *Anarquistas, imigrantes*, pp. 19–22.

20. Initial quotation from "Os acontecimentos do Rio e do Ceará," *O Amigo do Povo* (January 17, 1904), p. 1. The rest, from *O Amigo do Povo* (December 6, 1903), *Il Pungulo* (May 1, 1909), *Avanti!* (July 25 and November 28, 1914), are taken from Michael Hall, "Immigration and the Early São Paulo Working Class," *Jahrbuch für Geschichte von Staat, Wirtschaft, und Gesellschaft Lateinamerikas* 12 (1975), pp. 397–399.

21. "1 de maio," *O Grito do Povo* (May 1, 1900); "O salariato é a forma moderna da escravidão," *O Amigo do Povo* (August 14, 1903); "Entre operários," *O Amigo do Povo* (June 21, 1902); "13 de maio," *A Lucta Proletária* (May 16, 1908). *A Terra Livre* (May 6, 1916) stressed the similarities between the slave trade and the subsidized immigration program. "It used to be that private enterprise, the slave trader, took charge of going to hunt or buy the blacks. . . . Today the entrepreneur who runs this business is the State. It doesn't buy the slave, but it pays his passage. And the slave is called a contract laborer [*colono*]." Quoted in Silvia I. L. Magnani, *O movimento anarquista em São Paulo* (São Paulo, 1982), p. 154.

22. Maria Lúcia Caira Gitahy, "Os trabalhadores do porto de Santos, 1889–1910" (*tese de mestrado*, Universidade Estadual de Campinas, 1983), pp. 67–68, 79, 109–110, 290–291, 302.

23. On the antiforeigner campaigns of the late 1910s, see Maram, *Anarquistas, imigrantes*, pp. 60–89; Fausto, *Trabalho urbano*, pp. 233–243.

24. "Pela propaganda," *O Amigo do Povo* (February 14, 1903); "Jornal Operário," *Jornal Operário* (September 17, 1905).

25. Maram, *Anarquistas, imigrantes*, p. 67; "O preto Simeão," *O Combate* (May 13, 1915); "O velho anarquista Rodrigues," *Folha de São Paulo* (October 27, 1984), p. 46.

26. "Azafama clerical," *A Lucta Proletária* (March 7, 1908); "O sol da liber-

dade," *Aurora Social* (special anniversary issue, no date; internal evidence suggests January 1911); "Os brasileiros e a questão social," *O Grito Operário* (December 28, 1919). The militance of native-born Brazilian workers was also emphasized by paulista activist Everardo Dias in his account of a visit to the northeastern city of Recife in the late 1910s, where he found a vigorous, well-organized labor movement. Despite the fact that in Recife "the foreign element is non-existent, . . . this very Brazilian working class demonstrates more class consciousness and enthusiasm than São Paulo's 'foreign' proletariat." Quoted in June Hahner, *Poverty and Politics: The Urban Poor in Brazil, 1870–1920* (Albuquerque, 1986), p. 86.

27. Gitahy, "Trabalhadores do porto," p. 44; "Sociedade Trabalhadores em Café," *Progresso* (April 1931), p. 4; "Salvador de Paula," *Progresso* (September 26, 1929), pp. 3, 7; "O inimigo do preto é o preto," *O Clarim da Alvorada* (May 13, 1924), p. 2; "Ironia sangrenta," *Elite* (March 2, 1924), pp. 3–4; *Getulino* (March 30, 1924), p. 2; "A situação económica social do negro," *Progresso* (August 30, 1931), p. 2.

28. On black participation in early labor unions elsewhere in Brazil, see Hahner, *Poverty and Politics*, pp. 98–105, 251–252, 271–272, 282–283; Francisco Foot Hardman, "Trabalhadores e negros no Brasil," *Folha de São Paulo* (May 16, 1982); Maram, *Anarquistas, imigrantes*, pp. 31, 89; Fausto, *Trabalho urbano*, pp. 36, 55.

29. "Pobre povo brasileiro," *O Amigo do Povo* (December 27, 1903); "No reino da Senegambia," *A Plebe* (September 15, 1917); "A escala," *Aurora* (April 1, 1905); "Os negros," *A Sorocabana* (September 1, 1918). For an insightful analysis of racial and ethnic tensions within the Brazilian working class during this period, see Sidney Chalhoub, *Trabalho, lar e botequim: O cotidiano dos trabalhadores no Rio de Janeiro da Belle Époque* (São Paulo, 1986), passim.

30. One black newspaper noted that strikebreaking had been the means by which black men had finally penetrated the ranks of conductors and drivers for the São Paulo Tramway, Light, and Power Company, which before the strike of 1919 had restricted black men to laying track. *Getulino* (December 9, 1923), p. 1. For a reply which argued that Afro-Brazilians should make common cause with white workers rather than undermine them, see the short essay by Moacyr Marques, *Getulino* (March 30, 1924).

31. "O 13 de maio," *A Plebe* (May 15, 1920).

32. "Escravos e selvagens da Europa," *Jornal Operário* (October 15, 1905); "O emigrante," *A Pátria* (January 3, 1904).

33. Denis, *Brazil*, pp. 314, 316; Holloway, *Immigrants on the Land*, p. 63; Beiguelman, *Formação do povo*, pp. 72–73, 108–109. For a detailed discussion of the labor situation in the Paraíba region, see Stanley J. Stein, *Vassouras: A Brazilian Coffee County, 1850–1900* (2nd edition, Princeton, 1985), pp. 259–274.

34. Dean, *Rio Claro*, pp. 172, 152; Holloway, *Immigrants on the Land*, p. 63; Beiguelman, *Formação do povo*, p. 108; see also Vangelista, *Braccia per la fazenda*, pp. 51–55, 92–96, 106–114.

35. *Relatório apresentado ao . . . Secretário dos Negócios do Interior do Estado de São Paulo pelo Director da Repartição de Estatística e Arquivo . . . em 31 de julho de 1894* (Rio de Janeiro, 1894), pp. 82–83; Beiguelman, *Formação*

do povo, pp. 117–121; "Condições do trabalho na indústria textil do Estado de São Paulo," *Boletim do Departamento Estadual do Trabalho* 1, 1–2 (1912), pp. 35–80.

36. Figures from Directoria Geral de Estatística, *Recenseamento realizado em 1º de setembro de 1920* (Rio de Janeiro, 1926), 4, pp. 170–173. On Brazilian-born offspring of immigrant parents, see Hall, "Immigration," pp. 394–395; and Fernandes, *Integração do negro*, 1, pp. 139–140. Inspectors from the State Department of Labor reported visiting a textile factory in 1912 which employed 20 adults, 151 foreign-born minors, and 112 Brazilian minors. Of this last group, 106 were children of Italian parents. "Condições de trabalho na indústria textil," p. 60. While carrying out research in the personnel files of the Jafet textile factory in São Paulo (see chapter 4), I found numerous Italian-surnamed Brazilian-born minors and young adults working in the factory in the 1910s and 1920s, many of them related to older Italian-born employees.

37. Fernandes, *Integração do negro*, 1, pp. 60–97.

38. "Os jornais dos netos de escravos," *Jornal da Tarde* (June 12, 1975), p. 17; "Frente Negra Brasileira, 1930–1937," (unpublished collaborative *trabalho de pesquisa*, Pontifícia Universidade Católica–São Paulo, 1985), anexo 2, unpaginated.

39. On São Paulo Light, see "Frente Negra Brasileira," anexo 2. For factory workers in the black press, see, for example, *A Rua* (February 24, 1916), p. 3, which mentions "certain young women from the Trapani Factory," and "certain young women from the Silk Factory"; or the obituary of Deodato de Moraes, employed at "the hat factory in Vila Prudente . . . Workers from various factories attended his funeral." *O Alfinete* (September 22, 1918), p. 2. My own 20 percent sample of workers hired at the Jafet textile plant between 1905 and 1930 showed that, of those Brazilian-born workers of known race, 10.9 percent were Afro-Brazilian. However, the first Afro-Brazilian worker does not appear on the company's rolls until 1922—though some may be included among the workers of unknown race recorded during the 1910s—and over 90 percent of the black workers hired by the firm during this period were taken on only after 1925.

40. On Brazilian domestic service during this period, see Sandra Lauderdale Graham, *House and Street: The Domestic World of Servants and Masters in Nineteenth-Century Rio de Janeiro* (Cambridge and New York, 1988).

41. Eclea Bosi, *Memória e sociedade: Lembranças de velhos* (São Paulo, 1977), pp. 123, 301, 312. One couple in the state capital used their control over their domestic slave Anna to keep her in ignorance of the Golden Law until 1892, when some abolitionists learned of her plight and prevailed on the police to rescue her. "Anna declared her complete ignorance of the law of May 13 . . . [and] that she knew nothing about abolition because whenever the family left the house, they left her locked in her room." "Locaes: Escravisação," *O Estado de São Paulo* (May 15, 1892).

42. "Serviço doméstico," *O Estado de São Paulo* (June 2, 1892); see also *A Província de São Paulo* (February 6, 1889), which contains a short item discussing how *fazendeiros'* wives were replacing black domestics with Italian women, "who, moved by the desire for wages and better food, learn the necessary skills quickly and give good service."

43. For criticisms in the black press of want ads for domestics specifying

"whites preferred," see *Getulino* (November 11, 1923), p. 1, and "Prefere-se branca," *Progresso* (September 26, 1929), p. 5. On the continuing use of such ads in the 1940s, and employers' attitudes concerning race, see Oracy Nogueira, "Atitude desfavorável de alguns anunciantes de São Paulo em relação aos empregados de cor," *Sociologia* 4, 4 (1942), pp. 328–358.

44. "Frente Negra Brasileira," anexos 2 and 3; Fernandes, *Integração do negro*, 1, pp. 210–211; "E por aqui," *Elite* (March 2, 1924), "Não querem trabalhar," *O Kosmos* (November 16, 1924); Bosi, *Memória e sociedade*, pp. 312, 317.

45. Bosi, *Memória e sociedade*, p. 317; "E por aqui," *Elite* (March 2, 1924); "Ciudae de vossas filhas," *Getulino* (April 13, 1924); "Reparando," *O Alfinete* (September 28, 1921).

46. For a listing of Fernandes's work, see chapter 1, note 12.

47. This argument appears repeatedly in chapter 1 of Fernandes, *Integração do negro*, pp. 15–97. The oft-quoted line about blacks' "inability to feel, think, and act" like free men appears on page 95.

48. Fernandes's evidence concerning turn-of-the-century conditions is based mainly on interviews conducted some fifty years after the fact, in the late 1940s and early 1950s. The interviewees tended to be middle-class and upwardly mobile Afro-Brazilians, many of whom held a very low opinion of what they saw as the black *lumpen*. For further discussion of class divisions within the black population, and black middle-class attitudes toward lower-class blacks, see chapters 5 and 6. On how Fernandes's research was conducted, see Roger Bastide and Florestan Fernandes, *Brancos e negros em São Paulo* (3rd edition, São Paulo, 1971), pp. 13–17.

49. I am not the first to take aim at the Fernandes thesis. For other criticisms, see Azevedo, *Onda negra*, pp. 22–24; Chalhoub, *Trabalho, lar e botequim*, pp. 52–54; Boris Fausto, *Crime e cotidiano: A criminalidade em São Paulo (1880–1924)* (São Paulo, 1984), p. 58; Carlos Hasenbalg, *Discriminação e desigualdades raciais no Brasil* (Rio de Janeiro, 1979), pp. 72–77.

50. The census of 1872 assigned São Paulo a total population of 837,354: 433,432 whites, 39,465 *caboclos*, 207,845 free blacks and mulattoes, and 156,612 slave blacks and mulattoes. Samuel Harman Lowrie, "O elemento negro na população de São Paulo," *Revista do Arquivo Municipal de São Paulo* 4, 48 (1938), table 1, p. 12.

51. Fernandes, *Integração do negro*, 1, pp. 64–66; Roberto J. Haddock Lobo and Irene Aloisi, *O negro na vida social brasileira* (São Paulo, 1941), p. 29. On free black urban workers and artisans in Brazil more generally, see Herbert Klein, "Nineteenth-Century Brazil," in David W. Cohen and Jack P. Greene, *Neither Slave nor Free: The Freedmen of African Descent in the Slave Societies of the New World* (Baltimore, 1972), pp. 325–330.

52. Directoria Geral de Estatística, *Synopse do recenseamento de 31 de dezembro de 1890* (Rio de Janeiro, 1898), pp. 145, 373. The figures on immigrant literacy correspond very closely to similar data for European immigrants to the United States during the 1890s. Fifty-three percent of Italian immigrants to the United States were literate, and 40 percent of Portuguese immigrants were. Stanley Lieberson, *A Piece of the Pie: Blacks and White Immigrants since 1880* (Berkeley, 1980), p. 171.

53. In 1940 the literacy rates among blacks aged fifty and over (i.e., those born before 1890) were 21.7 percent for pretos, and 29.0 percent for pardos. Among whites fifty and over, the rate was 47.9 percent. IBGE, *Recenseamento geral de 1940. Censo demográfico: Estado de São Paulo* (Rio de Janeiro, 1950), table 18, pp. 16–17.

54. On literacy among the São Paulo slave population, see Schwarcz, *Retrato em branco e negro*, pp. 110, 180–182.

55. José Murilo de Carvalho, *Os bestializados: O Rio de Janeiro e a República que não foi* (São Paulo, 1987), p. 45; Joseph L. Love, *São Paulo in the Brazilian Federation, 1889–1937* (Stanford, 1980), pp. 92–96.

56. Cleber da Silva Maciel, *Discriminações raciais: Negros em Campinas (1888–1921)* (Campinas, 1988), pp. 100–102; "Pedra que rola da montanha," *Progresso* (March 24, 1929); "Salvador de Paula," *Progresso* (September 26, 1929), pp. 3, 7. It is interesting to note that none of these schools was racially exclusive; all of them accepted white and Asian students as well as black.

57. Fernandes, *Integração do negro*, 1, pp. 74; Michael Hall, "Immigration," p. 395; Rudolph M. Bell, *Fate and Honor, Family and Village: Demographic and Cultural Change in Rural Italy since 1800* (Chicago, 1979), p. 198. Further supporting these findings is Virginia Yans-McLaughlin's book *Family and Community: Italian Immigrants in Buffalo, 1880–1930* (Ithaca, 1971), which concludes that the overwhelming majority of immigrants were agricultural workers: "Those few immigrants who had engaged in manufacturing did not compose an industrial proletariat." P. 27. See also Beiguelman, *Formação do povo*, p. 122.

58. "Condições do trabalho," pp. 38–39.

59. Directoria Geral de Estatística, *Recenseamento da população do Império do Brasil a que se procedeu no dia 1º de agosto de 1872. Quadros geraes* (Rio de Janeiro, 1873), table 5. On the use of slave labor in nineteenth-century industry, see Beiguelman, *Formação do povo*, p. 122; Costa, *Senzala à colônia*, p. 21; Douglas Cole Libby, *Trabalho escravo e capital estrangeiro no Brasil: O caso do Morro Velho* (Belo Horizonte, 1984); Jorge Siqueira, "Contribuição ao estudo da transição do escravismo colonial para o capitalismo urbano-industrial no Rio de Janeiro: A Companhia Luz Stearica (1854/1898)" (*dissertação de mestrado*, Universidade Federal Fluminense, 1984).

60. A recent study of workers at textile, dock, urban transport, and electric power firms in Rio de Janeiro during this period found the overwhelming majority of their employees to be Brazilian; the percentage of Afro-Brazilians in each firm's work force varied between 30 and 40 percent. Sam Adamo, "The Broken Promise: Race, Health, and Justice in Rio de Janeiro, 1890–1940" (Ph.D. dissertation, University of New Mexico, 1983), p. 55; see also Eileen Keremetsis, "The Early Industrial Worker in Rio de Janeiro, 1870–1930" (Ph.D. dissertation, Columbia University, 1982). English traveler Lilian Elliott reports visiting a textile mill in the heavily Afro-Brazilian northeastern state of Pernambuco employing thirty-five hundred workers, almost all of them locally born. "The manager of the mills, an Englishman, spoke highly of the Brazilian operatives; the company has never taken any measures to import other labour than that of the district." Lilian E. Elliott, *Brazil: Today and Tomorrow* (rpt., 2nd edition, New York, 1922), pp. 231–232.

61. Kowarick, *Trabalho e vadiagem*, pp. 117–118; see also Hasenbalg, *Discriminação*, pp. 165–166.

62. Dean, *Rio Claro*, pp. 173–174.

63. Fernandes, *Integração do negro*, 1, chapter 2, "Pauperização e anomia social," pp. 98–245.

64. This point is made by Sidney Chalhoub in *Trabalho, lar e botequim*, p. 53.

65. Quoted in Maciel, *Discriminações raciais*, p. 84.

66. Fernandes himself suggested that the image may not have corresponded to the reality, but in the sense that the reality was even worse than the image. He discussed "the whole mythology concerning the poverty, promiscuity, and abandonment in which some three-fifths of the black population of the state capital normally lived. That mythology circulated as much among whites as among blacks and mulattoes. Nevertheless, it only did partial justice to reality. The recollections and testimony that we gathered paint dark,. disturbing scenes that are shocking and almost inconceivable in a Brazilian historical context." *Integração do negro*, 1, p. 147.

67. Robert Slenes argues that marriage rates among slaves in São Paulo approached those of the free population during the final years of slavery; see his "The Demography and Economics of Brazilian Slavery, 1850–1888" (Ph.D. dissertation, Stanford University, 1976), chapter 9; and his "Escravidão e família: Padrões de casamento e estabilidade familiar numa comunidade escrava (Campinas, século XIX)," *Estudos Econômicos* 17, 2 (1987), pp. 217–228. In the same issue of *Estudos Econômicos*, see also João Luis R. Fragoso and Manolo G. Florentino, "Marcelino, filho de Inocência Crioula, neto de Joana Cabinda: Um estudo sobre famílias escravas em Paraíba do Sul (1853–1872)," pp. 151–174; and Iraci del Nero de Costa, Robert W. Slenes, and Stuart B. Schwartz, "A família escrava em Lorena (1801)," pp. 245–296. Also on the slave family, see Stuart B. Schwartz, *Sugar Plantations in the Formation of Brazilian Society: Bahia, 1550–1835* (Cambridge and New York, 1985), pp. 379–412; and Richard Graham, "Slave Families on a Rural Estate in Colonial Brazil," *Journal of Social History* 9, 3 (1976), pp. 382–402.

68. Stein, *Vassouras*, p. 262, fn. 39; Fausto, *Crime e cotidiano*, p. 58. Fausto's findings coincide with those of anthropologist Moema Poli Teixeira Pacheco, who finds that in present-day *favelas* (slums) in Rio de Janeiro "the black family, one perceives, is as attached to such values as family and marriage as are so-called middle-class families; the 'incompleteness' or 'instability' [of the former], to quote Florestan Fernandes, if it exists, does not threaten these values so prized by the society." " 'Aguentando a barra': A questão da família negra" (manuscript, Museu Nacional, Rio de Janeiro, 1982), p. 16. For a considerably more negative view of the black family during this period, see Adamo, "The Broken Promise," pp. 101–108.

69. In the state of São Paulo in 1890, 36.6 percent of whites had been married at some point in their lives; among blacks the rate was 34.7 percent (36.8 percent for pretos, and 32.9 percent for pardos). In 1950, among individuals aged fifteen and older, 66.1 percent of whites had been married at some point in their lives, versus 60.9 percent of blacks (60.4 percent of pretos, and 62.2 percent of pardos). Directoria Geral de Estatística, *Recenseamento, 1890*, pp. 136–137; IBGE, *Recenseamento geral de 1950. Censo demográfico: Estado de São Paulo* (Rio de Janeiro, 1954), table 7, pages 6–7.

Divorce was illegal in Brazil at the time both censuses were taken, and only a very small proportion of the population fell into that category: 0.1 percent in 1890, and 0.6 percent in 1950. In my calculations I included these individuals in the "ever married" category.

70. Fernandes, *Integração do negro*, 1, pp. 162–163, 198. Fernandes admitted that many immigrant families were "disorganized" as well, but that "even the Italian 'disorganized family,' for example, possessed decided advantages over the 'black family'. . . ." 1, p. 216.

71. Fausto, *Crime e cotidiano*, pp. 13–14, 51–57, 119, 167–172; "Estatística criminal," A *Illustração Brasileira* (October 1, 1912), pp. 119–121.

72. "Grave erro!" *O Bandeirante* (September 1918), pp. 2–3.

73. On the editorship and readership of the black and labor presses, see, respectively, Roger Bastide, "A imprensa negra do Estado de São Paulo," in his *Estudos afro-brasileiros* (São Paulo, 1973); Miriam Nicolau Ferrara, A *imprensa negra paulista (1915–1963)* (São Paulo, 1986); and Maria Nazareth Ferreira, A *imprensa operária no Brasil, 1880–1920* (Petrópolis, 1978).

74. "Sin creencias," *El Grito del Pueblo* (August 20, 1899).

75. "O alcoolismo," *Jornal Operário* (October 29, 1905); "O dia dos operários," *O Grito do Povo* (May 1, 1900).

76. Articles on alcoholism appeared regularly in the black press; in the labor and immigrant press, see "O alcoolismo," *Jornal Operário* (October 29, 1905); "Abaixo o alcool!" *O Carpinteiro* (June 1, 1905), which argues that "alcoholism is, unhappily, one of the most pernicious plagues affecting the working class"; "O alcoolismo," *O Proletário* (October 1, 1911); "Contra l'alcoolismo," *Palestra Social* (January 12, 1901); and others. On dancing and parties, see "Depois do baile," *O Grito Operário* (February 4, 1920); "O Carnaval," *O Internacional* (February 6, 1921); "Carnaval," *O Internacional* (January 17, 1922); "Carnaval," *O Grito Operário* (February 18, 1920). On notorious dance halls, "Carta aberta," *O Alfinete* (October 12, 1918).

77. "A aleijada," *O Dois de Fevereiro* (August 1905). On the perils of domestic service, "Uma menor violentada," *O Proletário* (July 15, 1911); "Cuidae de vossas filhas," *Getulino* (April 13, 1924); "Reparando," *O Alfinete* (September 28, 1921). On prostitution, "O fenómeno da prostituição," *A Plebe* (January 19, 1935).

78. "O pobre é um vadio," *A Plebe* (June 9, 1917).

79. See, for example, Fernandes's essay "Representações coletivas sobre o negro: O negro na tradição oral," or his devastating analysis of the "prejudice of having no prejudice," Brazilians' assumption that their nation is completely free of racism despite obvious indications to the contrary. Florestan Fernandes, *O negro no mundo dos brancos* (São Paulo, 1972), pp. 21–44, 201–216. He was ambivalent, however, on how important this racism was in excluding black people from employment in turn-of-the-century São Paulo. See, for example, the previously cited quotation on the inability of blacks "to feel, think, and act" like free men, in which he argued that São Paulo's "rejection" of black people was caused, not by racism, but by Afro-Brazilians' failure to adopt "the psycho-social and moral attributes of 'family head,' of 'salaried worker,' of 'capitalist entrepreneur,' of 'citizen,' etc. . . . Sociologically speaking, the rejection would have had a specifically racial character if blacks had had these qualities and,

despite having them, had been rejected. But the evidence presented suggests the contrary. To the degree that they possessed the rudiments of these attributes or showed themselves capable of acquiring them, blacks found the door open, and became part of class society." Fernandes, *Integração do negro*, 1, p. 95. Later, however, he presented cases of black people who did in fact possess those qualities, and continued to suffer rejection or exclusion on racial grounds. He concluded that "the 'orderly, well behaved black' had to accept a hard, sad fate. The only possibilities open to him were defined by a sort of tacit specialization, involuntary and almost insuperable, that kept him forever tied to 'black people's work' offering minimal remuneration and an existence as painful as it was uncertain." *Integração do negro*, 1, p. 145.

80. On racial ideology, see Thomas Skidmore, *Black into White: Race and Nationality in Brazilian Thought* (New York, 1974); Thomas Skidmore, "Racial Ideas and Social Policy in Brazil, 1870–1940," in Richard Graham, ed., *The Idea of Race in Latin America, 1870–1940* (Austin, 1990); Renato Ortiz, "Memória coletiva e sincretismo científico: As teorias raciais do século XIX," in *Cultura brasileira e identidade nacional* (São Paulo, 1985); Schwarcz, *Retrato em branco e negro*. See also the sources on the *ideologia da vadiagem* cited in chapter 2, note 67.

81. Stolcke and Hall, "Introduction of Free Labour."

82. João Pedro da Veiga Filho, *Estudo econômico e financeiro sobre o Estado de São Paulo* (São Paulo, 1896), p. 69.

83. For analysis of the economic consequences of the "saturation" of the São Paulo labor market by an "unlimited" supply of immigrants, see Vangelista, *Braccia per la fazenda*, pp. 67–140.

84. Robert Foerster, *The Italian Emigration of Our Times* (Cambridge, Mass., 1919), p. 316.

85. Denis, *Brazil*, pp. 196, 216; Beiguelman, *Formação do povo*, p. 79; Holloway, *Immigrants on the Land*, p. 55.

86. On the importance of female and child labor on the plantations, see Verena Stolcke, "The Exploitation of Family Morality: Labor Systems and Family Structure on São Paulo Coffee Plantations, 1850–1979," in Raymond T. Smith, ed., *Kinship Ideology and Practice in Latin America* (Chapel Hill, 1985), pp. 266–274; Zuleika M. Forcioni Alvin, "Emigração, família e luta: Os italianos em São Paulo, 1870–1920" (*dissertação de mestrado*, Universidade de São Paulo, 1983), pp. 97–157; Vangelista, *Braccia per la fazenda*, pp. 146–151. See also the 1884 *colono* contract reproduced in Costa, *Senzala à colônia*, the first line of which obligates "the heads of family, jointly with their wives, children, and relatives" to fulfill the terms of the contract. Pp. 205–208.

On women and children in the industrial sector, see "O trabalho dos menores," *Boletim do Departamento Estadual do Trabalho* 2, 6 (1913), pp. 21–34; Beiguelman, *Formação do povo*, pp. 127–128, 190, 213; Love, *São Paulo*, p. 19. Commenting on the rapid industrial development of São Paulo City during the 1910s, Lilian Elliott noted that "to see this and to watch the crowds of pretty chattering Italian girls pouring out of Braz and Mooca factories at noon or evening is to obtain a revelation of the newer South America." Elliott, *Brazil*, p. 268.

87. Holloway, *Immigrants on the Land*, pp. 141–142; Maria Célia Paoli, "Working Class São Paulo and Its Representations," *Latin American Perspectives* 14, 2 (1987), p. 209; see also Vangelista, *Braccia per la fazenda*, pp. 242–243. In the textile industry, as of 1912 adult males (aged sixteen or older) composed only 19.3 percent of the labor force. Adult women made up half the work force (49.4 percent), and the remaining third (31.2 percent) were children aged fifteen or younger. "Condições do trabalho," pp. 38–39.

88. Foerster, *Italian Emigration*, p. 319. For studies on the United States which indicate Italian families' "very strong propensity to send their children to work as soon as it was possible," see Lieberson, *A Piece of the Pie*, p. 173; Yans-McLaughlin, *Family and Community*, pp. 189–194.

89. Quotation from *A Província de São Paulo* (February 6, 1889). On libertos' antipathy toward female and child labor, see Francisco de Paula Lazaro Gonçalves, *Relatório apresentado à Associação Promotora de Immigração em Minas* (Juiz de Fora, 1888),p. 11; Stein, *Vassouras*, p. 262; and for evidence of black families' reluctance to send their children into the factories, see chapter 4 in this volume. The apparent desire of black families to protect women and children from the rigors of the labor market would seem to undercut Fernandes's observations concerning the lack of family feeling among Afro-Brazilians.

90. On the use of coercion and violence by planters against immigrants, see Hall, "Origins of Mass Immigration," pp. 121–140; Vangelista, *Braccia per la fazenda*, pp. 195–215 passim; Alvin, "Emigração, família e luta," pp. 130–146. Even Holloway's relatively positive portrayal of conditions on the *fazendas* indicates that the use "of armed ruffians in the service of the landowner" continued into "the first years of the twentieth century," after which "reports of capanga [private gunmen] brutality diminished, as positive incentives replaced the vestiges of the coercive slave regime." Holloway, *Immigrants on the Land*, p. 103.

91. Holloway, *Immigrants on the Land*, pp. 42–43; Vangelista, *Braccia per la fazenda*, p. 83.

92. The impact of an abundant labor supply on São Paulo's industrialization is discussed in Wilson Cano, *Raizes da concentração industrial em São Paulo* (2nd edition, São Paulo, 1977), pp. 126–128. Cano notes that industrial wages in São Paulo lagged significantly behind those of Rio de Janeiro and Rio Grande do Sul, giving paulista industry a competitive edge over the rest of the country. P. 248, fn. 24.

93. The American consul is quoted in Paulo Sérgio Pinheiro and Michael Hall, eds., *A classe operária no Brasil, 1889–1930. Documentos*, Volume 2, *Condições de vida e de trabalho, relações com os empresários e o estado* (São Paulo, 1981), p. 126; "Increased Salary of Motormen and Conductors" (no date, but internal evidence suggests early 1920s), Arquivo, Eletricidade de São Paulo, pasta 29.005 (1906–1924).

94. On these various strategies of resistance, see Holloway, *Immigrants on the Land*; Alvin, "Emigração, família e luta"; Stolcke and Hall, "Introduction of Free Labour," and Fausto, *Trabalho urbano*. Historians have tended to underestimate the importance of strikes in the countryside because of their lack of success. For evidence that they occurred not infrequently, and were taken quite seriously by planters, see Stolcke and Hall, "Introduction of Free Labour";

pp. 185–186; Dean, *Rio Claro*, pp. 179–180; and Holloway, *Immigrants on the Land*, pp. 104–108.

95. Quotes from Denis, *Brazil*, p. 22. For articles on the "inconstancy" of immigrant workers, see *Revista Agrícola* (1899), pp. 50, 350–352, 382–386; (1901), pp. 166–167, 311; (1902), pp. 75–84; (1904), pp. 218–221. The observation from *O Combate* is quoted in Alba Maria Figueiredo Morandini, "O trabalhador migrante nacional em São Paulo, 1920–1923" (*tese de mestrado*, Pontifícia Universidade Católica–São Paulo, 1978), p. 78. On immigrants' purchases of smallholdings, see Holloway, *Immigrants on the Land*, pp. 139–166; Verena Stolcke, *Coffee Planters, Workers and Wives: Class Conflict and Gender Relations on São Paulo Plantations, 1850–1980* (New York, 1988), pp. 36–43.

96. For an 1895 report by the Secretariat of Agriculture arguing that "the introduction of thousands of immigrants of a single nationality into this or that State must cease," see Morandini, "O trabalhador migrante," p. 37, fn. 30. In the *Boletim do Departamento Estadual do Trabalho* see: "O Departamento Estadual do Trabalho em 1914," 3, 12 (1915), pp. 471–472; "A legislação do trabalho sob o ponto de vista immigratorio," 6, 23 (1917), p. 270; "O trabalhador nacional," 5, 20 (1916), p. 352; "Localização dos trabalhadores nacionais," 7, 27 (1918), pp. 301–340; and others. These articles acknowledge quite openly the labor market preference granted to the immigrants over Brazilians. "Abandoned to their fate, with no assistance from the government, [the libertos and caboclos] were easy and defenseless prey to the illnesses which conquered them, wasting their bodies, reducing their capacity for work, and destroying their race. While this was happening, we opened our pocketbook to the European immigrants, who have no love for this land and their eyes fixed on their distant Fatherland, where many of them return after having saved some money. We gave them everything: land, housing, food, tools, medical assistance, and guaranteed work." "O saneamento da população agrária do Brasil," *Boletim do Departamento Estadual do Trabalho* 6, 23 (1917), pp. 245–246.

Lúcio Kowarick nicely captures the "rehabilitation" of the Brazilian worker during the war years. "His lack of ambition came to be seen as the parsimony of one who is content with little, is not after easy gain, and above all, does not make demands; lack of constancy was translated into versatility and aptitude for new kinds of work, while lack of discipline was metamorphosed into stoutheartedness and dignity. The former wanderer was ready to go wherever he was needed. His love of adventure and brawling were transformed into fearlessness and courage to perform risky tasks, while his wariness and suspiciousness became a sound characteristic with which to reject spurious ideas, so much in vogue at the time. His indolence came not from sloth or a vagabond nature, but from lack of opportunity to work, while his vices were now seen as a result of the misery in which he had been bogged down for centuries and from which he must now be removed." *Trabalho e vadiagem*, p. 124. Lilian Elliott, visiting São Paulo during the war years, received the same message. "Intelligent and apt, docile if conciliated and stubborn if crossed, the *mestizo* has some excellent qualities; the indolence of which he is often accused is sometimes want of direction, and sometimes the result of ill-health in certain regions, disappearing when the enervating malaria and akulostomiasis [*sic*] are conquered, exactly as in the South of the United States, where the same troubles are common. With better sanitation in the crowded warm regions, and persistence in good schooling, the *brasileiro* of the labouring classes would not need supplanting with introduced immigrants." Elliott, *Brazil*, p. 82.

97. Morandini, "O trabalhador migrante," p. 76; "Immigração," *Boletim do Departamento Estadual do Trabalho* 12, 42–43 (1922), p. 14; Love, *São Paulo*, pp. 11, 75.

98. Love, *São Paulo*, pp. 12; Vangelista, *Braccia per la fazenda*, p. 110.

99. "Pequenas considerações," *O Clarim da Alvorada* (January 6, 1929).

100. Fernandes, *Integração do negro*, 1, p. 157. Afro-Brazilian entry into the industrial labor force was further assisted by state action at the national level in the form of the Lei de Nacionalização do Trabalho (the Nationalization of Labor Law), enacted by the Vargas regime in 1931, which required at least two-thirds of the labor force in industrial and commercial establishments to be native-born Brazilians. Agriculture was explicitly exempted from this requirement. *Diário Oficial dos Estados Unidos do Brasil* (August 25, 1931), pp. 13,552–13,558.

101. Hasenbalg, *Discriminação*, p. 254.

Chapter 4. Working, 1920–1960

1. On Brazilian industrialization, see Warren Dean, "A industrialização durante a República Velha," in Boris Fausto, ed., *O Brasil republicano: Estrutura de poder e economia* (3rd edition, São Paulo, 1982), pp. 249–283; John P. Dickenson, *Brazil* (Boulder, 1978); Rollie Poppino, *Brazil: The Land and the People* (New York, 1968), pp. 238–283. Figures from E. Bradford Burns, *A History of Brazil* (New York, 1970), p. 259; Richard Nyrop, ed., *Brazil: A Country Study* (Washington, D.C., 1983), pp. 181, 228, 354; Dickenson, *Brazil*, p. 204; and George Thomas Kurian, *The New Book of World Rankings* (New York, 1984), p. 199.

2. Figures from Dean, "Industrialização," pp. 260–262; and Joseph L. Love, *São Paulo in the Brazilian Federation, 1889–1937* (Stanford, 1980), p. 58. See also Warren Dean, *The Industrialization of São Paulo, 1880–1945* (Austin, 1969); Wilson Cano, *Raízes da concentração industrial em São Paulo* (2nd edition, São Paulo, 1977).

3. For research making use of such records in Rio de Janeiro and Santa Catarina, see Sam Adamo, "The Broken Promise: Race, Health, and Justice in Rio de Janeiro, 1890–1940" (Ph.D. dissertation, University of New Mexico, 1983); Eileen Keremetsis, "The Early Industrial Worker in Rio de Janeiro, 1870–1930" (Ph.D. dissertation, Columbia University, 1982); Valentim Lazzarotto, *Pobres construtores de riqueza: Absorção da mão-de-obra e expansão industrial na Metalúrgica Abramo Eberle, 1905–1970* (Caxias do Sul, 1981).

4. "Condições do trabalho na indústria têxtil do Estado de São Paulo," *Boletim do Departamento Estadual do Trabalho* 1, 1–2 (1912), pp. 35–80. Statistics on the textile industry from June Hahner, *Poverty and Politics: The Urban Poor in Brazil, 1870–1920* (Albuquerque, 1986), p. 192; Kenneth Erickson, *The Brazilian Corporative State and Working-Class Politics* (Berkeley, 1977), p. 13. See also Stanley J. Stein, *The Brazilian Cotton Manufacture: Textile Enterprise in an Underdeveloped Area, 1850–1950* (Cambridge, Mass., 1957).

5. Dean, *Industrialization of São Paulo*, p. 31. The Jafet factory is discussed in

the "Condições do trabalho" article. Of the thirty-three factories surveyed, it was the largest in terms of size (50,000 square meters), and the fourth largest in terms of capitalization. The number of workers employed is not mentioned; Paula Beiguelman and Boris Fausto estimate its work force at the time of the general strike of 1917 as between fifteen hundred and sixteen hundred, which would have made it one of the largest factories of any kind in the state. Boris Fausto, *Trabalho urbano e conflito social, 1890–1920* (São Paulo, 1977), p. 193; Paula Beiguelman, *Formação do povo no compleixo cafeeiro: Aspectos políticos* (2nd edition, São Paulo, 1977), p. 198.

A nice comparison with the Jafet company is provided by Peter Winn's *Weavers of Revolution: The Yarur Workers and Chile's Road to Socialism* (New York, 1986), which deals with a Chilean textile firm founded by Palestinian immigrants in 1937.

6. Lilian E. Elliott, *Brazil, Today and Tomorrow* (rpt., New York, 1922), p. 268.

7. For the 1910–1930 period as a whole, minors (children fifteen or younger) composed essentially the same proportion of the work force at Jafet: 31.4 percent. The youngest workers encountered in the personnel files were four six-year-old girls hired in 1910.

8. "Condições do trabalho," pp. 43–44. The worst offender in terms of child labor was the Caielli factory, where of 293 employees only 20 were adults. "In spite of [the owners'] declaration to the contrary, we found 12-year-old children in service." Conditions in the textile factories apparently inspired an accompanying article, "O trabalho dos menores," in the same issue of the *Boletim*, which argued for the enforcement of the laws prohibiting employment for children under the age of ten, and urged that children be permitted to work only after a thorough medical examination.

9. For a history of São Paulo Light, see Edgard de Souza, *História da Light: Primeiros 50 anos* (São Paulo, 1982); see also Judith Tendler, *Electric Power in Brazil: Entrepreneurship in the Public Sector* (Cambridge, Mass., 1968), pp. 7–34; and the periodical publications of Eletricidade de São Paulo's Departamento de Patrimônio Histórico, *Boletim Histórico* (1985–1987) and *Memória* (1988–). Payroll figures taken from "Demonstration of Total Cost of Payrolls" (July 22, 1931), and "Demonstrações das folhas de pagamento" (1948–1949), Arquivo, Eletricidade de São Paulo, pasta 29.004

10. For the period before 1920, a 5 percent sample of São Paulo Light's pre–Social Security records turned up twenty-nine Brazilian-born workers, thirty-five immigrants, and fifteen of unknown birthplace. For the same period, a 20 percent sample of Jafet's pre–Social Security records produced seventy-four Brazilian-born workers and seventy-three immigrants.

The records become considerably more abundant after 1920. The 20 percent Jafet sample produced 2,772 persons of known birthplace hired between 1921 and 1930. For the same decade, the 5 percent São Paulo Light sample produced 868 persons of known birthplace.

11. Such second-generation Brazilians were numerous in São Paulo by the 1920s. According to the state census of 1934, among Brazilian-born residents of the state capital aged nineteen or over, 41.5 percent were the offspring of a

foreign-born father and mother; an additional 11.0 percent had either a foreign-born father or mother. Offspring of foreign parents constituted 73.3 percent of the industrial labor force in the capital; an additional 8.1 percent of those working in industry had one foreign parent. "Estatística," *Boletim do Departamento Estadual de Estatística*, 1, 1 (1939), pp. 97, 102. My thanks to Thomas Holloway for calling this source to my attention.

12. "Frente Negra Brasileira, 1930–1937" (unpublished collaborative *trabalho de pesquisa*, Pontifícia Universidade Católica–São Paulo, 1985), anexo 2.

13. See chapter 3, note 100.

14. "Frente Negra Brasileira," anexo 2; *Getulino* (December 23, 1923), p. 1, and (January 23, 1924), p. 2.

15. As in the earlier state-sponsored recruiting programs, the firm paid new workers' transportation costs to São Paulo City, and often provided subsidized company-owned housing. One of the former employees with whom I spoke, the son of Italian immigrants to the coffee zone in western São Paulo, had himself been hired under this program in 1952. He recalled that the recruiting agent's offer of high wages and a subsidized apartment persuaded him, along with several of his brothers and sisters, to leave their family farm and come to the capital. Given the hardships and uncertainties of rural life, he says, none of them ever had cause to regret their decision. "The factory was like a prison," he recalls, "but it was better than the farm!" This opinion is seconded by a black woman who left her home in the countryside in 1936 to come to São Paulo and work in a textile factory. "The work was lighter, not so dirty as farm work, where you got covered with dust." Conselho Estadual da Condição Feminina, *Mulheres operárias* (São Paulo, 1985), p. 33.

16. On the growth of these newer industries, see Dickenson, *Brazil*, pp. 105–131; John Humphrey, *Capitalist Control and Workers' Struggle in the Brazilian Auto Industry* (Princeton, 1983), pp. 31–35 and passim.

17. IBGE, *Recenseamento geral de 1950. Censo demográfico: Estado de São Paulo* (Rio de Janeiro, 1954), table 11, p. 10; IBGE, *Recenseamento geral de 1960. Censo demográfico: Estado de São Paulo* (Rio de Janeiro, n.d.), table 7, p. 11.

18. IBGE, *Recenseamento geral de 1940. Censo demográfico: Estado de São Paulo* (Rio de Janeiro, 1950), table 62, p. 472; IBGE, *Recenseamento, 1950. São Paulo*, table 37, p. 73.

19. IBGE, *Recenseamento, 1940. São Paulo*, table 30, p. 24; IBGE, *Recenseamento, 1950. São Paulo*, table 23, p. 30.

20. The 1940 census shows 39,383 pardos and pretos working in the industrial sector, 18,294 in domestic service, and 56,396 "inactive, in activities not included in other categories, or in ill-defined or undeclared occupations." This does not include housewives and schoolchildren, who were listed separately. Comparable figures for whites in 1940 were 376,829 employed in industry, 151,424 in domestic service, and 359,735 inactive, etc. IBGE, *Recenseamento, 1940. São Paulo*, table 30, pp. 24–25.

21. IBGE, *Recenseamento, 1950. São Paulo*, table 23, p. 30.

22. The number of white industrial workers grew from 376,829 in 1940 to 674,502 in 1950.

23. *Evolução. Revista dos homens pretos de São Paulo* (May 13, 1933).

24. "Entre e veja se ahi ha negros como você," *Progresso* (November 15, 1931), p. 2; "Protesto da Assembleia contra a discriminação racial," *O Mutirão* (June 1958), p. 1; "Aqui é como nos EE.UU.," *Hífen* (February 1960), p. 1; "Empresas discriminam trabalhadores negros," *Notícias Populares* (October 21, 1982).

25. The reader is here reminded that the workers in these samples represent a 1 percent sample of the white labor force at each firm, and a 4 percent sample of the nonwhite labor force. Obviously, as indicated in Tables 4.1 and 4.2, whites formed the great majority of workers at each firm.

26. The proportion of pardos hired at São Paulo Light is probably somewhat overstated. As indicated in Appendix C, 40 of the 327 black workers in the sample were identified solely by their photographs, and had no racial label indicated in their files. Though these workers were assigned to an "unspecified Afro-Brazilian" category, a number of indicators—birthplace, time at which they entered the firm, appearance in photograph—suggest that most of them were pretos, which would reduce the pardo-preto ratio cited in the text, and make the racial composition of the black workers at São Paulo Light more similar to that at Jafet.

In the remainder of this chapter, statistics on the black work force will be presented separately for pardos and pretos whenever there is a significant difference between those two populations. When no such figures are provided, it means that statistical indicators were essentially the same for pardos and pretos.

27. In 1940, São Paulo City contained 45,135 pardos and 63,546 pretos. IBGE, *Recenseamento, 1940. São Paulo*, table 62, p. 472. In 1950 the capital contained 55,342 pardos and 169,564 pretos. IBGE, *Recenseamento, 1950. São Paulo*, table 37, p. 73.

28. IBGE, *Recenseamento, 1940. São Paulo*, table 30, pp. 24–25; IBGE, *Recenseamento, 1950. São Paulo*, table 23, p. 30.

29. This reflects the relative racial composition of São Paulo State and the Northeast. In São Paulo, pretos outnumbered pardos in 1950 by a ratio of 2.5:1 (727,789 to 292,669). In the Northeast, pardos outnumbered pretos by a ratio of 3.9:1 (5,399,729 to 1,374,899). IBGE, *Recenseamento geral de 1950. Censo demográfico: Estados Unidos do Brasil* (Rio de Janeiro, 1956), table 39, p. 69.

30. One indication of the higher levels of experience demanded at São Paulo Light is that in 1945 the company began asking for, and recording, detailed information on workers' previous work history, even for unskilled common laborers. No such job histories were ever requested at Jafet.

31. Even if these figures exaggerated somewhat, they still reflect a work force considerably better educated than the population as a whole. In 1950, of São Paulo State's male population, 61.8 percent of whites and 47.4 percent of blacks were literate. Among females, 47.4 percent of whites and 36.6 percent of blacks were literate. IBGE, *Recenseamento, 1950. São Paulo*, table 17, p. 20.

32. More pardos than pretos came to São Paulo Light from the agricultural sector. Of pardos, 21.8 percent had a background in agriculture, as compared with 13.4 percent of pretos, and 7.1 percent of whites.

33. The company's reluctance to place preto employees in service positions

involving regular contact with the public is suggested by the firing in 1941 of Pedro Assumpção S., a preto trolley driver who had worked for the company since 1937. One evening he become involved in an altercation with three white men who, upon discovering that they had boarded the wrong tram by mistake, "insulted the driver, calling him a *negro*, and attacked him with a knife." The company's investigation of the resulting fracas concluded that the driver was in no way to blame, and had defended himself from an unprovoked attack. Nevertheless, he was fired shortly thereafter for his "incompatibility with public service." Arquivo, Eletricidade de São Paulo, envelope 26, pacote 2081-V.

34. Jacquelyn Dowd Hall et al., *Like a Family: The Making of a Southern Cotton Mill World* (Chapel Hill, 1987), pp. 205–206, 69.

35. The record for suspensions was set by a white worker, Manoel G., who between 1947 and 1964 was suspended thirty-six times, usually for excessive absences. At no point did his supervisors discuss firing him (at least in writing), and he eventually resigned from the firm. Arquivo, Eletricidade de São Paulo, envelope 11, pacote 120–746.

36. Senado Federal, *Consolidação das leis do trabalho* (Brasilia, 1974), pp. 196–203.

37. Of those workers fired at Jafet, 51.4 percent of whites, and 51.2 percent of blacks, were let go before completing their first year; at São Paulo Light, the comparable percentages were 56.3 for whites, and 61.3 percent for blacks.

38. Arquivo, Eletricidade de São Paulo: envelope 6, pacote 2073-V; envelope 25, pacote 120–056; envelope 3, pacote 120–1276.

39. Between 1940 and 1970, there were only four years in which the rate of inflation in Brazil fell below 10 percent. The peaks of each inflationary period were reached in 1944 (27.5 percent), 1955 (23.3 percent), and 1959–1966, during which prices rose by a factor of twenty. Cláudio Contador and Cláudio Haddad, "Produção real, moeda e preços: A experiência brasileira no período 1861–1970," *Revista Brasileira de Estatística* 36 (1975), p. 435.

40. This summary of firing and resignation practices at Jafet is based on material contained in the files themselves, and on conversations with former employees of the firm. The involuntary nature of these resignations is further indicated by the fact that, of the sixty-five workers who left the firm in this way, only three indicated a reason for their resignation (in all three cases, "personal interest"). Of those workers who appear to have resigned voluntarily, two-thirds specified their reasons for doing so.

41. Light conductors were notorious for shortchanging the company. A collection of reminiscences of life in São Paulo during the early decades of the century includes a recollection by one gentleman of how conductors used to siphon off fares: "Ding-ding, two for Light and one for me." Eclea Bosi, *Memória e sociedade: Lembranças de velhos* (São Paulo, 1977), p. 131.

In light of the previously discussed *ideologia da vadiagem*, it is ironic to note in the "generally unsatisfactory" category of firings the presence of four white workers, and no blacks, fired *por ser vadio* (for being a bum).

42. The reader will note the absence of retirements in the Jafet work force. After I had completed my research at the factory, I learned that the files of individuals who had retired from the firm are kept in a separate depository,

apart from the records with which I had been working. By the time I made this discovery, I was on the verge of leaving São Paulo, and was unable to begin the coding of this additional body of material. As Table 4.7 indicates, at São Paulo Light retirees represented less than a tenth of the labor force, and it is my impression, from a quick survey of the retiree files at Jafet, that a similar proportion obtained at the textile firm. Clearly the inclusion of these workers would have had an impact on the composition of the sample, particularly in fleshing out the cohort hired during the 1930s. Judging from the São Paulo Light data, however, I doubt that it would have significantly altered the similarities and disparities between racial groups (e.g., differences in birthplace, time with the firm, literacy, etc.) documented in the sample of workers who did not reach retirement.

43. In 1957 the company brought a team of Italian consultants to the factory to advise it on how to increase productivity while reducing labor costs. The team instituted a Taylorization program which made it possible to reduce the work force by a third while maintaining pre-1957 levels of production. As a result, of those workers who resigned from Jafet involuntarily, 60 percent did so in 1957, and another 25 percent in 1958 and 1959. These reductions did not restore the firm to profitability however, and in 1961 it closed its doors, and the factory was converted to a warehouse. On the competitive pressures which aging textile factories in Latin America faced during the 1950s and 1960s, and on their efforts to meet those pressures by importing Taylor-inspired management and production techniques, see Winn, *Weavers of Revolution*, pp. 22–24, 44–46.

44. Maria Célia Paoli, "Working-Class São Paulo and Its Representations," *Latin American Perspectives* 14, 2 (1987), p. 209. A 1959 description of working conditions at Jafet seconds this testimony. "In the workplace there were large quantities of cotton dust, the floor was cement, very damp; the environment was very hot and sweltering . . . ; there was an air conditioner in the workplace which produced an artificial mist which soaked the head and clothes of [the workers] throughout [their] daily shift. When it rained, the place was completely soaked and the workers were obliged to remove the rainwater. . . ." Raul de Carvalho to the Juiz de Direito da 2a Vara de Accidentes de Trabalho (March 23, 1959), Jafet, prontuário 19857. Working conditions at textile factories of the Jafet mill's vintage are vividly described in Hall, *Like a Family*, pp. 44–113.

45. Paoli, "Working-Class São Paulo," p. 210.

46. Jafet, prontuário 30869.

50. R. H. Bowles to Edgard de Souza (March 5, 1929), Arquivo, Eletricidade de São Paulo, pasta 29.004.

51. Arquivo, Eletricidade de São Paulo, envelope 12, pacote 2131.

52. This proportion is so low that one has to question the reliability of the documents on this score. Promotions or changes in job were supposed to be entered on the worker's *ficha*, a summary record of service which also included information on salary changes. Recordkeepers at Jafet, however, seem to have been lackadaisical about recording either, since only 5.5 percent of workers at Jafet had any raise at all recorded in their files—a figure which seems improbably low, especially when one considers that the years covered by the sample were

a period of intense inflation, during which workers at São Paulo Light, for example, received annual raises like clockwork. Further undermining one's confidence in the records is the fact that most of the promotions and pay raises which I did find and code were recorded not on the *fichas* but on small slips of paper thrust randomly into the files. One suspects, then, that there was more movement in both wages and job assignments at Jafet than shows up in the files.

53. Given their substantial vocational achievement, it is worth looking at these black foremen in more detail. The fifteen individuals involved come close to constituting a generational cohort; most of them joined São Paulo Light between 1925 and 1930, with all but one of the remainder joining during the 1930s. Since they were hired prior to the creation of the Social Security recordkeeping system, most did not have race noted on their personnel forms, but rather were identified through the use of photographs (and thus cannot be categorized as pardos or pretos). The majority were natives of São Paulo. They served a median period of nine years with the company before being promoted to foreman status. And most of them went on to serve until retirement in the 1960s.

Black workers do not always look up to black foremen and supervisors as people to be emulated. A black union director at one of the auto plants in São Bernardo, an industrial suburb of São Paulo City, says of black foremen that "for the most part they are worse than the whites, because in order to remain in their position they have to produce twice the output that a white would have to, so they exploit their workers much more." "Organização incipiente na região," *Caderno C, Diário do Grande ABC* (November 24, 1985).

Chapter 5. Living in a Racial Democracy, 1900–1940

1. Thomas Holloway, *Immigrants on the Land: Coffee and Society in São Paulo, 1886–1934* (Chapel Hill, 1980), p. 160. Small and medium-sized holdings are defined as those less than 50 *alqueires* (approximately 300 acres) in size. See also Verena Stolcke, *Coffee Planters, Workers and Wives: Class Conflict and Gender Relations on São Paulo Plantations, 1850–1980* (New York, 1988), pp. 36–43.

2. Décio Saes, *Classe média e política na Primeira República brasileira (1889–1930)* (Petrópolis, 1975); Steven Topik, "Middle-Class Brazilian Nationalism, 1889–1930," *Social Science Quarterly* 59, 1 (1978), pp. 93–103.

3. Herbert S. Klein, "Nineteenth-Century Brazil," in David W. Cohen and Jack P. Greene, *Neither Slave nor Free: The Freedman of African Descent in the Slave Societies of the New World* (Baltimore, 1972), pp. 325–330; Gilberto Freyre, *The Mansions and the Shanties: The Making of Modern Brazil* (New York, 1963), pp. 368–423 passim; Manuel Raimundo Querino, *A raça africana e os seus costumes* (Salvador, 1955), pp. 153–172.

4. Afro-Brazilians composed 12.2 percent of the working-age population in São Paulo in 1940, and 8.8 percent of public employees.

5. "Meus rascunhos," *Getulino* (December 23, 1923), p. 2.

6. "O concurso de Itapetininga: Bairrismo e preconceitos de cor," *O Combate* (May 24, 1915), p. 4. Apparently stung by the accusation of racism, the school superintendent responded that, while black candidate Henrique de Araujo did

have a more advanced degree than his white competitor, "when one tries to gauge intellectual abilities, one does not and must not think in terms of [academic] degrees. . . . Titles and diplomas only impress those who, in evaluating and judging, skate over the surface." "O concurso de Itapetininga," *O Combate* (May 25, 1915), p. 3.

7. "Patronage formed the connecting web of politics in nineteenth-century Brazil and sustained virtually every political act. . . . By their actions Brazilians signaled that for them an impersonal state remained a pipe dream, that the provision of employment and the distribution of authority constituted the true and lasting function of the state." Richard Graham, *Patronage and Politics in Nineteenth-Century Brazil* (Stanford, 1990), pp. 1, 272. See also Emília Viotti da Costa, *The Brazilian Empire: Myths and Histories* (Chicago, 1985), pp. 189–90, 196–197. On the continuation of patronage into the twentieth century, see Lawrence Graham, *Civil Service Reform in Brazil* (Austin, 1970); James M. Malloy, *The Politics of Social Security in Brazil* (Pittsburgh, 1979), pp. 77–79, 98–100.

8. See, for example, the social columns of *Getulino* for 1923, or *Progresso* for 1928; see also "Nomeações," *A Liberdade* (March 7, 1920), which reports on appointments of Afro-Brazilians to jobs in municipal and state government around the state, including eight clerks and ten school inspectors.

9. "Os jornais dos netos de escravos," *Jornal da Tarde* (June 12, 1975), p. 17. State employment was particularly important to the editors of the black papers, who were unable to support themselves through their journalistic work alone, and whose high levels of literacy made them suitable for clerical and secretarial work in bureaucratic offices. A humorous poem on a visit to the editorial offices of *A Liberdade* in 1919 reports on the sources of income of its editors: "Baptista is at the Law School, Gastão at City Hall." "Chegando," *A Liberdade* (November 23, 1919). "Baptista" is Frederico Baptista de Souza, who wrote for a number of black papers during the 1920s and 1930s, and worked as a clerk-secretary at the Law School. See his obituary, *Niger* (August 1960), p. 11. Arlindo Veiga dos Santos, frequent contributor to the black papers, and president of the Palmares Civic Center and Brazilian Black Front, also worked as a secretary at the Law School. "Dr. A. J. Veiga dos Santos," *O Clarim da Alvorada* (January 6, 1929), p. 4.

10. The basic source on the black press is Miriam Nicolau Ferrara, *A imprensa negra paulista (1915–1963)* (São Paulo, 1986); see also Roger Bastide, "A imprensa negra do Estado de São Paulo," in *Estudos afro-brasileiros* (São Paulo, 1973). I am deeply grateful to Professor Ferrara for making available to me her extensive personal collection of black newspapers, which she has subsequently donated to the University of São Paulo. Political scientist Michael Mitchell has prepared a microfilm, *The Black Press of Brazil*, on deposit at the Firestone Library of Princeton University, which includes many of these papers. See also the facsimile edition of several issues of these papers, *Imprensa negra* (São Paulo, 1984), published by the state Secretariat of Culture with an accompanying text by Clóvis Moura.

11. Ferrara, *Imprensa negra*, pp. 246, 256.

12. Florestan Fernandes, "O mito da democracia racial," in *A integração do*

negro na sociedade de classes (3rd edition, São Paulo, 1978), 1, pp. 249-269; Emília Viotti da Costa, "The Myth of Racial Democracy," in *Brazilian Empire*, pp. 234-246; Thales de Azevedo, *Democracia racial* (Petrópolis, 1975). For an examination of the racial democracy concept in Venezuela, see Winthrop R. Wright, *Café con Leche: Race, Class, and National Image in Venezuela* (Austin, 1990).

13. Louis Couty, *L'esclavage au Brésil* (Paris, 1881), quoted in Célia Maria Marinho de Azevedo, *Onda negra, medo branco: O negro no imaginário das elites—século XIX* (São Paulo, 1987), p. 78.

14. See Herbert Klein's assessment of the position of free blacks in nineteenth-century society: "Although this free colored class was the largest single grouping in imperial Brazil, its existence clearly did not mean the end of racial discrimination in Brazilian society. From the colonial period on, there was constant opposition on the part of the white elite to that class's increasing self-assertiveness. . . . racial tensions were prominent enough for free men of color like Luis Gama and other intellectuals, especially those who were Negro, to be forced to identify with the largely black slave community for their self-realization." Klein, "Nineteenth-Century Brazil," pp. 332-333.

15. Theodore Roosevelt, "Brazil and the Negro," *Outlook* 106 (1914), pp. 410-411, quoted in Nelson do Valle Silva, "Black-White Income Differentials: Brazil, 1960" (Ph.D. dissertation, University of Michigan, 1978), p. 50.

16. Robert Conrad, *Children of God's Fire: A Documentary History of Black Slavery in Brazil* (Princeton, 1983), pp. 285, 453.

17. The idea that slaves were better protected and less exploited in Brazil and Spanish America than in the United States formed the core of Frank Tannenbaum's influential comparative study, *Slave and Citizen: The Negro in the Americas* (New York, 1946). Historical research carried out during the last twenty years has called much of Tannenbaum's argument into question, and has led historians to discard most of it.

18. Lívio de Castro, "Questões e problemas: Ódio entre raças," *A Província de São Paulo* (February 6, 1889). Despite recognizing its barbarous qualities, abolitionist Joaquim Nabuco agreed that "slavery never poisoned the mind of the slave toward the master—fortunately for us—nor did it arouse between the two races that two-way loathing which naturally exists between oppressor and oppressed. For this reason, the contact between the two races outside slavery was never bitter, and the man of color found every avenue open before him." Joaquim Nabuco, *Abolitionism: The Brazilian Antislavery Struggle* (Urbana, 1977), p. 21.

19. For such proposals, see Azevedo, *Onda negra*, pp. 100-104. Richard Graham has argued that one such proposal in particular, that of an agrarian reform which would make land available to the libertos, played a direct role in provoking the overthrow of the monarchy in 1889. Richard Graham, "Landowners and the Overthrow of the Empire," *Luso-Brazilian Review* 7, 2 (1970), pp. 44-56.

20. Even Gilberto Freyre admitted the high levels of "sadism," a word he used repeatedly, which characterized master-slave relations. *The Masters and Slaves: A Study in the Development of Brazilian Civilization* (New York, 1946),

pp. 349–352, 368, 390–394. As he concluded in the final paragraph of his book, "The lives of the Negro slaves who served the white *ioiôs* and *iaiás* was not altogether a merry one." p. 474.

21. The temporal juxtaposition between emancipation and the declaration of racial democracy is remarked on by Hélio Santos in "O presidente negro," *Veja* (October 31, 1984), p. 138.

22. Swedish sociologist Gunnar Myrdal made this contradiction the starting point of his classic work on United States race relations. See Gunnar Myrdal, *An American Dilemma: The Negro Problem and Modern Democracy* (New York, 1944), pp. xlv–xlix, and chapter 1, "American Ideals," pp. 3–25.

23. For some of the most interesting analyses of these contradictions and this struggle, see the work of anthropologist Roberto da Matta: *Carnavais, malandros, e heróis* (Rio de Janeiro, 1978), and *A casa e a rua: Espaço, cidadania, mulher e morte no Brasil* (São Paulo, 1985). In the field of political science, see Francisco Weffort's reflections on the "enormous distance" in Brazil "between that which intentions proclaim and which actions do," and on the "sharp contrasts between the 'legal country,' ruled by anachronistic laws and institutions, and the 'real country,' experiencing a process of rapid modernization." *Por que democracia?* (São Paulo, 1984), pp. 53, 57. (This short book is available in English translation under the title "Why Democracy?" in Alfred Stepan, ed., *Democratizing Brazil: Problems of Transition and Consolidation* [New York, 1989], pp. 327–350.) In the field of history, see the work of José Murilo de Carvalho, *Teatro de sombras: A política imperial* (São Paulo, 1988), and *Os bestializados: O Rio de Janeiro e a República que não foi* (São Paulo, 1987); and Emília Viotti da Costa's illuminating essay "Liberalism: Theory and Practice," on which the next several paragraphs are based. *Brazilian Empire*, pp. 53–77.

24. Carvalho, *Os bestializados*, pp. 38, 159–60. On declining voter participation, see his chapter 2, notes 51 and 53.

25. Weffort, *Por que democracia?*, pp. 21–31.

26. "Porque queremos a confederação," *O Clarim da Alvorada* (April 25, 1926), p. 2; "Os homens pretos e a evolução social," *Auriverde* (April 29, 1928), p. 2; "A situação económica social do negro," *Progresso* (August 30, 1931), p. 2.

27. "Quem somos," *O Clarim da Alvorada* (November 14, 1926), p. 3. See also "Reparando," *O Alfinete* (November 1921); "A questão da raça," *Auriverde* (April 29, 1928), p. 3; "O ódio de raça," *Progresso* (January 13, 1929), p. 2. For an extended critique of United States race relations by mulatto lawyer and intellectual Evaristo de Moraes, parts of which were reprinted in the black newspaper *Getulino*, see his *Brancos e negros nos Estados Unidos e no Brasil* (Rio de Janeiro, 1922).

28. "Grave erro!" *O Bandeirante* (September 1918), p. 3.

29. "Os pretos em São Paulo," *O Kosmos* (November 16, 1924), p. 2, reprinted from *Getulino* (September 28, 1924).

30. On the whitening thesis, see Thomas Skidmore, *Black into White: Race and Nationality in Brazilian Thought* (New York, 1974).

31. For an interim report on *branqueamento* in progress, published as part of the national census of 1920, see [F. J. Oliveira Viana,] "Evolução da raça," in

Directoria Geral de Estatística, *Recenseamento do Brasil realizado em 1º de setembro de 1920* (Rio de Janeiro, 1922), 1, pp. 313–344.

32. "Grave erro!" *O Bandeirante* (September 1918), pp. 2–3; "Cartas d'um negro," *Getulino* (September 23, 1923); "Fusão de raças," *Getulino* (October 7, 1923), p. 1. But see also the occasional short stories in the black papers in which black men fall hopelessly in love with white women. These romances never produce offspring, and usually conclude with the death of the male. They seem to imply that race mixture, while a desired ideal, is difficult if not impossible to achieve in practice; and that whitening will take place not through such mixture, but rather through the elimination of black people. For examples of these stories, see "Episódio da revolta da Ilha de São Domingos," *Menelick* (January 1, 1916), p. 1; "Archinimigo de Camargo," *Getulino* (September 30, 1923); "A quem me entender," *O Clarim da Alvorada* (February 3, 1924), p. 1.

33. "O grande problema nacional," *Evolução* (May 13, 1933), pp. 9, 13; "Congresso da Mocidade Negra Brasileira," *O Clarim da Alvorada* (June 9, 1929), p. 1. See also *Getulino's* response to the Reis bill of 1923, which proposed to bar Afro-American, or any black, immigration into Brazil. While agreeing that "we are convinced that [the presence of] more blacks in Brazil would increase the misfortunes of that unhappy race," the paper went on to say that "what wounds our soul like a red-hot iron is the manner in which a certain Congressman justified this bill, which will appear in the annals of Congress for all eternity. Yes, for all eternity it will be clear that black blood is a disorder in our national ethnic formation." "Echos de projecto F. Reis," *Getulino* (January 20, 1924), p. 1. The Reis bill is discussed in Skidmore, *Black into White*, pp. 192–196. For a discussion of Afro-American interest in migrating to Brazil, and evidence that Brazilian consuls sought to frustrate such migration, see Teresa Meade and Gregory Alonso Pirio, "In Search of the Afro-American 'Eldorado': Attempts by North American Blacks to Enter Brazil in the 1920s," *Luso-Brazilian Review* 25, 1 (1988), pp. 85–110.

34. "Na terra do preconceito," *O Clarim da Alvorada* (March 4, 1928), p. 3; "Eduquemos nosso povo," *O Clarim da Alvorada* (September 28, 1931), p. 4. See also "Aos nossos leitores," *O Alfinete* (September 3, 1918), p. 1.

35. "Cartas d'um negro," *Getulino* (October 21, 1923), p. 3; "Preto e branco," *O Kosmos* (April 18, 1923), p. 1. On Abbott's vision of Brazilian race relations, and his visit to Brazil, see David J. Hellwig, "A New Frontier in a Racial Paradise: Robert S. Abbott's Brazilian Dream," *Luso-Brazilian Review* 25, 1 (1988), pp. 59–67.

36. "Os pretos em São Paulo," *O Kosmos* (October 19, 1924), p. 1. See also the following issues of *Getulino:* September 9, 1923, p. 2; December 9, 1923, p. 1; October 5, 1924, p. 1. Also see the following articles in *Progresso:* "Prefere-se branca" (September 26, 1929), p. 5; "A Guarda Civil" (February 1931), p. 3; "Entre e veja se ahi ha negros como você" (November 15, 1931), p. 2.

37. "Restaurant Giocondo," *O Clarim da Alvorada* (January 25, 1930), p. 2. On conditions in Campinas and other western towns, see Cleber da Silva Maciel, *Discriminacões raciais: Negros em Campinas (1888–1921)* (Campinas, 1988); "O protesto de Campinas," *Alvorada* (June 1946); "Problemas e aspirações," *Diário*

Trabalhista (May 16, 1946), p. 5; Thomas W. Walker, "From Coronelism to Populism: The Evolution of Politics in a Brazilian Municipality, Ribeirão Preto, São Paulo, 1910–1960" (Ph.D. dissertation, University of New Mexico, 1974), p. 64; Edgard T. Santana, *Relações entre pretos e brancos em São Paulo* (São Paulo, 1951), pp. 7–8; Irene Maria F. Barbosa, *Socialização e relações raciais: Um estudo de família negra em Campinas* (São Paulo, 1983), pp. 26–28; Michael Mitchell, "Racial Consciousness and the Political Attitudes and Behavior of Blacks in São Paulo, Brazil" (Ph.D. dissertation, Indiana University, 1977), p. 128; "Edificante!" *Progresso* (January 13, 1929).

38. "A costume fa's leis," *Getulino* (March 9, 1924); the article fails to mention the city where this incident took place, referring to it as "a progressive city in the Mogiana zone," in the north-central part of the state. On segregation in the public parks and squares of small cities in western São Paulo, see Eclea Bosi, *Memória e sociedade: Lembranças de velhos* (São Paulo, 1977), p. 17; and "Problemas e aspirações," *Diário Trabalhista* (May 16, 1946), p. 5.

39. "Para os nossos leitores," *O Alfinete* (September 22, 1918), p. 1; "Na terra do preconceito," *O Clarim da Alvorada* (March 4, 1928), p. 3; "13 maio," *O Clarim da Alvorada* (May 13, 1930), p. 1.

40. Historian Joel Rufino dos Santos draws the distinction between the myth of racial democracy and the hope or desire for racial democracy. "Democracia racial, o mito e o desejo," *Folhetim*, *Folha de São Paulo* (June 8, 1980), p. 7.

41. On associational life among Brazilian slaves, see Mary C. Karasch, *Slave Life in Rio de Janeiro, 1808–1850* (Princeton, 1987), pp. 82–87, 254–301; A.J.R. Russell-Wood, *The Black Man in Slavery and Freedom in Colonial Brazil* (New York, 1982), pp. 128–160; Julita Scarano, *Devoção e escravidão: A Irmandade de Nossa Senhora do Rosário dos pretos no distrito diamantino no século XVIII* (São Paulo, 1976).

42. On the Irmandade dos Remédios, see "Pequenino templo," *Progresso* (December 31, 1929), p. 5; and Robert Conrad, *The Destruction of Brazilian Slavery, 1850–1888* (Urbana, 1970), pp. 242–243. On the Irmandade do Rosário, see Raul Joviano Amaral, *Os pretos do Rosário de São Paulo* (São Paulo, 1954). The Largo do Paissandu also houses a statue honoring the Black Mother (see chapter 8), erected by the municipality in 1955, and is the frequent site of rallies and demonstrations by present-day black organizations. See also Maciel's discussion of the Irmandade de São Benedito in Campinas, *Discriminações raciais*, p. 99.

43. Iêda Marques Britto, *Samba na cidade de São Paulo (1900–1930): Um exercício de resistência cultural* (São Paulo, 1986). The newspaper *Progresso*, which published from 1923 through 1931, and which I have quoted frequently in this chapter, was the organ of G. C. Campos Elíseos, and contains much information on the activities of the organization.

44. "A propósito de um texto," *O Kosmos* (April 20, 1924), p. 1; "Offerta," *O Kosmos* (March 15, 1923), p. 3.

45. "Relatório de 1923," *O Kosmos* (January 20, 1924); "Relatório," *O Kosmos* (January 25, 1925).

46. On the black athletic clubs, see "O São Geraldo," *O Clarim da Alvorada* (July 26, 1931), p. 3; "O negro e o esporte" and "Club Athletico Brasil," *Evolução* (May 13, 1933), pp. 8, 16; "Tudo preto," *Progresso* (February 1931), p. 4.

On the beginnings of soccer in São Paulo, and its segregated character through the 1930s, see "O negro no futebol brasileiro," *Placar* (May 13, 1988), pp. 36-42. This last article says that the first black players were not hired in São Paulo until 1940, though *Evolução* said (in 1933) that, after repeated defeats at the hands of the Rio teams, "some of our clubs began to accept black paulistas." See also "Bixiga, de italianos e negros," *Folha de São Paulo* (December 6, 1983).

47. For discussion of the gathering political crisis of the Republic during the 1920s, see Peter Flynn, *Brazil: A Political Analysis* (Boulder, Colo. 1979), pp. 41-50; Boris Fausto, *A revolução de 1930* (São Paulo, 1970), pp. 92-104; Silvio Duncan Baretta and John Markoff, "The Limits of the Brazilian Revolution of 1930," *Review* 9, 3 (1986), pp. 416-435.

48. On the millenarian movement of Antônio Conselheiro in the northeastern state of Bahia (1893-1897), see Euclides da Cunha, *Rebellion in the Backlands* (Chicago, 1944); and Robert M. Levine, "'Mud-Hut Jerusalem': Canudos Revisited," *Hispanic American Historical Review* 68, 3 (1988), pp. 525-572. On the Vaccination Riots of 1904 in Rio de Janeiro, see Jeffrey D. Needell, "The *Revolta contra Vacina* of 1904: The Revolt against Modernization in *Belle Époque* Rio de Janeiro," *Hispanic American Historical Review* 67, 2 (1987), pp. 223-270; Teresa Meade, "'Civilizing Rio de Janeiro': The Public Health Campaign and the Riot of 1904," *Journal of Social History* 20, 2 (1986), pp. 301-322; Carvalho, *Os bestializados*, pp. 91-139.

49. The naval mutiny of 1910, known as the Revolt of the Whip, was touched off by the refusal of sailors (50 percent of whom were pretos, and 30 percent pardos) to continue to submit to whippings, which they associated with slavery. Petitions from the sailors to the president stated that they could "no longer bear slavery in the Brazilian navy" or officers "who make us their slaves." June Hahner, *Poverty and Politics: The Urban Poor in Brazil, 1870-1920* (Albuquerque, 1986), pp. 271-272; see also Alvaro Bomilcar, *O preconceito de raça no Brasil* (Rio de Janeiro, 1916), pp. 7-45, 96-101; Gilberto Freyre, *Order and Progress: Brazil from Monarchy to Republic* (New York, 1970), pp. 399-401. On the Contestado Rebellion, see Todd Alan Diacon, "Capitalists and Fanatics: Brazil's Contestado Rebellion, 1912-1916" (Ph.D. dissertation, University of Wisconsin-Madison, 1987).

50. Though survivors of the 1924 São Paulo rebellion, and of an accompanying uprising in Rio Grande do Sul, undertook a three-year "long march" across fourteen thousand miles of Brazilian territory, during which they tried unsuccessfully to raise the peasantry against the republic. On this astonishing episode, see Neill Macaulay, *The Prestes Column: Revolution in Brazil* (New York, 1974).

51. On the Democratic Party, see Fausto, *Revolução de 1930*, pp. 32-38.

52. Glicério quotation from Joseph L. Love, *São Paulo in the Brazilian Federation, 1889-1937* (Stanford, 1980), p. 112.

53. Joseph Love's study of São Paulo's political elite during the Republic found only two Afro-Brazilians, both mulatto Republicans, in an elite of 263 people. One was Francisco Glicério, who played an important role in the conspiracy to overthrow the monarchy in 1889, and who subsequently served as minister of agriculture in the federal government. The other was Armando Prado, an illegitimate member of the prominent Prado family, who is frequently

mentioned in the black newspapers of the 1910s and 1920s. For a time he even ran his own paper aimed at an Afro-Brazilian audience, *A Sentinella*. Love, *São Paulo*, pp. 85, 156; Darrell E. Levi, *The Prados of São Paulo, Brazil: An Elite Family and Social Change, 1840–1930* (Athens Ga., 1987), p. 120.

Of all the political parties of the Republic, only the Communist Party seems to have made a serious effort to recruit Afro-Brazilians. The Communists appealed to the black population to join them in the creation of "a broad democracy, a government truly of the people, because only a democracy will be able to eliminate once and for all the privileges of race, color, and nationality, and to give the blacks of Brazil the . . . liberty and equality, free of reactionary prejudice, for which they have so bravely struggled over more than three centuries." Edgar Carone, *O PCB (1922–1943)* (São Paulo, 1982), 1, pp. 167, 178; see also Edgar Carone, *Movimento operário no Brasil (1877–1944)* (São Paulo, 1979), pp. 333–336; Robert M. Levine, *The Vargas Regime: The Critical Years, 1934–1938* (New York, 1970), pp. 63, 73; Flynn, *Brazil*, pp. 78, 92, fn. 34. Levine argues, however, that these efforts produced little response among the black population. Certainly the black middle class was avowedly anti-Communist. See, for example, *Progresso's* response to Soviet appeals for blacks to join them in their struggle against capitalism. "Do the Soviets really believe that the blacks will set sail with them in a leaky canoe?" *Progresso* (April 28, 1929), p. 5.

54. "A esmola," *O Clarim da Alvorada* (November 15, 1925), p. 1; Fernandes, *Integração do negro*, 1, pp. 301, 330; "Preconceito tolo e absurdo," *Progresso* (October 12, 1928), p. 1; *Progresso* (December 16, 1928), p. 3; "Pedra que rola da montanha," *Progresso* (March 24, 1929). The center attracted considerable support, enrolling over seven hundred members. "Centro Cívico Palmares," *O Clarim da Alvorada* (October 27, 1929), p. 4.

55. "O negro deve ser político?" *O Clarim da Alvorada* (October 27, 1929).

56. On the political struggles of this period, see Thomas Skidmore, *Politics in Brazil, 1930–1964: An Experiment in Democracy* (New York, 1968), pp. 3–47; Levine, *The Vargas Regime*; and Flynn, *Brazil*, pp. 59–93. Vargas adopted the term "New State" from Portuguese dictator Antônio de Oliveira Salazar, whose regime had coined it in 1930 and then applied it to the Portuguese constitution of 1933, a document heavily influenced by Italian Fascism. A. H. de Oliveira Marques, *History of Portugal* (New York, 1976), 2, p. 181.

57. "A arrancada para o Infinito," *Progresso* (November 30, 1930), p. 1.

58. *Diário Oficial dos Estados Unidos do Brasil* (August 25, 1931), pp. 13,552–13,558; Arthur Hehl Neiva, "Getúlio Vargas e o problema da imigração e a colonização," *Revista de Imigração e Colonização* 3, 1 (April 1942), pp. 24–70.

59. On the widespread support for Vargas among the black population of São Paulo, see Bosi, *Memória e sociedade*, pp. 312–314. Concerning his support among the poor and working class more generally, see pp. 115, 117, 178–179, 372–375. On continuing black electoral support for Vargas and his Brazilian Labor Party into the 1940s and 1950s, see Amaury de Souza, "Raça e política no Brasil urbano," *Revista de Administração de Empresas* 11, 4 (1971), pp. 61–70.

60. "Vivemos sem lar," *O Clarim da Alvorada* (January 25, 1925), p. 3.

61. On Arlindo Veiga dos Santos and the founding of the Front, see *O Clarim da Alvorada* (January 6, 1929), p. 4; "Congresso da Mocidade Negra Brasileira,"

O Clarim da Alvorada (June 9, 1929), p. 1; "Movimento de arregimentação da raca negra no Brasil," Diário de São Paulo (September 17, 1931), p. 5; "Frente Negra do Brasil," O Clarim da Alvorada (September 28, 1931), p. 2; "Estatutos da Frente Negra Brasileira," A Voz da Raça (August 1936).

62. "Movimento de arregimentação de raça negra no Brasil," Diário de São Paulo (September 17, 1931), p. 5; "Depoimentos," Cadernos Brasileiros 47 (1968), p. 21; "Frente Unica," Progresso (November 15, 1931), p. 3.

63. On local chapters of the Front in São Paulo State and elsewhere, see the frequent reports which appear in A Voz da Raça. On fronts in other states, see "Concentração frentenegrina em São Paulo," A Voz da Raça (October 1936); "A Frente Negra e o ano de 1937," A Voz da Raça (December 1936); "Discurso do representante da Frente Negra Pelotense," in Estudos afro-brasileiros (Rio de Janeiro, 1935), pp. 269–271; Maria de Azevedo Brandão, "Conversa de branco: questões e não-questões da literatura sobre relações raciais," Revista de Cultura Vozes 73, 3 (1979), pp. 33–35.

64. Fernandes, Integração do negro, 2, p. 19; "Frente Negra Brasileira, 1930–1937" (collaborative trabalho de pesquisa, Pontifícia Universidade Católica–São Paulo, 1985), anexo 3; "A Frente Negra Brasileira trabalha pela victória do seu candidato," Correio de São Paulo (May 1, 1933), p. 7.

65. On the Front's educational and mutual-aid activities, see various issues of A Voz da Raça. On the movement to the suburbs, see Ferrara, Imprensa negra, p. 67; "Frente Negra Brasileira," anexo 2; and Raquel Rolnik, "Territórios negros em São Paulo: Uma história" (unpublished paper presented at the International Congress of the Latin American Studies Association, Albuquerque, N.M., 1985), p. 14.

66. Mitchell, "Racial Consciousness," p. 131.

67. All members of the Front's leadership for whom professions can be ascertained were professionals or office workers. These include Arlindo Veiga dos Santos (clerk-secretary), Raul Joviano Amaral (accountant), Antônio Martins dos Santos (engineer), and Francisco Lucrécio (dentist). Deocleciano Nascimento was a prominent figure in the black press (editor of O Menelik [1916] and Auriverde [1928], and Anibal de Oliveira may have been the "A. Oliveira" who edited O Alfinete in 1918.

68. "Por acaso," A Voz da Raça (August 31, 1935), p. 4. However, the Front seems to have had difficulty recruiting middle-class Afro-Brazilians as well. A 1936 article criticized "those colored brothers who, having obtained their degrees in medicine, law, engineering, education, and dentistry, look with indifference on this magnificent initiative [to provide] culture, work, and education for poor, humble blacks," and urged them to join in the Front's work. "Alvorada da 'Frente Negra,'" A Voz da Raça (July 1936), p. 2.

69. "Inscripta como partido a Frente Negra," A Raça (December 21, 1935).

70. Fernandes, Integração do negro, 1, p. 301.

71. Ferrara, Imprensa negra, pp. 74–75; "A Frente Negra Brasileira faz reviver o caso da regência," Folha de São Paulo (April 8, 1932), p. 5; "Frente Negra Brasileira," anexo 3.

72. Fausto, Revolução de 1930, pp. 36–37.

73. It is striking to see, by the late 1920s, newspapers which thirty years

earlier had acclaimed immigration as the salvation of Brazil, now shaking their heads over how "São Paulo, this cosmopolitan city, found itself flooded, from one moment to the next, by strange people, bizarrely dressed . . . unacclimated, expressing themselves only in their mother tongue," who had little or nothing to contribute to the city's development. "Uma praga . . . e outra," *A Gazeta* (August 7, 1928), p. 8. The concept of a "tropical Belle Époque" is suggested by Jeffrey D. Needell, *A Tropical Belle Époque: Elite Culture and Society in Turn-of-the-Century Rio de Janeiro* (Cambridge and New York, 1987).

74. On middle-class nativism, see Hahner, *Poverty and Politics* pp. 150–155; and Topik, "Middle-Class Brazilian Nationalism," pp. 93–103. The quote on Integralism is from Levine, *The Vargas Regime*, p. 99; on the social origins (Brazilian-born, predominantly middle- and lower-middle-class) of the Integralists, see Hélgio Trindade, *Integralismo: O fascismo brasileiro na década de 30* (2nd edition, São Paulo, 1979), pp. 130–149.

75. "Os pretos em São Paulo," *O Kosmos* (December 21, 1924), reprinted from *Getulino* (October 12, 1924); "Que atrevimento!" *Getulino* (November 4, 1923), p. 2.

76. "Na terra do preconceito," *O Clarim da Alvorada* (March 4, 1928), p. 3; "Preconceito que não se justifica," *Progresso* (January 31, 1930); "O grande problema nacional," *Evolução* (May 13, 1933), pp. 9, 13.

77. The Front's statutes are reprinted in Ferrara, *Imprensa negra*, pp. 64–67, and "Estatutos da Frente Negra Brasileira," *A Voz da Raça* (August 1936); Fernandes, *Integração do negro*, 2, p. 49; "Apelo à economia," *A Voz da Raça* (October 28, 1933), p. 1; "A afirmação da raça," *A Voz da Raça* (June 10, 1933), p. 1. As Fernandes notes, the Front's paper offers "abundant material" along these lines.

78. "A afirmação da raça," *A Voz da Raça* (June 10, 1933), p. 1; "Apreciando," *A Voz da Raça* (October 1936), p. 1; for essays by Pedro Paulo Barbosa, see "Apreciando," and "O perigo vermelho," *A Voz da Raça* (November 1936), p. 1.

Arlindo Veiga dos Santos had been a prominent monarchist in São Paulo during the 1920s, and in 1930 and 1931 took part in the founding of several of the Fascist-inspired organizations which preceded Integralism. "Gentileza," *Progresso* (February 24, 1929); "D. Pedro Henrique," *Progresso* (September 28, 1930); Trindade, *Integralismo*, pp. 114 fn. 72, 118 fn. 85. During the 1960s he was still promoting the monarchist cause through a monthly newspaper, *Monarquia*, which divided its coverage between endorsements of monarchy as the ideal form of government, and lengthy denunciations of international Bolshevik Masonic conspiracies.

79. On these splits within the movement, see Mitchell, "Racial Consciousness," pp. 135–137. On the Socialist Party, "É o cúmulo," *A Voz da Raça* (January 20, 1934), p. 1; on the attacks on the anti-Front newspaper *Chibata*, "Foi empastellado o jornal 'Chibata'," *Diário Nacional* (March 20, 1932), p. 8; "O empastellamento d'A Chibata," *Diário Nacional* (March 22, 1932).

80. "Presidentes, Deputados," *A Voz da Raça* (June 1937), p. 5; "O momento político," *A Voz da Raça* (August 1937), p. 4.

81. "O negro em face da situação atual," *A Voz da Raça* (November 1937), p. 1.

82. Fernandes, *Integração do negro*, 2, pp. 66–69.

83. In 1935 Vargas's government began to crack down on the National Liberation Alliance, a Communist-dominated Popular Front organization. This repression triggered a leftist uprising among military forces stationed in Rio de Janeiro and northeastern Brazil, which the government successfully suppressed. The Integralist movement then launched a rightist uprising in May 1938, seeking to overthrow the recently declared New State. Their attempted coup was defeated, and the movement dissolved when its leader, Plínio Salgado, went into exile. On this turbulent period in Brazilian history see Levine, *The Vargas Regime*.

84. For articles rejecting proposals for a black political party, see "Advertência," *Senzala* (January 1946), pp. 14, 28; "Problemas e aspirações," *Diário Trabalhista* (July 12, 1946), p. 4; "Nem tudo que reluz é ouro," *Alvorada* (April 1946), p. 4.

Chapter 6. Blacks Ascending, 1940–1988

1. Figures from IBGE, *Recenseamento geral de 1940. Censo demográfico: Estado de São Paulo* (Rio de Janeiro, 1950), tables 29 and 49, pp. 22, 56–60; IBGE, *Recenseamento geral do Brasil—1980. Censo demográfico—dados gerais, migração, instrução, fecundidade, mortalidade—São Paulo* (Rio de Janeiro, 1982), table 1.11, pp. 106–119; IBGE, *Recenseamento geral do Brasil—1980. Censo demográfico—mão-de-obra—São Paulo* (Rio de Janeiro, 1983), table 1.9, pp. 47–56.

2. IBGE, *Recenseamento, 1940. São Paulo*, table 32, pp. 26–29; IBGE, *Recenseamento, 1980. Mão de obra—São Paulo*, table 1.9, pp. 47–56.

3. The precise figure is 1.9 percent. IBGE *Recenseamento, 1940. São Paulo*, table 24, p. 18. While this proportion is quite low, it compares favorably with that for Brazil as a whole. In 1940, only 1.1 percent of the national population had graduated from either high school or college. IBGE, *Recenseamento geral de 1940. Censo demográfico: Estados Unidos do Brasil* (Rio de Janeiro, 1950), table 24, p. 30.

4. On recent developments in Brazilian higher education, see Cláudio de Moura Castro, "O que está acontecendo com a educação no Brasil?" in Edmar Lisboa Bacha and Herbert S. Klein, eds., *A transição incompleta: Brasil desde 1945* (São Paulo, 1986), 2, pp. 103–161; figure on the 1970s enrollments from p. 130. Most of that increase, Castro notes, took place in the private *faculdades*. During the early 1980s, there was an average of forty-two applicants for each opening in the state and federal universities; those who were turned down had little choice but to enroll in the less selective private schools. "O 'diplomismo' furado," *Folha de São Paulo* (June 9, 1985), p. 43.

5. IBGE, *Recenseamento, 1980. Dados gerais—São Paulo*, table 3.4, pp. 526–528. The comparable rate for Brazil as a whole at that time was 6 percent. IBGE, *Recenseamento geral do Brasil—1980. Censo demográfico—dados gerais, migração, instrução, fecundidade, mortalidade—Brasil* (Rio de Janeiro, 1983), table 3.4, pp. 138–140.

6. IBGE, *Recenseamento, 1940. São Paulo*, table 25, p. 18; IBGE, *Recensea-

mento geral de 1950. Censo demográfico: Estado de São Paulo (Rio de Janeiro, 1954), table 21, p. 24. As in the white population, in both 1940 and 1950 almost all the black college graduates were men. In 1940 only forty-one were female; in 1950, only twenty-one. Among black women in São Paulo in 1950, only one in twenty-five thousand was a college graduate.

7. Richard M. Morse, "The Negro in São Paulo, Brazil," *Journal of Negro History* 38, 3, (1953), p. 297; Florestan Fernandes, *A integração do negro na sociedade de classes* (3rd edition, São Paulo, 1978), 2, p. 262; on racial strictures in Church-related schools in São Paulo, see Edgard T. Santana, *Relações entre pretos e brancos em São Paulo* (São Paulo, 1951), p. 18.

8. "Os negros brasileiros e suas aspirações," *Senzala* (February 1946), p. 19; "Os negros brasileiros lutam por suas reivindicações," *Diário Trabalhista* (January 15, 1946), p. 5.

9. IBGE, *Recenseamento, 1980. Dados gerais—São Paulo*, table 1.5, pp. 12–13. The census provides no racial data on the actual obtaining of diplomas and degrees.

10. By 1980, 10.5 percent of the white population had completed eleven years of education or more. Among the black population, only 2.2 percent (2.2 percent of pardos, and 2.1 percent of pretos) had achieved the same level of schooling.

11. "A crua discriminação racial no mercado de trabalho," *Caderno C, Diário do Grande ABC* (November 24, 1985); "Negros," *Veja* (May 11, 1988), p. 30; "Negros," *Dossiê CPV* 18 (São Paulo, 1984), p. 28; interview with Luis Luzzi, former president of the Associação Paulista de Administração de Pessoal (November 27, 1984); interview with staff members of the Grupo de Orientação e Interferência em Situações de Discriminação Racial no Trabalho (GOISDRT), Secretaria de Estado de Relações do Trabalho (May 19, 1988).

12. "Na Grande São Paulo, 200 mil jovens procuram vagas," *Folha de São Paulo* (November 25, 1984).

13. As an accompanying article indicates, "good appearance . . . mainly means being white." "Ao menor pobre, resta apenas esperança," *Folha de São Paulo* (November 25, 1984). See also Irene Maria F. Barbosa, *Socialização e relações raciais: Um estudo de família negra em Campinas* (São Paulo, 1983), pp. 108–110.

14. "Negros," *Veja* (May 11, 1988), p. 28. A former president of the São Paulo bakery workers' union noted that pardos and pretos are hired in large numbers to work in the city's bakeries but are virtually never employed as shop workers, selling bread and pastries to the public. Bakery owners admit that this is racial discrimination, he said, but argue that they are forced into it by their customers' preferences. This labor leader, himself a preto, said that he found this difficult to quarrel with, since, "as you know, the paulista public can be quite racist." Interview (May 2, 1985).

15. Muniz Sodré, "O negro e os meios de informação," *Revista de Cultura Vozes* 73, 3 (April 1979), p. 41.

16. On the role of Afro-Brazilians in the electronic media in São Paulo, see João Baptista Borges Pereira, *Côr, profissão e mobilidade: O negro e o rádio de São Paulo* (São Paulo, 1967); Solange M. Couceiro, *O negro na televisão de São Paulo: Um estudo de relações raciais* (São Paulo, 1983).

17. Flávio Gut, "A negra beleza prohibida," *Afinal* (September 23, 1986), pp. 44–52. Just two years before she was chosen the first black Miss Brazil, parda model Deise Nunes suffered the humiliation of being yanked at the last minute from a fashion show by an executive who announced that "blacks don't model for my company." "Denunciado racismo em RS," *Folha de São Paulo* (September 22, 1984), p. 20. One of the events in São Paulo marking the centennial of the abolition of slavery was a fashion show in a downtown pedestrian mall by black models protesting "what they identify as racial discrimination in their labor market." "Modelos fazem desfile contra discriminação no trabalho," *Folha de São Paulo* (May 13, 1988), p. 11.

18. Gut, "A negra beleza prohibida."

19. Nelson do Valle Silva, "Black-White Income Differentials: Brazil, 1960" (Ph.D. dissertation, University of Michigan, 1978), pp. 244, 283. The data presented in Silva's dissertation also contradicted the notion that pardos tend to occupy an intermediate position on the social scale between pretos and whites. When comparing preto and pardo (which he translates as "black" and "mulatto") salary performance, he found that "not only are their marginal returns to schooling [i.e., increase in salary per years of additional schooling] very similar, but if anything, blacks seem to enjoy greater rates of returns than mulattoes at the higher levels of schooling. In fact, the rate of returns to schooling for blacks is larger than that for mulattoes (11.1 percent increase per year of schooling for blacks, 10.4 percent for mulattoes), contradicting clearly the usual assumption of considerably more mobility for mulattoes." White salaries increased at a rate of 12.4 percent per year of schooling. Pp. 206–207.

20. Nelson do Valle Silva, "Updating the Cost of Not Being White in Brazil," in Pierre-Michel Fontaine, ed., *Race, Class, and Power in Brazil* (Los Angeles, 1985); Lúcia Elena Garcia de Oliveira et al., *O lugar do negro na força de trabalho* (Rio de Janeiro, 1985), pp. 47–53; Jeffrey W. Dwyer and Peggy A. Lovell, "The Cost of Being Nonwhite in Brazil," *Sociology and Social Research* 72 (1988), pp. 136–142; Peggy A. Lovell, "Racial Inequality and the Brazilian Labor Market" (Ph.D. dissertation, University of Florida, 1989), pp. 136–139. Carlos Hasenbalg also reports on a 1973 survey conducted in Rio de Janeiro which showed earnings by black men with an elementary school education to be larger, in absolute terms, than earnings by black men with secondary and college educations. Carlos Hasenbalg, *Discriminação e desigualdades raciais no Brasil* (Rio de Janeiro, 1979), p. 214.

21. The *salário mínimo* was instituted in 1940 as part of Getúlio Vargas's program of labor reforms. It is set by the government, and is roughly comparable to the American minimum wage, except that it is expressed in terms of a monthly salary rather than an hourly wage. Depending on the rate of inflation, and on how much time has elapsed since it was last adjusted upward, during the 1980s the *salário mínimo* oscillated in value between twenty-five and seventy-five dollars per month in U.S. figures.

22. It is important to note that educational deficiencies are by no means an insuperable barrier to upward mobility in Brazil. Data from the 1973 National Household Survey (PNAD) "show that there are still a large number of individuals well-placed in the social structure whose level of formal education is

relatively rudimentary. For example, about 20% of the upper stratum individuals in 1973 had finished only grade school or less. Among the members of the upper-middle stratum, this percentage reached about 36%." José Pastore, *Inequality and Social Mobility in Brazil* (Madison, 1982), p. 80. These figures may be lower in São Paulo State, with its better-educated population and more technically demanding job market. Nevertheless, it is striking to see such a high rate of upward mobility among poorly educated Brazilians, and to juxtapose it with the much lower rates of upward mobility, and much higher rates of downward mobility, among well-educated Afro-Brazilians. On racial differences in intergenerational mobility, see Carlos A. Hasenbalg, "Race and Socioeconomic Inequality in Brazil," in Pierre-Michel Fontaine, ed., *Race, Class and Power in Brazil* (Los Angeles, 1985).

23. This individual is the previously mentioned Luis Luzzi (see note 11), who heads his own human resources consulting firm in São Paulo. In addition to talking with me, Luzzi presented his findings at the public Seminar on Racial Discrimination in the Workplace, sponsored by the state government and held in São Paulo City on December 3, 1984.

24. Similar reasons were cited by the owner of a São Paulo bar accused of refusing to admit black people. "I'm not the one who chooses the people who frequent my bar. The public selects them. If I let two colored girls in here, that same day ten people are going to complain and start talking about how the place is going downhill. You know what the paulista middle class is like." (See also the comments expressed in note 14.) The bar owner then went on to reveal that he probably shares the attitudes of his customers. "There's nothing personal in any of this. My secretary, who is my right arm, is also, pardon the expression, dark. You should see her boyfriend. He's terrifying! If you ran into him at night, you'd tremble for fear that he is going to attack you!" "Negras impedidas de entrar em bar por preconceito," *Folha de São Paulo* (February 3, 1985), p. 20.

25. In one such survey, 59 percent of whites stated that whites are "very prejudiced" against blacks; only 4 percent, however, admitted to holding such prejudices themselves. "This survey . . . shows how intolerable prejudice is considered to be: the majority says that it exists, but individual respondents will not admit to it[;] prejudice is always someone else's, never one's own." "Pesquisa confirma disimulação," *Folha de São Paulo* (May 9, 1988), p. 12; see also "Para maioria dos paulistanos, negro é marginalizado" and "Entrevistado raramente assume preconceito," *Folha de São Paulo* (March 25, 1984).

26. Morse, "The Negro in São Paulo," pp. 298, 304. Interviews conducted by Octávio Ianni in the late 1950s also give evidence of white interest in the idea of segregation. One respondent justified such ideas in terms reminiscent of South African justifications for apartheid: "I would be in favor of Brazil being like the United States. I don't want to go back to slavery, but yes, make some kind of division, separate. Because separation would give more opportunities to the whites, and even more to the blacks, for them to show and develop their possible qualities." Octávio Ianni, *Raças e classes sociais no Brasil* (2nd edition, São Paulo, 1988), p. 57.

Morse's comments on the difficulties in detecting Brazilian-style discrimination were echoed twenty years later by another U.S. historian, John Hope

Franklin, who was traveling through the country on a lecture tour. "I have been assured that there is no color prejudice in Brazil. This may be true. But as a visitor from outside, I am struck by the very small number of blacks in responsible positions of influence and power. It may be that there are Brazilian blacks occupying those positions, but I did not find them. . . . There is something undefined, which I would almost describe as a feeling of color [*"sentimento de cor"*], but which I would not say is at all similar to what happens in the United States. I have many doubts about the way things actually happen in Brazil. When I note the absence of blacks in so many areas of Brazilian life, I begin to wonder what this can really mean. . . ." "Onde estão os negros? O preconceito de cor visto no Brasil por um historiador negro dos EUA," *Veja* (May 9, 1973), pp. 3–4.

27. Roger Bastide and Florestan Fernandes, *Brancos e negros em São Paulo* (3rd edition, São Paulo, 1971), pp. 168–169.

28. "Este mundo é dos brancos?" *Afinal* (July 23, 1985), p. 9; "Foram 100 anos de resistência. E estamos aqui," *Manchete* (May 21, 1988), p. 6; Haroldo Costa, *Fala, crioulo* (Rio de Janeiro, 1982), p. 81.

29. "Afro-brasileiros apoiam aproximação com a África," *O Globo* (January 9, 1978).

30. "Ferraz: Abolição é a nossa maior data," *O Estado de São Paulo* (May 14, 1971).

31. Ianni, *Raças e classes sociais*, pp. 65–66, 77–94. These points were nicely illustrated by an exchange I witnessed one evening at dinner in an upper-middle-class São Paulo household. One of the individuals present cited the Brazilian proverb that "in Brazil, we don't have a racial problem; here the black knows his place." To which another person responded, "Yes, but nowadays they're forgetting what that place is—and that's the problem!"

32. On racial stereotypes in Brazil, and their diffusion among the population at large, see Ianni, *Raças e classes sociais*, pp. 77–109; Clóvis Moura, *O preconceito de cor na literatura do cordel* (São Paulo, 1966); Florestan Fernandes, *O negro no mundo dos brancos* (São Paulo, 1972), pp. 201–216; Maria Suely Kofes de Almeida, "Entre nós, os pobres, eles, os negros" (*dissertação de mestrado*, Universidade Estadual de Campinas, 1976), pp. 100–132. A recent study of racial attitudes among schoolchildren in Rio found very high levels of negative stereotyping among children of all races; "the indices of rejection of blacks are practically the same among blacks as among whites." "Calvário da cor," *Veja* (March 30, 1988), p. 92.

For graphic evidence of the role of such stereotypes in preventing the hiring of Afro-Brazilians, see the interviews with radio executives in Pereira, *Côr, profissão e mobilidade*, pp. 176–180. To quote just one: "You've touched on a point that I think about a lot. Sometimes we get a black applicant who doesn't even seem black: serious, poised, intelligent, responsible. I'm almost inclined to give him a chance. But I'm afraid to take the risk. Sometimes they look like that on the outside, and then when you least expect it they reveal themselves for what they really are. And then what am I going to say to my superiors?" Pp. 178–179.

33. Discussing the roots of the degraded status of manual labor, Lúcio Kowarick recalls how, in nineteenth-century São Paulo, physical labor "led

nowhere at all, and rather than ennobling the person who performed it, the effort of doing so tended, on the contrary, to bring him closer to the rules of domination and submission [of slavery]. . . . Work continued to be seen—as in fact it was—as the most debased form of existence, as something which only a slave could and should undertake." "The Subjugation of Labour: The Constitution of Capitalism in Brazil" (unpublished manuscript, 1985), p. 60. Such attitudes are widely diffused throughout Latin America; on similar feelings among the Argentine middle class, see James Scobie, *Buenos Aires: From Plaza to Suburb, 1870–1910* (New York, 1974), pp. 218–220.

34. Workers' Party president Luis Inácio da Silva ruefully recalls his unsuccessful 1982 candidacy for governor of São Paulo State. He tried to capitalize on his working-class background, presenting himself to working-class voters as "ex–dye factory assistant, ex–lathe operator, ex–trade unionist, ex–prisoner, ex–I don't know what else, a Brazilian just like you. I imagined that the working class would understand by this: 'Wow, this guy is all this and is a candidate: we could do this, too.' But it seems that workers understood exactly the opposite: nobody wanted to be a Brazilian just like me. They wanted to be Brazilians with a university degree; they wanted to be Brazilians with better living conditions, with better intellectual training, with a better quality of life." Margaret Keck, "Lula and the Workers' Party: Emergence of a New Politics?" *Camões Center Quarterly* 2, 1–2 (1990), p. 14.

35. On second- and third-generation Brazilians' embrace of discrimination and prejudice, see Bastide and Fernandes, *Brancos e negros*, pp. 152–158; and Santana, *Relações*, pp. 22–24.

36. As earlier in the century, about the only area of the white-collar economy where it does not rule absolutely is in the state bureaucracy, where the legally mandated use of "blind" examinations for hiring enables black job candidates to compete against whites under conditions of relative equality. Ianni, *Raças e classes sociais*, pp. 63–65. Black lawyer Eurídice Aparecida de Jesus observes that "if private enterprises do not accept blacks, they can become public servants and thus acquire a certain amount of status." "Artistas e intelectuais lutam contra a discriminação," *Folha de São Paulo* (March 25, 1984). A black employment counselor concurs, but notes that in the public sector as well discrimination can come into play. "Many blacks go to work as a public servant, since the public examinations do not discriminate on the basis of color, race, or creed. But even in the public sector, blacks have to depend on the good will of their supervisor at promotion time." "A crua discriminação racial no mercado de trabalho," *Caderno C, Diário do Grande ABC* (November 24, 1985). And, a third informant notes, state salaries are often much lower than in the private sector. "This is why state employment is the only alternative for blacks. Who else would work for so little?" "Na luta com Zumbi," *Folhetim, Folha de São Paulo* (June 8, 1980), p. 14.

37. Examining a series of public surveys on racial attitudes in Brazil, one study concludes that they "reveal a rejection of persons of color in the two situations involving the greatest intimacy and least social distance. These are the family and social club." R. Penn Reeve, "Race and Social Mobility in a Brazilian Industrial Town," *Luso-Brazilian Review* 14, 2 (1970), pp. 243–244.

38. Roberto da Matta, *A casa e a rua: Espaço, cidadania, mulher e morte no Brasil* (São Paulo, 1985), pp. 55–80 passim; Roberto Schwarz, *Ao vencedor as batatas* (São Paulo, 1977), p. 16.

39. On the importance of personal contacts and networks in gaining employment, see Anthony Leeds, "Brazilian Careers and Social Structure: An Evolutionary Model and Case History," *American Anthropologist* 66 (1964), pp. 1321–1347. Brazilians have a proverb which nicely illustrates this principle: When you apply for a job, what matters most is not your I.Q. but your Q.I. (*quem indicou*—who recommended you).

40. Santana, *Relações*, p. 19; Bastide and Fernandes, *Brancos e negros*, pp. 166–167; "Clubes e negros," *O Novo Horizonte* (November–December 1954), p. 2; Roberto J. Haddock Lobo and Irene Aloisi, *O negro na vida social brasileira* (São Paulo, 1941), p. 81; "Presidente do Tietê fala em 'subversão'," *Folha de São Paulo* (May 17, 1978). In his article on a steel town in Minas Gerais State, Reeve finds that social clubs constitute "the one example of blatant racism in the town." Reeve, "Race and Social Mobility," p. 244.

41. Reeve, "Race and Social Mobility," p. 244. Such contacts are especially important for black job seekers, whose access to employment is already severely limited by their race. Each of the individuals interviewed in a study of black workers in Rio Grande do Sul emphasized "the importance of having someone to open doors. All of them, at key moments in their careers, had had someone who introduced them, who recommended them, who spoke on their behalf, who asked a favor for them." Petronilha Beatriz Gonçalves e Silva, "A formação do operário negro," *Educação e Sociedade* 22, 7 (1985), p. 69.

42. Costa, *Fala, crioulo*, pp. 104–105. A number of other individuals interviewed by Costa tell similar stories of being barred from club dances and social functions.

43. See Carl Degler's reflections on "the genius of Brazilian race relations: individual, rather than group mobility." *Neither Black nor White: Slavery and Race Relations in Brazil and the United States* (New York, 1971), p. 275. Roger Bastide invokes a kind of trickle-up theory, observing that under these conditions "black upward mobility cannot take any other form than that of infiltration, one black droplet after another passing through the filter held in the hands of the whites." Bastide and Fernandes, *Brancos e negros*, p. 227.

The inconsistency and unpredictability of Brazilian discrimination is perfectly illustrated by the previously cited case of Milton Gonçalves being stopped at the door of the São Paulo Athletic Association. First, Gonçalves had attended several previous dances at the club. Second, the director who barred Gonçalves's entry was himself a pardo, a prominent athlete who had competed in the 1938 Olympics. Third, when Gonçalves met the director the next day, the latter, "with the most cynical air in the world, almost smiling, said calmly, 'Hey look, yesterday it was no good, but come on back today and I'll bend the rules for you.' . . . I wanted to tell him to fuck himself, to stick the club up his ass—but it wasn't the moment to say anything. The best thing to do was just to leave." Costa, *Fala, crioulo*, p. 106.

While some blacks benefit from this inconsistency and unpredictability, others find it infuriating. Businessman Alberto Ferreira describes it as "the worst kind of discrimination. . . . The best would be for the people to take a definitive position: either stand once and for all alongside the black, understanding him as a human being equal to anyone else, or make discrimination official, eliminating the hypocrisy that now exists." "Discriminação ainda existe, diz o negro," *Diário do Grande ABC* (November 22, 1984).

44. Costa, *Fala, crioulo*, pp. 38–39. Another of Costa's informants recalls his mother's frequently repeated advice to "not put your foot where your hand won't reach"; in other words, don't try to push higher in life than you're meant to go. A black journalist recalls his childhood in the slums. "My brothers and sisters, tired and resigned to the situation, couldn't understand why I worked all morning at the market and then went to school. Why study? It was never going to get me anywhere, they said." Pp. 118, 94. For similar comments, see Barbosa, *Socializa-ção e relações raciais*, pp. 65, 105; Bastide and Fernandes, *Brancos e negros*, p. 191.

45. "As antenas da raça," *Caderno B, Jornal do Brasil* (May 8, 1988), p. 10.

46. Neusa Santos Souza, *Tornar-se negro: As vicissitudes da identidade do negro brasileiro em ascensão social* (Rio de Janeiro, 1983), pp. 39–43.

47. Costa, *Fala, crioulo*, p. 96. One of Neusa Santos Souza's informants echoes this point. Middle-class blacks have a choice, she says: "You can be part of the black community—which I have been out of for quite some time—or you can become part of the white milieu, which is unsatisfying. It's a place where everything is an examination, where they're always testing you." Souza, *Tornar-se negro*, pp. 66–67.

48. See, for example, "Salão da rua Glycério," *A Liberdade* (April 4, 1920), p. 3; "Prefere-se branca," *Progresso* (September 26, 1929), p. 5; *Getulino* (September 9, 1923), p. 1.

49. "Os personagens e suas histórias," *Folha de São Paulo* (July 9, 1978).

50. Anthropologist Irene Barbosa reports on the "great anxiousness" with which middle-class blacks "search for solutions to racial problems which will not undermine the hard-won position of the [black] 'elite.'" *Socialização e relações raciais*, p. 133.

51. I did not conduct systematic interviews with black people in São Paulo, nor did I keep a close record of the opinions and ideas which emerged in my conversations with them. My impression is that as many as a third, or perhaps slightly more, of the people I talked to said that they had never suffered discrimination directly. A similar proportion applies to the written material I covered, which I have used extensively in this chapter.

52. "Branco e preto: Uma ligação condenada," *Última Hora* (July 22, 1976).

53. For some of these studies, see Virgínia Leone Bicudo, "Atitudes raciais de pretos e mulatos em São Paulo," *Sociologia* 11, 3 (1947), pp. 195–219; Bastide and Fernandes, *Brancos e negros*, pp. 180–188; Ianni, *Raças e classes sociais*, pp. 95–109; Costa, *Fala, crioulo;* Souza, *Tornar-se negro*, pp. 28, 36. For a poignant expression of this desire, see the interview with an economically successful middle-class family in São Paulo City. The three children of this family describe themselves as morenos (see Appendix B); the oldest, eight years old, who attends an exclusive private school where she is one of only five black students, notes, "I'm not white, but I'm not black *[pretona]* either." "Casal negro sente preconceito no cotidiano," *Folha de São Paulo* (May 9, 1988), p. 11.

54. A paper by a black psychologist on his efforts, along with several other professionals, to organize a black consciousness group in the northeastern city of Recife describes their shock at realizing that they had virtually no Afro-Brazilian friends in their professional or social circles. "We soon realized that we knew practically no other blacks or mulattoes who formed part of our circles of friends. This was, why not admit it, a tremendous surprise, and even a great shock and a blow." Sylvio José B. R. Ferreira, "A questão racial em Pernambuco: A necessidade e os impasses de uma ação política organizada" (unpublished paper presented at the annual conference of the Associação Nacional de Pós-Graduação e Pesquisa em Ciências Sociais, ANPOCS, Novo Friburgo, 1981), p. 12.

55. According to the 1980 census, 21 percent of married couples in Brazil were of mixed race. However, research on marriage registries for São Paulo City between 1948 and 1957 found that only 3 percent of marriages were interracial. Nelson do Valle Silva, "Distância social e casamento inter-racial," *Estudos Afro-Asiáticos* 14 (1987), pp. 62, 73.

56. Silva, "Distância social."

57. "Um ator contra os preconceitos," *Folha de São Paulo* (May 13, 1978), p. 29. This preference for whiteness is widespread among blacks at all social levels, not just the middle class. What makes the black middle class distinctive is that its better-educated and more affluent members form more attractive partners for whites than do working-class blacks. As a result, Nelson do Valle Silva finds racial endogamy strongest at the working-class level, and intermarriage more frequent (though still far below the statistically expected level) in the middle class. Nelson do Valle Silva, "Endogamia de cor ou endogamia de classe?" (unpublished paper presented at the annual conference of the Associação de Pós-Graduação e Pesquisa em Ciências Sociais, ANPOCS, Novo Friburgo, 1981), p. 12.

58. Costa, *Fala, crioulo,* p. 196. This informant, the holder of a graduate degree in history, describes the process of whitening: "You nullify yourself as a black, you start to live another life, you float without any place to rest, with no reference or relationship to what should be your own particular way of being." A successful black singer concurs: "A black who comes up in the world is like a confused cockroach, not knowing where to step; he feels as though he's divided into sections, cut up into strips. . . ." Pereira, *Côr, profissão e mobilidade,* p. 242; for an extended discussion of the ambiguous social position of upwardly mobile Afro-Brazilians, see the concluding chapter of that book, pp. 237–261. See also the comments of anthropologist Lélia Gonzalez on the "process which any upwardly mobile black experiences, of distancing oneself from one's roots, of alienation." "Negro," *Istoé* (May 17, 1978), p. 45.

To have an idea of what this process involves, white readers might contemplate the prospect of living in a racially mixed society dominated by black people, in which the basic prerequisites for rising in the world were to value blackness as an ideal, to marry a black spouse, to produce black children, and, in general, to deny the fact of one's whiteness and seek to become accepted as "black." This is a rough capsule description, in reverse, of life as it is lived by millions of pardos and pretos in Brazil.

59. Souza, *Tornar-se negro,* p. 48.

60. Roger Bastide, *Estudos afro-brasileiros* (São Paulo, 1973), pp. 143–144; Bastide and Fernandes, *Brancos e negros,* p. 168. For other comments on preto-

pardo hostility, see Santana, *Relações*, p. 23; Costa, *Fala, crioulo*, pp. 113, 154; Fernando Henrique Cardoso, *Capitalismo e escravidão no Brasil meridional: O negro na sociedade escravocrata do Rio Grande do Sul* (São Paulo, 1962), pp. 301–303. For expressions in the black press of this tension between pretos and pardos, see "Parece incrível," *O Alfinete* (September 22, 1918), p. 3; "Vagando," *A Liberdade* (December 14, 1919), pp. 1–2; "Carta aberta," *Getulino* (November 2, 1924), p. 1; "Parabens, Viriato!" *Progresso* (April 28, 1929), p. 3.

61. Such efforts took visible form in the mulatto social clubs of the beginning of the century, which whites were welcome to join but from which pretos were barred. On one of these clubs, the Valete de Copas (Jack of Hearts) in Campinas, see Eclea Bosi, *Memória e sociedade: Lembranças de velhos* (São Paulo, 1977), p. 308; "Carta aberta," *Getulino* (November 2, 1924), p. 1. See also the observations by Neusa Santos Souza's informants: for example, "There are two types of mulattoes: those who wish to be white, and those who wish to acknowledge that they are black, but a different kind of black—that's what we are, a different kind of black." Souza, *Tornar-se negro*, p. 64.

62. Writing in 1938, Samuel Lowrie describes these gatherings as a relatively recent phenomenon in the city. Lowrie, "O elemento negro na população de São Paulo," *Revista do Arquivo Municipal de São Paulo* 4, 48 (1938), p. 34. Bastide and Fernandes indicate that prior to the 1930s blacks had gathered for their footings in the Largo do Arouche, where a statue of black abolitionist Luis Gama was erected in 1932. They moved to the Rua Direita allegedly in retaliation for an episode in which students at the nearby Law School taunted and harassed a pregnant black woman in the street. Bastide and Fernandes, *Brancos e negros*, p. 160. Merchants' protest quoted in Morse, "The Negro in São Paulo," p. 301. On the police sweeps of the 1940s, see Sebastião Rodrigues Alves, *A ecologia do grupo afro-brasileiro* (Rio de Janeiro, 1966), p. 36; "Problemas e aspirações," *Diário Trabalhista* (March 14, 1946), p. 7.

63. Costa, *Fala, crioulo*, pp. 107–108; Joel Wolfe, "The Rise of Brazil's Industrial Working Class: Community, Work, and Politics in São Paulo, 1900–1955" (Ph.D. dissertation, University of Wisconsin–Madison, 1990), p. 309.

64. "Deplorável," *A Voz da Raça* (March 1937), p. 1; "A Rua Direita," *A Voz da Raça* (April 1937), p. 1; "Os negros! Ora . . . os negros . . . ," *Alvorada* (November 1947), p. 2; Bastide and Fernandes, *Brancos e negros*, p. 160. By the 1970s and 1980s the Rua Direita area, including the Praça da Sé and the Viaduto do Chá, was still a popular gathering place for black people on weekend evenings, and the frequent site of black (and other) political meetings.

65. For an interesting study of the members of one such organization in Campinas, see Barbosa, *Socialização e relações raciais*. The newspaper *Hífen*, which was published in Campinas for several years during the early 1960s, is a representative expression of this black elite class.

The most important of the black middle-class clubs in São Paulo City is the Aristocratic Club, reported in 1984 to have thirty-five hundred members. "Movimento negro avalia sua importância," *Folha de São Paulo* (April 15, 1984).

66. See, for example, the petition signed by various black organizations and circulated in connection with the elections of 1950, quoted in Fernandes, *Integração do negro*, 1, p. 90. On the specific Afro-Brazilian individuals and organi-

zations that collaborated in the UNESCO-sponsored research headed in São Paulo by Bastide and Fernandes, see Bastide and Fernandes, *Brancos e negros*, 13–17. One of those informants, preto Dr. Edgard Santana, gathered his testimony into a book, the previously cited *Relações entre pretos e brancos*, which is frequently disparaging toward its lower-class subjects. At one point he seeks to establish the validity of his claims concerning black anomie and social disorganization, and to discredit countercharges by black workers of snobbery and elitism among the black middle class. "It is easy for those on top to look down on what is taking place beneath them; but it is difficult for those who are low to see what is taking place on high. The first-class passengers on a ship can observe those in third class, but the reverse is not true." P. 6.

See also American anthropologist Ruth Landes's description of the late Edison Carneiro, a well-known student of Afro-Brazilian culture. Describing Carneiro as a "mulatto aristocrat" (though, as her book makes clear, one of limited financial means), she notes that "he was a liberal, and was even considered as a radical in some quarters; but he was distinctly not a man of the people. . . . Edison viewed the candomblé people [poor urban blacks in Salvador] as from across a gap. To him they were specimens, although of course human beings with an inalienable right to live as they chose." Ruth Landes, *The City of Women* (New York, 1947), pp. 59–60.

Chapter 7. Organizing, 1945–1988

1. On the continuing existence of these organizations, see the social columns of *Alvorada* for 1946 and 1947, and in particular "Homenagem do movimento recreativo ao 13 de maio" (May 13, 1946). On the relationships between the samba schools and the Vargas dictatorship, see Alison Raphael, "Samba and Social Control: Popular Culture and Racial Democracy in Rio de Janeiro," (Ph.D. dissertation, Columbia University, 1980), pp. 89–122.

2. The association's efforts are described in Oracy Nogueira, "Atitude desfavorável de alguns anunciantes de São Paulo em relação aos empregados de cor," *Sociologia* 4, 4 (1942), pp. 328–358. Its members wrote to Vargas in 1941; eighteen months later, in March 1943, the national Department of Press and Propaganda banned such ads. See the correspondence in the Arquivo Nacional do Brasil, Secretaria do Presidente da República, Ministério de Trabalho, Indústria, e Comércio, lata 410, PR 107839/43. My thanks to Joel Wolfe for this citation.

3. The tension between the New State's efforts to establish firm control over Brazilian workers, and the efforts by workers to turn the New State's programs and policies to their own individual and collective advantage, is explored in John David French, "Industrial Workers and the Origins of Populist Politics in the ABC Region of Greater São Paulo, Brazil, 1900–1950" (Ph.D. dissertation, Yale University, 1985). See also Kenneth Erickson, *The Brazilian Corporative State and Working-Class Politics* (Berkeley, 1977); and James M. Malloy, *The Politics of Social Security in Brazil* (Pittsburgh, 1979).

4. On black organizational efforts during this period, see the black publications mentioned, and Miriam Nicolau Ferrara, *A imprensa negra paulista (1915–1963)* (São Paulo, 1986), pp. 141–162. In 1950 the small Brazilian Socialist

Party ran black candidates for Congress and the state Assembly; four years later the Afro-Brazilian Movement for Education and Culture nominated candidates to the same offices; all were defeated. See the issues of *O Novo Horizonte* for those years, and *Mundo Novo* (New World) for 1950. See also Florestan Fernandes, *A integração do negro no sociedade de classes* (3rd edition, São Paulo, 1978), 2, pp. 88–90.

5. "O preconceito existe!" *Correio Paulistano* (July 16, 1950). For similar articles, see Roger Bastide and Florestan Fernandes, *Brancos e negros em São Paulo* (3rd edition, São Paulo, 1971), p. 210. For responses by the black press to attacks by the mainstream São Paulo newspapers on black organizations, see "Os negros devem organizar-se," *Alvorada* (June 1947), p. 6; "Um ponto de vista," *Alvorada* (August 1947), p. 3; "Ha males que vêm para bem," *O Novo Horizonte* (May 1947), p. 2.

6. Such racism is often labeled *racismo às avessas*, a significant and revealing phrase. "*Racismo às avessas*" would be translated literally as "upside-down racism," or "racism the wrong way round." As in the previously cited quotation, it implies that white prejudice against blacks is "normal"; black prejudice against whites is perverse, "paradoxical," and contrary (another possible translation of "*às avessas*")to the established order of things. *Novo Michaelis dicionário ilustrado: Português-inglês* (rpt., São Paulo, 1984), p. 133. Black social scientist Helena Theodoro comments on the phrase. "Why 'contrary racism'? Why not simply 'racism,' if this is in fact the case? Even in this, whites and the dominant system see blacks as something perverse, backwards, and contrary." "Movimento negro já conta 400 entidades e cresce no Brasil," *Jornal do Brasil* (May 12, 1985).

7. "Negros e brancos em São Paulo," *O Estado de São Paulo* (July 24, 1955); "O crime do preconceito de côr," *Jornal do Comércio* (August 10, 1967). Sociologist Florestan Fernandes recalled that, when the work of the UNESCO researchers first appeared in print in 1953 and 1954, "there were those who considered it *dangerous*, as if the researchers were responsible for the latent or open tensions which we simply described and interpreted." Bastide and Fernandes, *Brancos e negros*, p. 10; emphasis in original. For a more recent expression of such fears from the 1980s, see the 1982 incident documented in chapter 8, note 47.

8. "Consciência negra," *Folha de São Paulo* (November 25, 1979), p. 3.

9. Carl Degler, *Neither Black nor White: Slavery and Race Relations in Brazil and the United States* (New York, 1971), p. 138.

10. "Medidas legislativas para impedir a imitação do preconceito racial norte-americano," *Correio Paulistano* (July 18, 1950); Bastide and Fernandes, *Brancos e negros*, p. 256. Note that the title of this article, like Franco's previously quoted statement, places the blame for race prejudice on foreigners, and declines to acknowledge it as a Brazilian problem.

11. "Uma lei à brasileira," *Folhetim*, *Folha de São Paulo* (June 8, 1980), p. 13. During my research I did uncover a single instance of a conviction under the Afonso Arinos Law, in Minas Gerais in 1975, in a case in which the doorman of a bar was found guilty of denying entry to a female college student. He paid a fine equivalent to $1.85 in U.S. figures, and received a suspended sentence. Several days later a group of young black men, enraged by the lightness of the sentence,

sacked the bar. "Porteiro racista so pagará multa," *Folha de São Paulo* (September 23, 1975); "Grupo destroi bar em represalia a racismo," *Folha de São Paulo* (October 2, 1975).

12. "Os ardis da Lei Afonso Arinos," *Caderno B, Jornal do Brasil* (May 8, 1988), p. 5. On the antiracism article in the Constitution of 1988, "Racismo é crime," *O Estado de São Paulo* (February 3, 1988).

13. The publisher of black journalist Haroldo Costa's collection of interviews with Afro-Brazilians, *Fala, crioulo* (Rio de Janeiro, 1982), apparently felt it necessary to reassure the book's readers, on the jacket copy, that "this is not a book which is racist *às avessas*. Haroldo Costa and his interviewees are not radicals, they're not looking for revenge. They are Brazilians who love their country and help to make it great."

A businessman interviewed by Costa acknowledges these white fears. "I think the white community in general was always afraid that blacks would acquire power, thinking that when we did, we would call for revenge, that we would want to be paid back. But we're not into that. I think that they're seeing that now." P. 26.

14. Emília Viotti da Costa, *Da senzala à colônia* (2nd edition, São Paulo, 1982), p. 403; "Movimento de arregimentação da raça negra no Brasil," *Diário de São Paulo* (September 17, 1931), p. 5; Virginia Bicudo, "Atitudes raciais de pretos e mulatos em São Paulo," *Sociologia* 11, 3 (1947), pp. 212–213. As we have seen, Rebouças's promise not to agitate among the slave population was subsequently foresworn by Antônio Bento and the radical abolitionists of São Paulo.

15. For examples of close relationships between black newspapers and certain unions, see the reports in *Mundo Novo* (1950) on the activities of the printers' union; or *Niger* (1960), the editorial offices of which were in the headquarters of the construction workers' union, and which ran frequent ads by the union aimed directly at black construction workers. For articles on black social and cultural events held in union halls, see "I Salão Campineiro dos Amigos das Belas Artes," *Hífen* (April 1960), p. 1; "A respeito do TENSP," *Niger* (July 1960), p. 5; "Convescote da ACN," *Niger* (August 1960), p. 13. During the 1980s black organizations continued to make use of union facilities; the Unified Black Movement, discussed later in this chapter, held numerous meetings at union halls in Campinas and São Paulo, and public meetings held by the Council for the Development and Participation of the Black Community (also discussed later in this chapter) were often held at union halls.

Concerning blacks in leadership positions in São Paulo unions, see Robert Alexander's 1954 interviews with Benedetto Silva, preto treasurer of the metalworkers' union, and with Edgar Martins, pardo special assistant to the general secretary of the union. Robert Alexander Papers, Rutgers University Library. In other unions, Antônio Chamorro, a long-time organizer in and former director of the textile workers' union, recalls that Afro-Brazilians did not appear on the union's board until the 1960s, but that they currently constitute a quarter of the directorate. Interview (June 10, 1988). The bakery workers' union elected preto Raimundo Rosa de Lima to the presidency in 1969, a post which he held until 1984. At several points during his presidency and since, the board of directors has been majority black. Interview (May 2, 1985). In 1984 black activist Osvaldo

Ribeiro was elected president of the São Paulo airline workers' union; two years later he became president of the one of the two labor federations in São Paulo, the Confederação Geral dos Trabalhadores (CGT). "Osvaldo Ribeiro: 1° Secretário de Estado negro," *Jornal do Conselho da Comunidade Negra* (May 1988), p. 3; "O que propõem os dirigentes da nova CGT?" *Debate Sindical* (May 1986), pp. 13–15.

16. The competition among these parties for working-class votes in São Paulo during the postwar years is well covered in French, "Industrial Workers," pp. 302–521. Adhemar de Barros had made somewhat of an effort to court the black population of São Paulo during his 1938–1941 term as Vargas's "interventor" in the state. See *O Clarim da Alvorada* (September 28, 1940), p. 1; "Novos tempos," *Alvorada* (February 1947), p. 1. During the early 1950s he used *O Novo Horizonte* as a medium through which to recruit black voters for the Social Progressive Party. See, for example, "Mensagem aos negros," *O Novo Horizonte* (September 1954), p. 5; and Michael Mitchell, "Racial Consciousness and the Political Attitudes and Behavior of Blacks in São Paulo, Brazil" (Ph.D. dissertation, Indiana University, 1977), pp. 156–157. On efforts by the Brazilian Communist Party to attract the black vote, see chapter 5, note 53. This party was officially banned in 1947, after which it could no longer run candidates in elections. It continued to exist as an organized force, however, and retained considerable influence in the labor movement.

17. On black support for Vargas and the Brazilian Labor Party during this period, see Amaury de Souza, "Raça e política no Brasil urbano," *Revista de Administração de Empresas* 11, 4 (1971), pp. 61–70. Souza's data, based on interviews carried out in Rio de Janeiro in 1960, show black middle-class voters supporting the Brazilian Labor Party even more strongly than black workers, whereas the tendency among white voters was the opposite.

18. On the Black Cultural Association, see Clóvis Moura, "Organizações negras," in Paul Singer and Vinícius Caldeira Brant, eds., *São Paulo: O povo em movimento* (São Paulo, 1980), pp. 157–159; "Embora perto (e às vezes junto), o negro brasileiro está muito longe do branco," *Última Hora* (October 17, 1973); and the issues of the association's newspaper, *O Mutirão*, which began publication in May 1958. For information on the two theater groups, see *O Mutirão* and the monthly magazine *Niger*, published from July through September 1960. Both the theater groups were offshoots of organizations first established in Rio: Abdias do Nascimento's Teatro Experimental do Negro, founded in 1944, and Solano Trindade's Teatro Popular Brasileiro, founded in 1950.

19. On the alienation of elite and middle-class support from the Second Republic, see René Armand Dreifuss, *1964: A conquista do estado* (2nd edition, Petrópolis, 1981), especially chapters 5–7; and Alfred Stepan, *The Military in Politics: Changing Patterns in Brazil* (Princeton, 1971), pp. 134–152. On the coup of 1964 and the first years of the dictatorship, see Thomas E. Skidmore, *Politics in Brazil, 1930–1964: An Experiment in Democracy* (New York, 1967), pp. 253–321; Thomas E. Skidmore, *The Politics of Military Rule in Brazil, 1964–1985* (New York, 1988), pp. 3–65; Peter Flynn, *Brazil: A Political Analysis* (Boulder, Colo., 1979), pp. 226–365.

20. On the repression of this period, see Maria Helena Moreira Alves, *State*

and Opposition in Military Brazil (Austin, 1985), pp. 34–38, 123–131, 155–159; Joan Dassin, ed., *Torture in Brazil* (New York, 1986); Paulo Sérgio Pinheiro, *Escritos indignados: Polícia, prisões e política no estado autoritário* (São Paulo, 1984).

21. These opposition forces are described and analyzed in Bernardo Sorj and Maria Hermínia Tavares de Almeida, eds., *Sociedade e política no Brasil pós-64* (São Paulo, 1983); Skidmore, *Politics of Military Rule;* Alves, *State and Opposition,* pp. 153–210; and Alfred Stepan, ed., *Democratizing Brazil: Problems of Transition and Consolidation* (New York, 1989), pp. 143–296. On São Paulo in particular, see Singer and Brant, *São Paulo.*

22. Luis Inácio "Lula" da Silva, head of the Workers' Party and a former metalworker, came in second in the first round of voting in November 1989, and then took 47 percent of the national vote in the run-off election against Fernando Collor de Melo in December.

23. Margaret E. Keck, "The New Unionism in the Brazilian Transition," in Stepan, *Democratizing Brazil,* table 3, p. 270. Using data from São Paulo alone, Wood and Carvalho calculate that the minimum wage during the miracle years had 77–80 percent of the buying power which it had in 1964. They also note that, as the minimum wage declined in value, infant mortality in São Paulo rose from 67.6 per 1,000 in 1964 to 94.6 in 1974. Charles H. Wood and José Alberto Magno de Carvalho, *The Demography of Inequality in Brazil* (Cambridge and New York, 1988), p. 115.

24. The following discussion focuses on São Paulo State, where black mobilization was most intense. Caetana Damasceno et al., *Catálogo de entidades de movimento negro no Brasil* (Rio de Janeiro, 1988) lists 343 organizations, 138 of them located in São Paulo, 76 in Rio de Janeiro, 33 in Minas Gerais, 27 in Bahia, and the rest scattered throughout the country.

25. Recognizing the need to defuse potential white hostility toward a black organization, the Working Group emphasized in its public announcements that its "initial goal of improving the image of the black population does not necessarily imply [racial] segregation." "Grupo que age em prol da valorização do negro," *Diário Popular* (May 8, 1974). See also João Baptista Borges Pereira, "Aspectos do comportamento político do negro em São Paulo," *Ciência e Cultura* 34, 10 (1982), pp. 1287–1288.

26. "Ao leitor" and "Comunidade negra e alienação," *Jornegro* 2, 6 (unknown month, 1979); "Conquistas poéticas dos Cadernos Negros," *Folha de São Paulo* (October 14, 1984), p. 51; "Negros," *Folha de São Paulo* (May 31, 1977), p. 31. For a discussion of a comparable Rio de Janeiro organization during this period, the Institute for Research on Black Cultures, see Joel Rufino [dos Santos], "IPCN e Cacique de Ramos: Dois exemplos de movimento negro na cidade do Rio de Janeiro," *Comunicações do ISER* 7, 28, (1988), pp. 5–20. The importance of the early black newspapers as part of the historical and cultural heritage of black São Paulo is suggested by the fact that, like Eduardo de Oliveira e Oliveira in 1977, the Black Cultural Association had held a similar exhibition of black newspapers, also at the São Paulo Municipal Library, in 1972. "Imprensa negra em exposição," *O Estado de São Paulo* (May 12, 1972).

27. These points are made in Joel Rufino dos Santos, "O movimento negro e a

crise brasileira" (unpublished manuscript, 1985). See the periodic reports on black movements in the United States and Africa in the monthly magazine *Versus* (1976–1980), to which a number of young black journalists contributed. See also theater director Teresa Santos's account of her sojourn in revolutionary Angola as an employee of the Ministry of Culture. Costa, *Fala, crioulo,* pp. 218–220.

28. Luz's death went unreported in the mainstream press. The ejection of the boys from Tietê Boating Club is reported in "Presidente do Tietê fala em 'subversão'," *Folha de São Paulo* (May 17, 1978).

29. As we have seen, Afro-Brazilians are routinely denied admission to Brazilian athletic clubs. Concerning torture, "scholars of the history of police enforcement in Brazil agree that at least since the late nineteenth century physical torture has been routine in interrogating non-elite prisoners." Skidmore, *Politics of Military Rule,* pp. 126–127. Such practices continue to the present: "Five years after the end of military rule, the police in Brazil continue to routinely torture and sometimes kill prisoners." "Brazil Police Accused of Torture and Killing in Rights Report," *New York Times* (June 19, 1990), p. 3. See also Pinheiro, *Escritos indignados,* pp. 71–106 passim.

30. The founding of the MNU is discussed in Moura, "Organizções negras," pp. 171–175; and Lélia Gonzalez, "The Unified Black Movement: A New Stage in Black Political Mobilization," in Pierre-Michel Fontaine, ed., *Race, Class and Power in Brazil* (Los Angeles, 1985).

31. See Gonzalez, "Unified Black Movement"; Movimento Negro Unificado, *Programa de ação* (Campinas, 1984); and "Negro: A luta continua," *Cadernos do CEAS* 72 (March–April 1981), pp. 18–28.

32. Actress Zezé Motta recalls that she joined the Unified Black Movement when it was first founded, but left because she "had run-ins with people who were a little too radical." "Foram 100 anos de resistência. E estamos aqui," *Manchete* (May 21, 1988), p. 6. Even a sympathetic observor describes the MNU as a "notoriously rigid" organization. Santos, "IPCN e Cacique de Ramos," p. 6. One of its founders, Hamilton Cardoso, recalled how the movement "kept getting narrower and narrower ideologically, characterizing itself increasingly as a movement of the left. . . . After a year, it started to lose militants and strength." "Movimento negro avalia sua importância," *Folha de São Paulo* (April 15, 1984). The MNU forms an interesting contrast to the Black Front of the 1930s: the former alienated its initial supporters by pushing too far to the left, while the latter produced the same result by pushing too far to the right. Each movement reflected the oppositional political climate of the time: the popularity of antirepublicanism and Fascism in the 1930s, culminating in the creation of the New State; and the Marxism of the 1970s, which assumed particular strength in student circles in opposition to the military governments of those years.

33. The jockeying of the parties for the black vote is described in Pereira, "Aspectos do comportamento político," and the M.A. thesis written by his student, Ana Lúcia E. F. Valente, *Política e relações raciais: Os negros e as eleições paulistas de 1982* (São Paulo, 1986). See also the interviews with the Afro-Brazilian spokespeople of the various parties, "Os negros e os partidos políticos," *Folhetim, Folha de São Paulo* (June 13, 1982), pp. 10–11. The four black officeholders who left the PMDB in 1981 and joined the Democratic Social

Party were Congressman Adalberto Camargo, state assemblywoman Teodosina Ribeiro, and São Paulo City councilmen Paulo Ruy de Oliveira and Mário Américo Castro. For extensive interviews with Camargo, see Valente, *Política e relações raciais*, pp. 145–172; Costa, *Fala, crioulo*, pp. 60–66.

34. Such a position is expressed by Clóvis Moura in a debate with Father Batista Laurindo. "A luta dos negros contra a opressão," *O São Paulo* (May 11, 1984), p. 6. At its Third Congress in April 1982 the MNU adopted this position as its own, declining to endorse or enter into alliance with any particular party. It did, however, leave its members free to join and work for any party or candidate of their choice. "É preciso avançar o movimento negro," *Em Tempo* (April 22, 1982), p. 13. Along these lines, see also Abdias do Nascimento's tract *Quilombismo* (Petrópolis, 1980).

35. These points are made in Joel Rufino dos Santos's lucid essay "O movimento negro e a crise brasileira," and echoed by Rio de Janeiro activist Carlos Alberto Oliveira, elected to Congress in 1986 on the Democratic Labor Party ticket. "The right always mystified the problem [of race], saying there was no racial discrimination in the country, and the left, principally the Communist Party, refused to discuss the problem, saying that it would be a divisive factor within the working class." "Pesquisa mostra: Negro trabalha mais e ganha menos," *Nas Bancas* (November 21, 1985).

Largely in response to the resurgence of the black movement, during the 1980s the Communist Party intensified its denunciations of racial inequality, and attacked the concept of racial democracy as "a fundamental part of a reactionary ideology which is used to justify the worst forms of oppression. . . . The absence of racial democracy, a permanent fact in Brazil, serves the de facto suppression of democracy for all, and above all for the poor and exploited." *Uma alternativa democrática para a crise brasileira* (São Paulo, 1984), p. 121, 120–122, and 202; see also "O mito da democracia racial," *Voz da Unidade* (June 30, 1983), p. 15. After considerable internal debate, the newly formed Workers' Party also recognized the importance of racial issues; see its brochure "O negro e o Partido dos Trabalhadores," prepared for the 1982 elections.

36. This is a point recognized by Florestan Fernandes in his observation that Brazilian elites regard black activism "as the worst kind of protest, after worker protest. . . ." Florestan Fernandes, *Circuito fechado* (São Paulo, 1977), p. 78.

37. The Brizola administration placed high priority on the expansion of public primary schools, an item of immediate and direct concern to the poor white and black populations. It also sharply reduced police mistreatment of poor white and black arrestees, and the notorious police death squads which operated in the poverty-stricken suburbs of the Baixada Fluminense. Skidmore, *Politics of Military Rule*, p. 410.

An important symbolic act of the Brizola administration was the passage by the state Assembly in 1985 of a law banning racial discrimination in elevators, stairwells, and other common areas in apartment buildings. This was a law of particular interest to black people, who are routinely consigned to the "service elevator" in such buildings and forbidden to ride in the "social elevator." "Entra em vigor no Rio a lei que dá acesso livre a elevador social," *Folha de São Paulo* (January 2, 1986). Political scientist Paulo Sérgio Pinheiro notes that "Brazil is the only country in the world (besides South Africa) in which buildings have a 'social elevator' and another elevator for workers, blacks, and dogs, not always in that order." "Joana e o paraiso da opressão," *Folha de São Paulo* (September 23, 1984), p. 68.

38. "Movimento negro avalia sua importância, "*Folha de São Paulo* (April 15, 1984). On black electoral support for the Democratic Labor Party in Rio de Janeiro, see Glaucio Ary Dillon Soares and Nelson do Valle Silva, "Urbanization, Race, and Class in Brazilian Politics," *Latin American Research Review* 22, 2 (1987), pp. 155–176. It is worth noting that Rio de Janeiro's population is 38.7 percent pardo and preto, while São Paulo's is only 23.0 percent pardo and preto.

39. Valente, *Política e relações raciais*, p. 139.

40. Valente, *Política e relações raciais*, pp. 128–130. Even among middle- and higher-income voters, over 80 percent were unable to name any of the black candidates. By election day those proportions had apparently been reduced substantially, to judge by the postelection survey.

41. Valente, *Política e relações raciais*, pp. 125, 128, 135. A survey of black workers in a large electrical utility in Rio de Janeiro found a similar lack of interest in political action. "In addition to placing no credence in the effective-ness of anti-racism laws or government action of any kind, as several interviewees indicated, the possibility of using existing political parties, or creating new ones on the basis of the city's black movement, was not even mentioned." Jorge Aparecido Monteiro, "Cor e trabalho na empresa pública: Uma introdução," *Série Estudos IUPERJ* 56 (1987), p. 75.

This skepticism about political action to remedy societal problems extends well beyond the area of race, and is widespread among lower-class Brazilians of all races. "As a rule, the popular sectors are somewhat skeptical about the possibility of effecting political change. Politics is seen as an elite struggle, and the State is perceived as a realm beyond the popular sectors. . . . In the limited spare time they have, poor people typically focus on a range of issues that have little to do with politics: family life, sports, relaxing." As the author of this passage notes, given the traditionally exclusionary character of Brazilian pol-itics, such attitudes are not unreasonable or unrealistic assessments of the situa-tion. They "nevertheless limit the possibility of collective action, for only at the point when people believe in the legitimacy and efficacy of collective action is it possible to organize a social movement." Scott Mainwaring, "Grassroots Popular Movements and the Struggle for Democracy," in Stepan, *Democratizing Brazil*, p. 183. Mainwaring also cites survey data taken prior to the elections of 1986 which showed relatively few voters able to name any of the competing parties. When set in this context, black voters' inability to name any of the black candidates looks less like a characteristic of Afro-Brazilians in particular, and more like a characteristic of lower-class Brazilian voters in general.

42. Again, see Mainwaring, "Grassroots Democracy."

43. See, for example, Carolina de Jesus's *Child of the Dark* (New York, 1962), the diary of a poverty-stricken black woman living in the São Paulo *favela* of Canindé during the 1950s. Jesus indicates only occasional passing interest in racial matters; the dominant theme of the book is hunger, and getting enough to eat. Writing on May 13, 1958, for example, she said that "today is a nice day for

me, it's the anniversary of the Abolition. The day we celebrate the freeing of the slaves." But she spent most of the day hunting for food, and concluded that "that is the way on May 13, 1958 I fought against the real slavery—hunger!" Pp. 33–34.

See also the comments by the leader of a community organization in a poor, black neighborhood of Rio, who finds the black movement too "discursive" in character, spending too much time on ideological debates and insufficient time on addressing the immediate, pressing needs of people in poor communities. "Movimento negro já conta 400 entidades e cresce no Brasil," *Jornal do Brasil* (May 12, 1985). See also the criticisms of the black movement expressed by members of a domestic servants' association in Rio de Janeiro. Celma Rosa Vieira, "Negra: Mulher e doméstica," *Estudos Afro-Asiáticos* 14 (1987), pp. 154–156.

44. When asked whether racial prejudice exists in Brazil, 65 percent of the low-income black voters surveyed by Valente answered yes (compared with 69 percent of middle-income respondents, and 91 percent of high-income respondents). Valente, *Política e relações raciais*, p. 125. In a survey of black workers at a Rio de Janeiro electrical utility, 52 percent of low-income black workers said that they had experienced prejudice directly (versus 50 percent of middle-income workers, and 60 percent of high-income employees). Monteiro, "Cor e trabalho," p. 45.

45. See, for example, the declarations of veteran congressman Afonso Arinos de Melo Franco, author of Brazil's 1951 antidiscrimination law. "In Brazil we have an advantage: race prejudice is much greater among the elites; the lower classes have hardly any. In England or the United States black workers are discriminated against by members of their own class. But not here. Here it's just a question of the elite." "Arinos: Uma questão cultural," *O Globo* (June 4, 1980), p. 9; see also "Uma lei á brasileira," *Folhetim, Folha de São Paulo* (June 8, 1980), p. 13.

46. On the basis of her research in a poor neighborhood in São Paulo's *periferia*, anthropologist Teresa Pires do Rio Caldeira argues that "prejudices against Blacks are generalized among all social classes, and can assume extreme forms among poor people. . . ." "Houses of Respect" (unpublished paper presented at the International Congress of the Latin American Studies Association, Boston, October 1986), p. 20. Historian Boris Fausto agrees. "In the Brazilian lower classes being poor is one thing, and being poor and black is even worse." "Democracia racial, o mito e o desejo," *Folhetim, Folha de São Paulo* (June 8, 1980), p. 8. Anthropologist Maria Suely Kofes de Almeida develops this point at length in "Entre nós, os pobres, eles, os negros" (*dissertação de mestrado*, Universidade Estadual de Campinas, 1976), based on extensive interview research carried out in a lower-class housing project in Campinas. And Carolina de Jesus reports being the target of racial epithets and insults directed at her by fellow *favelados*. Jesus, *Child of the Dark*, pp. 30, 88, 136.

Anthropologist Moema de Poli T. Pacheco tries to downplay the importance of race in interpersonal relations among the poor, but her informants' declarations suggest otherwise. Many resisted her efforts to get them to talk about an obviously painful subject, one of them protesting, "I never thought about that, about skin color. I never paid attention to it. . . . I never let it take charge of me."

If race is not important, why does one have to make an effort to prevent its "taking charge of" him or her? Another informant insists that race has no importance in the *favela:* "We all grew up together, and by the time we got into the habit of thinking of one person as black and another as white, we were already such good friends that it didn't make sense for us to fight about it." Again, if race is unimportant, why should anyone fight about it? "A questão da cor nas relações de um grupo de baixa renda," *Estudos Afro-Asiáticos* 14 (1987), pp. 86, 92.

47. Samuel Harman Lowrie, "O elemento negro na população de São Paulo," *Revista do Arquivo Municipal de São Paulo* 4, 48 (1938), p. 33; Nelson do Valle Silva, "Endogamia de cor ou endogamia de classe?" (unpublished paper presented at the annual conference of the Associação Nacional de Pós-Graduação e Pesquisa em Ciências Sociais, ANPOCS, Novo Friburgo, October 1981), p. 13.

48. See, for example, Monteiro, "Cor e trabalho," pp. 38–39, 42; Ramatis Jacino, *Histórico de uma candidatura operária* (São Paulo, 1987), p. 81; Bastide and Fernandes, *Brancos e negros*, p. 164. White union activist Antônio Chamorro concurs that one often hears racist jokes among white workers, and sometimes among black ones as well. Interview (June 10, 1988). One of Monteiro's informants characterizes such teasing as a way for white workers "to hide their racism behind jokes." "Cor e trabalho," p. 42.

49. "O protesto de Campinas," *Alvorada* (June 1946), p. 4; "Problemas e aspirações," *Diário Trabalhista* (May 10, 1946), p. 5; Bastide and Fernandes, *Brancos e negros*, p. 164; Octávio Ianni, *Raças e classes sociais no Brasil* (2nd edition, São Paulo, 1988), p. 67.

50. Santos, "O movimento negro e a crise brasileira," p. 15; Valente, *Política e relações raciais*, p. 77. The most visible politician of this type is Benedita da Silva, first elected to the Rio city council in 1982 and then to Congress in 1986, both times on the Workers' Party ticket. A black woman who grew up in one of Rio's *favelas*, she presents herself as the representative of women, the poor, and black people (not necessarily in that order; each group receives equal weight in her political work). "One Woman's Mission: To Make Brasilia Sensitive," *New York Times* (February 9, 1987), p. 4.

51. On the general question of inequality in Brazil, see Wood and Carvalho, *Demography of Inequality.*

52. Fernandes, *Integração do negro*, 1, p. 10; see also Octávio Ianni, "Diversidades raciais e questão nacional," in *Raças e classes sociais*, pp. 338–356.

53. "Censo-80 vai pesquisar cor, decide o IBGE," *Folha de São Paulo* (November 9, 1979), p. 6. The National Association of Post-Graduate Education and Research in Social Sciences, itself a creation of the boom in higher education during the miracle years, created a working group on themes and problems of the black population, which meets at the association's annual conventions, and since 1978 has produced a number of extremely useful papers on various aspects of racial inequality in Brazil.

54. "Irmãos, a Igreja pecou," *Afinal* (July 14, 1987), pp. 17–18; "Cisão pastoral," *Veja* (February 24, 1988). Not until 1984 did the Franciscan order ordain its first black priest in northeastern Brazil. Frei Hugo Fragoso, OFM, "Uma dívida que a Província de Santo Antônio ainda não pagou," *Santo Antônio* (May 1984), p. 59.

55. "Irmãos, a Igreja pecou"; Grupo de União e Consciencia Negra, *Escrevendo a nossa história* (São Paulo, 1983); Comissão dos Religiosos, Seminaristas e Padres Negros—Rio de Janeiro, *"Ouvi o clamor deste povo"* . . . *negro* (Petrópolis, 1987).

56. On the church's role in recent Brazilian politics and the base community movement, see Scott Mainwaring, *The Catholic Church and Politics in Brazil, 1916-1985* (Stanford, 1986). For a fascinating article on the community-organizing work of a young black priest in a poor suburb of Rio de Janeiro, see Jane Kramer, "Letter from the Elysian Fields," *The New Yorker* (March 2, 1987), pp. 40-74.

57. On the internal struggle within the church, see Mainwaring, *The Catholic Church*; and Ralph della Cava, "The 'People's Church,' the Vatican, and *Abertura*," in Stepan, *Democratizing Brazil*, pp. 143-167. That struggle emerged into the open during the Brotherhood Campaign of 1988, when the conservative archbishop of Rio de Janeiro, Dom Eugénio Sales, expressed his unhappiness with the CNBB's decision by launching his own separate, independent campaign, also focused on the question of race, but presenting the more traditional, Freyrean point of view. This was the first time that a Brazilian bishop had publicly dissociated himself from an annual Lenten campaign, and led to further discussions, debates, and conflict within the church hierarchy. My thanks to Ralph della Cava for this information.

58. In May 1987, for example, the Rio de Janeiro Commission of Black Religious, Seminarians, and Priests announced that it had documentary evidence of more than twenty cases of discrimination by the church against black priests, which it planned to present to church authorities. "Frei acusa a Igreja Católica de 'racista'," *Folha de São Paulo* (May 20, 1987).

59. Kramer, "Letter from the Elysian Fields," p. 66. Members of the Rio Commission, mentioned in note 58, were dismayed several months later when the CNBB disowned a popular history booklet which they had prepared on "false heroes who contributed to the massacre of blacks in Brazil" by maintaining slavery. When public uproar erupted over the presence of abolitionist Ruy Barbosa, the duke of Caxias (commander of the Brazilian army during the war with Paraguay, 1864-1870, and a major Brazilian military hero), and Princess Isabel in the book, the CNBB made pains to describe the publication as "an autonomous booklet prepared by the black movement, not by the CNBB." "Padres negros consideram duque de Caxias 'falso herói'," *Folha de São Paulo* (July 30, 1987).

60. For example, one of the Workers' Party's black militants, although considering the party to have the most progressive position on race, nevertheless finds it to be "full of disinformation and serious prejudices" concerning this topic. Jacino, *Histórico de uma candidatura operária*, the chapter "A questão racial," pp. 68-83.

61. The struggle for these positions is described in Valente, *Política e relações raciais*, pp. 97-105; and "Negros querem participar do secretariado municipal," *Folha de São Paulo* (May 5, 1983).

62. Decreto no. 22.184, May 11, 1984, *Diário Oficial do Estado de São Paulo* (May 12, 1984). The council is composed of nineteen members who are all

appointed by the governor and serve two-year terms. They are assisted in their work by a small administrative staff.

63. While Governor Montoro had represented the party's liberal left wing, Governor Quércia, former mayor of Campinas, represented its right wing. By mid-1988 tensions between these two factions drove the leftist reformers, the so-called *tucanos*, to secede and form the Brazilian Social Democratic Party. Partly as a result of this split, in the mayoral elections of that November the left-wing Workers' Party came from behind to win the mayoralty of São Paulo City, which thus became the largest city in the world governed by a Marxist mayor, former social worker Luiza Erundina.

64. On the Council for the Participation and Development of the Black Community and its activities (as well as for numerous items of interest on the black movement in São Paulo), see its newspaper *Jornal do Conselho da Comunidade Negra*, published from January 1985 through the present. The black offices in the Secretariats of Education and Labor are, respectively, the Working Group for Afro-Brazilian Affairs, and the Group for Orientation and Intervention in Situations of Racial Discrimination in the Workplace. Osvaldo Ribeiro, the head of the Special Secretariat of Social Relations, had served as president of both the airline workers' union and the São Paulo CGT.

65. Critics might respond that the federal government took action in combatting racism in 1951, by passing the Afonso Arinos Law. It is important to note, however, that while a handful of congressmen did acknowledge the existence of a racial problem in Brazil at that time, the overwhelming majority voted for the law without ever making such an admission. Responsibility for enforcing the law was then placed in the hands of police and state prosecutors, none of whom have displayed much diligence in this area.

66. For some of the data prepared by SEADE, see the two-part article "Os negros no mercado de trabalho na Grande São Paulo," *Pesquisa de Emprego e Desemprego na Grande São Paulo* 9 (1985), pp. 8–16, and 10 (1985), pp. 8–19; and Miguel W. Chaia, "Discriminação racial," *Revista Fundação SEADE* 2, 2–3 (1986), pp. 7–14. Staffers at the black office in the Secretariat of Labor used these data at their meetings with union officials, who, they report, were "very surprised" by the levels of inequality documented in the SEADE reports. Some of those union officials were willing to consider ways to eliminate such inequality. Others, however, became defensive, arguing that raising such issues with the membership at large would tend to divide workers along racial lines, and lead to conflict which would undermine the union movement. Interview with staffers of the Group for Orientation and Intervention in Situations of Racial Discrimination in the Workplace (May 19, 1988).

67. This disparity between the resources available to the state agencies and those available to the organizations of the black movement is one of the prime causes of friction among these groups. The Unified Black Movement has been particularly vehement in its criticism of the Council for the Participation and Development of the Black Community, attacking it as "an organ linked to the government, which does not place itself at the service of the black movement, trying to put band-aids on subjects like discrimination and violence, as well as

not contributing to us financially." "Conselho busca adesões e apoio," *Caderno C, Diário do Grande ABC* (November 24, 1985).

68. *Imprensa negra* (São Paulo, 1984).

69. *Salve o 13 de maio?* (São Paulo, 1988).

Chapter 8. One Hundred Years of Freedom: May 13, 1988

1. The Emancipation Proclamation of January 1, 1863, freed all slaves held in areas controlled by Confederate forces. But "from a legal point of view, it was really the Thirteenth Amendment, approved by Congress in February 1865 and ratified in December, that actually emancipated all the slaves." As in Brazil, slavery as an institution in the United States had largely disintegrated by the moment of formal emancipation. August Meier and Elliott Rudwick, *From Plantation to Ghetto* (3rd edition, New York, 1976), pp. 159-160.

William Wiggins finds that Afro-Americans celebrate emancipation on at least fifteen different dates, varying from one part of the country to another. William H. Wiggins, Jr., *O Freedom! Afro-American Emancipation Celebrations* (Knoxville, 1987), p. xix and passim.

2. It is worth noting that May 13, 1888, was the final act of slave emancipation in the Americas as a whole. In abolishing the last, and largest, slave system in the hemisphere, the Golden Law transcended national boundaries and was genuinely international in its significance.

3. "As festas de hontem," and "Manifestação," *Diário Popular* (May 14, 1889); "Arbitrariedade," *A Província de São Paulo* (May 16, 1889).

4. "Dia a dia," *O Estado de São Paulo* (May 13, 1892). In the downtown neighborhood of Bixiga, a resident who was born in 1890 recalls that *batuques* celebrating May 13 continued in that neighborhood to the beginning of the 1950s, and then died out. "O velho Scaramuzza lembra as origens do Bexiga," *Folha de São Paulo* (May 14, 1985), p. 19.

5. On commemorations of May 13 by immigrant (particularly Italian) and labor organizations, see "Notícias diversas—13 de maio," *O Estado de São Paulo* (May 14, 1901); "Noticiário—Antônio Bento," *Diário Popular* (May 14, 1897). For radical critiques of abolition and May 13, see "O 13 de maio e a situação operária," *O Combate* (May 14, 1918); "13 de maio," *Germinal!* (May 13, 1913); "13 de maio," *A Lucta Proletária* (May 16, 1908). For reflections on the slaves' heroism in the struggle for abolition, see "O preto Simeão," *O Combate* (May 13, 1915).

6. On the May 13 celebrations in the 1890s and early 1900s, see "Noticiário— Estrella de Maio," *Diário Popular* (May 22, 1889); "Noticiário—Estrella de Maio," *Diário Popular* (May 27, 1889); "Notícias diversas—13 de maio," *O Estado de São Paulo* (May 14, 1901); "As commemorações cívicas de hontem," *O Combate* (May 14, 1928), p. 3; Cleber da Silva Maciel, *Discriminações raciais: Negros em Campinas (1888-1921)* (Campinas, 1988), pp. 87-91. In 1931 a monument to Gama was erected in the downtown Largo do Arouche, which then became the endpoint of the annual march. For photos of marchers gathered at the Consoloção cemetery and the Largo do Arouche, see "No 44° anniversário da

abolição," *Folha da Noite* (May 13, 1932). On the visits to the media, see "Apos a grande romaria da saudade," *O Clarim da Alvorada* (June 9, 1929).

7. "Pretos x brancos," *A Gazeta* (May 14, 1928), p. 6; "A grande partida de hontem," *O Combate* (May 14, 1928), p. 6.

8. Brazilian anthropologist Roberto da Matta has suggested that one reason for the immense popularity of soccer in Brazil is that it is one of the few competitive settings in the country in which the rules of competition are clearly established, are known to all, do not change over the course of the competition, and are fairly enforced. This is in marked contrast to "everyday" Brazilian life (in politics, business, work, academia, etc.), where the rules are enforced arbitrarily, or not at all, and are constantly being rewritten or reinterpreted so as to favor the interests of powerful elites. Soccer thus becomes one of the few areas of Brazilian life in which all participants compete on an equal basis, and are rewarded strictly on the basis of their talents and achievements. Not coincidentally, it is also one of the areas of Brazilian life most open to black initiative and upward mobility. On the significance of soccer in Brazilian society, see Janet Lever, *Soccer Madness* (Chicago, 1983).

9. "Promette revestir-se de grande brilho a Semana Esportiva da Mocidade Negra," *Correio de São Paulo* (May 12, 1933); "Esportes," *A Voz da Raça* (May 1937).

10. See, for example, the May 13, 1946, issue of *Alvorada*, or the coverage of the seventieth anniversary of abolition in the black newspaper *O Mutirão* (May 1958).

11. "Apontamento social," *Correio d'Ébano* (June 16, 1963). The 1963 contest was honored by the presence of President João Goulart. On the 1966 contest, see "Mariza é a bonequinha," *Jornal da Tarde* (May 13, 1966). On the difficulty of Afro-Brazilian women winning beauty contests in Brazil during this period, see the interview with Vera Lúcia Couto dos Santos, the Miss Renaissance who scored an upset victory to become Miss Guanabara (Miss de Janeiro) in 1964. At the subsequent Miss Brazil competition, a woman in the audience, "yelling hysterically, completely possessed," shouted at her to get off the stage and back into the kitchen. She managed to retain her composure and was voted first runner-up. Haroldo Costa, *Fala, crioulo* (Rio de Janeiro, 1982), pp. 26–31. In 1986 Deise Nunes, a parda model from Rio Grande do Sul, became the first Afro-Brazilian Miss Brazil.

12. Not everyone sees the Black Mother in such a positive light. Many nineteenth- and twentieth-century whites deplored the "corrupting" effect that an upbringing by black wetnurses and maids had on white children, even going so far as to suggest that whites drank in the vices of black life, not to mention the diseases, through the Black Mother's milk. For comments from the 1800s and early 1900s, see Robert Conrad, *Children of God's Fire: A Documentary History of Black Slavery in Brazil* (Princeton, 1983), pp. 135–140, 221–225; Sandra Lauderdale Graham, *House and Street: The Domestic World of Servants and Masters in Nineteenth-Century Rio de Janeiro* (Cambridge and New York, 1988), pp. 35, 117–120. Other whites rejected the idea of the Black Mother's contributions entirely, arguing that "a few black slaves who suckled the children of their masters did not contribute anything toward the formation of our race and our

nationality." They claimed that the Black Mother gave a completely inaccurate image of Brazil, "degrading us in the eyes of the Nation and the world." "Monumento a Mãe Preta," *Diário Nacional* (November 1, 1928), p. 8.

From another perspective, present-day black militants see the Black Mother as a symbol which badly distorts the realities of slave labor and domestic service, and which seeks to justify and excuse the exploitation of black women under slavery. Hamilton Cardoso reflects on how the Black Mother "was transformed into a national heroine when she stopped nursing her own children to feed with 'mother's milk' the child of the slaveowner, allowing white mothers to keep beautiful their small, 'superior' breasts. The *mãe negra*, in the image of a fat old woman with enormous breasts, resembling a dairy cow, even earned a statue in the Largo do Paissandu, in São Paulo." Hamilton Cardoso, "Passado: Branco e sem mácula," *Istoé* (September 26, 1979), pp. 36–42. Cardoso's description of the São Paulo statue is an accurate one. It is also worth noting the fevered inscription on the statue's base, which recalls how "enslaved by love, [in order] to bring up children not her own, like the pelican she tore her entrails, and gave to the Fatherland the sacrifice of her breasts."

13. "Ferraz: Abolição é a nossa maior data," *O Estado de São Paulo* (May 14, 1971); "A mãe preta, a homenagem do presidente," *O Estado de São Paulo* (May 14, 1972); "O pequeno clube dos negros, o 220, e seu grande orgulho: O president vem visitá-lo," *Jornal da Tarde* (May 12, 1972); "Presidente condena a discriminação racial," *O Estado de São Paulo* (March 8, 1975).

14. R. K. Kent, "Palmares: An African State in Brazil," *Journal of African History* 6, 2 (1965), pp. 161–175; Edison Carneiro, *O quilombo dos Palmares* (São Paulo, 1947); Décio Freitas, *Palmares, a guerra dos escravos* (rpt., São Paulo, 1982).

15. For example, São Paulo's Palmares Civic Center, founded in 1927, which served as a precursor to the Black Front, took its name from the experience of Palmares.

16. Quilombhoje, *Reflexões* (São Paulo, 1985), p. 82.

17. On the early Zumbi festivals, see "FECONEZU," *Jornegro* 2, 6 (no month, 1979). Despite the resurgent black movement's antagonism toward May 13, black poet Cuti (Luiz Silva) notes the surge of mobilization which took place in São Paulo in response to the ninetieth anniversary of abolition, May 13, 1978. The Unified Black Movement was formed at that time, three black newspapers came into existence (*Jornegro, Abertura,* and *Tição*), the first *Caderno Negro* (an annual collection of poetry and short stories by black authors) was published, and plans were begun for that fall's Zumbi festival. "Conquistas poéticas dos Cadernos Negros," *Folha de São Paulo* (October 14, 1984), p. 51.

18. This vision of Palmares is most vividly communicated in Carlos Diegues's 1983 film *Quilombo,* an account of Palmares and its eventual destruction. See also the National Labor Front's 1982 pamphlet "Escravidão e libertação"; "O velho anarquista Rodrigues," *Folha de São Paulo* (October 27, 1984), p. 46; Hamilton Cardoso, "A contribuição de Palmares," *Folha de São Paulo* (December 5, 1983), p. 3. The closing lines in the paragraph are from Milton Nascimento's *Missa dos quilombos,* the Quilombo Mass prepared as part of the efforts of the progressive wing of the Catholic church to respond to the black movement (see chapter 7).

19. "Negros unem-se e obtem vitória contra racismo," *Folha de São Paulo* (January 10, 1981); "Negro luta contra discriminação na escola," *Jornal do País* (May 9–15, 1985), p. 9; "No 'Projeto Zumbi,' a voz da cultura negra," *Folha de São Paulo* (November 15, 1984), p. 33; "No brilho da cor," *Istoé,* (November 28, 1984), p. 49. A black cultural week was also held in Rio during November 16–25, 1984, to coincide with Zumbi Day. Though no state support was forthcoming for the event, a number of Brazil's most important companies, including the Pão de Açucar supermarket chain and Braspetro, contributed. "A Kizomba de Martinho, festa das artes negras," *Folha de São Paulo* (October 31, 1984), p. 39.

20. The ministry's planning for the centennial got off to a rough start when it appointed a commission headed by the grandson of Princess Isabel, and containing not a single Afro-Brazilian member. After protests from black organizations, the planning commission was dissolved and reconstituted under the directorship of black lawyer Carlos Moura.

21. So intense was this debate that it even attracted attention in the United States press, which would not normally report on the celebration of a national holiday in a Latin American country. "Brazil's Blacks Pressing for Real Equality," *Wall Street Journal* (May 11, 1988), p. 18; "Brazil's Blacks Feel Prejudice 100 Years after Slavery's End," *New York Times* (May 14, 1988), pp. 1, 6; "Brazil's Blacks Look Anew at the Issue of Race," *Washington Post* (May 13, 1988), p. A25; "Brazil: No Equality for Blacks Yet," *Los Angeles Times* (April 9, 1988), p. 1; and the report "Slavery in Brazil," *Morning Edition*, National Public Radio (May 29, 1988).

22. This skepticism is nicely conveyed by the title of a magazine produced by the Working Group on Afro-Brazilian Affairs of the São Paulo Secretariat of Education. Intended for distribution to teachers and students in the São Paulo public schools, the magazine was entitled *Salve o 13 de maio?,* thus turning the traditional cheer ("Long live May 13," or "[God] save May 13") into a question.

23. *Sambas de enredo* (Rio de Janeiro, 1988). Clearly times had changed since 1962, when the same school had paraded to "Casa grande e senzala," a samba inspired by Gilberto Freyre's classic work:

> Black slaves and masters
> made brothers by the same ideal—
> to tame the vast unconquered corners,
> attempting to evolve,
> to achieve together their emancipation,
> working in the canefields,
> mines and coffee plantations.
>
> In the fields and on the farms
> they struggled valiantly,
> consolidating their sovereignty.
> And these brave men with love and tenderness
> forgot their hard life in parties of rare splendor.
> In elegant salons the young ladies and masters danced.
> And in the slave quarters the slaves sang,
> beating on their drums.

Praise and glory to these strong people   -
who helped to build the riches of our Brazil,
my Brazil.

Alison Raphael, "Samba and Social Control: Popular Culture and Racial Democracy in Brazil" (Ph.D. dissertation, Columbia University, 1980), p. 214.

24. See, for example, the broadside distributed at the May 13 march in São Paulo by the Black Union and Consciousness Group, an organization connected with the progressive wing of the Catholic church. "We carry in the streets today our sign of denunciation, and the affirmation of ONE HUNDRED YEARS OF A LIE." "13 de maio de 1988," Grupo de União e Consciéncia Negra–São Paulo.

25. "A República Negra da Bahia," *Afinal* (February 9, 1988), pp. 53–61; "Inspiração na África," *Istoé* (April 20, 1988), pp. 34–38; "Na Bahia ha protestos em outdoors," *Folha de São Paulo* (May 9, 1988), p. 13; "Negros queimam retrato da princesa," *Folha de São Paulo* (May 13, 1988), p. 13.

26. See chapter 7, note 59.

27. "Marcha dos negros mobiliza grande aparato militar," *Jornal do Brasil* (May 12, 1988), p. 14-a; "Quatro mil negros saem em passeata contra o 13 de maio," *O Globo* (May 12, 1988), p. 8; "No Rio, marcha de negro é barrada pela polícia," *Folha de São Paulo* (May 12, 1988), p. 14.

28. "TV Educativa cancela debate sobre abolição," *O Estado de São Paulo* (May 14, 1988), p. 36.

29. "Queremos trabalho, queremos emprego! O 13 de maio não é dia de negro!" "Congresso comemora abolição," *O Globo* (May 13, 1988), p. 6.

30. "Abolição é exemplo de congraçamento e união," *O Globo* (May 14, 1988), p. 2.

31. Florestan Fernandes, "O 13 de maio," *Folha de São Paulo* (May 13, 1988), p. 3.

32. The International Congress on Slavery did include sessions on postabolition conditions and present-day race relations in Brazil, but, as its title suggests, its emphasis was overwhelmingly on the experience of slavery. On the initial planning for the event, see "A escravidão nas Américas," in the *Caderno de Programas e Leituras, Jornal da Tarde* (January 5, 1985), p. 5. For a survey of the scholarly studies that were published in conjunction with the centennial which makes quite clear those studies' focus on slavery, see Robert M. Levine, " 'Turning on the Lights': Brazilian Slavery Reconsidered One Hundred Years after Abolition," *Latin American Research Review* 24, 2 (1989), pp. 201–217.

33. One of the more curious articles was an interview with Dr. Eliane Azevedo, the rector of the Federal University of Bahia, who responded to a series of questions concerning which stereotypes about blacks were true and which were not. For example, according to Dr. Azevedo, blacks do not have larger penes than whites, but they do tend to have longer legs, which makes them more suited for sports. "Médica diz o que é verdade nos mitos sobre os negros," *Folha de São Paulo* (May 9, 1988), p. 12.

34. The theme of *alegria* found its way into President Sarney's radio address. "I remember a sunny morning when I visited the Cape Verde Islands: the multitudes in the plaza, their colorful dress. And I discovered there, in the midst

of those chanting people, that Brazil's *alegria* came from Africa." Sarney had made a similar point two days earlier, upon being presented with the first copy of the *Guide to Sources on the History of Africa*, prepared by the National Archive in honor of May 13. "One cannot understand the *alegria* of the Brazilian people unless one understands that it came on the winds from Africa." "Maestro acusa a Bossa Nova de racista," *Folha de São Paulo* (May 12, 1988), p. 14. The *alegria* theme emerged in particularly undiluted form in an ad taken out by General Motors of Brazil to commemorate the centennial and black contributions to Brazilian life: "That smile, that walk, that music, that spice of life, that accent, that dancing, that *alegria*. . . ."

35. On the role of racial democracy as a defuser of racial and social tension, see Bolivar Lamounier, "Raça e classe na política brasileira," *Cadernos Brasileiros* 47 (1968), pp. 39–50.

36. For an example of such efforts, see the collection of essays *Reflexões*, by the black writers' collective Quilombhoje (a combination of the Portuguese words "*quilombo*" and "*hoje*," "today"). The collective's members denounce the Brazilian tendency "to 'sell' blacks as eternally happy, smiling beings, treated as the court jester: 'dance the samba for me, blacks, I know you're good at that.'" One of the challenges facing black writers, they argue, is for them to find a way to destroy this stereotype and display their anger, "spitting in the face of those who wish to keep us eternally submerged in a foolish and alienating happiness." P. 65; see also 13–14. Concerning the image of Afro-Brazilians as happy *sambistas*, see noted black songwriter and performer Gilberto Gil's caustic comments on the constant pressure he has experienced during his career to be "o bom crioulo puxador de samba." Anélio Barreto, "Este mundo é dos brancos?" *Afinal* (July 23, 1985), p. 13.

37. ". . . e o Sr. Ministro," *O Globo* (May 13, 1988), p. 4.

38. Clearly the Second Republic came much closer than the First to meeting the minimum requirements of a democratic political system. Even under the Second Republic, however, illiterates, who remained a majority of the population through the 1950s, were denied suffrage and thus excluded from political participation.

39. This point is stressed in Silvio Duncan Baretta and John Markoff, "Brazil's *Abertura*: A Transition from What to What?" in James M. Malloy and Mitchell A. Seligson, eds., *Authoritarians and Democrats: Regime Transition in Latin America* (Pittsburgh, 1987), particularly pp. 53–57.

40. See chapter 1, note 11.

41. Furtado, an economist, had served as minister of planning under the left-wing populist administration of President João Goulart (1961–1964), and had spent much of the period of the dictatorship in exile in France.

42. "Vem ai cem anos de ebulição," *A Gazeta* (May 13, 1988), p. 13; "Prêmio Nobel cobra mais ação contra apartheid," *Folha de São Paulo* (May 13, 1988), p. 11. Furtado resigned his position as minister of culture a month after the centennial; I have no evidence that his proposal was ever put into practice.

43. "Cem anos, sem quasi nada," *Istoé* (April 20, 1988), pp. 30–33; "Na segunda classe," *Veja* (May 11, 1988), pp. 22–30.

44. "Cem anos depois," *Folha de São Paulo* (May 13, 1988), p. 2; "Cem anos

de solidão," *Caderno B, Jornal do Brasil* (May 8, 1988), p. 8; "Another Myth Bites the Dust," *The Brasilians* (May-June 1988), p. 2. For other denunciations of racial inequality in Brazil, see the supplements "Abolição: 100 anos," *Diário Popular* (May 12, 1988); "Vem ai cem anos de ebulição," *A Gazeta* (May 13, 1988), pp. 13-18; "Brasil: Os negros, hoje," *Manchete* (May 21, 1988), pp. 4-9; and the press release prepared by the São Paulo state statistical service, SEADE, "Os negros e a discriminação racial no mercado de trabalho" (May 12, 1988).

45. "A verdadeira discriminação," *O Globo* (May 13, 1988), p. 4; "A mulata e Dom Miguel," *Caderno B, Jornal do Brasil* (May 8, 1988), p. 2.

46. "Qual é a cor do racismo," *Senhor* (May 20, 1986), pp. 11-12. This white fear of black crime is deftly satirized in Luis Fernando Veríssimo's short story "The Robbery," in which a white middle-class couple mistake a black delivery boy for a robber and insist on giving the bewildered teenager all the money and jewels in the apartment in order to save their lives. After he leaves, still insisting that all he wanted was to pick up some soda bottles, "the maid spread word of the robbery through the building. The wife had an attack of nerves which lasted for days. The husband said that it was impossible to live in the city any more. But all in all, he felt that things had worked out well. He hadn't panicked. He had won the bandit over. He had protected his home from violence." Luis Fernando Veríssimo, "O assalto," *O analista de Bagé* (Porto Alegre, 1984), pp. 75-78.

47. "Sob acusação de racismo, GAP afasta integrante," *Folha de São Paulo* (August 11, 1982). When the contents of the report were made public, Governor Maluf fired its author, economist Benedito Pio da Silva. The report was erroneous, incidentally, in asserting that residents of Washington, D.C., do not vote. They elect local officials and nonvoting delegates to Congress, and also vote in presidential elections.

48. "Quatro mil negros saem em passeata contra o 13 de maio," *O Globo* (May 12, 1988), p. 8; "Os ardis da Lei Afonso Arinos," *Caderno B, Jornal do Brasil* (May 8, 1988), p. 5. See also São Paulo's *Diário Popular*, which expressed support for the black movement, but only as long as the movement conducts itself "in an easy-going manner, in keeping with our [Brazilian] way of being." Blacks must "orient their struggle correctly, so that their racial and cultural characteristics can be integrated tranquilly into our social fabric, like so many other races and cultures that came here and live together with us." "A luta pela liberdade," *Abolição: 100 anos, Diário Popular* (May 12, 1988), p. 2.

49. "Democracia racial, o mito e o desejo," *Folhetim, Folha de São Paulo* (June 8, 1980), p. 7.

50. "Romance entre Marcos Paulo e Zezé Motta divide opinião pública," *Contigo* (February 11, 1985), pp. 3-5; "Discussão sobre racismo em horário nobre," *Jornal do Brasil* (May 26, 1985).

51. This is a paraphrase of King's comments following his 1957 visit to Ghana. David J. Garrow, *Bearing the Cross: Martin Luther King, Jr., and the Southern Christian Leadership Conference* (New York, 1986), p. 91.

52. For accounts of the day, see "Negros divididos denunciam racismo," *O Estado de São Paulo* (May 14, 1988), p. 36; "Caminhada de luta leva seis mil a Sé," *Diário Popular* (May 14, 1988), p. 12; "Divergências marcam atos do 13 de maio," *Folha de São Paulo* (May 14, 1988), p. 13.

Chapter 9. Looking Back, Looking Forward

1. Charles H. Wood and José Alberto Magno de Carvalho, *The Demography of Inequality in Brazil* (Cambridge and New York, 1988).

2. Fundação Carlos Chagas, *Diagnóstico sobre a situação educacional de negros (pretos e pardos) no Estado de São Paulo* (São Paulo, 1986); *Raça negra e educação, Cadernos de Pesquisa* 63 (Fundação Carlos Chagas) (São Paulo, 1987).

3. See the studies cited in chapter 6, note 20.

4. If anything, Brazilian state agencies are formally committed to the rigorous combatting of negative racial stereotypes. On occasion, however, they do slip up. During the early 1980s, as part of an advertising campaign to persuade paulistas to pay their taxes, the municipality of São Paulo tried to capitalize on white fears of black crime by running a photograph of a black teenager aiming a handgun at the camera, with the caption "This is the least agreeable way to pay your taxes." And feminists and black activists both object to state tourist boards' exploitation of the image of the hot-blooded, sensual mulatta in their advertising campaigns to promote international and internal tourism.

5. The Brazilian census of 1990 should yield interesting data on this score.

6. See the articles cited in chapter 1, note 16.

7. "Tem muita favela? Vai ter mais," *Folha de São Paulo* (May 12, 1988), p. 15; "Brazil's Street Children: New Attempt at Rescue," *New York Times* (May 11, 1987), p. 7; "Racial Inequalities Are Now Being Challenged in Brazil," *Boston Globe* (September 3, 1987). See also Rosa Maria Fischer Ferreira, *Meninos da rua: Valores e expectativas de menores marginalizados em São Paulo* (São Paulo, n.d.).

8. José Arthur Gianotti, "Política pela política," *Folhetim, Folha de São Paulo* (March 10, 1985), p. 2.

9. "Governo constata trabalho escravo no interior do país," *Folha de São Paulo* (October 4, 1985), p. 11; "A escravidão hoje no Brasil," *Folha de São Paulo* (May 13, 1986), p. 3; "A escravidão no país do latifúndio," *Retrato do Brasil* (January 22, 1987), pp. 11–14.

10. "Projeto de Abdias defende acesso do negro ao trabalho," *Folha de São Paulo* (June 10, 1983); "Mobilização, a arma contra o preconceito," *Abolição: 100 anos, Diário Popular* (May 12, 1988), p. 7.

11. Blacks and "other races" constituted 12.3 percent of the national population in 1970: 25.1 million people out of a total population of 203.2 million. United States Bureau of the Census, *Statistical Abstract of the United States, 1975* (Washington, D.C., 1975), table 39, p. 34.

12. Similar perceptions among the white electorate in the United States appear to have played a significant role in the election of Republican administrations in the 1980s committed to rolling back the affirmative action and equal opportunity programs of the previous decade. On the undoing of those programs see the series of front-page articles in the *Wall Street Journal* (October 22, 24, 28, 1985). This change in orientation in federal policy did not escape the notice of the Brazilian press; on the racial policies of the Reagan years, see "A volta (discreta) do racismo," *Jornal do Brasil* (September 23, 1987).

Former São Paulo black congressman Adalberto Camargo (1967–1983) expresses the zero-sum feeling which characterizes much of Brazilian life, and which motivates white resistance to black advancement. "The spaces within the organization of Brazilian society are all occupied. On the day that we [blacks] succeed in occupying one, we're going to dislodge somebody." Haroldo Costa, *Fala, crioulo* (Rio de Janeiro, 1982), p. 65.

13. "Let's say that that cynicism is born on the right. But the truth is that it then generalizes itself [throughout the society] and ends up affecting everyone." Francisco Weffort, *Por que democracia?* (São Paulo, 1984), p. 53. Historian José Murilho de Carvalho discusses the Brazilian "mentality of irreverence, mockery, sarcasm. . . . Those who let themselves be guided by appearances were *naifs*. They could only be objects of mockery and scorn." *Os bestializados: O Rio de Janeiro e a República que não foi* (São Paulo, 1987), pp. 159–160.

14. J. G., "Racismo," *Folha de São Paulo* (June 5, 1980), p. 2.

15. The most recent example of such consequences can be seen in the events following the extension of suffrage to illiterates in 1985, which instituted universal adult suffrage for the first time in Brazilian history. The results of this development were the unexpected victories of Workers' Party candidates in the mayoral elections of 1988, and the surprisingly strong performance in the 1989 presidential elections of Workers' Party candidate Luis Inácio "Lula" da Silva. A former metalworker with a grade-school education, and a committed socialist, Silva is the antithesis of Brazil's traditional political elite and of the presidential candidates fielded by that elite. He nevertheless confounded all expectations by winning 47 percent of the national vote, nearly becoming Brazil's first worker-president.

Selected Bibliography

Archives
See Appendix C.

Newspapers and Periodicals
I found many of the newspaper and magazine articles cited in the text in clipping files maintained by the newspaper *O Estado de São Paulo* (see Appendix B, note 12), and by the Centro Pastoral Vergueiro. The files maintained by those two entities complement each other nicely. The archivists at *O Estado* clip mainly from mainstream, establishment publications, whereas the librarians at the Centro Pastoral Vergueiro draw much of their material from the alternative press produced by labor unions, the progressive wing of the Catholic church, and community and civic organizations.

In addition to those two sources, I also read the following publications for the years indicated.

Mainstream, establishment press

Correio de São Paulo. São Paulo. 1933
Diário de São Paulo. São Paulo. 1931.
Diário Nacional. São Paulo. 1928, 1932.
Diário Popular. São Paulo. 1889, 1897.
O Estado de São Paulo. São Paulo. 1892–1893, 1898–1901, 1917.
Folha da Noite. São Paulo. 1932.
A Gazeta. São Paulo. 1928, 1933.

State publication

Boletim do Departamento Estadual do Trabalho. São Paulo. 1912–1922.

Afro-Brazilian press

O Alfinete. São Paulo. 1918–1919, 1921.
Alvorada. São Paulo. 1945–1948.

Árvore das Palavras. São Paulo. 1974.
Auriverde. São Paulo. 1928.
O Baluarte. Campinas. 1904.
O Bandeirante. São Paulo. 1918–1919.
Chibata. São Paulo. 1932.
O Clarim. São Paulo. 1935.
O Clarim da Alvorada. São Paulo. 1924–1932.
Correio d'Ébano. Campinas. 1963.
Cruzada Cultural. São Paulo. 1948.
Elite. São Paulo. 1924.
O Estímulo. São Carlos. 1935.
Evolução. São Paulo. 1933.
Getulino. Campinas. 1923–1924. São Paulo. 1926.
Hífen. Campinas. 1960–1962.
Jornal do Conselho da Comunidade Negra. São Paulo. 1985–1988.
Jornegro. São Paulo. 1979.
O Kosmos. São Paulo. 1922–1925.
A Liberdade. São Paulo. 1919–1920.
O Menelik. São Paulo. 1915–1916.
Mundo Novo. São Paulo. 1950.
O Mutirão. São Paulo. 1958.
Niger. São Paulo. 1960.
Nosso Jornal. Piracicaba. 1961.
Notícias de Ébano. Santos. 1957.
O Novo Horizonte. 1946, 1947, 1954, 1958, 1961.
O Patrocínio. Piracicaba. 1928.
Progresso. São Paulo. 1928–1931.
Quilombo. Rio de Janeiro. 1950.
A Raça. Uberlândia, Minas Gerais. 1935.
Redenção. Rio de Janeiro. 1950.
A Rua. São Paulo. 1916.
A Sentinella. São Paulo. 1920.
Senzala. São Paulo. 1946.
Sinba. Rio de Janeiro. 1977, 1979.
Tribuna Negra. São Paulo. 1935.
União. Curitiba. 1948.
A Voz da Raça. São Paulo. 1933–1937.
O Xauter. São Paulo. 1916.

Labor press

O Amigo do Povo. São Paulo. 1902–1904.
Aurora. São Paulo. 1905.
Aurora Social. Santos. 1910–1911.
O Carpinteiro. São Paulo. 1905.
O Combate. São Paulo. 1915–1918, 1928.
Diário Trabalhista. Rio de Janeiro. 1946.

O Dois de Fevereiro. Santos. 1905.
Folha do Braz. São Paulo. 1899–1901.
Germinal! São Paulo. 1913.
El Grito del Pueblo. São Paulo. 1899.
O Grito do Povo. São Paulo. 1900.
O Grito Operário. São Paulo. 1919–1920.
O Internacional. São Paulo. 1921–1922.
Jornal Operário. 1905.
A Lucta Proletária. 1908.
Palestra Social. São Paulo. 1901.
A Plebe. São Paulo. 1917–1920, 1935.
O Proletário. Santos. 1911.
Rebate. São Paulo. 1898.

Other Sources

Adamo, Sam. "The Broken Promise: Race, Health, and Justice in Rio de Janeiro, 1890–1940." Ph.D. dissertation, University of New Mexico, 1983.
Alden, Dauril. "Late Colonial Brazil." In Leslie Bethell, ed., *Cambridge History of Latin America*, Vol. 2. Cambridge and New York, 1984.
Almeida, Maria Suely Kofes de. "Entre nós, os pobres, eles, os negros." *Dissertação de mestrado*, Universidade Estadual de Campinas, 1976.
Uma alternativa democrática para a crise brasileira. São Paulo, 1984.
Alves, Maria Helena Moreira. *State and Opposition in Military Brazil.* Austin, 1985.
Alvin, Zuleika M. Forcioni. "Emigração, família e luta: Os italianos em São Paulo, 1870–1920." *Dissertação de mestrado*, Universidade de São Paulo, 1983.
Amaral, Raul Joviano. *Os pretos do Rosário de São Paulo.* São Paulo, 1954.
Andrews, George Reid. "Comparing the Comparers: White Supremacy in the United States and South Africa." *Journal of Social History* 20, 3 (1987): 585–599.
Andrews, George Reid. "Latin American Workers." *Journal of Social History* 21, 2 (1987): 311–326.
Andrews, George Reid. "Race and State in Colonial Brazil." *Latin American Research Review* 19, 3 (1984): 203–216.
Arcaya U., Pedro M. *Insurrección de los negros de la serranía de Coro.* Caracas, 1949.
Azevedo, Célia Maria Marinho de. *Onda negra, medo branco: O negro no imaginário das elites—século XIX.* Rio de Janeiro, 1987.
Azevedo, Thales de. *Democracia racial.* Petrópolis, 1975.
Barbosa, Irene Maria F. *Socialização e relações raciais: Um estudo de família negra em Campinas.* São Paulo, 1983.
Baretta, Silvio Duncan, and John Markoff. "Brazil's *Abertura:* A Transition from What to What?" In James M. Malloy and Mitchell A. Seligson, eds.,

Authoritarians and Democrats: Regime Transition in Latin America. Pittsburgh, 1987.

Baretta, Silvio Duncan, and John Markoff. "The Limits of the Brazilian Revolution of 1930." *Review* 9, 3 (1986): 416–435.

Barman, Roderick J. *Brazil: The Forging of a Nation, 1798–1852.* Stanford, 1988.

Bastide, Roger. "The Development of Race Relations in Brazil." In Guy Hunter, ed., *Industrialisation and Race Relations: A Symposium.* London, 1965.

Bastide, Roger. *Estudos afro-brasileiros.* São Paulo, 1973.

Bastide, Roger, and Florestan Fernandes. *Brancos e negros em São Paulo.* 3rd edition, São Paulo, 1971.

Beiguelman, Paula. *Os companheiros de São Paulo.* São Paulo, 1977.

Beiguelman, Paula. *Formação do povo no compleixo cafeeiro: Aspectos políticos.* 2nd edition, São Paulo, 1977.

Bell, Rudolph M. *Fate and Honor, Family and Village: Demographic and Cultural Change in Rural Italy since 1800.* Chicago, 1979.

Bethell, Leslie. *The Abolition of the Brazilian Slave Trade: Britain, Brazil, and the Slave Trade Question, 1807–1869.* Cambridge and New York, 1970.

Bethell, Leslie, ed. *Cambridge History of Latin America.* 4 vols. Cambridge and New York, 1984–1986.

Bethell, Leslie, and José Murilo de Carvalho. "Brazil from Independence to the Middle of the Nineteenth Century." In Bethell, *Cambridge History of Latin America,* Vol. 3. Cambridge and New York, 1985.

Bicudo, Virgínia Leone. "Atitudes raciais de pretos e mulatos em São Paulo." *Sociologia* 11, 3 (1947): 195–219.

Bomilcar, Alvaro. *O preconceito de raça no Brasil.* Rio de Janeiro, 1916.

Bosi, Eclea. *Memória e sociedade: Lembranças de velhos.* São Paulo, 1977.

Brandão, Maria de Azevedo. "Conversa de branco: Questões e não-questões da literatura sobre relações raciais." *Revista de Cultura Vozes* 73, 3 (1979): 27–36.

Britto, Iêda Marques. *Samba na cidade de São Paulo (1900–1930): Um exercício de resistência cultural.* São Paulo, 1986.

Bruno, Ernani Silva. *História e tradições da cidade de São Paulo.* 3 vol. 3rd edition, São Paulo, 1984.

Burns, E. Bradford. *A History of Brazil.* New York, 1970.

Caldeira, Teresa Pires do Rio. "Houses of Respect." Paper presented at the International Congress of the Latin American Studies Association, Boston, October 1986.

Cándido Mello e Souza, Antônio. *Os parceiros do Rio Bonito.* São Paulo, 1979.

Cano, Wilson. *Raizes da concentração industrial em São Paulo.* 2nd edition, São Paulo, 1977.

Cardoso, Fernando Henrique. *Capitalismo e escravidão no Brasil meridional: O negro na sociedade escravocrata do Rio Grande do Sul.* São Paulo, 1962.

Cardoso, Fernando Henrique, and Octávio Ianni. *Côr e mobilidade social em Florianópolis.* São Paulo, 1960.

Carneiro, Edison. *O quilombo dos Palmares.* São Paulo, 1947.

Carone, Edgar. *Movimento operário no Brasil, 1877–1944.* São Paulo, 1979.

Carone, Edgar. *O PCB (1922-1943)*. São Paulo, 1982.

Carvalho, José Murilo de. *Os bestializados: O Rio de Janeiro e a República que não foi*. São Paulo, 1987.

Carvalho, José Murilo de. *A construção da ordem: A elite política imperial*. Rio de Janeiro, 1980.

Carvalho, José Murilo de. *Teatro de sombras: A política imperial*. São Paulo, 1988.

Castro, Cláudio de Moura. "O que está acontecendo com a educação no Brasil?" In Edmar Lisboa Bacha and Herbert S. Klein, eds., *A transição incompleta: Brasil desde 1945*. 2 vols. São Paulo, 1986.

Cell, John W. *The Highest Stage of White Supremacy: The Origins of Segregation in South Africa and the American South*. Cambridge and New York, 1982.

Chaia, Miguel W. "Discriminação racial." *Revista Fundação SEADE* 2, 2-3 (1986): 7-14.

Chalhoub, Sidney. "Slaves, Freedmen and the Politics of Freedom in Brazil: The Experience of Blacks in the City of Rio." Paper presented at the Conference on the Meaning of Freedom, Greensburg, Pa., August 1988.

Chalhoub, Sidney. *Trabalho, lar e botequim: O cotidiano dos trabalhadores no Rio de Janeiro da Belle Époque*. São Paulo, 1986.

Comissão dos Religiosos, Seminaristas e Padres Negros—Rio de Janeiro. "*Ouvi o clamor deste povo*". . . *negro*. Petrópolis, 1987.

Conrad, Robert E. *The Destruction of Brazilian Slavery, 1850-1888*. Berkeley, 1972.

Conrad, Robert E. *World of Sorrow: The African Slave Trade to Brazil*. Baton Rouge, 1986.

Conrad, Robert E., ed. *Children of God's Fire: A Documentary History of Black Slavery in Brazil*. Princeton, 1983.

Conselho Estadual da Condição Feminina. *Mulheres operárias*. São Paulo, 1985.

Contador, Cláudio, and Cláudio Haddad. "Produção real, moeda e preços: A experiência brasileira no período 1861-1970." *Revista Brasileira de Estatística* 36 (1975): 407-440.

Costa, Emília Viotti da. *A abolição*. São Paulo, 1982.

Costa, Emília Viotti da. *The Brazilian Empire: Myths and Histories*. Chicago, 1985.

Costa, Emília Viotti da. *Da senzala à colônia*. 2nd edition, São Paulo, 1982.

Costa, Haroldo. *Fala, crioulo*. Rio de Janeiro, 1982.

Costa, Iraci del Nero da, Robert W. Slenes, and Stuart B. Schwartz. "A família escrava em Lorena (1801)." *Estudos Econômicos* 17, 2 (1987): 245-296.

Couceiro, Solange M. *O negro na televisão de São Paulo: Um estudo de relações raciais*. São Paulo, 1983.

Couty, Louis. *O Brasil em 1884: Esboços sociológicos*. Rio de Janeiro, 1984.

Cunha, Euclides da. *Rebellion in the Backlands*. Chicago, 1944.

Curtin, Philip. *The Atlantic Slave Trade: A Census*. Madison, 1969.

Daffert, F. W. *Coleção dos trabalhos agrícolas extraidos dos relatórios annuaes de 1888-1893, do Instituto Agronômico do Estado de S. Paulo (Brasil) em Campinas*. São Paulo, 1895.

Damasceno, Caetana, et al. *Catálogo de entidades de movimento negro no Brasil*. Rio de Janeiro, 1988.

da Matta, Roberto. *Carnavais, malandros, e heróis*. Rio de Janeiro, 1978.

da Matta, Roberto. *A casa e a rua: Espaço, cidadania, mulher e morte no Brasil*. São Paulo, 1985.

Dassin, Joan, ed. *Torture in Brazil*. New York, 1986.

Davies, Robert H. *Capital, State and White Labour in South Africa, 1900–1960*. Atlantic Highlands, N.J., 1979.

Davis, David Brion. *The Problem of Slavery in the Age of Revolution, 1770–1823*. Ithaca, 1975.

Davis, David Brion. *Slavery and Human Progress*. New York, 1984.

Dean, Warren. "A industrialização durante a República Velha." In Boris Fausto, ed., *O Brasil republicano: Estrutura de poder e economia*. 3rd edition, São Paulo, 1982.

Dean, Warren. *The Industrialization of São Paulo, 1880–1945*. Austin, 1969.

Dean, Warren. *Rio Claro: A Brazilian Plantation System, 1820–1920*. Stanford, 1976.

Degler, Carl. *Neither Black nor White: Slavery and Race Relations in Brazil and the United States*. New York, 1971.

della Cava, Ralph. "The 'People's Church,' the Vatican, and *Abertura*." In Alfred Stepan, *Democratizing Brazil: Problems of Transition and Consolidation*. New York, 1989.

Denis, Pierre. *Brazil*. London, 1911.

DeShazo, Peter. *Urban Workers in Chile, 1902–1927*. Madison, 1983.

Diacon, Todd Alan. "Capitalists and Fanatics: Brazil's Contestado Rebellion, 1912–1916." Ph.D. dissertation, University of Wisconsin–Madison, 1987.

Dickenson, John P. *Brazil*. Boulder, 1978.

Directoria Geral de Estatística. *Recenseamento da população do Império do Brasil a que se procedeu no dia 1º de agosto de 1872. Quadros geraes*. Rio de Janeiro, 1873.

Directoria Geral de Estatística. *Recenseamento do Brasil realizado em 1º de setembro de 1920*. 5 vols. Rio de Janeiro, 1922–1926.

Directoria Geral de Estatística. *Synopse do recenseamento de 31 de dezembro de 1890*. Rio de Janeiro, 1898.

"Discurso do representante da Frente Negra Pelotense." In *Estudos afro-brasileiros*. Rio de Janeiro, 1935.

Dreifuss, René Armand. *1964: A conquista do estado*. 2nd edition, Petrópolis, 1981.

Drescher, Seymour. "Brazilian Abolition in Comparative Perspective." *Hispanic American Historical Review* 68, 3 (1988): 429–460.

Dwyer, Jeffrey W., and Peggy Lovell. "The Cost of Being Nonwhite in Brazil." *Sociology and Social Research* 72 (1988): 136–142.

Dwyer, Jeffrey W., and Peggy Lovell Webster. "Wage Differentials and Racial Discrimination in São Paulo, Brazil." Manuscript, 1987.

Elliott, Lilian E. *Brazil: Today and Tomorrow*. Rpt., New York, 1922.

Erickson, Kenneth. *The Brazilian Corporative State and Working-Class Politics*. Berkeley, 1977.

"Estatística." *Boletim do Departamento Estadual de Estatística* 1, 1 (1939): 74–105.

Fausto, Boris. *Crime e cotidiano: A criminalidade em São Paulo (1880–1924)*. São Paulo, 1984.

Fausto, Boris. *A revolução de 1930*. São Paulo, 1970.

Fausto, Boris. *Trabalho urbano e conflito social, 1890–1920*. São Paulo, 1977.

Fernandes, Florestan. "Beyond Poverty: The Negro and the Mulatto in Brazil." In Robert Brent Toplin, *Slavery and Race Relations in Latin America*. New York, 1974.

Fernandes, Florestan. *Circuito fechado*. São Paulo, 1977.

Fernandes, Florestan. "Immigration and Race Relations in São Paulo." In Magnus Morner, ed., *Race and Class in Latin America*. New York, 1970.

Fernandes, Florestan. *A integração do negro na sociedade de classes*. 2 vols. 3rd edition, São Paulo, 1978.

Fernandes, Florestan. *The Negro in Brazilian Society*. New York, 1969.

Fernandes, Florestan. "The Negro in Brazilian Society: Twenty-Five Years Later." In Maxine L. Margolis and William E. Carter, eds., *Brazil: Anthropological Perspectives*. New York, 1979.

Fernandes, Florestan. *O negro no mundo dos brancos*. São Paulo, 1972.

Fernandes, Florestan. *A revolução burguesa no Brasil*. São Paulo, 1974.

Fernandes, Florestan. "The Weight of the Past." In John Hope Franklin, ed., *Color and Race*. Boston, 1969.

Ferrara, Miriam Nicolau. *A imprensa negra paulista (1915–1963)*. São Paulo, 1986.

Ferreira, Maria Nazareth. *A imprensa operária no Brasil, 1880–1920*. Petrópolis, 1978.

Ferreira, Rosa Maria Fischer. *Meninos da rua: Valores e expectativas de menores marginalizados em São Paulo*. São Paulo, n.d.

Ferreira, Sylvio José B. R. "A questão racial em Pernambuco: A necessidade e os impasses de uma ação política organizada." Paper presented at the annual conference of the Associação Nacional de Pós-Graduação e Pesquisa em Ciências Sociais (ANPOCS), Novo Friburgo, 1981.

Flory, Thomas. *Judge and Jury in Imperial Brazil, 1808–1871*. Austin, 1981.

Flynn, Peter. *Brazil: A Political Analysis*. Boulder, Colo., 1979.

Foerster, Robert F. *The Italian Emigration of Our Times*. Cambridge, Mass., 1919.

Foner, Eric. *Nothing But Freedom: Emancipation and Its Legacy*. Baton Rouge, 1983.

Foner, Philip S., and Ronald L. Lewis, eds. *Black Workers: A Documentary History from Colonial Times to the Present*. Philadelphia, 1988.

Fontaine, Pierre-Michel. "Research in the Political Economy of Afro-Latin America." *Latin American Research Review* 12, 1 (1980): 111–141.

Fontaine, Pierre-Michel, ed. *Race, Class, and Power in Brazil*. Los Angeles, 1985.

Fox-Genovese, Elizabeth, and Eugene Genovese. "The Political Crisis of Social History: A Marxian Perspective." *Journal of Social History* 10, 2 (1976): 205–220.

Fragoso, João Luis R., and Manolo G. Florentino. "Marcelino, filho de Inocência Crioula, neto de Joana Cabinda: Um estudo sobre famílias escravas em Paraíba do Sul (1835–1872)." *Estudos Econômicos* 17, 2 (1987): 151–174.

Franco, Maria Sylvia de Carvalho. *Homens livres na ordem escravocrata*. São Paulo, 1969.

Fredrickson, George M. *White Supremacy: A Study in American and South African History*. New York, 1981.

Freitas, Décio. *Palmares, a guerra dos escravos*. Rpt., São Paulo, 1982.

French, John David. "Industrial Workers and the Origins of Populist Politics in the ABC Region of Greater São Paulo, Brazil, 1900–1950." Ph.D. dissertation, Yale University, 1985.

"Frente Negra Brasileira, 1930–1937." Collaborative *trabalho de pesquisa*, Pontifícia Universidade Católica–São Paulo, 1985.

Freyre, Gilberto. *Brazil: An Interpretation*. New York, 1945.

Freyre, Gilberto. *The Mansions and the Shanties: The Making of Modern Brazil*. New York, 1963.

Freyre, Gilberto. *The Masters and the Slaves: A Study in the Development of Brazilian Civilization*. New York, 1946.

Freyre, Gilberto. *New World in the Tropics*. New York, 1959.

Freyre, Gilberto. *Order and Progress: Brazil from Monarchy to Republic*. New York, 1970.

Fundação Carlos Chagas. *Diagnóstico sobre a situação educacional de negros (pretos e pardos) no Estado de São Paulo*. São Paulo, 1986.

Garrow, David J. *Bearing the Cross: Martin Luther King, Jr., and the Southern Christian Leadership Conference*. New York, 1986.

Gitahy, Maria Lúcia Caira. "Os trabalhadores do porto de Santos, 1889–1910." *Tese de mestrado*, Universidade Estadual de Campinas, 1983.

Gonçalves, Francisco de Paula Lázaro. *Relatório apresentado à Associação Promotora de Immigração em Minas*. Juiz de Fora, 1888.

Gonzalez, Lélia. "The Unified Black Movement: A New Stage in Black Political Mobilization." In Pierre-Michel Fontaine, ed., *Race, Class and Power in Brazil*. Los Angeles, 1985.

Gorender, Jacob. *O escravismo colonial*. 3rd edition, São Paulo, 1980.

Graham, Lawrence. *Civil Service Reform in Brazil*. Austin, 1970.

Graham, Richard. "Brazilian Slavery Re-examined: A Review Article." *Journal of Social History* 3, 4 (1970): 431–453.

Graham, Richard. *Britain and the Onset of Modernization in Brazil, 1850–1914*. Cambridge and New York, 1968.

Graham, Richard. "Landowners and the Overthrow of the Empire." *Luso-Brazilian Review* 7, 2 (1970): 44–56.

Graham, Richard. *Patronage and Politics in Nineteenth-Century Brazil*. Stanford, 1990.

Graham, Richard. "Slave Families on a Rural Estate in Colonial Brazil." *Journal of Social History* 9, 3 (1976): 382–402.

Graham, Richard. "Slavery and Economic Development: Brazil and the United States South in the Nineteenth Century." *Comparative Studies in Society and History* 23, 4 (1981): 620–655.

Graham, Sandra Lauderdale. *House and Street: The Domestic World of Servants and Masters in Nineteenth-Century Rio de Janeiro*. Cambridge and New York, 1988.

Greenberg, Stanley B. *Race and State in Capitalist Development: Comparative Perspectives*. New Haven, 1980.

Haberly, David T. *Three Sad Races: Racial Identity and National Consciousness in Brazilian Literature*. Cambridge and New York, 1983.

Hahn, Steve. "Class and State in Postemancipation Societies: Southern Planters in Comparative Perspective." *American Historical Review* 95, 1 (1990): 75–98.

Hahner, June. *Poverty and Politics: The Urban Poor in Brazil, 1870–1920*. Albuquerque, 1986.

Hall, Jacquelyn Dowd, et al. *Like a Family: The Making of a Southern Cotton Mill World*. Chapel Hill, 1987.

Hall, Michael. "Immigration and the Early São Paulo Working Class." *Jahrbuch für Geschichte von Staat, Wirtschaft, und Gesellschaft Lateinamerikas* 12 (1975): 393–407.

Hall, Michael. "The Origins of Mass Immigration in Brazil, 1871–1914." Ph.D. dissertation, Columbia University, 1969.

Harris, Marvin. *Patterns of Race in the Americas*. New York, 1964.

Harris, William J. *The Harder We Run: Black Workers since the Civil War*. New York, 1982.

Hasenbalg, Carlos. *Discriminação e desigualdades raciais no Brasil*. Rio de Janeiro, 1979.

Hasenbalg, Carlos. "Race and Socioeconomic Inequality in Brazil." In Pierre-Michel Fontaine, ed., *Race, Class and Power in Brazil*. Los Angeles, 1985.

Hasenbalg, Carlos. "Race Relations in Post-Abolition Brazil: The Smooth Preservation of Racial Inequalities." Ph.D. dissertation, University of California–Berkeley, 1978.

Hays, Samuel. "Society and Politics: Politics and Society." *Journal of Interdisciplinary History* 15, 3 (1985): 481–499.

Hellwig, David J. "A New Frontier in a Racial Paradise: Robert S. Abbott's Brazilian Dream." *Luso-Brazilian Review* 25, 1 (1988): 59–67.

Holloway, Thomas. "The Brazilian 'Judicial Police' in Florianópolis, Santa Catarina, 1841–1871." *Journal of Social History* 20, 4 (1987): 733–756.

Holloway, Thomas. *Immigrants on the Land: Coffee and Society in São Paulo, 1886–1934*. Chapel Hill, 1980.

Holloway, Thomas. "Immigration and Abolition: The Transition from Slave to Free Labor in the São Paulo Coffee Zone." In Dauril Alden and Warren Dean, eds., *Essays Concerning the Socioeconomic History of Brazil and Portuguese India*. Gainesville, 1977.

Humphrey, John. *Capitalist Control and Workers' Struggle in the Brazilian Auto Industry*. Princeton, 1983.

Ianni, Octávio. *Escravidão e racismo*. São Paulo, 1978.

Ianni, Octávio. *Raças e classes sociais no Brasil*. 2nd edition, São Paulo, 1988.

Ianni, Octávio. *As metamorfoses do escravo: Apogeu e crise da escravatura no Brasil meridional*. São Paulo, 1962.

Imprensa negra. São Paulo, 1984.

Instituto Brasileiro de Geografia e Estatística (IBGE). *Recenseamento geral de 1940. Censo demográfico: Estado de São Paulo.* Rio de Janeiro, 1950.

Instituto Brasileiro de Geografia e Estatística (IBGE). *Recenseamento geral de 1940. Censo demográfico: Estados Unidos do Brasil.* Rio de Janeiro, 1950.

Instituto Brasileiro de Geografia e Estatística (IBGE). *Recenseamento geral de 1950. Censo demográfico: Estado de São Paulo.* Rio de Janeiro, 1954.

Instituto Brasileiro de Geografia e Estatística (IBGE). *Recenseamento geral de 1950. Censo demográfico: Estados Unidos do Brasil.* Rio de Janeiro, 1956.

Instituto Brasileiro de Geografia e Estatística (IBGE). *Recenseamento geral de 1960. Censo demográfico: Estado de São Paulo.* Rio de Janeiro, n.d.

Instituto Brasileiro de Geografia e Estatística (IBGE). *Recenseamento geral do Brasil—1980. Censo demográfico—dados gerais, migração, instrução, fecundidade, mortalidade—Brasil.* Rio de Janeiro, 1983.

Instituto Brasileiro de Geografia e Estatística (IBGE). *Recenseamento geral do Brasil—1980. Censo demográfico—dados gerais, migração, instrução, fecundidade, mortalidade—São Paulo.* Rio de Janeiro, 1982.

Instituto Brasileiro de Geografia e Estatística (IBGE). *Recenseamento geral do Brasil—1980. Censo demográfico—mão-de-obra—São Paulo.* Rio de Janeiro, 1983.

Jacino, Ramatis. *Histórico de uma candidatura operária.* São Paulo, 1987.

Jacobson, Julius, ed. *The Negro and the American Labor Movement.* Garden City, 1968.

Jesus, Carolina de. *Child of the Dark.* New York, 1962.

Johnstone, Frederick A. *Class, Race and Gold: A Study of Class Relations and Racial Discrimination in South Africa.* Lanham, Md., 1976.

Judt, Tony. "A Clown in Regal Purple: Social History and the Social Historians." *History Workshop* 7 (1979): 66–94.

Karasch, Mary C. *Slave Life in Rio de Janeiro, 1808–1850.* Princeton, 1987.

Keck, Margaret. "Lula and the Workers' Party: Emergence of a New Politics?" *Camões Center Quarterly* 2, 1–2 (1990): 13–15.

Keck, Margaret. "The New Unionism in the Brazilian Transition." In Alfred Stepan, ed., *Democratizing Brazil: Problems of Transition and Consolidation.* New York, 1989.

Kent, R. K. "Palmares: An African State in Brazil." *Journal of African History* 6, 2 (1965): 161–175.

Keremetsis, Eileen. "The Early Industrial Worker in Rio de Janeiro, 1870–1930." Ph.D. dissertation, Columbia University, 1982.

Kiernan, James P. "The Manumission of Slaves in Colonial Brazil: Paraty, 1789–1822." Ph.D. dissertation, New York University, 1976.

Klein, Herbert S. *The Middle Passage: Comparative Studies on the Atlantic Slave Trade.* Princeton, 1978.

Klein, Herbert S. "Nineteenth-Century Brazil." In David W. Cohen and Jack P. Greene, *Neither Slave nor Free: The Freedmen of African Descent in the Slave Societies of the New World.* Baltimore, 1972.

Kowarick, Lúcio. "The Subjugation of Labour: The Constitution of Capitalism in Brazil." Manuscript, 1985.

Kowarick, Lúcio. *Trabalho e vadiagem: A origem do trabalho livre no Brasil.* São Paulo, 1987.

Kramer, Jane. "Letter from the Elysian Fields." *The New Yorker* (March 2, 1987): 40–74.

Lamberg, Maurício. *O Brasil.* Rio de Janeiro, 1896.

Lamounier, Bolivar. "Raça e classe na política brasileira." *Cadernos Brasileiros* 47 (1968): 39–50.

Landes, Ruth. *The City of Women.* New York, 1947.

Lang, James. *Portuguese Brazil: The King's Plantation.* New York, 1979.

Lazzarotto, Valentim. *Pobres construtores de riqueza: Absorção da mão-de-obra e expansão industrial na Metalúrgica Abramo Eberle, 1905–1970.* Caxias do Sul, 1981.

Leeds, Anthony. "Brazilian Careers and Social Structure: An Evolutionary Model and Case History." *American Anthropologist* 66 (1964): 1321–1347.

Lever, Janet. *Soccer Madness.* Chicago, 1983.

Levi, Darrell E. *The Prados of São Paulo, Brazil: An Elite Family and Social Change, 1840–1930.* Athens, Ga., 1987.

Levine, Robert M. "'Mud-Hut Jerusalem': Canudos Revisited." *Hispanic American Historical Review* 68, 3 (1988): 525–572.

Levine, Robert M. "'Turning on the Lights': Brazilian Slavery Reconsidered One Hundred Years after Abolition." *Latin American Research Review* 24, 2 (1989): 201–217.

Levine, Robert M. *The Vargas Regime: The Critical Years, 1934–1938.* New York, 1970.

Lewin, Boleslao. "La 'conspiración de los franceses' en Buenos Aires (1795)." *Anuario del Instituto de Investigaciones Históricas* 4 (Rosario, 1960): 9–58.

Lewis, Jon. "South African Labor History: A Historiographical Assessment." *Radical History Review* 46–47 (1990): 213–236.

Libby, Douglas Cole. *Trabalho escravo e capital estrangeiro no Brasil: O caso do Morro Velho.* Belo Horizonte, 1984.

Lieberson, Stanley. *A Piece of the Pie: Blacks and White Immigrants since 1880.* Berkeley, 1980.

Litwack, Leon F. *Been in the Storm So Long: The Aftermath of Slavery.* New York, 1979.

Lobo, Roberto J. Haddock, and Irene Aloisi. *O negro na vida social brasileira.* São Paulo, 1941.

Love, Joseph L. "Political Participation in Brazil, 1881–1969." *Luso-Brazilian Review* 7, 2 (1970): 3–24.

Love, Joseph L. *São Paulo in the Brazilian Federation, 1889–1937.* Stanford, 1980.

Lovell, Peggy A. "Racial Inequality and the Brazilian Labor Market." Ph.D. dissertation, University of Florida, 1989.

Lowrie, Samuel Harman. "O elemento negro na população de São Paulo." *Revista do Arquivo Municipal de São Paulo* 4, 48 (1938): 5–56.

Macaulay, Neill. *The Prestes Column: Revolution in Brazil.* New York, 1974.

Machado, Maria Helena P. T. *Crime e escravidão: Trabalho, luta, resistência nas lavouras paulistas, 1830–1888.* São Paulo, 1987.

Maciel, Cleber da Silva. *Discriminações raciais: Negros em Campinas (1888–1921)*. Campinas, 1988.

Magnani, Silvia I. L. *O movimento anarquista em São Paulo*. São Paulo, 1982.

Mainwaring, Scott. *The Catholic Church and Politics in Brazil, 1916–1985*. Stanford, 1986.

Mainwaring, Scott. "Grassroots Popular Movements and the Struggle for Democracy." In Alfred Stepan, ed., *Democratizing Brazil: Problems of Transition and Consolidation*. New York, 1989.

Mallon, Florencia. *The Defense of Community in Peru's Central Highlands: Peasant Struggle and Capitalist Transition, 1860–1940*. Princeton, 1983.

Malloy, James M. *The Politics of Social Security in Brazil*. Pittsburgh, 1979.

Maram, Sheldon Leslie. *Anarquistas, imigrantes, e o movimento operário brasileiro, 1890–1920*. Rio de Janeiro, 1979.

Marcílio, Maria Luiza. "The Population of Colonial Brazil." In Leslie Bethell, ed., *Cambridge History of Latin America*, Volume 2. Cambridge and New York, 1984.

Marques, A. H. de Oliveira. *History of Portugal*. 2 vols. New York, 1976.

Mattoso, Katia M. de Queirós. *Ser escravo no Brasil*. São Paulo, 1982.

Meade, Teresa. "'Civilizing Rio de Janeiro': The Public Health Campaign and the Riot of 1904." *Journal of Social History* 20, 2 (1986): 301–322.

Meade, Teresa, and Gregory Alonso Pirio. "In Search of the Afro-American 'Eldorado': Attempts by North American Blacks to Enter Brazil in the 1920s." *Luso-Brazilian Review* 25, 1 (1988): 85–110.

Meier, August, and Elliott Rudwick. *From Plantation to Ghetto*. 3rd edition, New York, 1976.

Menucci, Sud. *O precursor do abolicionismo no Brasil: Luiz Gama*. São Paulo, 1938.

Merrick, Thomas W., and Douglas H. Graham. *Population and Economic Development in Brazil: 1800 to the Present*. Baltimore, 1979.

Mitchell, Michael. "Racial Consciousness and the Political Attitudes and Behavior of Blacks in São Paulo, Brazil." Ph.D. dissertation, Indiana University, 1977.

Monteiro, John M. "São Paulo in the Seventeenth Century: Society and Economy." Ph.D. dissertation, University of Chicago, 1985.

Monteiro, Jorge Aparecido. "Cor e trabalho na empresa pública: Uma introdução." *Série Estudos IUPERJ* 56. Rio de Janeiro, 1987.

Monteiro, Jorge Aparecido. "A questão racial e a administração de recursos humanos nas empresas brasileiras." *Revista de Administração de Empresas* 29, 1 (1989): 53–59.

Moraes, Evaristo de. *Brancos e negros nos Estados Unidos e no Brasil*. Rio de Janeiro, 1922.

Morandini, Alba Maria Figueiredo. "O trabalhador migrante nacional em São Paulo, 1920–1923." *Tese de mestrado*, Pontifícia Universidade Católica–São Paulo, 1978.

Morse, Richard M. "The Negro in São Paulo, Brazil." *Journal of Negro History* 38, 3 (1953): 290–306.

Moura, Clóvis. "A herança do cativeiro." *Retrato do Brasil* 1, 10 (1984): 109–113.

Moura, Clóvis. *O negro: De bom escravo a mau cidadão?* Rio de Janeiro, 1977.

Moura, Clóvis. "Organizações negras." In Paul Singer and Vinícius Caldeira Brant, eds., *São Paulo: O povo em movimento*. São Paulo, 1980.

Moura, Clóvis. *O preconceito de cor na literatura do cordel*. São Paulo, 1966.

Moura, Clóvis. *Rebeliões de senzala: Quilombos, insurreições, guerrilhas*. 3rd edition, São Paulo, 1981.

Moura, Clóvis. *Sociologia do negro brasileiro*. São Paulo, 1988.

Movimento Negro Unificado. *Programa de ação*. Campinas, 1984.

Myrdal, Gunnar. *An American Dilemma: The Negro Problem and Modern Democracy*. New York, 1944.

Nabuco, Joaquim. *Abolitionism: The Brazilian Antislavery Struggle*. Urbana, 1977.

Nascimento, Abdias do. *O genocídio do negro brasileiro: Processo de um racismo mascarado*. Rio de Janeiro, 1978.

Nascimento, Abdias do. *Quilombismo*. Petrópolis, 1980.

Nascimento, Abdias do, ed. *O negro revoltado*. Rio de Janeiro, 1982.

Needell, Jeffrey D. "Making the Carioca *Belle Époque* Concrete: The Urban Reforms of Rio de Janeiro under Pereira Passos." *Journal of Urban History* 10, 4 (1984): 383–422.

Needell, Jeffrey D. "The *Revolta contra Vacina* of 1904: The Revolt against Modernization in *Belle Époque* Rio de Janeiro." *Hispanic American Historical Review* 67, 2 (1987): 223–270.

Needell, Jeffrey D. *A Tropical Belle Époque: Elite Culture and Society in Turn-of-the-Century Rio de Janeiro*. Cambridge and New York, 1987.

Neiva, Arthur Hehl. "Getúlio Vargas e o problema da imigração e a colonização." *Revista da Imigração e Colonização* 3, 1 (April 1942): 24–70.

"Negro: A luta continua." *Cadernos do CEAS* 72 (March–April 1981): 18–28.

"Negros." *Dossiê CPV* [Centro Pastoral Vergueiro] 18. São Paulo, 1984.

"Os negros no mercado de trabalho na Grande São Paulo." *Pesquisa de Emprego e Desemprego na Grande São Paulo* 9 (1985): 8–16; and 10 (1985): 8–19.

Nogueira, Oracy. "Atitude desfavorável de alguns anunciantes de São Paulo em relação aos empregados de cor." *Sociologia* 4, 4 (1942): 328–358.

Nyrop, Richard, ed. *Brazil: A Country Study*. Washington, D.C., 1983.

Oliveira, Francisca Laíde de, et al. "Aspectos da situação sócio-econômica de brancos e negros no Brasil." Internal report, IBGE, Rio de Janeiro, 1981.

Oliveira, Lúcia Elena Garcia de, et al. *O lugar do negro na força de trabalho*. Rio de Janeiro, 1985.

Ortiz, Renato. *Cultura brasileira e identidade nacional*. São Paulo, 1985.

Pacheco, Moema de Poli Teixeira. "'Aguentando a barra': A questão da família negra." Manuscript, Museu Nacional, Rio de Janeiro, 1982.

Pacheco, Moema de Poli Teixeira. "A questão da cor nas relações de um grupo de baixa renda." *Estudos Afro-Asiáticos* 14 (1987): 85–97.

Paoli, Maria Célia. "Working Class São Paulo and Its Representations." *Latin American Perspectives* 14, 2 (1987): 204–225.

Pastore, José. *Inequality and Social Mobility in Brazil*. Madison, 1982.

Patai, Daphne. *Brazilian Women Speak: Contemporary Life Stories*. New Brunswick, 1988.

Pereira, João Baptista Borges. "Aspectos do comportamento político do negro em São Paulo." *Ciência e Cultura* 34, 10 (1982): 1286–1294.

Pereira, João Baptista Borges. *Côr, profissão e mobilidade: O negro e o rádio de São Paulo.* São Paulo, 1967.

Petrone, Maria Thereza Schorer. *A lavoura canavieira em São Paulo.* São Paulo, 1968.

Pierson, Donald. *Negroes in Brazil: A Study of Race Contact in Bahia.* Chicago, 1942.

Pinheiro, Paulo Sérgio. *Escritos indignados: Polícia, prisões e política no estado autoritário.* São Paulo, 1984.

Pinheiro, Paulo Sérgio, and Michael Hall, eds. *A classe operária no Brasil, 1889–1930. Documentos.* 2 vols. São Paulo, 1979, 1981.

Poppino, Rollie. *Brazil: The Land and People.* New York, 1968.

Queiroz, Suely Robles Reis de. *Escravidão negra em São Paulo: Um estudo das tensões provocadas pelo escravismo no século XIX.* Rio de Janeiro, 1977.

Querino, Manuel Raimundo. *A raça africana e os seus costumes.* Salvador, 1955.

Quilombhoje. *Reflexões.* São Paulo, 1985.

Raça negra e educação. Cadernos de Pesquisa 63 (Fundação Carlos Chagas). São Paulo, 1987.

Raffard, Henrique. *Alguns dias na Pauliceia.* São Paulo, 1977.

Ramos, Alberto Guerreiro. *Introdução crítica à sociologia brasileira.* Rio de Janeiro, 1957.

Raphael, Alison. "Samba and Social Control: Popular Culture and Racial Democracy in Rio de Janeiro." Ph.D. dissertation, Columbia University, 1980.

Reeve, R. Penn. "Race and Social Mobility in a Brazilian Industrial Town." *Luso-Brazilian Review* 14, 2 (1970): 236–253.

Reich, Michael. *Racial Inequality: A Political-Economic Analysis.* Princeton, 1981.

Reis, João José. *Rebelião escrava no Brasil: A história do levante dos malês (1835).* São Paulo, 1986.

Relatório apresentado ao Exm. Sr. Presidente da Província de São Paulo pela Comissão Central da Estatística. São Paulo, 1888.

Relatório apresentado ao . . . Secretário dos Negócios do Interior do Estado de São Paulo pelo Director da Repartição de Estatistica e Arquivo . . . em 31 de julho de 1894. Rio de Janeiro, 1894.

Rodrigues Alves, Sebastião. *A ecologia do grupo afro-brasileiro.* Rio de Janeiro, 1966.

Rolnik, Raquel. "Territórios negros em São Paulo: Uma história." Paper presented at the International Congress of the Latin American Studies Association, Albuquerque, N.M., March 1985.

Rout, Leslie. "Sleight of Hand: Brazilian and American Authors Manipulate the Brazilian Racial Situation, 1910–1951." *The Americas* 29, 4 (1973): 471–488.

Russell-Wood, A.J.R. *The Black Man in Slavery and Freedom in Colonial Brazil.* New York, 1982.

Saes, Décio. *Classe média e política na Primeira República brasileira (1889–1930).* Petrópolis, 1975.

Salve o 13 de maio? São Paulo, 1988.

Santana, Edgard T. *Relações entre pretos e brancos em São Paulo*. São Paulo, 1951.

Santos, Joel Rufino dos. "IPCN e Cacique de Ramos: Dois exemplos de movimento negro na cidade do Rio de Janeiro." *Communicações de ISER* [Instituto de Estudos da Religião] 7, 28 (1988): 5–20.

Santos, Joel Rufino dos. "O movimento negro e a crise brasileira." Manuscript, 1985.

Scarano, Julita. *Devoção e escravidão: A Irmandade de Nossa Senhora do Rosário dos pretos no distrito diamantino no século XVIII*. São Paulo, 1976.

Schwarcz, Lília Moritz. *Retrato em branco e negro: Jornais, escravos, e cidadãos em São Paulo no final do século XIX*. São Paulo, 1987.

Schwartz, Stuart B. "Plantations and Peripheries." In Leslie Bethell, ed., *Cambridge History of Latin America*, Volume 1. Cambridge and New York, 1984.

Schwartz, Stuart B. "Recent Trends in the Study of Slavery in Brazil." *Luso-Brazilian Review* 25, 1 (1988): 1–25.

Schwartz, Stuart B. *Sugar Plantations in the Formation of Brazilian Society: Bahia, 1550–1835*. Cambridge and New York, 1985.

Schwarz, Roberto. *Ao vencedor as batatas*. São Paulo, 1977.

Scobie, James. *Buenos Aires: From Plaza to Suburb, 1870–1910*. New York, 1974.

Scott, Rebecca J. "Comparing Emancipations: A Review Essay." *Journal of Social History* 20, 3 (1987): 565–584.

Scott, Rebecca. "The Meaning of Freedom: Postemancipation Society in Sugar-Producing Regions of Brazil, Cuba, and Louisiana." Paper presented at the Seminar on Social History and Theory, University of California–Irvine, March 1986.

Scott, Rebecca J. *Slave Emancipation in Cuba: The Transition to Free Labor, 1860–1899*. Princeton, 1985.

Senado Federal. *Consolidação das leis do trabalho*. Brasília, 1974.

Silva, Nelson do Valle. "Black-White Income Differentials: Brazil, 1960." Ph.D. dissertation, University of Michigan, 1978.

Silva, Nelson do Valle. "Distância social e casamento inter-racial." *Estudos Afro-Asiáticos* 14 (1987): 54–84.

Silva, Nelson do Valle. "Endogamia de cor ou endogamia de classe?" Paper presented at the annual conference of the Associação de Pós-Graduação e Pesquisa em Ciências Sociais (ANPOCS), Novo Friburgo, 1981.

Silva, Nelson do Valle. "Updating the Cost of Not Being White in Brazil." In Pierre-Michel Fontaine, ed., *Race, Class, and Power in Brazil*. Los Angeles, 1985.

Silva, Petronilha Beatriz Gonçalves e. "A formação do operário negro." *Educação e Sociedade* 22, 7 (1985): 57–83.

Singer, Paul, and Vinícius Caldeira Brant, eds. *São Paulo: O povo em movimento*. São Paulo, 1980.

Siqueira, Jorge. "Contribuição ao estudo da transição do escravismo colonial para o capitalismo urbano-industrial no Rio de Janeiro: A Companhia Luz Stearica (1854/1898)." *Dissertação de mestrado*, Universidade Federal Fluminense, 1984.

Skidmore, Thomas. *Black into White: Race and Nationality in Brazilian Thought*. New York, 1974.

Skidmore, Thomas. "Gilberto Freyre (1900–1987)." *Hispanic American Historical Review* 68, 4 (1988): 803–805.

Skidmore, Thomas. *Politics in Brazil, 1930–1964: An Experiment in Democracy*. New York, 1968.

Skidmore, Thomas. *The Politics of Military Rule in Brazil, 1964–1985*. New York, 1988.

Skidmore, Thomas. "Race and Class in Brazil: Historical Perspectives." In Pierre-Michel Fontaine, ed., *Race, Class, and Power in Brazil*. Los Angeles, 1985.

Skidmore, Thomas. "Racial Ideas and Social Policy in Brazil, 1870–1940." In Richard Graham, ed., *The Idea of Race in Latin America, 1870–1940*. Austin, 1990.

Skidmore, Thomas. "Toward a Comparative Analysis of Race Relations in the United States and Brazil since Abolition." *Journal of Latin American Studies* 4, 1 (1972): 1–28.

Skidmore, Thomas. "Workers and Soldiers: Urban Labor Movements and Elite Responses in Twentieth-Century Latin America." In Virginia Bernhard, ed., *Elites, Masses and Modernization in Latin America, 1850–1930*. Austin, 1979.

Skocpol, Theda. "Bringing the State Back In." In Peter Evans, Dietrich Rueschemeyer, and Theda Skocpol, eds., *Bringing the State Back In*. Cambridge and New York, 1985.

Slenes, Robert Wayne. "The Demography and Economics of Brazilian Slavery, 1850–1888." Ph.D. dissertation, Stanford University, 1976.

Slenes, Robert Wayne. "Escravidão e família: Padrões de casamento e estabilidade familiar numa comunidade escrava (Campinas, século XIX)." *Estudos Econômicos* 17, 2 (1987): 217–228.

Slenes, Robert Wayne. "O que Rui Barbosa não queimou: Novas fontes para o estudo da escravidão no século XIX." *Estudos Econômicos* 13, 1 (1983): 117–149.

Soares, Glaucio Ary Dillon, and Nelson do Valle Silva. "Urbanization, Race, and Class in Brazilian Politics." *Latin American Research Review* 22, 2 (1987): 155–176.

Sodré, Muniz. "O negro e os meios de informação." *Revista de Cultura Vozes* 73, 3 (April 1979).

Sorj, Bernardo, and Maria Hermínia Tavares de Almeida, eds. *Sociedade e política no Brasil pós-64*. São Paulo, 1983.

Souza, Amaury de. "Raça e política no Brasil urbano." *Revista de Administração de Empresas* 11, 4 (1971): 61–70.

Souza, Edgard de. *História da Light: Primeiros 50 anos*. São Paulo, 1982.

Souza, Laura de Mello e. *Desclassificados do ouro: A pobreza mineira no século XVIII*. Rio de Janeiro, 1982.

Souza, Neusa Santos. *Tornar-se negro: As vicissitudes da identidade do negro brasileiro em ascensão social*. Rio de Janeiro, 1983.

Stein, Stanley J. *The Brazilian Cotton Manufacture: Textile Enterprise in an Underdeveloped Area, 1850–1950.* Cambridge, Mass., 1957.

Stein, Stanley J. *Vassouras: A Brazilian Coffee County, 1850–1900.* 2nd edition, Princeton, 1985.

Stepan, Alfred. *The Military in Politics: Changing Patterns in Brazil.* Princeton, 1971.

Stepan, Alfred, ed. *Democratizing Brazil: Problems of Transition and Consolidation.* New York, 1989.

Stephens, Thomas H. *Dictionary of Latin American Racial and Ethnic Terminology.* Gainesville, 1989.

Stern, Steve J. *Peru's Indian Peoples and the Challenge of Spanish Conquest: Huamanga to 1640.* Madison, 1982.

Stolcke, Verena. *Coffee Planters, Workers and Wives: Class Conflict and Gender Relations on São Paulo Plantations, 1850–1980.* New York, 1988.

Stolcke, Verena. "The Exploitation of Family Morality: Labor Systems and Family Structure on São Paulo Coffee Plantations, 1850–1979." In Raymond T. Smith, ed., *Kinship Ideology and Practice in Latin America.* Chapel Hill, 1985.

Stolcke, Verena, and Michael M. Hall. "The Introduction of Free Labour on the São Paulo Coffee Plantations." *Journal of Peasant Studies* 10, 2–3 (1983): 170–200.

Tannenbaum, Frank. *Slave and Citizen: The Negro in the Americas.* New York, 1946.

Taylor, William B. "Between Global Process and Local Knowledge: An Inquiry into Early Latin American Social History, 1500–1900." In Olivier Zunz, ed., *Reliving the Past: The Worlds of Social History.* Chapel Hill, 1985.

Tendler, Judith. *Electric Power in Brazil: Entrepreneurship in the Public Sector.* Cambridge, Mass., 1968.

Tilly, Charles. "Retrieving European Lives." In Olivier Zunz, ed., *Reliving the Past: The Worlds of Social History.* Chapel Hill, 1985.

Topik, Steven. "Middle-Class Brazilian Nationalism, 1889–1930." *Social Science Quarterly* 59, 1 (1978): 93–103.

Topik, Steven. *The Political Economy of the Brazilian State, 1889–1930.* Austin, 1987.

Toplin, Robert Brent. *The Abolition of Slavery in Brazil.* New York, 1971.

Trevelyan, G. M. *English Social History.* London, 1944.

Trindade, Hélgio. *Integralismo: O fascismo brasileiro na década de 30.* 2nd edition, São Paulo, 1979.

United States Bureau of the Census. *Negro Population in the United States, 1790–1915.* Washington, D.C., 1918.

United States Bureau of the Census. *Statistical Abstract of the United States, 1975.* Washington, D.C., 1975.

United States Bureau of the Census. *Statistical Abstract of the United States, 1987.* Washington, D.C., 1986.

Valente, Ana Lúcia E. F. *Política e relações raciais: Os negros e as eleições paulistas de 1982.* São Paulo, 1986.

Van den Berghe, Pierre. *Race and Racism: A Comparative Perspective.* New York, 1967.

Vangelista, Chiara. *Le braccia per la fazenda: Immigrati e "caipiras" nella formazione del mercato del lavoro paulista.* Milan, 1982.

Veiga Filho, João Pedro da. *Estudo econômico e financeiro sobre o Estado de São Paulo.* São Paulo, 1896.

Veríssimo, Luis Fernando. *O analista de Bagé.* Porto Alegre, 1984.

Vieira, Celma Rosa. "Negra: Mulher e doméstica." *Estudos Afro-Asiáticos* 14 (1987): 141–158.

Wagley, Charles, ed. *Race and Class in Rural Brazil.* New York, 1963.

Walker, Thomas W. "From Coronelism to Populism: The Evolution of Politics in a Brazilian Municipality, Ribeirão Preto, São Paulo, 1910–1960." Ph.D. dissertation, University of New Mexico, 1974.

Weffort, Francisco. *Por que democracia?* São Paulo, 1984.

Weffort, Francisco. "Why Democracy?" In Alfred Stepan, ed., *Democratizing Brazil: Problems of Transition and Consolidation.* New York, 1989.

Wiggins, Jr., William H. *O Freedom! Afro-American Emancipation Celebrations.* Knoxville, 1987.

Williamson, Joel. *New People: Miscegenation and Mulattoes in the United States.* New York, 1980.

Wilson, William J. *The Declining Significance of Race: Blacks and Changing American Institutions.* 2nd edition, Chicago, 1980.

Winn, Peter. *Weavers of Revolution: The Yarur Workers and Chile's Road to Socialism.* New York, 1986.

Wolfe, Joel. "The Rise of Brazil's Industrial Working Class: Community, Work, and Politics in São Paulo, 1900–1955." Ph.D. dissertation, University of Wisconsin–Madison, 1990.

Wood, Charles H. "Census Categories and Subjective Classifications of Race in Brazil: An Empirical Assessment." Paper presented at the Seminário Internacional sobre Desigualdade Racial no Brasil Contemporâneo, Belo Horizonte, March 1990.

Wood, Charles H., and José Alberto Magno de Carvalho. *The Demography of Inequality in Brazil.* Cambridge and New York, 1988.

Woodward, C. Vann. *The Strange Career of Jim Crow.* 3rd edition, New York, 1974.

Wright, Winthrop R. *Café con Leche: Race, Class, and National Image in Venezuela.* Austin, 1990.

Yans-McLaughlin, Virginia. *Family and Community: Italian Immigrants in Buffalo, 1880–1930.* Ithaca, 1971.

Yudelman, David. *The Emergence of Modern South Africa: State, Capital and the Incorporation of Organized Labor in the South African Gold Fields.* Westport, Conn., 1983.

Zieger, Robert H., ed. *Organized Labor in the Twentieth-Century South.* Knoxville, forthcoming 1991.

Index

Abbott, Robert, 137
Abertura, 189–206 *passim*, 239; defined, 263
Abertura (newspaper), 331
Abolition of slave trade: in 1831, 31, 32, 35; in 1850, 33, 40
Abolition of slavery, 38–39; immediate causes of, 39–41; revolutionary implications of, 52; impact on European immigration of, 57; historical interpretations of, 211–212, 213, 219–223, 274, 276; in United States, 329; mentioned, 3, 18, 32, 243
—anniversary of: in 1889, 212; in 1892, 213; during early 1900s, 213–214; during 1920s, 214–215; in 1938, 155; during 1940s and 1950s, 215; in 1958, 188, 324–325; in 1960s and 1970s, 215–216; in 1978, 193, 331; in 1988, 205, 206, 218–233 *passim*, 276, 332–335 *passim*
Abolitionism: as mass-based movement, 40–41, 52, 211–212, 237–238, 276. *See also* Abolitionists
Abolitionists, 28, 32, 34–35; increasing radicalism of, 38–39; calls for agrarian reform by, 44, 131, 299; mentioned, 180, 277, 280, 319
Adamo, Sam, 253, 254
Advisory Group for Afro-Brazilian Affairs, 204

Afonso Arinos Law, 174, 184–185, 318–319, 328
Africa, 192, 239, 334
Afro-Brazilian Movement for Education and Culture, 318
Agriculture. *See* Plantation agriculture
Aguiar, Jayme de, 128, 147
Aguinaldo, Timoteo, 196
Alagoas, 218
Alcoholism, 75, 78, 80, 287
Alden, Dauril, 267
Alegria, 223–224, 333–334
Alexander, Robert, 319
Alfinete, O, 80, 139
Almeida, Suely Kofes de, 251, 325
Alves, João, 224
Alves, José Maria Rodrigues, 195, 199
Alvorada, 182
Amado, Jorge, 223
Amaral, Raul Joviano, 305
Amarelos: as racial category, 250; defined, 263
Américo Castro, Mário, 176, 323
Amigo do Povo, O, 61, 64
Anomie: among Afro-Brazilians, 75–81, 286, 317; among immigrants, 79–81
Anti-Semitism, 152, 153
Apartheid. *See* South Africa
Araraquara, 192, 212
Araujo, Henrique de, 297–298

357